Culture Matters

Culture Matters

Essays in Honor
of Aaron Wildavsky

edited by

Richard J. Ellis
Willamette University

and

Michael Thompson
The Musgrave Institute

WestviewPress

A Division of HarperCollins*Publishers*

Copyright © 1997 by Westview Press, A Division of HarperCollins Publishers, Inc.

Published in 1997 in the United States of America by Westview Press, 5500 Central Avenue, Boulder, Colorado 80301-2877, and in the United Kingdom by Westview Press, 12 Hid's Copse Road, Cumnor Hill, Oxford OX2 9JJ

Library of Congress Cataloging-in-Publication Data
Culture matters : essays in honor of Aaron Wildavsky / edited by
  Richard J. Ellis and Michael Thompson.
    p.   cm.
  Includes bibliographical references and index.
  ISBN 0-8133-3117-X — ISBN 0-8133-3118-8 (pbk)
  1. Political culture.   2. Culture.   I. Wildavsky, Aaron B.
II. Ellis, Richard (Richard J.)   III. Thompson, Michael.
JA75.7.C87   1997
306.2—dc21   97-17440
                                                                        CIP

The paper used in this publication meets the requirements of the American National Standard for Permanence of Paper for Printed Library Materials Z39.48-1984.

10   9   8   7   6   5   4   3   2   1

Contents

Foreword, Gabriel A. Almond   vii

Preface: Remembering Aaron Wildavsky, the Cultural Theorist   xiii

Acknowledgments   xix

Introduction, *Michael Thompson and Richard J. Ellis*   1

Part I
Rational Choice and Cultural Choice

1   Social Science as Cultural Science,
Rational Choice as Metaphysics, *Harry Eckstein*   21

2   Rational Choice and Culture: Clashing Perspectives
or Complementary Modes of Analysis? *Sun-Ki Chai*   45

Part II
Institutions and Culture

3   A Cultural Theory of Organizations, *Dennis J. Coyle*   59

4   Cultures: Frameworks, Theories, and Models,
Vincent Ostrom and Elinor Ostrom   79

Part III
Cultural Theories of Change

5   Political Culture and Political Change, *Charles Lockhart*   91

6   A Proposed Fragmentation of the Theory
of Cultural Change, *Arthur L. Stinchcombe*   105

Part IV
Risk and Culture

7   The Depoliticization of Risk, *Mary Douglas*   121

8   What's Special About Cancer? *Howard Margolis*   133

Part V
Culture and the Environment: Empirical Studies

9   Cultural Theory, Postmaterialism, and
    Environmental Attitudes, *Gunnar Grendstad and Per Selle*   151

10 Seeing Green: Cultural Biases and
    Environmental Preferences,
    Richard J. Ellis and Fred Thompson   169

Part VI
Cultural Theory and Practical Policies

11 Applying Cultural Theories to Practical Problems,
    Robert Klitgaard   191

12 Rewriting the Precepts of Policy Analysis,
    Michael Thompson   203

References   217
About the Book   241
About the Editors and Contributors   243
Index   245

Foreword

GABRIEL A. ALMOND

Like the mythical phoenix that rises from its ashes, political culture rises intermittently from the reductionist ashes to which its antagonists consign it. There have been four creative periods and about a half dozen reductionist episodes in the intellectual history of political culture. It has been on a positive and creative course for several decades, and the signs are for continued creativity.

Reductionism No. 1: Christianity. When Christianity conquered the classical world of Greece and Rome, the works of Herodotus, Plato, Aristotle, Polybius, and Plutarch, among others, with their insights into the differences among cities, nations, elites, and leaders, were lost to view in a homogenization of thought that divided humankind into the gross categories of the saved and the damned. It took the Islamic world in its secular and cosmopolitan moment, almost a thousand years later, to dust off the classics and make them available to a reawakening Europe. These rediscovered classics fed into the Renaissance, reviving speculation about the cultures and institutions of cities and nations, past and present, their causes and consequences. Thus Machiavelli's *Prince* and *Discourses on Livy* rehabilitated the classical insights into culture and personality, the conditions that shape them, and their consequences.

Systematic recognition of the importance of national differences reached a high point in the work of French Enlightenment philosophe Montesquieu. His *Essay on Causes Affecting Minds and Characters* first fully broached these themes in modern times, and his *The Spirit of Laws* fully elaborated a theory of national character.

"Men are influenced by various causes," he observed in his famous Book XIX of *The Spirit of Laws*, "by the climate [he has additional chapters in the *Essay on Causes* that deal with other physical factors, such as soil, terrain, food, and the like], the religion, the laws, the maxims of government, by precedents, morals and customs, from whence is formed a general spirit that takes its rise from these. In proportion, as in every nation any one of these causes acts with more force, the others are in the same degree weak. Nature and the climate rule almost alone over the savages; customs govern the Chinese; the laws tyrannize in Japan; morals had formerly all their influence at Sparta, maxims of government, and the ancient simplicity of manners, once prevailed at Rome" (1977, 287).

Durkheim, stressing his multicausal approach to cultural explanation as well as his functionalism, viewed Montesquieu as the father of modern social science (1965, 56–57). Montesquieu himself viewed his role as that of bringing to the study of history and human affairs the objectivity and rigor that Newton had brought to the study of the cosmos. It was Montesquieu's analytic model that lay behind the social-scientific claims of the authors of the *Federalist Papers*. Montesquieu's ideas constituted an important part of the intellectual heritage of Tocqueville, whose studies of eighteenth-century France and nineteenth-century America are perhaps the greatest classics of political culture research. Indeed, the contributions of both Montesquieu and Tocqueville to the theories of national character and political culture call for acknowledgment of the importance of the "French connection" (Montesquieu-Rousseau-Tocqueville-Durkheim) in these intellectual developments. For Montesquieu political culture was "the spirit of the laws"; for Tocqueville it was "the habits of the heart."

Reductionisms Nos. 2, 3, 4: Historicism, Economism, Biologism. The nineteenth century was rich in reductionist interpretations. Enlightenment anticipation of the universal spread of rational-secular knowledge and culture was elaborated in the work of "historicists" such as Comte and Spencer. In this perspective cultural uniqueness tended to be viewed as residual, as comprising traditions doomed to be superseded by humane progress and secular culture.

Marxist materialism, in its various forms and permutations, was the most pervasive form of reductionism in the nineteenth and twentieth centuries. Marx himself allowed for national differences that would explain different forms and degrees of class struggle. The Netherlands and the United States, for example, because of their specific historical experiences, might escape the violence of the inevitable, proletarian-capitalist confrontation. Revisionist Marxism assumed a political learning process, rather than a necessary violent revolution, that might produce the desired socialist outcome. Lenin reduced national and cultural differences to "strong" and "weak" links in the imperialist-capitalist chain. But for all the varieties of Marxism class struggle was the engine that moved history. Culture was either residual, or it was the mirror of class structure.

The grotesque biological reductionism of Nazi racialism was only an extreme form of a more diffuse biologism among many nineteenth-century historians and political scientists. Political scientist William B. Munro counted the Anglo-Saxon "race" as part of the explanation of the stable parliamentarism of Britain. The "eugenics" movement of the late nineteenth and early twentieth centuries accorded a large causal power to genetic constitution and to the possibilities of genetic selection for the "improvement of the race." By improvement was meant the superseding of unique cultures by rational-secular values and attitudes.

Reductionism No. 5: The German Connection and the Psychocultural Approach. The psychological reductionism of the 1930s and 1940s was in considerable part, though not entirely, a response to the fall of the Weimar Republic and to National Socialism. Freud and his followers had already begun to apply libido and "psychological mechanism" theory in interpretations of the state, politics, war, and religion in the first decades of the twentieth century. But it was the shocking fall of the Weimar Republic and the grotesque barbarism of National Socialism that challenged and discredited prevailing doctrines of political progress. Liberal Enlightenment theory predicted democratization in Germany, one of the most educated and knowledgeable peoples in the civilized world. Marxist theory predicted the development of socialist democracy in Germany, one of the most advanced capitalist powers, with a mature, organized working class and the largest Social Democratic Party in the world. What happened in Germany forced social theorists to rethink their explanatory strategies. Individual rationality and class rationality could not begin to explain the collapse of Weimar and National Socialism. The phenomena of German politics seemed to invite the sciences of the irrational and the nonrational to join forces in efforts to explain them.

There are stacks full of books and journal articles interpreting National Socialism and the "German problem" in psychocultural terms. Psychocultural theory interpreted German politics (and Japanese, American, Russian, French, and British politics as well) in terms of family structure, childhood socialization, and subconscious processes. The German patriarchal, authoritarian family was supposed to explain the mix of servile obedience and hostility that produced German nationalism, ethnocentrism, anti-Semitism. There was little room in this interpretation of national differences for adult experience, for the impact of history and political experience, and for autonomous cognitive processes.

In this extreme form the psychocultural approach was soon discredited and rejected. A more empirically grounded and quantitatively sophisticated political culture approach emerged in the decades after World War II, a research approach that continues with vitality to the present. Among the distinctive products of this literature in the 1950s to the 1970s were the voting studies of Paul Lazarsfeld and his associates (1944), the University of Michigan studies on the American voter (Campbell, Gurin, and Miller 1954; Campbell, Converse, Miller, and Stokes 1960), the cross-national political culture studies of Gabriel Almond and Sidney Verba (1963), the changing culture studies of Ronald Inglehart (1971), and the modernization studies of Alex Inkeles and Donald Smith (1974).

Reductionisms Nos. 6 and 7: Neomarxism and Rational Choice. The politics of the Vietnam War and the "cultural revolution" sought to elbow cultural variables aside in the late 1960s and 1970s, but only with partial success. It was argued by the "dependency" school that there was nothing problematic about political values and attitudes. They could be inferred from the international political economy. Good research was defined as that which illuminated and exposed this system of exploitation—a hierarchy of oppression centered in high capitalism in the United States and Europe and extending throughout the globe through the semiperiphery to the periphery. Studies of political attitudes were not only pointless; they were positively harmful, since they attributed solid reality to what were really the products of this exploitative and false-consciousness creating system (Packenham 1992).

But political culture research was attacked in those years from the methodological side as well. Rational choice theory in its earlier manifestations also viewed culture and attitudes as unproblematic. All that one required in order to explain social, cultural, and political phenomena was rational man, the short-run, hard-nosed calculator, and the mathematics and statistics that he needed in order to make cost-effective choices. The extraordinary success of the public choice movement can only be accounted for by its rigor and parsimony in an age dominated by the reductionist triumphs of physics and biology. And it did indeed illuminate such phenomena as aspects of decisionmaking in committees, the decisions of voters and politicians, the formation of cabinets, and diplomatic and strategic choices as well as choices of occupations, mates, and the like (Alt and Shepsle 1990). That these were only partial contributions to the explanation of social and political phenomena is now being generally acknowledged in the "new institutionalism." In its earlier manifestations rational choice theory claimed to be the only promise of a powerful, parsimonious, and rigorous social science.

A Renaissance in Political Culture Studies. While political culture research was whipsawed in those decades from the dependency left and the rational-choice right, it was too well rooted to be overwhelmed, as had been the case in earlier reductionist episodes. It lost some of its audience, and perhaps some of its half-hearted practitioners. But it has displayed robustness, increasing rigor, and an irrepressible creativity. Here are a number of examples of this vitality.

In the early 1970s Ronald Inglehart (1971) forecast developments in the culture of advanced industrial societies that would trigger basic changes in party systems and the voting behavior of these societies. He offered a theory of socialization and value change to explain these transformations. He and his associates at the University of Michigan and abroad monitored these developments systematically over time, adding new countries, refining and defending his hypotheses with a solid marshaling of evidence and inference (Inglehart 1977, 1981, 1990). He is among the small number of social scientists who have successfully practiced predictive political science, meeting all comers in professional polemic. Following on Inglehart's work, another group of European and American scholars trained in University of Michigan election survey research explored the deterioration of European parties and party systems that Inglehart's work had forecast. Samuel Barnes, Max Kaase, and their associates (Barnes and Kaase 1979) explored the new patterns of protest and unconventional political action that spread in Europe in the 1960s and 1970s. Another group of scholars, both American and European (Dalton, Flanagan, and Beck 1984; Dalton 1994), investigated the impact of attitude change on political institutions—political parties, pressure groups, and new issue movements in advanced industrial democracies.

Sidney Verba, with students and colleagues drawn from a career at Princeton University, Stanford University, the University of Chicago, and finally Harvard University, has produced a rigorous theory of political participation, tested and refined it cross-nationally, demonstrated the importance of issues in American political behavior, and explored the political culture of inequality, race, ethnicity, and caste (Verba and Nie 1972; Verba, Nie, and Kim 1978; Verba, Schlozman, and Brady 1995).

Robert Putnam and his students and associates at the University of Michigan, at Harvard University, and in Italy broke the barrier to systematic elite interviewing of European parliamentarians and members of the higher civil service, illuminating the political processes and public policy trends of European politics. Putnam's most recent book, *Making Democracy Work* (1993), reports the results of a twenty-year study of a "natural political experiment" in Italy. In the early 1970s Italy devolved substantial powers on its twenty regions. Putnam's team of scholars followed these developments with a combination of historical research, anthropological field studies, elite interviewing, and general attitude surveys, conducted at several points in the twenty-year span. They demonstrated that the relative success in political and economic performance in the northern regions of Italy could be explained by the higher levels of social trust in those regions and the consequent greater capacity for cooperative pooling of resources in community and economic ventures. Putnam refers to this combination of attitude and behavior as "social capital," and he is engaged at present in an investigation of what seems to be declining "social capital" in the United States.

While these methodologically innovative research programs broke new ground in the study of political culture, the earlier sociological and psychological investigative traditions continued to produce work rich in findings and implications. These include such work as Seymour Martin Lipset's studies of Canadian and American political culture (1995, 1996), Samuel Huntington's study of historical changes in American political culture (1981), Lucian Pye's studies of Asian political cultures (Pye and Pye 1985), Larry Diamond and his colleagues' studies of political culture in the processes of democratization (1993), and many others.

It is not too much to describe political culture studies as one of the major investigative fields in contemporary political science. It has drawn some of the leading talents of political science into creative polemics likely to challenge the imaginations of younger scholars (see Wildavsky 1987a; Eckstein 1988; Inglehart 1988; Laitin 1988; Wildavsky 1988b; and Werlin and Eckstein 1990). That "culture matters" is clearly evident on the record.

Preface:
Remembering Aaron Wildavsky,
the Cultural Theorist

Aaron Wildavsky first taught his graduate seminar on political culture in 1984. Over the next decade he would teach that course every year, until his death in 1993. At the University of California at Berkeley, he would still teach, on occasion, the Presidency or Budgeting or American Politics, but his heart (as well as his head) was now in what he called "cultural theory."[1] During that last decade of his life he taught three National Endowment for the Humanities summer seminars on Cultural Theory, as a way of spreading the faith. When he had visiting appointments, at American University in Washington, D.C., or the University of Bergen in Norway, he taught Cultural Theory. American interest in Cultural Theory, such as it is, is due in large part to Aaron's labor of love in those seminars.

Back in the early 1980s, Aaron's Berkeley colleagues, who knew him as an internationally renowned scholar of budgeting, public policy, and the American presidency, must have been more than a little perplexed to find him proposing to teach a course on Cultural Theory. More surprising still must have been the exotic syllabus, which included a host of anthropological readings on the Kwakiutl, the Comanche, the Cherokee, the Zuni, the Dobu, the Kapauku, the Hadza, the Bunyoro, the Igbo, and, of course, the Nuer, those paragons of self-regulation. Indeed, even conventional students of political culture would probably have found much of this reading list a little strange. Although most political scientists interested in culture would have acknowledged the origins of the culture concept in anthropology, few would have bothered to read much, if any, of this ethnography, believing that the lives of such primitives could not possibly be relevant to political culture in the advanced industrial societies of the West.

Aaron's course did have a smattering of the conventional names: Gabriel Almond, Lucian Pye, Clifford Geertz, even Claude Lévi-Strauss. But Aaron quickly made it clear that he really was not much interested in debating the merits of what these authors had to say about culture. He found the endless definitional squabbling over the meaning of culture to be barren. Instead of being prelude to explanation, definitional discussions seemed to serve as a substitute for the task of understanding and explaining the world around us. Instead of leading the seminar through the myriad alternative definitions and conceptualizations of culture, then, Aaron's course on political culture plunged straight into Cultural Theory, as pioneered by Mary Douglas. Aaron's enormous energy was focused not on dissecting the weaknesses of past works on culture but rather on building up a predictive theory of culture that could be tried out on the world. Although committed to theory, Aaron had little sympathy for that sort of rarefied theory that never seems to touch down in the world of real, live human beings. Cultural Theory, Aaron believed, should be a daily aid rather than, as he put it, "a put-on just for company" (1987c, 27).

Aaron believed in "learning by doing" (1987c, 24; 1988c, 3). Only by trying out Cultural Theory, by applying it to some phenomenon, could one move from passive understanding to active analysis.[2] In this spirit, his early classes applied Cultural Theory to the political debates over nuclear energy and the Mediterranean fruit fly, to the question of why governments grow, and to the so-called ungovernability crisis in Western democracies. At the end of the course everyone was asked to analyze a social or political phenomenon of their choosing to see how Cultural Theory fared in comparison with some other theory.[3] Aaron himself, as anyone who talked or walked with him knows, tried out Cultural Theory on virtually every aspect of human existence. He not only thought about categories of cultural analysis, as he explained in his (only?) unpublished paper, "From Political Economy to Political Culture," but he also thought *through* these categories (1987c, 25).

Originally drafted in 1984, "From Political Economy to Political Culture" was the first paper he assigned the following year to his 1985 seminar. The subtitle of that version was "Or Rational People Defend Their Way of Life," but its later subtitle—"Or Why I Like Cultural Analysis"—better communicates the purpose of the paper, namely, to explain to his doubting colleagues and to clarify for himself why a world-famous expert on budgeting and public policy had taken up this seemingly bizarre theory.

"Until coming across cultural analysis," Aaron explained, "I had no independent stance for viewing the world. . . . I had values [but] I lacked . . . a theory of my own I could use to come to my own conclusions about anything that seemed important" (1987c, 26). Coming from such an original, unconventional mind, such an admission hardly seems credible. Aaron did not need Cultural Theory, or any other theory for that matter, to come to his own conclusions about a phenomenon. Some of this, then, must be put down to Aaron's disarming self-deprecation (which was often strategic prelude or postscript to some extravagant claim on behalf of Cultural Theory). Yet some of it was absolutely genuine. As a scholar and involved citizen Aaron felt that Cultural Theory allowed him to better understand the world around him. And as a teacher he found that Cultural Theory enabled even quite ordinary students to write some extraordinary or at least more interesting papers.

There was of course a danger—if not for Aaron, then for the rest of us—that Cultural Theory might become a substitute for independent and creative thought rather than a stimulus to it. If everything had a cultural interpretation, then perhaps it explained nothing. A wide scope was one thing, a Gumby-like elasticity quite another.

There was also the danger that one might mistake the discovery of something new for a sterile relabeling of the old. Related to this was the temptation to make categorization and classification an end in and of itself. "*Any* criterion," Robert Brown cautioned, "will organize data—will order items in classes—but only some classifications will be scientifically useful" (1963, 169). We could, for example, classify the entire population of the world into four categories based on two criteria: height and weight. If our goal is to explain political or social phenomena, however, such a classification scheme is likely to be of little help. The lesson is that those who seek to apply Cultural Theory cannot rest satisfied with placing people into categories; they must also ask how this classification aids explanation of some phenomenon.

Aaron understood these pitfalls—indeed, in view of the constant barrage of criticism and disparagement that he and the theory received, he could hardly have failed to be aware of them. What, then, made Aaron forsake the safe harbors of budgeting and public policy and risk his reputation on the uncharted and perilous waters of Cultural Theory? In "From Political Economy to Political Culture," Aaron explained that he wanted a theory that would allow him to go beyond a political economy approach in which people's preferences were given and social context "was either nonexistent or implicitly assumed to be uniform" (1987c, 12).[4] Cultural Theory appealed to Aaron because it embedded people's choices in preferred patterns of social relations.

But the driving motive for Aaron's shift was less abstract.[5] It was the feeling that the theoretical perspectives he had relied on did not help him make sense of the great "cultural revolution" he saw occurring around him—the rise of environmentalism, animal rights, children's rights, and affirmative action, the adversarial media, the decline of political parties, the routine trashing of presidents, and the fall of academic standards (1987c, 30; also 15).[6] Cultural Theory, particularly the category of egalitarianism (originally called sectarianism), offered Aaron a way of seeing a common cultural dynamic that united these disparate phenomena. Or at least, as Aaron would have preferred to put it, Cultural Theory did better than any of the rival theories he had tried out or looked into, for example, the ill-fated theories of "the new class," the arid literature on fanaticism, or the unhelpful appellation of "purism."[7]

More concretely still, Aaron was drawn to Cultural Theory through his work on energy and environmental policy. In a 1976 review essay of a book entitled *The Uncertain Search for Environmental Quality,* Aaron suggested that conventional social science categories could not make sense of environmentalists' demands for purification. Their behavior could not be understood in terms of economic profit or political gain. Rather than call them irrational, Aaron reported that he was "trying to find a way to call them rational" (1976, 123). Drawing extensively on

Mary Douglas's seminal essay, "Environments at Risk" (1975), Aaron suggested that the environmental debate could not be understood without reckoning with the social relations that people valued. Charges of pollution, he echoed Douglas, were ways of protecting certain ideas and institutions from challenge.

Because "From Political Economy to Political Culture" stresses the discontinuity between Aaron the early budget analyst and Aaron the later cultural analyst, it is perhaps worth noting an important continuity between these two halves of Aaron's career. In Aaron's early work on budgeting and public policy he had been a relentless critic of cost-benefit analysis, and thus quite naturally he found a soulmate in Mary Douglas, whose own work contained a withering critique of economic models as question begging. If we ask, moreover, what it was that was so significant about *The Politics of the Budgetary Process* (1964), the answer must be in large part that the book showed that beneath the surface of arcane budgets were political struggles, fascinating ones at that. Just as in the 1960s and early 1970s Aaron the budgetary analyst argued that battles over the budget were essentially political struggles, so in the late 1970s and the 1980s Aaron the cultural theorist insisted that beneath mundane political struggles were battles between ways of life or cultures. Beneath discreet individual choices, as he explained Cultural Theory to Robert Dahl in 1982, people were "choosing among ways of life or types of rule."[8] That was and is the fundamental insight of Cultural Theory, and in this respect Cultural Theory can be seen as radically extending the logic that made Aaron such an astute analyst of the budgetary process and public policy.

In other ways, of course, Cultural Theory did represent a departure from Aaron's earlier understanding of American politics, especially as laid out in *The Politics of the Budgetary Process*. Incrementalism as a political theory left the clash of ultimate values alone, submerging rival visions of the good life in pragmatic agreements. Cultural Theory, in contrast, insisted on understanding politics in terms of ultimate values. For Aaron, politics in America had changed, and so too must the theory used to make sense of that politics. So dramatic were these changes that yet another edition of *The Politics of the Budgetary Process* was unthinkable; instead he would have to write an entirely new book, *The New Politics of the Budgetary Process* (1988a), from an entirely new theoretical vantage point. "The old politics," Aaron explained, "had been about increments because the base had been mostly accepted; the new politics was about the base because [the base] was no longer acceptable." Cultural Theory was Aaron's way of understanding disagreements about the base. Because Cultural Theory directed attention to fundamentally different schemes of values, Aaron felt that it was the theory for our times.

Changes in American politics attracted Aaron to Cultural Theory, but Cultural Theory also shaped the way Aaron thought about American politics and indeed all politics. Under the influence of Cultural Theory, Aaron became sensitized not only to the conflict of ultimate values in contemporary America but in all times and places. And under the influence of Cultural Theory he also became more pessimistic about our society's ability to handle conflict. In the face of irreconcilable cultural differences, incrementalism no longer seemed sufficient to resolve disagreements. If we are deeply separated by distinct cultures, not just by different parties or even ideologies, then how can we come to agreement and resolve our differences? Moreover, under the influence of Cultural Theory, Aaron seemed to focus with ever greater alarm on the rise of radical egalitarianism and its deleterious consequences on all the major institutions of American life, especially the universities he so cherished. If, as Aaron suggested in "The Rise of Radical Egalitarianism and the Fall of Academic Standards" (1991d, 239), there is a "massive onslaught of egalitarianism" in our society, then how will the institutions of liberal democratic capitalism survive?[9]

A reader of "The Rise of Radical Egalitarianism and the Fall of Academic Standards" may find it difficult to believe Aaron's insistence in "From Political Economy to Political Culture" that his search was "for a theory exposing the contradictions at the core of all possible cultures, not just those I don't like" (1987c, 21). That reader might conclude instead that it is the pathologies and contradictions of egalitarianism that interested (even obsessed) Aaron. Such a conclusion would not be far wrong. But the weakness, if weakness it is, is Aaron's, not the theory's. The theory does what Aaron said it does, namely, illuminate the contradictions and dilemmas of different ways of organizing social life. Aaron never hid his personal preference for competitive individualism, nor his dislike of radical egalitarianism (except in limited doses), but he always insisted that Cultural Theory could be just as readily used by those with other political axes to grind (1987c, 30). Here again we think he was right, although perhaps we won't know for sure until an egalitarian with Aaron's imagination and energy tries his or her hand at Cultural Theory.

Although Aaron worried a great deal about what he saw as a growing cultural divide in the United States between individualists and egalitarians and sought to understand how one might close that divide (1991a), his attitude to cultural dissensus was more complex than simple aversion. There was a part of Aaron that seemed genuinely to revel in the dissensus and debate over first principles. Aaron loved to argue about the big questions, about one's fundamental cultural commitments—no muddling through for him. Moreover, in much of his work, there was a deep appreciation for the inevitability and desirability of cultural variety and diversity (by which he did not mean ethnicity or skin color). In *Cultural Theory* (Thompson, Ellis, and Wildavsky 1990), for instance, Aaron insisted that a pluralism of cultural biases promoted and in fact were necessary to democracy. Egalitarianism, he allowed, was essential to democracy.

Finally, it should be said that while Aaron was certainly a fierce partisan of capitalism, his commitment to scholarship and teaching transcended that particular cultural preference. He never judged students or colleagues on the basis of their political beliefs. As a cultural theorist he believed that knowledge was socially constructed and that we could never totally escape our own subjectivity, but he never accepted the postmodern crock that one could not differentiate between politics and scholarship or that individual subjectivity made science impossible.

Throughout his life and career as a scholar and teacher he remained steadfast in his dedication to an academic excellence that transcended politics and trumped diversity. His was always an unmistakable and relentless voice of intellectual honesty and wisdom. We still miss that voice.

Richard J. Ellis
Michael Thompson

Notes

1. In order to distinguish the general enterprise of theorizing about culture from the specific "cultural theory" espoused by Wildavsky, we capitalize Cultural Theory when referring to Wildavsky's cultural theory. This usage is also adopted in the Introduction and Chapters 5, 9, and 12. The term "grid-group theory" or "grid-group cultural theory" is used in Chapters 2, 3, and 7.

2. In his essay "Teaching and Talking," Aaron noted that "hours and hours of discussion do more to straighten out thought than any amount of reading" (1988c, 3). This should not be misunderstood. In the classroom, Aaron distrusted endless discussion that seemed to be going nowhere, just as in collaborations he wanted help, not advice. In and out of the classroom he would tune out a meandering discussion or abruptly terminate a discussion that he felt was not fruitful. Aaron believed in talking to clarify one's thinking, but it was always "talking with a purpose," talking as a prelude to the doing.

3. "This comparison of theories is valuable," Aaron explained, because "on one side, it prevents students from being impaled upon a single theory not of their own choosing; on the other, it suggests that cultural theory may be inadequate but not necessarily compared to alternatives" (1987c, 29).

4. The question of preference formation (together with references to the work of Mary Douglas) made a prominent appearance in an essay entitled "Strategic Retreat on Objectives: Learning from Failure in American Public Policy" that was written for *Speaking Truth to Power* (1979).

5. This is even clearer in the earlier 1984 version of "From Political Economy to Political Culture."

6. For those who see culture as necessarily static, it is worth noting, as Charles Lockhart does in Chapter 5, that what drew Aaron to Cultural Theory was a desire to account for change, not stability.

7. In private correspondence at the beginning of 1980, Aaron described the book that would be published under the title *Risk and Culture* (Douglas and Wildavsky 1982) as "in some ways an extension of purism to environmental politics."

8. Wildavsky to Robert Dahl, August 27, 1982.

9. The vision is even darker but also more measured and compelling in "Politically Correct Hiring Will Destroy Higher Education" (1993–1994), a speech Aaron delivered at the national conference of the National Association of Scholars in April 1993, shortly before being diagnosed with lung cancer.

Acknowledgments

We wish to thank Jennifer Knerr for her initial interest and faith in this project. Others at Westview, particularly Leo Wiegman, Ryan Goldberg, and Brenda Hadenfeldt, also helped spirit the book along its way. John J. Guardiano's copyediting was truly exceptional. Brian Shipley, a Willamette University undergraduate student, deserves our special thanks for his invaluable assistance in helping to compile the bibliography. Jeff Eager aided in tracking down stray references toward the end. Completion of this project was facilitated by a Willamette University Atkinson grant in the summer of 1996 and by course release in the spring semester of 1997 courtesy of Willamette's Faculty Study Time Program. Finally, we would like to thank our contributors for their patience with the book's slow, tortuous path to publication. We hope it was worth the wait.

R.J.E.
M.T.

Introduction

MICHAEL THOMPSON
RICHARD J. ELLIS

Among the most promising developments in social science over the past decade has been the renewed attention to culture (Inglehart 1988; Eckstein 1988; Wuthnow and Witten 1988; Wildavsky 1989; Peterson 1990; Lamont and Wuthnow 1990; Wilson 1992; Tarrow 1992; During 1993; Putnam, 1993; Johnston and Klandermans 1995). Many social scientists have become dissatisfied with economistic approaches that take preferences as given and interests as self-evident. Rational choice models that would account for human behavior solely in terms of material self-interest are empirically inadequate (Green and Shapiro 1994), and defining self-interest more broadly as any preference, from self-expression to self-abnegation, borders on tautology. Yet renewed attention to culture is more a reaction to the perceived inadequacies of existing approaches than it is a positive endorsement of the culture concept. If the current revival of interest in culture is to be sustained, cultural theorists must demonstrate how cultural theories can avoid the pitfalls that led social scientists to relegate the culture concept to "the professional dog house for a generation" (Laitin 1995, 173).

The term "political culture" entered the lexicon of political science in the late 1950s and early 1960s. Intimately linked with the so-called behavioral revolution, the term signaled a turn away from the study of formal institutions to the informal behavior that breathed life into them. Political culture was heralded as a concept capable of unifying the discipline. By relating the behavior of individuals to the system of which the individual was a part, it promised to "bridge the 'micro-macro' gap in political theory" (Almond and Powell 1966, 51–52; also see Almond and Verba 1963, 32–36; and Pye 1965, 9). Yet within a decade, the concept of political culture had begun to fall out of fashion amid criticisms that, among other things, it was tautological, it was unable to explain change, it ignored institutions and power relations, and worst of all, it was unscientific.

Certainly it is true that culture has too often been conceptualized in terms of the unique configuration of values, beliefs, and practices that make the Russians different from the Chinese, the French different from the Americans, the Methodists different from the Quakers, or Toyota different from Audi. As long as culture is defined solely in terms of national, religious, ethnic, racial, or corporate distinctiveness, common measures are impossible and culture must remain a fancy name for what we do not understand. To get beyond using culture as a tautological conversation stopper (Why do Japanese children treat their parents more deferentially than American children? Because of their culture) or as the theory-busting anthropologist's veto ("Not in my tribe"), a theory of culture must identify common, generalizable cultural dimensions and types.

If the concept of culture is to be useful to social scientists, some classification of cultures is necessary. Any typology, of course, is doomed to failure in the sense that it will never precisely capture the full variety of social organization. Each historical setting is unique in countless ways. Each person has his or her own experiences, and any attempt to generalize across individuals or groups inevitably entails distortion. "General ideas," as Tocqueville explained, "do not bear witness to the power of human intelligence but rather to its inadequacy, for there are no beings exactly alike in nature, no identical facts, no laws which can be applied indiscriminately in the same way to several objects at once" (1969, 437). Since we lack the ability to perceive the full variety of the human experience, our choice must be either to abandon the quest for understanding, or to generalize (King, Keohane, and Verba 1994). And fundamental to generalization is typology (see Dryzek 1987, viii; Douglas 1982a, 200). "If we eschew explicit typologies which can be criticized and improved," Mary Douglas warns bluntly, we "expose the whole domain to undeclared, implicit typologies. Either way, behavior is going to be fitted into boxes" (1982b, 2).

Rethinking Cultural Theory

Douglas's (1970, 1982a) candidate for a typology of cultures was her "grid-group" typology (Figure I.1). The terms "group" and particularly "grid" have had the unfortunate consequence of making these ideas seem perhaps more arcane and exotic than they in fact are. Although the term "grid" is certainly unfamiliar to social scientists, the concept it denotes is not. In *Suicide*, Durkheim presented much the same idea in his discussion of social "regulation" (1951, bk. 2, chap. 5). A highly regulated (or high-grid) social context is signified by "an explicit set of institutionalized classifications [that] keeps [individuals] apart and regulates their interactions" (Douglas 1982a, 203). In such a setting, "male does not compete in female spheres, [and] sons do not define their relations with fathers" (1982a, 192). The further one moves "down-grid," the more individuals are expected to negotiate their own relationships with others. The "group" dimension, as Douglas explains, measures the extent to which "the individual's life is absorbed in and sus-

GRID

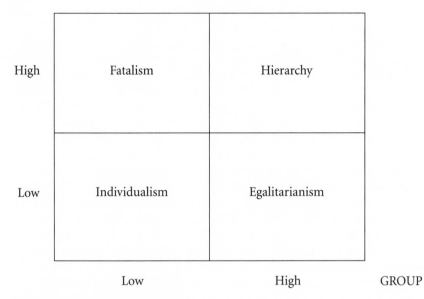

FIGURE I.1   The grid/group scheme

tained by group membership." A low group "score" would be given to an individual who "spends the morning in one [group], the evening in another, appears on Sundays in a third, gets his livelihood in a fourth" (1982a, 202). In contrast, a person who joined with others in "common residence, shared work, shared resources and recreation" would be assigned a high group rating (1982a, 191). The further to the right one moves along the group dimension, the tighter the control over admission into the group and the higher the boundaries separating members from nonmembers. From these two dimensions Douglas derived four cultural types: hierarchy (high group, high grid) egalitarian collectivism (high group, low grid), entrepreneurial individualism (low group, low grid), and fatalism (low group, high grid). She also distinguished a fifth type—the autonomy of the hermit—that is characterized by deliberate withdrawal (in contrast to the fatalist's involuntary exclusion) but, finding no place for it in her grid-group scheme, she had no option but to take the hermit "off the social map."

In her contribution to this volume, Douglas has reformulated the typology in ways that accent "the attitude to power and authority." Power may be exercised hierarchically, as in a bureaucracy, or power may be exercised through bargaining and exchange, as in competitive markets. These modes of organization can be resisted by either active criticism (the egalitarian stance) or passive resignation (the stance of the fatalist or "isolate"). The types remain basically the same, though how one derives the categories has changed. Also changed is the emphasis on overt competition between the different ways of life. Indeed, the types are now defined in part in terms of their opposition to one another.

Equally significant is the shift away from the primacy of social relations. In its original formulation (Douglas 1970, 1975) grid-group theory was often understood as a theory of how social relations shaped perceptions, how the life we lived with each other shaped the way we perceived the world. The types themselves were derived from social relations: grid and group. Douglas makes clear now, though, that the "typology of cultures is derived from cultural biases." It is "the *attitude* to power and authority" that is the "basic discriminator," not the authority relations themselves (emphasis added). To avoid giving the mistaken "impression of a culture as a sharply defined group of people," she now suggests "culture as a dialogue." The cultural analyst should treat the different ways of life as "cultural signal stations" and focus, for example, on the favorite words used by each culture or how "the choice of themes draws together the defenders of a cultural type against its opponents." None of this means that attitudes are free-floating—Douglas still insists, for example, that a "way of life depends heavily on the way of earning a living, and the social relations that are entailed." Social relations are "entailed," but it is cultural bias that is primary.

This newer version of Cultural Theory, sans "grid" and "group," is likely to be far more palatable, particularly to political scientists who confront the problem of explaining political conflict over a range of policy areas, from global warming to health care. We suspect that many have balked at Cultural Theory's gate because they do not see how going back to the social relations will necessarily help them make sense of the political contestation they observe. By making cultural bias primary, and by providing four coherent and politically relevant biases, Douglas has gone a long way toward making her typology useful for those who wish to make sense of the contentious policy disputes and "culture wars" so evident all around us.

But can we perhaps do still better? Typologies, as Douglas herself has always insisted, are not theories but merely "analytical schemes" or "heuristic devices." Their value, therefore, lies in their usefulness. A hydrodynamicist, for instance, may find it useful to place whales and submarines in the same category (in contradistinction to, say, halibut and stealth bombers), but he does not thereby arrive at a theory. His theory is a deep explanation for why his typology works: probably something to do with hypotheses about the ways in which solid objects can move through fluids and with the distinction between smooth and turbulent flow. What, then, is the theory behind the grid-group scheme? Where do we look for the deep explanation for why this typology works? The answer, as with the whales, the halibut, the submarines, and the stealth bombers, lies in the dynamics.

Inherent to the grid-group typology is the idea that social life is a flux—an endless tumult of people (social relations), values and beliefs (cultural biases), and transactions (behavior)—that continually generates a small number of recurrent regularities. It is these recurrent regularities that the grid-group typology captures, and the question that Cultural Theory has to answer is: How do these recurrent regularities come to be there? That, at any rate, is the pure, intellectual, curiosity-killed-the-cat way of working out where we should be looking for our theory. There is also a more practical route: one that is signaled by the shortcomings of the grid-group typology.

1. What happens in the middle? Is there a "gray mish-mash," or does a tiny shift from one side of a dotted line to the other result in a category jump whereas a much bigger shift that stays within a single box result in no change at all?
2. What about the hermit? Is there not some way of avoiding what Douglas has had to do, namely, taking the hermit "off the social map"?
3. What is being classified? Is it the individual (in which case that individual's social involvement must all take place in just one compartment) or is it the pattern of social relationships (together with its supporting cultural bias and the behavioral strategy that is justified and rendered rational by that cultural bias)? If it is the latter, then an individual may lead different parts of his or her life in different compartments.
4. Are the two dimensions really orthogonal? If "low group" corresponds to little or no involvement in grouped patterns, then what is to prevent an individual with low group from putting together an ego-focused network—an activity that is associated with the grid dimension?
5. What about causal priority? If social relations are prior, then cultural biases cannot be prior, and vice versa.

These five awkward questions have been raised, in one form or another, ever since the grid-group scheme was first proposed, and they are raised yet again in several of the chapters in this volume. Since these questions stem from certain shortcomings of the analytical scheme itself—its lack of any dynamical system to generate the typology, its use of continuous dimensions to generate discontinuous patterns, and so on—they cannot be resolved by reference to that analytical scheme. To resolve them we need a *theory*. And, turning the argument around, we will know we *have* a theory when it enables us to answer these five awkward questions.

Looking again at Douglas's account of the grid dimension, we see that "low grid" corresponds to a social setting in which transactions are *symmetrical*, and "high grid" to a social setting in which transactions are *asymmetrical* (Ostrander 1982). If we then make the bold hypothesis that social settings that would generate a relatively even mixture of symmetrical and asymmetrical transactions are simply not viable, then we have got rid of the idea of a continuous grid dimension. In its place we have an either/or dichotomy. It is an either/or, moreover, that allows for a third possibility: no transactions at all, symmetrical or asymmetrical.

Looking yet again at Douglas's account of the group dimension, we see that "low group" corresponds to a social setting in which there is *unfettered competition*, and "high group" to a social setting in which there are all sorts of *constraints*

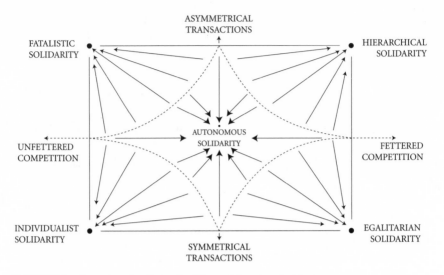

FIGURE I.2   Two tripartite discontinuities and five singularities

on competition. Again, we have an either/or dichotomy. If you are busy bidding and bargaining with whomsoever it pleases you to bid and bargain with, then you are not going to be able to devote yourself to the restraining of that sort of behavior, and vice versa. And, again, this either/or allows for a third possibility: no involvement with others, competitive or cooperative.

The grid-group scheme is now transformed into a plane that contains five points, each of which is altogether different from any of the other points on that plane. They are what mathematicians call *singularities.* If we then add arrows to indicate that these singularities are providing those who move toward them with more and more shared meaning, we can capture the idea that each of these five positions is always defining itself in opposition, or in contradistinction, to the other four: a contested terrain, in other words (Figure I.2). What we have here is not a static typology but the rudiments of a self-organizing dynamical system. Indeed, this diagram is a schematic representation of Cultural Theory's impossibility theorem (Thompson, Ellis, and Wildavsky 1990), which states that these five *social solidarities* or, as we called them in *Cultural Theory,* ways of life (patterns of social relationships together with their supporting sets of values and beliefs), are the only ones that are capable of achieving viability.

A proof of this impossibility theorem can be found in the work of Manfred Schmutzer and Wyllis Bandler (1980; see also Schmutzer 1994), who have demonstrated the process by which relationships can be built up into patterns in terms of a "transaction matrix" that can be solved only if certain conditions are met. They framed these conditions in terms of two notions: *openness* (which corresponds to Cultural Theory's "unfettered competition") and *strong connectedness* (which corresponds to Cultural Theory's "symmetrical transactions"). There are, in all, just four solutions—just four stationary points:

1. When there is openness and strong connectedness, the solution corresponds to the ego-focused networks that characterize market relationships.
2. When there is closure and weak connectedness, the matrix can be rearranged to be "upper triangular," which means that all relationships are hierarchically organized.
3. When there is closure and strong connectedness, we get what is technically an "insoluble matrix"; it is insoluble because instead of giving an across-the-board pattern, it results in a number of unconnected "polka dots." The members of each dot are strongly connected to one another, but each dot is so closed that there are no connections between any member of one dot and any members of the other dots.
4. Finally, there is a seemingly trivial solution in which you cannot really speak of either condition. This is where the matrix transforms into what is called an "all-zero matrix." Not open and not closed (neither unfettered nor fettered in Cultural Theory terms), not strongly connected and not weakly connected (neither symmetrical nor asymmetrical in Cultural Theory terms), this solution is at the absolute zero—no transactions between any individuals.

These four solutions, as Schmutzer and Bandler acknowledge, neatly fit the individualist, the hierarchist, the egalitarian, and the hermit, respectively. The remaining permutation—open but weakly connected—fits the fatalist: no organization and no pattern. (Schmutzer and Bandler show that this has no solution. If fatalists stabilized themselves, they wouldn't be fatalists.) They point out that these five outcomes (which, their proof makes clear, are all the outcomes there are) are "truly distinct types that cannot be transformed into each other unless the principal conditions are altered" (personal communication to Thompson).

This line of reasoning, we readily concede, may look strange to many social scientists. Nevertheless, it is a line of reasoning that we must follow if we are to have a theory and not just an analytical scheme. And it becomes a little less strange once we realize that it has a precedent: Arrow's (1951) justly famous impossibility theorem, which shows that there is no way of aggregating individual values to arrive at a social choice. Theorems, of course, set out from explicit assumptions, and the explicit assumptions from which Arrow sets out—essentially that preferences are inherent to individuals, and that no two individuals are alike—are the assumptions that are explicitly rejected by Cultural Theory. Individuality, Cultural Theorists insist, is not something that inheres in us (like our fingerprints); it is something that, to a considerable extent, we get from others. Without patterned involvement we would not know what we wanted; we discover our preferences by establishing our social relationships. Or, as Elster has it, individuality is "inherently relational" (1989, 6).

This is not a line of reasoning that only sprang into existence with Cultural Theory. It goes back a long way: to the transaction theory pioneered in the 1960s by Fredrik Barth (1966). Barth, like Cultural Theorists, was profoundly dissatisfied with the idea of taking preferences as given. Where, he asked himself, do preferences come from? He began with what present-day practitioners of artificial life modeling call a "soup": a large number of unconnected actors and a large number of things ("objects" as Barth calls them) that they can transact over, thereby becoming involved with others. The challenge Barth set himself, therefore, was to get culture (shared values and beliefs) and social organization (patterned relationships) to emerge from this cultureless and "presocial" setup. Translated into the language of political science, Barth's challenge was this: How do people who do indeed act in their interests come to know where their interests lie?

Initially, Barth's actor (we should be careful not to call him or her an individual yet[1]) does not know what he wants. Uninvolved with others, he has a ragbag of disparate values, and on the basis of those values he enters into transactions over objects that both he and those with whom he transacts happen to value. His ragbag of values provides him with a way of seeing the world and, thanks to that, he is able to discern (albeit dimly) what courses of action are available to him.[2]

He is also able (again, none too clearly) to predict their likely outcomes and hence to select the course that he assesses to be the most advantageous. Since those with whom he is transacting are likely to have rather differently constituted ragbags, the chances are that there will be a perceptible mismatch between what he expects to happen and what actually happens. In the light of this mismatch, he then rearranges his values in the hope of doing rather better next time. The eventual result of this rational behavior, across myriad and often overlapping transactions, is that his ragbag of values gradually becomes more systematized, more internally consistent, and more like those of the people with whom he transacts.

Barth's model of the transactional process matches the Cultural Theory idea that as you become socially engaged—that is, move toward any of the four corners of the diagram (Figure I.2)—you will simultaneously come to know more clearly what you want, and you will get more and more of it.[3] The one big difference, however, is that transaction theory has no directions—no different *kinds* of social involvement. It simply has this systematizing, integrating, and homogenizing process, and the idea is that we all follow it: We start off all over the place (the "soup"), and we all end up at the same place (culture and organization). Cultural Theory, by contrast, argues that there are five places, each of which emerges once the transacting starts, and that some of us end up at each of them. Of course, we do not all stay where we end up—there is always some movement of people between these destinations—but social life is absolutely not a one-way journey to a single destination.[4] Transaction theory, we can now see, has confused the local dynamic—the homing-in process—with the global outcome: the five solidarities or ways of life. It has assumed that because we all home in on something, there is only one something there for us to home in on. Extricating social science from that self-inflicted dead end, you could say, is what Cultural Theory is all about.

This, in many ways, is only the beginning of Cultural Theory. For instance, a diagram like that shown in Figure I.2 requires that there be what students of dynamical systems call a "morphogenetic field" (Thom 1972), of which this diagram is merely the projection onto two dimensions. It also requires that there be two sets of dynamics: a fast local dynamic (which is provided by Barth's transaction theory) and a slower global dynamic (which is provided by Cultural Theory's impossibility theorem). And then there is the question of evolution—history—which requires there to be irreversibilities—costs sunk into one preferred way of doing things: for instance, small-scale, decentralized renewable energy technologies (which is the egalitarian preference) rather than large-scale, centralized fusion technology (which is the hierarchist preference). But we do not want to go into all that here (see Thompson, Ellis, and Wildavsky 1990; Schwarz and Thompson 1990; Thompson 1996a). All we need for the purposes of this book is an explanation of how it is that this excursion into the sort of theory that can explain why the grid-group scheme works can extricate us from those five awkward questions that the scheme itself can never answer.

1. In the middle there is not a "gray mish-mash" but a fifth attractor, a fifth solidarity: the hermit's. And tiny shifts that are across a separatrix (separatrices are the "watersheds" between the various "basins of attraction") do result in a category change (because they bring the person under the thrall of a different attractor) whereas much larger shifts that happen not to cross a separatrix leave the solidarity unaltered.

2. The hermit is now firmly on the "social map," in a central position: a zone within which each of the four patterns of relationships is sufficiently dismantled to allow it then to be built up into one of the other three. Since there is no way of getting from any of these four to any of the others without passing through this central zone, we can begin to see how it is that the hermit is not an "optional extra" in the Cultural Theory typology. If this central zone was not there, then there would be no transactional niche where the four engaged social beings could pause to change their spots, recharge their batteries, lick their wounds, or do whatever it is that has to be done if they are to get from one corner to another. And since one of the tenets of Cultural Theory is that change is a necessary condition for stability, the hermit becomes a vital component of the whole dynamical system.

3. "A plague on both your houses" is the Cultural Theorist's verdict on the long-running dispute between methodological individualists and methodological collectivists. If you accept that false dichotomy, they point out, then you have sliced right through the vital strands—the solidari-

ties—that lace the whole caboodle together. Cultural dynamics, in other words, are independent of social scale, which means that insights gleaned from studies of, say, household consumption styles readily transfer to the international negotiations over carbon emissions in connection with global climate change (Dake and Thompson 1993; Thompson 1997). So it is the form of solidarity—the pattern of social relationships, together with the shared beliefs and values, and the behavioral strategy that is rendered rational by those beliefs and values—that is being classified. This means that if transactions fall into a number of fairly distinct spheres (workplace and home, for instance, or the Swiss villagers' communally owned pastures and private fields), there is no reason why an individual cannot be a vital part of several different forms of solidarity. Of course you cannot interview a form of solidarity—you have to talk to some of its constituent individuals, which is why (as Mary Douglas has always insisted) you have to be sensitive to the transactional context. You do not want your individual to be hopping about from one solidarity to another while you are trying to understand one of those solidarities by talking to him.

4. Grid and Group *are* orthogonal, and they do nicely distinguish between four of the five solidarities or ways of life. However, it is best not to use the term "orthogonal," because it leads one to think in terms of crossed dimensions rather than morphogenetic fields.

5. Causal priority is not the way to think about the relationship between social relations and cultural bias, because each (like the chicken and the egg—another far-from-simple dynamical system) is the cause of the other. The viability of certain comings-together of social relations and cultural biases (those that are pinpointed by the five singularities in Figure I.2), and the nonviability of all the rest, are the crucial features of human social life, features that simply cannot be grasped in terms of linear, cause-and-effect processes.

Culture Matters

Since only about half the chapters in this book are by partisans of Cultural Theory, we should pause here to explain why we have devoted so much time to explaining that theory (and its relationship to the grid-group scheme, which some proponents see as one and the same as Cultural Theory). Our argument is that to say that culture matters, though true, is not enough. Such an assertion all too easily leads us into one or another of two dead ends: the particularism of "thick description," and the vacuity of culture as an uncaused cause. Cultural Theory, whether one buys into it or not, does demonstrate that these two dead ends *are* avoidable—that those who argue that culture matters can, if they wish, gird themselves into a theoretical armor that is superior to that donned by those who hold that culture does not matter. Though the authors of this book are not all Cultural Theorists, they are certainly united around two contentions: that culture matters and that the dead ends of particularism and uncaused causes can be avoided.

The first two chapters address the relationship between rational choice and cultural theories. Social science, Harry Eckstein argues, has always been and should again be a cultural science, that is, a science concerned with enduring orientations to the world and the patterned meanings people attach to that world. Rational choice explanation, or, as Eckstein terms it, "utility-theory," is less social science than metaphysics. Utility-theory is metaphysical in its almost total disregard for empirical observation; the world, to the metaphysician, only gets in the way of one's ability to perceive fixed and abstract truths. Eckstein throws down the gauntlet: Utility-theory's assumptions about human behavior are untenable and its explanatory track record poor, even banal. Social scientists should stop squandering time and resources on a barren research program and begin attending to the empirical regularities of the social world.

The weaknesses of rational choice theory are also the starting point for Sun-Ki Chai. Foremost among these weaknesses, Chai points out, is rational choice theory's lack of curiosity about the origins of preferences and beliefs. Preferences are assumed rather than explained. Reductionist assumptions of selfish, materialist preferences and beliefs that are based on observation and logical inference lead to inaccurate predictions, and the alternative of leaving preferences and beliefs exogenous and unspecified makes rational choice theory indeterminate. Unlike Eckstein, Chai argues not that we should jettison rational choice theory altogether but rather that we should join rational choice theory with cultural theory so as to provide an explicit way of transforming culture into predictions about individual and group behavior in the presence of structural constraints. Cultural Theory, for instance, explains why there may be differences among cultures in their propensity to engage in violent behavior (Chai and Wildavsky 1994), and rational choice theory can explain why members of a single culture may act differently in the presence of different structural constraints. To take another example, Cultural Theory explains how the distribution of political preferences of voters may change over time (Chai and Wildavsky forthcoming), and rational choice theory can explain how these changes translate into changes in the success of different political parties. A synthesis of cultural theory and rational choice theory, Chai argues, can provide more powerful explanations than either theory can alone.

Whereas cultural theorists criticize rational choice theories for assuming preferences, critics of cultural explanations typically fault cultural theorists for assuming values. Culture, these critics insist, is a consequence, not (or at least not only) a cause of institutional structures. Typical is Brian Barry's argument (1970) that a democratic culture is a learned response to living under democratic institutions rather than—as he claimed Almond and Verba argued in their seminal work, *The Civic Culture* (1963)—a prerational commitment exerting a causal force upon those institutions. Similarly, Alessandro Pizzorno (1966) criticized Edward Banfield's classic study, *The Moral Basis of a Backward Society* (1958), for explaining the absence of collective action in southern Italy as a product of an irrational "ethos" rather than in terms of a rational response to their "marginalized" position in the economic and political structure. Such disputes, as we have already argued, miss the chicken-and-egg point.

To deny that culture is shaped by institutional structure, critics continue, makes the concept of culture deeply mysterious and unfathomable. As Peter Hall points out, "unless cultural theories can account for the origins of . . . attitudes by reference to the institutions that generate and reproduce them, they do little more than summon up a *deus ex machina* that is itself unexplainable" (1986, 34). We agree that culture must not be treated as an uncaused cause purportedly explaining why people behave as they do yet incapable of itself being explained. To do so is to posit a world in which values are disembodied, unattached to human subjects. A convincing cultural theory must also be a theory of institutions, of social relations. Cultural theories must provide a precise account of what types of institutions shape which preferences or interests in what kinds of ways, and vice versa.

Dennis Coyle attempts to provide just such a cultural theory of organizations in his chapter. Coyle shows that the categories generated by the grid and group dimensions possess the advantage of holding onto the best in previous organizational theory and research, thus cumulating findings, while opening up new areas of inquiry as well. Any theory of organizations must be able to account for the two modes of organizing—hierarchies and markets—that dominate social science theories. Charles Lindblom (1977) and Oliver Williamson (1975) are only two of the many scholars who have based entire bodies of theory on this fundamental distinction. Sensing that there may be more than markets and hierarchy, some organizational theorists occasionally mention "clans" (Ouchi 1980), "clubs" (Williamson 1975), or "collegiums" (Majone 1986), but these types do not come from the same matrix, are not built out of the same dimensions, as markets and hierarchies. A contribution of the grid-group typology is to derive the egalitarian and despotic modes of organization from dimensions that can also produce the more familiar categories of markets and hierarchy.

Elinor and Vincent Ostrom provide an opportunity for a reprise by outlining a little bit of culture formation: their long-running and spirited discourse with Aaron Wildavsky, Harold Lasswell, Robert Dahl, and Charles Lindblom—a high-powered effort to knit together disciplinary strands that for too long have gone their separate ways. The result, not surprisingly, is a contested terrain, with the Ostroms maintaining that a general theory is not possible and Wildavsky (and the other Cultural Theorists) insisting that it is. Much, however, depends on what a theory is. The Ostroms distinguish between models, theories, and frameworks, relying on Walter Eucken's idea that different systems of order (hunters and gatherers, say, and modern industrial societies) require different theories. Cultural Theory, by this criterion, cannot be a theory, because it explicitly applies to any society, any time, any place. For the

Ostroms, therefore, Cultural Theory is a framework. But how much contestation is entailed in these different usages of the word "theory"?

The answer may depend on whether you take Cultural Theory to be one and the same as the grid-group scheme. If you do, then the contestation is considerable, because the grid-group scheme is only a model in Ostromian terms, yet it is being used as a framework by its proponents. But if, as we have been arguing, Cultural Theory is the deep dynamical explanation for why the grid-group scheme works, then there is much less to contest. Indeed, to the extent that Cultural Theory is a theory of theories (which is the spirit in which Coyle has used it), then it is clearly a framework in terms of the Ostroms' division of the terrain. If we are right, then, the Ostroms' reservations apply not to Cultural Theory but to the grid-group scheme masquerading as Cultural Theory. Indeed, their reservations closely match the "shortcomings" we have already listed: "What happens in the middle?" and "Are the dimensions orthogonal?" The Ostroms also worry about cultural biases (which coexist within each and every conventional "culture") being too glibly referred to as cultures and about the fact that animal species have organization without having any culture to bias.

It would be too optimistic to say that all this contestation disappears once we have distinguished between the grid-group scheme (the model in Ostromian terms) and Cultural Theory (the framework in Ostromian terms), but at least we can claim progress. Culture and cultural bias *have* been too readily conflated; culture is *not* a prerequisite for organization, but if you have culture and you are organized, then you will have cultural biases. And these biases (and the ways of organizing and disorganizing that they accompany) are what Cultural Theory (or is it Cultural Framework?) is trying to get hold of. Put another way, the long-running, transdisciplinary discourse that the Ostroms both describe and contribute to is vital to social science.

The perennial question of culture's place in explanations of change is taken up by political scientist Charles Lockhart and by sociologist Arthur Stinchcombe. Drawing upon German, Japanese, and American history, Lockhart attempts to show that Cultural Theory can account for political change. Building on *Cultural Theory* (Thompson, Ellis, and Wildavsky 1990, chaps. 4 and 5), Lockhart emphasizes that no cultural bias is a thing for all seasons, good for all times and places. Thus as historical circumstances change, some cultural biases and modes of organizing are inevitably advantaged and others disadvantaged. The Great Depression, to take an extreme example, made it more difficult for self-reliant individualists to insist or persuade others that failure was the fault of the individual. In an era of massive unemployment those egalitarians who pinned the blame on "the system" became more persuasive and consequently gained adherents. Lockhart places special emphasis on the social pressures that lead cultural adherents to make and break alliances. By placing these unstable alliances at the heart of the matter, Lockhart shows that culture, far from being static, is constantly changing as adherents continually forge, break apart, and renegotiate alliances.

Stinchcombe takes another route altogether in accounting for cultural change. His is the path of the fox who knows many things rather than Lockhart's hedgehog, who knows one big thing. Rather than seek, as Lockhart does, a single, unified organizing principle, Stinchcombe wishes to "fragment" theory. Stinchcombe begins with a simple puzzle: Culture is said by theorists to be static and unchanging, and yet when we look around us we see rapid changes in values and attitudes across a wide range of issues, from premarital sex and smoking to capital punishment and partisan identification. Moreover, these changes in culture cannot be reduced to changes in objective social circumstances—crime rates, urbanization, industrialization, and the like. For all his differences with Lockhart, Stinchcombe agrees that the answer to this puzzle lies in greater attention to how people learn throughout their lives from current events (such as elections) and institutions (such as the Boy Scouts, Planned Parenthood, or universities). Stinchcombe also usefully points out that the puzzle is partly a product of the divorce between empirical studies of culture, which focus on changeable attitudes while slighting the unspoken assumptions of a culture, and cultural theories, which focus on the fixed and the constraining and slight the changeable attitudes and values. Only by bringing theory and empirical research together, Stinchcombe intimates, will we produce satisfactory accounts of cultural change.

Stinchcombe and Lockhart agree that just because culture is somehow "deep" does not make it stable, any more than tectonic plates buried deep in the earth's crust make for a surface free of earthquakes and volcanoes. They also agree that the juxtaposition of culture and change, as if the existence of the latter invalidated the importance of the former, is wrong-headed. Whether we shall advance further by fragmenting cultural theory, as Stinchcombe believes, or by building a more coherent, even unified cultural theory, as Lockhart believes, remains to be seen. It will likely entail both, since, as Stinchcombe shows, much that is at present unified needs to be fragmented and, as Lockhart shows, much that is at present fragmented needs to be unified.

Cultural theorists can pat themselves on the back for showing that culture is a "contested terrain" (Fantasia and Hirsch 1995, 145) upon which rival adherents are continually striving to advance their distinctive biases. But that culture is contested does not mean that everything in a culture is always politicized; only that it may *become* politicized (and that other parts that *are* politicized may cease to be so). Tariq Banuri has wagered that the price of pork on the world market could go to zero (or even become negative) and no Pakistani—hierarchist, individualist, egalitarian, fatalist, or hermit—would start eating it.[5] Yet we also know that deep-seated, across-the-board cultural components such as this *do* change. Indeed, it is precisely one of these changes that provides Stinchcombe with his point of departure: The accepted—in this case, advice on interracial association—becomes unacceptable. So things cultural do not stay the same, and often it is precisely those things that people are most convinced are unchangeable that change. It used to be said, to take another example, that a German joke is no laughing matter, yet that ponderousness (like the authoritarianism that was also believed to be so definitive of Germanness) is hard to find these days.

Here, then, for those who believe that culture matters, is a rich seam to open up. Moreover, if theorizing on culture has become so unified that it is insisting that changes like this cannot happen, then the sort of fragmentation Stinchcombe is calling for is badly needed. Indeed, it is a necessary step on the way toward the sort of reunification that Lockhart is calling for. The contested terrain that Cultural Theory gives us is not the sort of place where things change slowly or not at all. It is a place where adaptation—"social learning," as it is sometimes called—is always happening, often suddenly, and often in the places where it is least expected.

Perhaps nowhere is the contested terrain of culture more evident than in the area of risk perception. From ozone depletion to deforestation to hazardous waste, we find in the same society, among people with the same education or income levels, radically different perceptions of the significance of these risks and of who is to blame. Mary Douglas, in her chapter in this volume, indicts reigning approaches to risk perception for proceeding as if risk perceptions were formed independently of political conflicts. Psychometric approaches, she charges, have tried to cast risk assessment as properly being above mere politics, ignoring that risks and dangers are always used as political weapons. Cultural adherents reveal their true colors in the risks they accent and in whom they blame for those risks. The contest over risk, Douglas concludes, is part and parcel of the perennial struggle between rival ways of life, and no theory that slights the cultural dimension of risk perception can be taken seriously.

Howard Margolis concedes the importance of cultural bias and social construction, but rightly worries that the social constructivist approach at times becomes "an amorphous beast that wants to gobble far more than it reasonably ought to be fed." (Mary Douglas expresses similar concerns, suggesting that "social construal" might be preferable to "social construction.") Margolis attempts to carve out a role for individual cognition that avoids both the tautological "dread factor" (people, the cognitive psychologists tell us, dread the dreadful) and the social naïveté of "risk realism" (which assumes that risk perceptions reflect knowledge). Although Margolis uses the tools of cognitive psychometrics and Douglas the tools of Cultural Theory, their different approaches begin from a similar premise: "that qualitative aspects of risk dominate lay perception to the point that how much danger is really there can be treated as irrelevant." Margolis no less than Douglas opens up the acultural and apolitical understanding of risk that has dominated policy analysis in the United States over the past few decades. Cognition, Margolis shows, works in wondrous ways—ways that, far from excluding the cultural and the political from the processes of risk perception, make those involvements inevitable. Cultural and cognitive approaches are certainly distinct, but they are far more complementary than has hitherto been recognized.

Believing that a theory should not be judged against an impossible standard of perfection but rather by how well it performs in comparison with rival theories,

Gunnar Grendstad and Per Selle compare Cultural Theory with Ronald Inglehart's well-known cultural theory of postmaterialism. Inglehart's theory rests on Abraham Maslow's notion of a "hierarchy of needs" whereby the satisfaction of basic needs such as clothing, shelter, and food then allows people to pursue higher needs such as self-expression and spiritual fulfillment. Environmental protection, in Inglehart's theory, is one of these higher, derived needs that people pursue only after they have satisfied their basic, economic needs (Inglehart 1971, 1977, 1979, 1990). This is an elegant and attractive theory, but Grendstad and Selle, using a 1993 public opinion survey conducted in Norway, show that the hypothesized connection between environmentalism and postmaterialism is weak to nonexistent. They find, moreover, that Cultural Theory's categories do a much better job of accounting for variations in environmental values and beliefs. The category of egalitarianism, in particular, proves to be especially important in understanding environmental attitudes.

Grendstad and Selle's findings are corroborated by the research reported in Richard Ellis and Fred Thompson's chapter on environmental attitudes in the U.S. Northwest. It is tempting to view environmental attitudes as existing on a more lofty or elevated plane than grubby economic interests. Environmentalism, we are sometimes told, is above all this; ideologically autonomous, it transcends the conventional debates over equality and capitalism. Ellis and Thompson find this autonomy thesis sorely lacking; what they find instead is that environmental attitudes are deeply embedded in broader sociocultural orientations toward equality and markets. Human attitudes toward the environment, like other human attitudes, are powerfully joined to our preferences about how we wish to live with one another. Try as we might to separate them, perceptions of the environment and risk cannot be separated from cultural involvements.

The final section of this book begins with Robert Klitgaard's important challenge to cultural theorists. Klitgaard asks what cultural theories can tell us about practical empirical and normative problems, specifically problems of development and change in the so-called Third World. Granted that culture matters, how *should* one take cultural diversity into account when planning development projects? To say that we must take culture into account is to sidestep the hard question of whether policymakers should simply accept the local culture as it is, or should try to subvert or change it. Should one be a "trait-taker" or a "trait-maker"? The questions Klitgaard poses are both empirical—When and how can people adapt policies to existing cultures? When and how can people intentionally change or preserve aspects of culture?—and ethical—How should we take these culture-by-policy interactions into account?

There are two ways in which culture (or, rather, the relative strengths and patterns of interaction of the biases within culture) might be taken into account in policy work. The first is the way Klitgaard assumes it should happen: by somehow "factoring in" these currently disregarded variables so as to improve the already established ways of achieving development. This of course requires that we not question the idea of development. The second is much more wrathful, aiming not to augment and improve these established ways but to destroy them. Michael Thompson opts for the wrathful alternative and answers Klitgaard's challenge by rewriting the precepts of policy analysis—a bold undertaking that he quickly scales down to the more modest suggestion that Cultural Theory (unlike, say, rational choice theory) allows us to discern this enticing opportunity for a bout of creative destruction.

Thompson's argument is that the social science used in policy analysis represents a congenial coming together of the managerial predilections of policymakers and the one-way-journey-to-a-single-destination of the "masters." Social systems, conceived in this way, are *simple* (linear, deterministic, insensitive to initial conditions, predictable, and, with adequate knowledge, steerable). Cultural Theory rejects these assumptions, insisting instead that social systems (like ecosystems) are *complex* (nonlinear, indeterministic, highly sensitive to initial conditions, and unpredictable, even with complete knowledge, which of course is unattainable anyway). The policy tool kit that we routinely reach for—cost-benefit analysis, probabilistic risk assessment, single metrics, and all those approaches that assume that uncertainty is merely the absence of certainty—is of no use whatsoever if things are complex. Indeed, it is positively harmful (which begins to explain why the word "development" is best enclosed in quotation marks). In this exhilarating argument (and it is always nice to finish with an exhilarating argument) we have to do two things, neither of which will be easy. We have to put down the familiar tool kit, and we have to assemble and learn to use the tool kit appropriate to policy in a complex world.

To be useful in the real and complex world of public policy, the culture concept must be brought down from the rarefied plane of abstract definitions and conceptualizations in order to be measured and fitted. "Plenty of definitions but too little theory" was the verdict of anthropologists Alfred Kroeber and Clyde Kluckhohn in the early 1950s, one reaffirmed by political scientist Robert Tucker (1973, 174) a quarter century later. One can never have enough theory, but the verdict today might be more properly rendered: "Plenty of definitions, a few theories, far too little measurement, and precious few predictions."

That cultural variables are often difficult to measure does not mean that we should give up on building testable cultural theories. This is the seductive path taken by many of those who march under the currently fashionable banner of "cultural studies." Practitioners of "cultural studies" would dismiss Klitgaard's concerns about measurement, specification, and testing as a sorry relic of "positivist" science. Though we share cultural studies' vocabulary of "social construction," subjectivity, and meaning, we do not share its hostility to building testable empirical theories that help us explain the world around us. As we explained in the preface of *Cultural Theory,* "this rigid dichotomy between interpretation of meaning and scientific explanation is unjustified. It is true that human beings create meaning. But it is also true that it is possible to make statements of regularities that help in explaining and even predicting (or retrodicting) the human construction of meaning. Subjectivity need not rule out regularity as long as different sorts of people feel subjective in similar ways with regard to similar objects. . . . [S]ocial science and the interpretation of meaning are not only compatible but essentially also the same subject" (Thompson, Ellis, and Wildavsky 1990, xiii–xiv).

Is this faith in a rigorous science of culture naïvely optimistic? We think not. The promise of cultural theory is attested to by Robert Putnam and his colleagues' (1993) painstakingly careful work on Italian regional governance, the immense body of cross-national survey research that has been spawned by Ronald Inglehart's seminal work on postmaterialism (1971, 1977, 1981, 1990; Inglehart and Abramson 1994), the rigorous operationalization of the grid-group typology by Jonathan Gross and Steve Rayner (1985), and the quantitative work by Stephen Cornell and Joseph Kalt (1993) measuring the impact of cultural norms on self-government on American Indian reservations, to list only a few exemplars of cultural research. Works such as these do not just affirm that "culture matters" but set themselves to the much more difficult task of specifying the ways in which culture matters, the conditions under which it matters, and how much it matters. "Culture matters" is more than just a rallying cry, then; it is an insistence that we show how, when, and why culture matters in the real world.

Notes

1. For convenience, we will refer to this actor as "he" from now on.

2. The objection that Barth seems to be explaining how people get their preferences by assuming that they set off with some of them already in place has been rebutted by Robert Heiner (1993). Heiner uses simple mathematical arguments to show that, faced with an uncertain environment, it is advantageous ("rational," as Herbert Simon would say) to limit your choice of actions. That way you stand a chance of learning *something* about the world—an insight that is consistent with Barth's "ragbag" assumption and that is now routinely adopted by modelers of artificial life.

3. Actually, it is not quite as simple as this, because the center too is an "attractor," and it is in moving toward this (and away from social involvement) that the hermit learns what he wants and does not want. To represent all this correctly, we need a "morphogenetic field" (see Figure I.2).

4. Cf. those who follow Durkheim (mechanical to organic solidarity), Tönnies (gemeinschaft to gesellschaft), Maine (status to contract), or Marx (transfer of control over the means of production from the bourgeoisie to the proletariat). See Thompson, Ellis, and Wildavsky 1990, part two.

5. Tariq Banuri, director of the Sustainable Development Policy Institute in Pakistan, personal communication to Michael Thompson.

Part One

*Rational Choice
and Cultural Choice*

Chapter One

Social Science as Cultural Science, Rational Choice as Metaphysics

HARRY ECKSTEIN

The ideas of political culture and of rational choice—or, to use a more appropriate term, utility, or utility rationality[1]—underlie the currently dominant approaches to constructing theory in political science. The opposition between these approaches is nothing new. It goes back to the very beginning of the idea of positive (that is, empirical) social science in the early nineteenth century.

Starting then and continuing over a century or so, the idea of culture was worked out as a solution to a problem first raised by Auguste Comte in *The Positive Philosophy* (1830–1835). This was how the social sciences would differ from the other sciences when they finally developed. Comte had argued—convincingly, I think—that all of the sciences developed through three stages: first a theological stage, in which the natural was explained by the supernatural; then a metaphysical stage, in which understanding of experience is sought through pure thought; and finally a positive stage, in which explanations are constructed inductively. The progress of the positive sciences, Comte argued further, was a developmental order, in which the sciences of the simpler phenomena developed first, the more complex later, and the most complex, social science, last—a development that in Comte's time was still to come.

Comte thought that all of the sciences are a single enterprise in that they have the same fundamental aim: to discover the laws that govern experience. Different subject matters, however, require different tacks to accomplish that aim, although each science can learn from others. All of the sciences also have a single epistemology, the ultimate arbiter of the truth-value of scientific theories being observation. Special subject matters, however, also call for special methods of inquiry, although, again, inquirers should apply methods from other areas, if applicable.

The idea of culture was thus intended from the start to be a foundation concept for empirical social science, as against essentialist metaphysical thought, which disdained observation. Moreover, the idea was developed in explicit opposition to the rival notion of utility that underlies what we now call rational choice.

The most basic argument of the cultural approach is that actions have meaning to the agents who take them, and that explanations in social science therefore should characteristically be couched in terms of underlying meanings that "orient" agents to the situations in which they have to act. The most basic difference between cultural theory and utility theory is that in the former, orientations to situations are not fixed in human nature but are variable, whereas in the latter, they are invariable, always consisting of the calculation of cost-benefit ratios. It should be manifest that this difference compels choice between the two approaches, for it is impossible for the same thing to be both uniform and variable.

In this chapter I argue that the cultural conception of how empirical social science should proceed is correct and the utility approach deeply flawed. I will do this first by outlining the basic traits of cultural science as it can and should be practiced—*as* a science—and then by showing that utility theory, despite its claims to be proper science, is a regrettable reversion to prescientific, that is, metaphysical, thinking.

The second part of the argument is important because in justifying the cultural approach it does not suffice merely to argue that the cultural tack makes sense; it should also be shown that the cultural approach makes more sense than alternatives. The first part is important because basing political science, let alone the social sciences generally, on the notion of culture has often been perceived as contrary to the scientific spirit. Contemporary culturalists who practice "interpretation" and "phenomenology" take this position themselves, as if it were a virtue. It is thought, even more generally and by scholars who otherwise would be supportive of cultural science, that culturalism condemns one to the use of loose methods and inexact, impressionistic observations—exactly what the practice of science seeks most to avoid.

I will try to show here that these beliefs are unwarranted. Cultural science no doubt is difficult to practice; its proper practice requires discipline and ingenuity; its elaboration will be the work of many people over much time; and its early achievements will be woefully inadequate. But these statements can be made about all of the sciences.

Outline of the Nature of Cultural Science

The Axiomatic Basis of Cultural Theories

Every positive theory and system of theories makes certain assumptions about the nature of its subject matter that can and should be stated in axiomatic form. Doing so permits deductions from the theory that should be corroborated by observations if the assumptions are to receive assent. The assumptions are never just assumptions. They are claims that the surface appearance of observed phenomena has been penetrated to a deeper level that validly explains the surface.

Elsewhere I have argued that cultural theories rest on four related axioms at their "theoretical core"[2] and spelled out numerous empirically testable inferences that can be drawn from them about the nature of political change (Eckstein 1988). These axioms can also be regarded, jointly, as a complete technical definition of what exactly culture means as a scientific concept. I will summarize the axioms here, referring the reader to the cited article for elaboration.

The Postulate of Oriented Action.   This is the keystone of cultural theories. It says that actors have general dispositions to act in standardized ways in sets of situations. Orientations are not the same as attitudes. They are *general* dispositions evidenced in sets of attitudes. If, for example, an actor acts tolerantly toward some particular group, say, gay people, that is an attitude. To say that someone is tolerant is to say that he has a general disposition toward tolerance vis-à-vis groups (in the plural) perceived as "different" from normal. Thus statements about orientations are generalizations about how agents invest their world with meaning as a condition of acting in the situations that confront them.

In the case of individuals, the postulate says that their behavior follows a "mediated stimulus-response" model (Osgood 1958), with orientations doing the mediating. In the case of societies or subsocieties, it says that they manifest certain typical orientations that frequently occur in them.

Both individuals and collectives may manifest a relative lack of standard orientations; that is the essence of anomie. The postulate of oriented action implies that such a state of affairs will be accompanied by pathologies, because particular orientations to action and general sets of such orientations perform indispensable functions in the economy of human existence, individual and collective. These functions are principally twofold:

1. Orientations have an *economizing* function, so to speak: They relieve actors of the impossible burden of decoding and encoding every situation afresh before acting. When, for example, I feel drowsy late at night, I do not calculate whether, on balance, I should go to sleep, where, how, and for how long. I simply go through a routine: I check whether it is (culturally) normal bedtime, do my normal ablutions, don the normal sleeping uniform, go to the normal sleeping place,

and use the normal sleeping furniture. If I had been forced to calculate all this out, I would probably not have slept at all.

2. Orientations that are shared also make social interactions and relationships *predictable.* Without predictability the relationships could hardly exist at all. Orientations are an indispensable source of "negative entropy" in social relations and systems. You sleep better if you are reasonably sure that no one will telephone you after the (culturally) normal bedtime. Likewise, if you are telephoned later than that, the other party will generally know where and in what state to find you. Nearly everyone's life, happily, is replete with such observed routines. When that is not the case, troubles ensue.

Since these functions are vitally important, the postulate further implies that there will be a tendency, successful or not, to reduce anomie where it exceeds some threshold. Anomie is a force of social entropy; integrated culture is "negentropic." Like all the rest of existence, social life can be regarded as a battleground on which entropic and negentropic forces—in this case anomie and culture—constantly contest.

The Postulate of Orientational Variability.   This postulate says two things (which could also be stated as separate axioms). It says that orientations are not simply epiphenoma of objective situational conditions; that is, they cannot be inferred directly from situations. The same situations can be interpreted to mean a virtually unlimited variety of things. If this were not the case, one could simply reason directly from situations to action, bypassing a great deal of troublesome stuff, such as how to find out what actors' orientations actually are. The postulate also says, of course, that orientations are not all the same.

The postulate does not say that orientations must necessarily be appropriate to the situations actors face. However, since orientations furnish understandings of situations, problems must follow if for any reason the orientations come to be seen as having little utility for comprehending experience—for instance, as a result of noncultural social changes.

The Postulate of Socialization.   This postulate extends the second. It says that since orientations do not vary by objective conditions and are not fixed in human nature, then they must have an external cultural source; that is, they must be imparted by previously socialized carriers of culture. The postulate does not say that learning leaves no room for individual creativity. It does imply that creativity in regard to meaning is always tightly constrained, and indeed presupposes a great deal of prior learning.

The Postulate of Cumulative Learning.   This postulate says two things:

1. One is that early learning is more important than later learning; it acts as a sort of filter through which later learning must pass. No one is free at any point to

return to a state of infancy in regard to culture, or even to regress any great distance toward such a state. One reason for this is that if it were otherwise, culture would be infinitely malleable and fragile and therefore incapable of performing its functions. Another is that advanced and complex learning always builds on earlier and simpler learning. No doubt learning goes on in some measure throughout life; it must do so because orientations must be relevant to life-changes in situations in the normal course of life. But early learning limits greatly the extent and ease of later learning.

The related questions of just how much late learning is possible, how much early learning can be undone without incurring grave dysfunctions, and under what conditions substantial "reorientation" may be required and/or feasible, must be answered through research. Adaptation to changed conditions, which includes relearning, is critical to individual and social functioning, no matter what core axioms are used in theorizing. The axioms of cultural theory, however, lead one to suppose that reorientation is always difficult to accomplish and usually fraught with dangers of pathology.

2. The postulate also says that there is a tendency to make the bits and pieces of learning into a coherent (consistent, consonant) set. To the extent that orientations are contradictory, or even just eclectic, they cannot effectively serve their functions. The postulate does not say that all actors or cultures have consistent orientations, but it implies that, to the extent that this is not the case, problems ensue. A counterpart of anomie, then, is what we might call *cultural dissonance*, to which what I said earlier about anomie also applies.

The Inertia Theorem.   Even if we knew nothing about any specific culture, we would be able to develop a considerable body of testable hypotheses from these postulates. The postulates themselves, to some extent, may be directly testable as hypotheses—for instance, against the very large literature we have on socialization, general and political (Hyman 1959).

One deduction that may be made from the postulates and that is clearly of first importance is that cultures, other things being equal, will display a high degree of continuity, or "inertia." This does not mean that cultural changes do not occur, any more than the principle of physical inertia implies that there is never change in the direction or velocity of objects in motion. Both physical and cultural inertia, however, imply that continuity in motion is the "normal" state, and that changes are always a result of certain contingent forces and must always take certain forms. I developed this point in the article cited earlier (Eckstein 1988), in which a number of other hypotheses about cultural change and inertia were also developed from the core postulates. One of these is what might be called the adaptation theorem. This says that changes in culture "normally" are adaptive to changes in situations, unless large-scale radical change is deliberately pursued or unavoidable. Adaptive change is change that is made for the sake of continuity:

pattern-maintaining change. The two theorems, which appear to point in opposite directions—toward continuity and toward change—are thus reconciled, as logically they must be.

An important point that follows from the inertia theorem is that research into processes of reorientation will provide telling tests, perhaps even crucial tests, of cultural theory. If large-scale reorientation occurs readily, without the risk of serious dysfunctions, and especially if this is so even in cases that are not somehow "naturals" (most-likely cases) for reorientation, then cultural theories are refuted wholesale. This point should be elaborated separately, and then researched. I indicate it here to show that axiomatization can lead not just to pertinent research but directly to potentially severe empirical tests of theory.

A Technical Definition of Culture.   We are now in a position to formulate a concise definition of "culture" as a scientific concept: *Cultures are the variable and cumulatively learned patterns of orientations to action in societies.* The modifiers of "orientations"—"variable" and "cumulatively learned"—are required because orientations might not have these traits, in which case they would not constitute culture. This definition is elaborated in the four postulates in such a way that definition and theory are immediately linked.

Cultural Interpretations as Hypotheses

Every culture and subculture has its distinct signs, norms, and cognitive beliefs governing meaning. Each may be treated as a separate behavioral world. When we state what its signs, norms, and cognitions are, we "interpret" the culture; this includes describing it in concepts designed for comparison and generalization. We also interpret when we account for particular actions or action sets in a culture on the basis of the particular traits of the culture.[3]

In Weber's principal methodological writings on what he called "interpretive sociology," he insisted that any interpretation must be treated as a hypothesis. As such it can have no claim to validity except through testing against evidence. A cultural interpreter may be ever so steeped in the details of a culture; he or she may have observed it closely and over a long period of time as a participant observer; he or she may be ever so sensitive and clever; but while one may award an extra benefit of doubt for such virtues, the "proof" still is in the inductive pudding.

I mean this to apply especially to what has been called "thick description" (Geertz 1973). Thick description has sometimes been offered as an alternative to positive social science, and a preferable alternative. It involves an epistemology that is antiscientific and supposedly atheoretical. However, even in the hands of a Geertz interpreting Bali, thick description yields nothing more than plausible hypotheses, like every other theoretical construction. The claim that an interpretation is "thick" does not alter the fact that it is more than just description. It is a claim that something underlies surface appearances, and therefore it is theory. As long as no attempt is made to test thick descriptions as hypotheses, they are just surmises, or perhaps very high-level travel literature.

In the following I offer an example of interpretation in both senses of the term from my own work and through it try to show that interpretations of particular cultures, treated as hypotheses, can be part and parcel of positive social science.

Political cultures, and authority cultures more generally, contain as an important component certain decision rules: norms about the conditions under which collective decisions are considered to have been taken properly, so that they are binding on the collectivity. These may be rules stated explicitly in a constitution, but such formal rules may or may not be the operative rules.

In a book about Norway, written mainly in 1964 (Eckstein 1966), I argued that a kind of "consensual" decision rule prevails there. The rule says something like this: Agree widely, preferably unanimously; if this is not possible, appear in public to be widely agreed (take co-responsibility; stop criticizing); and if this is also not possible, drop the subject, if you can. This rule has cognitive elements ("anything widely agreed to is more likely to be right than anything not so agreed"); it also involves affect (Norwegians generally feel uncomfortable with disagreements). Saying that this is the Norwegian rule does not mean that all Norwegians subscribe to it as a personal value. It means that the rule is so widely shared that it constrains just about all Norwegians when they engage in collective decisionmaking.

This statement of the Norwegian decision-rule was a rather shallow empirical generalization, confined of course to Norway. Its basis in evidence was much unsystematic observation, from small neighborhood clubs to the parliamentary level. It could be, and it was, attacked as resting only on "anecdotal" evidence. I answered that criticism in a subsequent article, pointing out that what counts most is not the material out of which hypotheses are formulated, but how well they stand up to testing, especially by risky predictions of unknowns.

A fortunate occasion for such prediction—something like a natural experiment—arose just at that time. In 1965 a general election brought to power a so-called bourgeois coalition, after thirty years of continuous rule by the social-democratic Labor Party. The coalition was an odd combination of incompatible parties. It included a party that stood mainly for urban business interests; another that represented agricultural interests; a nonreligious and an antireligious party; a Christian fundamentalist party; and a small party that represented especially the ideas of liberal intellectuals. The parties represented views and interests that had been the source of Norway's deepest political cleavages. In the circumstances, almost all informed opinion was that the coalition had no chance of lasting any substantial length of time.

In the article that replied to the criticism of my hypothetical formulation of the Norwegian decision-rule I offered a test. This consisted of four predictions of the future of the new coalition, all obviously very risky given the background of informed belief: First, the coalition would endure by avoiding all divisive issues (some of these were specified). Second, it would work smoothly by concentrating on the most widely agreed subject (in this case, reducing taxes—always a useful subject for getting agreement). Third, it would do little or nothing to undo the welfare state that had been built by the Labor Party (which still had 40 percent of the parliamentary seats). And fourth, it would fall apart if it were forced to deal with any issue that would mobilize its fissions. This included the possibility that the coalition would have to deal with the potentially deeply divisive issue of whether or not Norway should join the European Economic Community. The reason that this issue would arouse deep latent divisions in Norway also was a matter of cultural interpretation that could be tested by the same prediction (Eckstein 1967).

Events corroborated all of these predictions. The predictions constituted "severe" tests of the hypothesis from which they were derived, and thus their outcomes were "strong corroborations" (see Watkins 1984, 294–297). They illustrate that there is no reason why cultural interpretations should not live up to high Popperian standards of inductive corroboration. If interpretations also display high sensitivity or are packaged in good literary prose, so much the better; bonus points for style may be awarded, but these things are in no way relevant to validity.

Cultural Nomothesis

Although each culture is distinct from every other, that does not preclude the formulation of general theories about culture, including theories that state universal laws. Every individual entity is in some sense unique. My cat is distinct from your cat, and my molecules are not yours. This does not mean that I cannot generalize about cathood, or that there cannot be any such field as molecular biology. It is the same with cultures.

Deductive-nomological explanation, as Hempel has called it (1966, 51–54), explains particular phenomena via invariant empirical laws, applied deductively to variable initial conditions. Cultural interpretation, of course, is also explanation, but it seems useful to keep interpretive and nomological explanations distinct, if only because some who accept the possibility of cultural explanation at the level of the particular deny it at the level of the general, especially if that level is the universal.

To discover general laws of culture, one must of course deal with characteristics that they share. Here special theoretical concepts are required, and this makes great demands on theoretical ingenuity and gives plenty of scope to theoretical imagination. Although the formation of concepts useful for generalizing broadly about cultures is still at a primitive stage, some beginnings have been made; this includes some of my own works. The kind of universals developed in these works are what one might call formal universals. They identify general "forms" that culture can exhibit despite great variability in their "contents." These concepts may serve as examples of what is required in a cultural science of universal scope.

Congruence-Incongruence.   A universal trait of cultures is the extent to which subcultures in them are congruent, that is, substantially similar in form. Particular degrees of congruence characterize particular cultures; degrees of congruence, large and small, characterize all. I have argued that high congruence of the authority-cultures found in societies is a necessary condition of high governmental stability and performance (Eckstein 1966, appendix). Potentially, congruence theory may explain even more than that. It may explain social stability in general or explain the stability and performance of any collectives, subsocietal, societal, and transnational. Obviously work needs to be done to make concepts like congruence operational and exact. Some work toward this end was in fact done, over a long period, by myself and collaborators (Eckstein and Gurr 1975).

Consonance-Dissonance.   Another such universal trait of cultures (including subcultures) is the extent to which their traits are consonant or dissonant. These concepts are trickier than congruence, so I will go into them a bit more extensively.

By consonance and dissonance I refer to how well the constituent elements of culture "fit" one another—the extent to which they are harmonious combinations or the opposite, just as in combinations of musical tones. This too is potentially a powerful explanatory notion. Like chemical compounds, some cultural compounds may be stable, unstable, volatile, or downright explosive; some may enable systems and subsystems to do work, and others may impede their energy.

To apply the notion of consonance, it is necessary to have some notions of the constituent elements of culture patterns. Conceivably, we may at some time in the future have a scheme for characterizing the elements of culture patterns (and also of social structures) analogous to the periodic table, which is a powerful device for both descriptive and theoretical purposes. We have nothing of the kind yet, not even a primitive beginning. This is not because we cannot have such a scheme but because we have not seriously tried to devise one.

Here too I tried to make a start (with Ted R. Gurr), by developing what we called an "analytic scheme" for characterizing authority relations in societies, as a special segment of their cultures (Eckstein and Gurr 1975). We tried, deliberately, to imitate a procedure from chemistry, from which, unlike biology or even physics, social scientists almost never borrow. It seemed sensible to do so in this case. Social scientists are forced to speak about components of compound social phenomena and how they interact, so why not try to do so in an emulation, however primitive, of the field that does this best?

Consonance is a concept that can be distinguished into several subconcepts, all of which are also universals. Consonance can refer to:

1. The degree of *uniformity* in culture patterns; that is, the extent to which orientations are in fact shared by members of a collectivity. A culture may be characterized by a high degree of uniformity or by little. Culture certainly is never anything so uniform as "national character." The degree of cultural uniformity can be expected to have significant consequences for

society; some degree of it may even be a necessary condition, or a functional prerequisite, for its existence.

2. The degree of *coherence* in culture patterns; that is, the extent to which their elements or constituent subcultures form stable and efficient or unstable and inefficient compounds.

3. *Complementarity*, or lack of it, among the orientations of members of collectives who have different social locations or "statuses." For example, it has been said that the British political elite, in the past and perhaps still, expected to be treated deferentially and that the nonelite gave it deference—a manifestly stable combination, whereas deference expected–deference denied is obviously potentially volatile.

4. The degree of *correspondence* of cultural norms to legal forms and actual practices. There is no reason why these should ever coincide, and deviations from their coincidence may be great. As some of my research has shown, this is likely to be an especially serious source of problems if norms and practices are for some reason out of sync, as they may be. It is also problematic where attempts are made to substitute legal forms, such as constitutions, for existing norms and practices in order to transform the norms and practices. Such a situation should be distinguished, however, from a case in which norms have disintegrated and forms are used as surrogates for the norms.

No doubt other universals of culture can be identified. Those discussed, however, should suffice to make the point that nothing prevents cultural theorizing even at the most general level.

Culture Types

Between the level of singular cultures and universals of culture are culture types: particular combinations of traits that occur in sets, or classes, of cultures. Here we are on more familiar ground than with universals, so the discussion can be more brief.

In the work that introduced the concept of "political culture" into the field of political science, Gabriel Almond and Sidney Verba (1963) devised a political culture type and used it in a hypothesis; this may serve for illustration. The type was the "civic culture," and the hypothesis in which it was used was that a civic culture is a necessary condition of stable democracy.

A civic culture is a mix of three disparate components in general political culture and in the orientations of individuals: parochial, subject, and participant orientations. Since these components can also exist unmixed or in other combinations, the Almond-Verba language allows us to generate seven culture types right off the bat, and Almond and Verba themselves in fact suggested hypotheses in which these culture types are used. An important concern that follows for theory is to identify mixes of orientations that can be stable and efficient and those that cannot. The same question, of course, arises with regard to culture types that closely approach being typologically pure.

A similar issue is whether just any mix of parochial, subject, and participant orientations constitutes a civic culture conducive to successful democracy, or whether there are also lethal compounds of the orientations. The relative strengths of the components of such orientational compounds can also be a basis for further typological differentiation. Almond and Verba, for instance, distinguished a civic culture in which subject orientations are relatively strong (Great Britain) from one in which participant orientations dominate (the United States). We may ask what consequences follow from such mixes that are variations within a single type.

The four cultural "ways of life" formulated by Michael Thompson, Richard Ellis, and Aaron Wildavsky (1990) on the basis of Mary Douglas's grid-group approach—the egalitarian, the hierarchical, the individualistic, and the fatalistic ways of life—seem to me to be especially promising constructions for cultural typology. The types can be useful for characterizing both overall political cultures and subcultures within them as well as individual orientations. Most important, each may constitute a coherent "orientational system": that is, something that works like an orientation to orientations, encapsulating a great many meanings in a limited set of supermeanings. Together the four types may in fact exhaust all possible such systems of political orientations.

The idea of a very limited set of superorientations seems plausible if orientations have an "economizing" function, as I argued earlier. Such superorientations would enable agents to act on little information and little processing of information. If so—an eminently testable hypothesis—then we would also be enabled to predict a number of attitudes and behaviors from little information. Moreover, general systems of orientations in which specific orientations are organized should be especially resistant to change and especially subject to the imperative of avoiding dissonance. They may then come to have consequences that are "functional-cultural" in nature—that is, they should come with devices for maintaining the systems as intact as possible. This idea of a "cultural functionalism" was in fact proposed by Wildavsky and his collaborators (Thompson, Ellis, and Wildavsky 1990, 107, 186, 202).[4]

The ways-of-life typology points to another possibility that may have important implications for theory, namely, that orientations can be generalized about at different levels of generality. The four ways of life exist at a very high level of generality. It might be interesting, and also a potentially powerful explanatory device, to identify species and subspecies of the four genera.

Culture-Themes

Culture-themes are aspects of culture considered especially important. There are two kinds:

A culture-theme may be thematic to a particular culture. This is so if an orientation occurs with especially great uniformity in a culture and if other orientations may be considered to load on it. For example, Tocqueville treated equality as the leitmotiv of the American culture he observed. This use of the notion of culture-themes comes from Margaret Mead and Rhoda Metraux (1954). Culture-themes, in this sense, occur in interpretation rather than in theories that state general cultural laws. Nevertheless, as pointed out earlier, statements of the themes are hypotheses, to be tested in the cultures in which they are held to obtain.

A culture-theme also may be a general component of cultures that is considered especially important for general theorizing: a leitmotiv in social scenarios (in the plural). For instance, the theme of social trust/distrust is widely considered to be of fundamental importance in political explanation, for example, by Almond and Verba (1963) and by Lucian Pye (1965). Robert Putnam's (1993) distinction between horizontally and vertically defined social relationships, in my view, deserves to be used just as widely, on an equally fundamental level. The ways-of-life typology may also be useful in identifying culture-themes, both in the particular and the general theoretic sense.

Method: The "Observation" of Culture

Cultural science surely has this allurement: It is possible to practice it at the level of extreme particularity, with all the sensitivity of perception, mastery of detail, and elegance of exposition associated with thick description at its best; it is also possible to practice it at the most universal theoretical level, with all the attractions of formally deductive yet empirically demanding theorizing; and much in between. When mature enough, cultural science should have no difficulty in linking any levels of particularity and generality, using theory to explain particulars, and using particulars as evidence or grounding for theories.

That promise, however, depends on our ability to devise valid, reliable, and exact methods for getting at orientations and culture. This, it has been argued, is the Achilles' heel of cultural science. Orientations and culture are, after all, subjective and never directly observable. They are, as Arthur Bentley said, "soul-stuff," or "mind-stuff," or "spooks." How could so inaccessible a subject matter be amenable to hard scientific methods?

The answer is simple—though the practice to which it leads will be difficult.[5] The social sciences are not precluded from positing the "real" existence of phenomena that are not directly observed, as long as they can be observed through their effects. Other sciences posit nonobservational variables routinely and make ontological claims for them. No one has directly seen, for instance, electricity, or a magnetic field, or a field of force, and yet we are quite accustomed to talking about them as though we could see them. We do not see electricity when the lights are turned on; we see an effect of something we call electricity. Likewise, we observe such an effect when we experience electric shock or read an electric meter. Electricity, however, and other such mind-things, are "seen" so reliably and exactly through their effects, including effects on measuring instruments, that we pay the power company exact amounts for the kilowatt-spooks we use, without raising ontological objections. Not only do the hard sciences use nonobservational concepts for which ontological claims are made, but also these concepts are arguably by far the most important concepts that they use.

Ontological claims that do not rest on direct observation are also familiar in jurisprudence and are often used to decide nothing less than life-and-death issues. The difference between direct and circumstantial evidence is precisely the difference between direct sense-experience of an entity or event and indirect evidence for something postulated and known through its effects. Other things being equal, direct evidence is always preferable. However, circumstantial evidence often is stronger and more conclusive. Reports of direct evidence can be willfully or otherwise erroneous. ("Never trust an experimental result," it has been said, "unless it is confirmed by a theory.") Observations may be made under inauspicious conditions—seen in a bad light, or fleetingly, or with strong self-confirming preconceptions. Circumstantial evidence, per contra, may be wholly convincing, because of its convergent nature or because from certain evidence, such as fingerprints, exact singular predictions can be deduced. The scientist, moreover, has an important advantage over the lawyer with regard to circumstantial evidence: He or she may decide the kind of indirect evidence to be obtained so that it will be particularly revealing, as in a well-designed experiment. Furthermore, direct and circumstantial evidence often turn out to be interchangeable; when we know by inference what to look for and how, it sometimes turns out to be the case that we can observe directly what earlier we only postulated.

The effects that lead to the inference of orientations are, of course, actions. Orientations are considered to underlie and to explain actions, just as all theoretical concepts are considered to underlie and explain surface phenomena. As a start, then, we may get at orientations by simple sense-observation. No doubt, however, we must also find technical instruments of observation with which to get at them better and more exactly than raw observation permits—cultural analogs of microscopes, thermometers, and the like.

We already have a good many such technical instruments, although we no doubt need more and better ones, as is the case in all of the sciences. The whole arsenal of psychological testing techniques is available. So are widely used techniques such as survey research, or techniques that formerly were widely used, such as content analysis. Particularly promising, and not nearly as familiar to political scientists as it ought to be, is the "semantic differential" technique for the "measurement of meaning," devised and applied with impressive successes by Charles Osgood and a number of his collaborators and students over time (Osgood, Suci, and Tannenbaum 1957). A strong case can also be made for adapting Donald Campbell's conception of a "multitrait-multimethod" approach to the requirements of cultural science (Campbell 1950; Campbell and Fiske 1959).

Finding good, discriminating instruments of observation and measurement is a critical task for cultural science. That task will require the ingenuity of many people over long periods, as it has in other sciences. The task may conceivably be more intricate in cultural science than in other sciences—although devices such as cloud-chambers or nuclear accelerators seem intricate enough. It is difficult, however, to see why the task should not, in principle, be discharged well enough.

Contra Utility Theory

The development of cultural science thus poses great and multifaceted tasks that can keep individuals and professions working busily over indefinite time. After Comte, it took well over a century to accomplish the conception of cultural science, and between the conception and its full development still lies almost infinite labor. No one says that practicing science—any science—is easy.

For just that reason, it seems especially regrettable that, at present, so much effort and intellect are being devoted in political science to the elaboration of a body of theory that is pseudoscience—or, as Comte would have said, prescientific metaphysics, against which the very idea of positive social science was originally defined. I refer of course to utility theory. It is important to take a stance against utility theory here, for the reason stated earlier: that a complete case for social science as cultural science must include a case against alternatives to it. The essence of my argument against utility theory is not just that it has few empirical successes to its credit and that it has been the source of much ludicrous reasoning (as argued powerfully in Green and Shapiro 1993), but also that this has been inevitable because it is not science but rather "essentialism" in thin disguise.

How Positive Theory Progresses

What follows is a very simple sketch of a very complicated subject: how theory develops in positive science. The sketch is based on Karl Popper's solution to the basic problem of his work (how science proceeds from theory to better theory), as interpreted and to an extent amended by his followers, most notably John Watkins (1984). It will be evident later that we need the sketch in order to judge whether utility theory should be considered a scientific theory in the first place.

Scientific theory progresses gradually, over long periods, toward a goal that is approachable but not attainable in finite time. In that progress, less adequate theory is replaced by more adequate theory. The process of change is sometimes more rapid, more fundamental, and more far-reaching than in its normally gradual course—though it is debatable whether any wholesale "scientific revolution" ever occurs. Certainly science never begins again at square one, and one may also wonder whether anything like a wholesale "paradigm shift" ever happens.

"More adequate" theory means theory that is closer to what may be called the Bacon-Descartes ideal for science, which includes the requisites that theory be certainly true; that it penetrate to some ultimate explanation of phenomena; that it be unified; that it have complete predictive power; and that it be perfectly exact. This is an ideal sprung from and very similar to metaphysical essentialism, for a perfect theory would realize the dream of every metaphysician: to state the form or essence of all things, past, present, and future. It is logically demonstrable as well as evident from the history of science that nothing remotely like the classical ideal for science is attainable. Science, however, can *progress* toward all aspects of the goal, much as one can progress meaningfully toward other intrinsically unattainable goals. It is possible, for instance, to accumulate constantly greater wealth without ever attaining the greatest amount of wealth possible, or to climb higher and higher mountains without ever being able to climb the highest mountain possible. So, too, can scientific theory progress toward an abstract end-state, despite the fact that, as can be demonstrated logically, its perfection will always still lie an infinite distance away.

When science progresses, it does so by theories that (1) penetrate ever deeper beneath surface appearances toward some ultimate reality and (2) become increasingly unified, (3) more predictively powerful, and (4) more exact. And, of course, scientific theories must also be, at every stage, and in some sense, "true."

The first of these goals, the ultimate-reality goal, was the characteristic aim of prescientific metaphysics. Theory meant "first principles," the essences that are hidden by sense-experience. The senses, it was thought, detect mere "phenomena," and the underlying forms of phenomenal content could be evident only to pure reason. In reference to this as a goal for science, Popper has written: "I do not think that we can ever describe, by our universal laws, an ultimate essence of the world. I do *not* doubt that we may probe deeper and deeper into the structure of our world or, as we might say, into properties of the world that are ever more essential, or of greater and greater depth" (cited in Watkins 1984, 132).

In this progress toward ultimate depth, unity, predictive power, and exactitude, the decisive role is always played by the testing of theory against observations. Surviving tests is the critical condition for theories' gaining assent, including theories suggested by experience itself. But not just any test for correspondence will do. The only close inductive equivalent to deductive proof is to be found in surviving *severe tests of theory, aimed at refutation.* That is the closest induction can come to establishing verity in some permanent or absolute sense.

There often is little or no difficulty in passing a test for correspondence. If a theory is defended on the ground that it was formulated to fit a body of data, it is not tested at all, because numerous hypotheses can always fit a body of data. If a theory is tested against data that are much the same as the data it was formulated to fit, the results of the test are likely to be the same, and little additional truth-value is acquired. If a theory is tested against anything likely to corroborate it, the test is weak at best. Theories can claim assent only to the extent that they have withstood concerted efforts to falsify them.

How can one tell whether a test is severe? Such a test *ideally* has the following form:

1. It involves a risky prediction, namely the prediction of something either *empirically novel* (not yet observed) or *theoretically novel* (an empirical regularity not previously formulated).
2. The empirical or theoretical novelty is a strict deductive consequence of the theory's core postulates.
3. The test is *theoretically challenging,* in that there is a rival theory that leads to the same test, with a predicted outcome different enough to permit a crucial experiment to decide between the competing theories.

The severity of tests depends, in general terms, on how close they come to this ideal.

The animating spirit of scientific inquiry thus consists of (1) skeptical caution toward theoretical ideas, especially ideas that go a large distance beneath, or beyond, what the observed phenomena will bear, or what already corroborated theory sustains; and (2) the accumulation of evidence and the constant testing of ideas against it in stiff tests at every stage.

Why Utility Theory Is Not Scientific

I will not present here a thorough critique of political utility theory; such a critique has already been published by Donald Green and Ian Shapiro (1994).[6] I fully agree with their critique, which is directed at the empirical status of utility theory. They sum their argument up as follows: "Our claim is that to date no innovative theoretical insights of rational choice theory have been subjected to serious empirical scrutiny and survived. The tests of the theory that have been attempted fall into one of three categories: They tend to disconfirm it; they . . . [are] irrelevant to evaluating the theory's truth; or they provide support for hypotheses that are banal" (Green and Shapiro 1993, 3). Subsequently they characterize the empirical progress made in one aspect of political utility theory over two decades as a "working up from nothing to a state of extreme poverty" (1993, 33)—which is not a bad description of the theory's overall empirical status.

Green and Shapiro direct their criticisms toward how political utility theory has actually been practiced in empirical studies, which leaves open an important question: whether the flaws they discuss are somehow inherent in the approach or are simply the result of avoidable bad practice. In my view, there is indeed a fatal intrinsic flaw in the utility approach that underlies and explains the bad practices that Green and Shapiro identify. As I noted earlier, the flaw is that, properly viewed, what is called rational choice theory is not positive social science at all but rather a reversion to prescientific metaphysics as Comte conceived it.

In an earlier paper (Eckstein 1996) I summarized the nature of metaphysical thought (literally, thought beyond the physical, the observable) as follows:

Metaphysics replaced . . . theological thought with something equally fanciful: pure ideas elaborated in pure abstraction. In metaphysical construction one sought the "essences" or "forms" manifested in experienced things and events, in the sense that these notions had in classical Greek philosophies: the "ideas" lying beyond experience, of which experiences are shadowy reflections, as in the Allegory of the Cave.... Attaining truth about the nature of things was regarded as a task for philosophic wisdom that could rise directly to fixed and eternal forms, and not be misled by mere ephemeral "content." The mere appearances that constitute observations were considered irrelevant to the discovery of these essences, or downright impediments to genuine wisdom.

We will see that this characterization fits political utility theory all too well.

It is evident that utility theory begins at a very deep level beneath observable experience—about as deep a level as is possible in social science. This is the quintessential start (and also end) of metaphysical thinking. The utility postulate is categorical. It comes without auxiliary hypotheses and without qualifying "ifs." Utility theorists in political science do not say that their ideas hold to the extent that specified conditions obtain—that they hold, for instance, if a polity is modern, or if it is a democracy, or if it comes coupled with a market economy, or if a political activity really is gamelike. The core postulate of utility theory, as John Ferejohn (1991, 281) concedes, is in fact an ultimate universal law that specifies exactly what, at bottom, any and all political behavior is about. If there is any level of explanation beneath that law, we would probably have to go to the brain to find its utility-optimizing circuitry.

To be sure, beginning at a level—any level—deep beneath surface phenomena is not necessarily damnable. One might have good reason to do so. From where, then, does the postulate of utility rationality come? What are the good reasons for proposing it?

It does not come from psychology. Psychological research might conceivably have found evidence pointing in the direction of the postulate, but, if anything, the opposite is the case.[7] Neither does it come from researches by political scientists directly into the credibility of the postulate. Again, if anything, the opposite obtains. Pertinent experimental research by political scientists has shown that actors are simply incapable of following mathematical optimizing strategies, except in the simplest, most obvious situations; that at best they vary in games-playing ability; and that they keep intruding into games "weird" variables like norms of fairness (Green and Shapiro 1993, 36).[8] Nor does the postulate come from reflection on how a deeper unified theory might deductively account for empirical regularities already found in the field. From the start, in fact, far from showing that established regularities in observations follow logically from the theory, its core postulate encountered difficulties in explaining even the most elementary observed regularities—for instance, that some people in democracies vote and others do not. One would have expected a seriously proposed theory to be capable of explaining such a simple matter easily, leaving the tough stuff for later.

The postulate comes, of course, from economics, which got it from the utilitarian philosophers. Has the postulate survived in economics because it has withstood efforts at refutation so well? Economics hardly seems notable for its predictive triumphs, or for any exacting tests of its theoretical propositions. The field is notable for elegant formalizations, as is its political science counterpart. Both might conceivably pass muster as special branches of abstract mathematics or logic. This would deserve applause if the formalizations were ever seriously tested, with the core postulate put at risk. They are not. Economics, in fact, seems to be two fields. There is empirical economics (econometrics), and there is the purely deductive elaboration of its core postulates. This division is certainly not bridged in the manner of theoretical and experimental physics. It seems difficult, then, to think of a good reason why utility economics, of all fields, should be regarded as a model for positive social science.

When utility theorists are asked to justify their core postulate, a common answer is that it is "merely an assumption." Surely, however, there must be some reason for thinking that the assumption would be fertile—that it would yield good testable theories. It is true that counterintuitive assumptions sometimes do have such results. But that does not mean that *any* far-out assumption is likely to pay off, and certainly not that the farther-out an assumption is, the bigger will be its payoff. We do not just randomly launch postulates for theory, hoping that they will astonish us by somehow arriving at their target. There are no "mere assumptions" in positive science. *Not* making "mere assumptions" is, if anything, the essence of the thing.

It is also said by utility theorists that they do not make reality claims for their core postulate. That may do well as a way of avoiding evidence, but it is inconsistent with positive science. Science always makes reality claims for its theoretical axioms, Milton Friedman (1953) notwithstanding.[9] If these claims are directly testable against observations (as the basic utility postulate probably is), so much the better. If they are only testable indirectly by deductions from theory—such as the deduction from Einsteinian relativity of the seeming shifting of position of a star whose light passes close to a massive object—that will also do very well. If postulates are not claimed to be "real" at all, that means that they have no testable empirical content—in which case the only possible claim that can be made for them must rest on some supposed metaphysical intuition.

It is also sometimes said that utility theory is only a "research programme," as Imre Lakatos (1978, volume 1) uses that concept. That also has an attractive consequence: As Lakatos has shown, research programmes cannot ever be refuted. The results arrived at when carrying out the programmes, however, can and should always be tested; and the results of the tests provide indications of whether it is worthwhile to follow a programme or better to abandon it. Hence that device also gets utility theorists nowhere.

In the same vein, it is common for utility theorists to say that they do not hold that people are in fact utility rational, but only that they behave as if they were. That also will not do. If people behave as if they were utility rational, then they are utility rational—just as, for instance, if people act, speak, and write as if they were intelligent, then they must be intelligent. The question remains of whether people do in fact behave according to the canons of utility theory, and whether they do so in a way that is deductively faithful to the utility postulate rather than to some "epicyclical" improvisation based on it, devised to fit observed behavior in the first place.[10]

It must be granted that scientific theories also make "metaphysical" assumptions in postulating things not immediately accessible to observation and thus "beyond the physical." Einstein actually called himself a "metaphysicist" (Holton 1968, 188), and Popper, as we saw, not only admits essentialist elements into scientific theories but also recommends them. Note, however, that Popper calls his position "modified essentialism," by which he means essentialism always mitigated by theoretical caution and subjected to tough attempts at empirical refutation.[11] The latter especially is so great a modification that it turns essentialism inside out.

Utility theory has certainly not been notable for a concern with empirical corroboration through severe tests, or indeed for much genuine testing at all.[12] A colleague of mine calls himself a "soft" utility theorist because he cares seriously about data and also does deductive modeling along utility lines. That, of course, should make him the hard-headed theorist, and the others the soft ones; but in the world of utility theory, one sees what he means. The significance that political utility theorists attach to empirical grounding is exemplified by a recent issue of *Rationality and Society* (vol. 4, no. 4, 1992, 380–469) that was wholly devoted to that subject; not one contributor addressed the empirical status of the theory in political science.

This should not be taken to mean that empirical fit is of no concern at all to political utility theorists. At this stage of the development of positive social science, the scientific culture no longer allows anyone to dismiss empirical evidence as irrelevant. Contemporary metaphysicians, however, reveal themselves by the way they treat evidence.

One way in which "evidence" enters political utility theory is for a utility theorist to select some established body of evidence and then "explain" it by some version of utility theory tailored to that purpose. Usually all that is demonstrated by this is that something *can* be explained in the language of utility. But if one is clever and disingenuous enough, one can always explain anything in any theoretical language, especially by fiddling with core postulates. Green and Shapiro (1993, 10) point out that in utility explanations of observed phenomena, factors are generally invoked ad hoc that have nothing to do with the core postulate of utility theory, or that even contradict it, just so that the observed facts will fit. Examples include "differences in the sources of utility (happiness, wealth, preferences), . . . the decision rules on which [people] are said to act (maximizing, satisficing, minimaxing), . . . and the perceptions and learning of actors." In positive science, on the contrary, theory always precedes the explanation of observations; these are used to test it, not just to demonstrate the possibility of explanation in a special language.

A choice example of this mode of operation by political utility theorists is their treatment of the voter turnout problem mentioned earlier, namely, that some people vote in elections and others do not. Much clever twisting and stretching of the utility postulate has been used to explain that fact, which has nevertheless shown strong resistance to explanations in the language of utility.

The manifest deductive inference from the utility postulate, following one of its first proponents in political science, Anthony Downs (1957), was that people just should not vote. A reasonable person would have concluded from this that the postulate is plainly wrong, but a devotee of the postulate would go to great lengths to rescue it. Hence when the paradox of voter turnout was discovered, an extensive, and rather comic, discussion of it followed. The issue of this discussion was not how to explain that some people vote and others do not but how to explain voting as a utility-rational act. That surely is a problem only for people who want to impose the utility postulate by hook or by crook.

The dodges used to "solve" the problem were almost worthy of the Scholastics. Downs himself, for instance, said that democracy requires voting, that people prefer democracy to other forms of government, and that therefore they vote out of a sense of democratic civic duty. This is absurd. For instance, it implies that voters are prodemocracy regardless of how they vote, and that in, say, 1932, more Americans were antidemocracy than were Germans.[13] It was also said that people vote to minimize regrets that might result from not voting, even if not to optimize utility. This seems better, but one still wonders why voters should feel such regrets and nonvoters not.[14] When this was realized, variables for saving the hypothesis were promiscuously introduced: for instance, intensity of partisanship (which sounds suspiciously like a meaning variable) or the misperception that one's vote matters after all, or the perceived closeness of elections. Others (e.g., Uhlaner 1989a; Fedderson 1992) have labored to produce models that could imply "positive turnout" in utility language, sometimes again adding meaning variables, such as group identity, from which the models' power seems mainly to derive.

One serious response to all this has been to rule voter turnout out of the domain of political utility theory. No one can have a problem with this—unless it is implied, as it is, that anything not demonstrably beyond the explanatory power of utility theory confirms the theory. This gives utility theory the status of a null hypothesis. The null hypothesis in science is always that a hypothesis is wrong, not that it is right unless definitively impugned. The latter is the way of metaphysics. But the debate over voter turnout continues, unresolved, as it also does over other problems and paradoxes posed by utility theory but not necessarily by the nature of things.

The one reason for such problems that is never seriously entertained is that the fault might lie in the postulate itself. The postulate is given every benefit of the doubt and the evidence none, which is exactly what unmodified essentialists do and exactly the reverse of what should be done in a positive science.

One is also astonished by the way political utility theorists treat evidence that might corroborate or refute their theories. Almost any evidence that matches theoretical expectations is considered to corroborate theory, and any evidence that does not is not counted against it; that way, of course, one can never lose, which makes winning trivial. Consider, for instance, the following results from experiments supposed to establish support for utility theories: One group (Berl, Mc-Kelvey, and Winer 1976, 467) found that only three of seventeen results fit the theoretical core they were "testing"; yet they considered the theory supported by their findings for the astonishing reason that they could not reject the hypothesis [*sic*] that the unexpected results just somehow turned up, for reasons irrelevant to the theory. Another group (McKelvey and Ordeshook 1984, 189) said that the theory they tested experimentally "receives considerable support" from the fact that expectations deduced from it occurred four times in nineteen trials. Yet another (Fiorina and Plott 1978, 583–584) drew comfort from four correct predictions in twenty trials. And so it goes, through a lengthy list. One wonders just how much worse a theory has to fare to flunk a test.

Despite all this, it might be useful to construct utility models as purely "ideal-typical" constructs, as Weber used that concept. By this is meant constructs that are not really to be tested against reality but that are used in comparison to observations. When so used, the constructs indicate the extent to which the observed world fits them and to what extent explanation requires other constructs. Sometimes models so used also indicate what sorts of other models are required for fuller explanation.

The fact is, however, that utility theorists do not so use their models. One suspects that the reason for this is that comparisons between abstract models and concrete observations really are also tests of theory, whatever their intended purpose. That would recommend the procedure greatly to positive theorists, such as Weber, but not to metaphysicians.

Markets and Market Cultures

Utility theory was developed principally to explain the operation of economic markets, and it remains the orthodoxy of theoretical economics. From the analysis of markets it has gradually been extended to the analysis of human behavior (and even some animal behavior) in all its aspects. But let us reconsider whether utility theory even serves its original purpose well. My remarks here apply to markets as they are, empirical markets, not abstract and fictitious markets conceived in terms of utility assumptions in the first place.

If markets are to operate effectively, they themselves require an appropriate culture. They would require this even if all people were perfectly utility rational. It has always been understood that markets require complex and reliable legal systems to operate properly; legal systems are essentially explicit norms, and since they cannot anticipate all contingencies, legal systems still need to be supplemented by implicit norms. Furthermore, laws will not serve well if they contradict norms. If laws and norms are inconsistent, strain and dysfunctions result. Hence, through the front door of markets, culture comes streaming in.

How else could one guarantee that the myriad contracts that markets involve will be reliably kept? How else could the cornering of markets by foul means be avoided? Effectively operating markets require more than just greed. The *auri sacra fames* is universal, not just capitalistic. Market economies require that gain be pursued in highly institutionalized, that is, normatively regulated, ways. These ways have no doubt been gradually worked out in successful market economies over long periods of time. Market economies did not always work as well as they do now in advanced societies, and probably they are still not optimally constructed. In well-established market economies a great deal of institutional learning from experience no doubt has occurred and has led to the gradual definition and redefinition of norms and laws appropriate to the economies. If such economies are to be exported, therefore, the relationship of markets to culture must be well understood, and not only markets but also market cultures must be fostered.

Besides, how could any rational calculation occur and succeed in a world lacking a fairly high degree of predictability? One could even argue that a universe of utility maximizers would particularly require a highly crystallized culture in which to operate. To the extent that the behavior of others is not predictable, rational calculation in interaction must fail.

Culture also defines value or benefit in the first place. Anything can have intrinsic exchange-value: cattle, wives, slaves, land, rank, money, or ability to give presents, stage ceremonies, or subsidize the arts. Without money as a generalized value, no complex market could operate. But even in money economies other values exist. Hence a crucial problem arises: What values, other than money and gaining money, do smoothly operating markets require? Weber's *Protestant Ethic and the Spirit of Capitalism* developed subtle hypotheses in regard to this issue, thus far unrivaled.

This is a problem worthy of scholarly exertion in a time of economic liberalization. Just as democracy can hardly work without democratic culture, so free markets will not work without market culture. We do not yet know much about what an appropriate market culture is, except for trivial ideas, such as that people pursue gain in markets. Without good hypotheses on market cultures, it is simply not possible to offer constructive advice to countries engaged in trying to transform command economies into market economies. In addressing problems of liberalization, economists have nothing to go on but common sense (or, as is sometimes the case, common nonsense). Economics, as the field is now, has nothing of theoretical value to say about these problems because economists, blinkered by their core postulate, simply do not raise them.

Weber at least began to raise and think about this issue, especially in *Economy and Society* (1978, esp. 2:311–338), though his views about it are scattered among observations on a great variety of other subjects and no doubt are dated. However, he did make a start that can serve as a basis for going further. His own professorship, after all, was in economics. His field was what was then called "social economics" (*Sozialökonomie*), meaning, roughly, economics as a specialized part of sociology. The "continental tradition" in economics, as it has sometimes been called, was exactly that: economics from a general sociological point of view. That tradition originally paralleled utility economics (which Weber understood and wrote about), but it was gradually displaced by the latter.

Surely much can still be said for the social economics tradition, and it needs particularly to be said now, when that tradition has for all practical purposes died from an overdose of utility economics. Economics is clearly one of the social sciences. Economies consist of interactions, roles and statuses, institutions, and meanings. They are not just abstract supply-demand curves or equilibria, without human agents or cultural contexts, playing themselves out in a transcendental logic-game. If the idea of social science as cultural science makes sense, it must apply to economics as well. There certainly should come to be, at least as a complement to "pure" utility economics, what might be called cultural economics.

Beyond Culture

It may, and probably will, turn out to be the case that there are theoretical levels deeper than the cultural. If so, as I argued earlier, they would best be found by reflecting on what might underlie cultural regularities and laws when these have been sufficiently formulated for narrower ranges and at less deep levels—in what Merton has called middle-range hypotheses. Still, it might be useful to indicate, and to keep in mind as cultural analysis proceeds, what might lie beyond culture, at deeper explanatory removes. I offer two suggestions here, without elaboration.

First, it might be that we will find an invariant cultural deep structure that underlies cultural variability, analogous to linguistic deep structure. Such a deep structure might exist because cultural variability, however great, must also be limited, for functional reasons. Just as any language must be intelligible, so no culture can exist that does not fulfill its function, which is to make situations intelligible. However, discovering such a deep structure, if indeed it exists, is not a matter for "mere assumptions" but rather for inference from observed cultures and for testing against the contents of empirical cultures.

Second, it might be that the "deeper" level of explanation is psychological, or, beyond that, it might lie in the structure of the brain and the fundamental organic imperatives of human existence. Comte argued long ago that every science builds on every other that developed earlier. Social science, he said, thus would grow out of and adapt the theories of biology and physiology, as has in fact been the case in social systems theory and in the "general theory of action." Social science might well continue to link itself to these older sciences. It might even help to develop them in providing social facts and theories for deeper explanation.

Notes

An earlier version of this chapter was presented for a panel in memory of Aaron Wildavsky at the 1994 Annual Meeting of the American Political Science Association in New York City.

1. For my reasons for preferring the term "utility" to "rational choice," see Eckstein 1996, note 1.

2. For the nature and uses of "theoretical cores," see Einstein 1920 and Watkins 1984.

3. Weber's word for this, *Deutung*, may be translated as interpretation, but it also carries the connotation of getting at significance. Weber's own most celebrated exercise in *Deutung* was his interpretation of the meanings that underlay the very distinctive behavior of early modern capitalists (Weber 1930). It is possible, similarly, to interpret individual meanings and to use reconstructions of such meanings in accounting for individual behaviors.

4. Elsewhere I have written about the proper way to construct typologies, suggesting that it is the "method of progressive differentiation," as exemplified by the way organisms are classified in biology—another example of how we might profit from emulating that adjacent field (Eckstein and Gurr 1974).

5. I have discussed the problem of cultural method and solutions for it in Eckstein 1992, 284–303.

6. The monograph by Green and Shapiro (1993) cited here has since become a book, bearing the same title (1994). The book was not yet published when this paper was written, and so references here are to the earlier work.

7. I consider Shawn Rosenberg's critique (1995) to be definitive for this purpose as well as a vindication of the cultural approach. For good summaries of other pertinent studies, see Luce and von Winterfeldt 1994, Schoemaker 1982, and Weber 1993.

8. Green and Shapiro (1993, 38) also point out that experimenters in political science generally do not even allow variables like social norms, ideological commitments, or group attachments to play a role in their experiments.

9. Friedman seems to say that "wildly unrealistic" postulates, like those of utility economics, may be admitted into positive theory if they yield theories that have great predictive power. The error here is simple: Postulates that yield theories of great empirical power should be considered "realistic" by virtue of that fact, as against any conventional view of reality. If postulates are in fact unrealistic, nothing "real" can be deduced from them.

10. For instance, the notion of "nested games," invented to account for facts resistant to explanation by utility theory, is a perfect social science replica of the improvised epicycles that ultimately spelled the doom of Ptolemaic astronomy (Tsebelis 1990).

11. Note also that concepts that are originally "metaphysical" may become accessible to observation, for instance, by the use of special instruments of observation. In "modified essentialism" this is always the aspiration.

12. By genuine tests I mean tests aimed at refutation.

13. Riker and Ordeshook, in a very limited study (1968), did find a positive relationship between measures of the sense of civic duty and voting. However, "sense of civic duty" surely is a meaning, or a cultural, variable.

14. Ferejohn and Fiorina (1975) explain this by strength of partisanship, a variable introduced ad hoc to handle the problem, and one that is certainly truistic.

Chapter Two

Rational Choice and Culture: Clashing Perspectives or Complementary Modes of Analysis?

SUN-KI CHAI

Cultural and rational choice analyses have long been seen as antithetical approaches, based on diametrically opposed views of human nature and theory construction. The late 1960s and the 1970s featured a struggle between cultural/psychological and rational choice approaches for the "soul" of theory in political science, with the latter gradually gaining the upper hand during this period. The 1980s and early 1990s have been a period of relative ascendancy for rational choice in political science, but this ascendancy has been accompanied by a growing number of critical examinations of the approach (e.g., Etzioni 1988; Mansbridge 1990; Cook and Levi 1990; Lane 1991; Monroe 1991; Green and Shapiro 1994) as well as by a notable renaissance of work within the cultural approach (e.g., Pye and Pye 1985; Eckstein 1988; Chilton 1988, 1991; Pye 1988; Gibbins 1989; Thompson, Ellis, and Wildavsky 1990; Inglehart 1990; Wilson 1992; Ellis 1993a; Putnam 1993; Diamond 1993; Abramson and Inglehart 1995).[1]

It is unclear how this latest round of methodological conflict will end, whether with the permanent ascendancy of one approach, an endless back and forth between the two, or a theoretical synthesis that combines elements of both approaches.[2] In this chapter I point the way to a possible reconciliation and synthesis of these two rival approaches. Conceptualizing culture as the basis for individual preferences (goals) and beliefs, I argue, allows cultural analysis to be compatible with the assumption of rational behavior. Furthermore, integrating the rationality assumption into a cultural approach can generate explanations of political behavior that combine the general applicability of the rational choice approach with the sensitivity to local context of the political culture approach.

The chapter begins by providing a brief overview of contemporary debates in the social sciences over the relative usefulness of cultural and rational choice approaches. The next section points to a small but growing literature that implicitly or explicitly integrates culture and rationality in the explanation of political behavior, dividing this literature into analysis in which culture is seen as directly shaping the way individuals calculate the costs and benefits of different actions, and analysis in which culture plays an indirect role in coordinating mutual expectations among individuals about one another's behavior. The final section discusses possible problems with too free a use of assumptions about culturally induced preferences and beliefs in rational choice explanations of specific behaviors, and describes ways in which such assumptions can be grounded in general theories that systematically account for culture across a wide range of environments, placing extended emphasis on grid-group cultural theory.

Culture Versus Rationality

Debates over culture and rationality in political science have revolved around opposing views of human nature and social science theory. The rational choice approach was originally imported to political science from microeconomics by a number of influential scholars, mostly economists (e.g., Arrow 1951; Downs 1957; Black 1958; Buchanan and Tullock 1962; Olson 1965; Riker 1962 is the most notable exception). In its conventional and by far most common form, rational choice theory takes a spare and unvarying view of human nature. The key assumption of rational choice is that people make choices that they expect will maximize their goals. Such an assumption, however, is nonfalsifiable without some specification of what these goals are and how these expectations are formed. In the conventional rational choice view, people are assumed to have preferences that are exclusively selfish and materialistic as well as beliefs that are based solely on direct observation and logical inference.[3] Although structure (the environmental constraints surrounding people) is left unaccounted for, these assumptions make it fairly clear a priori what internal mechanisms are thought to drive human behavior. Hence they can be used in a deductive manner to generate determinate and therefore falsifiable predictions about behavior given a wide range of structural conditions.

The cultural approach spans a number of research areas. Many of the formative works in this approach are explicitly located within the political culture literature within political science (e.g., Almond 1956; Almond and Verba 1963, 1980; Pye and Verba 1965), but they also include closely related work in systems theory (e.g., Easton 1953, 1957, 1965; Almond 1960, 1965) and modernization theory (e.g., Lerner

1958, Inkeles and Smith 1974). Because it was originally influenced by then-current trends in sociology, this approach has often been referred to as the "sociological approach" (Barry 1970), though this label has become somewhat anachronistic. Unlike the rational choice approach, it takes for granted that an individual's behavior is not based on unvarying internal mechanisms, but rather is a result of specific attitudes that can vary from individual to individual, group to group, and society to society. Unlike the rational choice approach, it does not contain a single model of human behavior and does not contain a core set of assumptions that are shared by all theories and that can be used to generate falsifiable predictions.

An inability to generate falsifiable predictions deductively from core assumptions has generally been seen as the main weakness of the cultural approach vis-à-vis the rational choice approach. The cultural approach, say critics, is not a theory but simply a set of categories and concepts (Harsanyi 1969; Mitchell 1969; Barry 1970; Holt and Turner 1975; Rogowski 1978; Gray 1987). Even empirical findings about individual, group, or societal attitudes have no clear implications for behavior, they argue, since the cultural approach does not provide a way to predict how attitudes interact with structure to generate behavior (Mitchell 1969, Rogowski 1974, Bates 1990). While specific theories within the approach can and often do generate falsifiable predictions, the critics argue that these theories as a whole lack coherence and consistency because they do not share a common deductive base.

These commentaries contributed to the rise of the rational choice approach in political science and the relative decline of the cultural approach during the 1970s and 1980s. Of course a number of other factors may have contributed to this trend as well, most notably the widespread attraction among social scientists to rational choice's highly developed formal techniques and the refinement of these formal techniques, especially game theory, for use in analyzing political phenomena. Whatever the reasons, rational choice theory has been touted as the basis for a unified social science encompassing economic, political, and social phenomena (Becker 1976; Hirshleifer 1985; Coleman 1986; Friedman and Hechter 1990; Lalman, Oppenheimer, and Swistak 1993), and the phenomenon of "economic imperialism" has loomed large over many social science disciplines.

Nonetheless, the path to the top for rational choice has been far from smooth or free of obstacles. In fact, its growth in prominence has generated a rising chorus of criticisms that have been telling enough to be taken to heart even by some of the most steadfast proponents of the approach. These criticisms are directed at the core of rational choice theory, its assumptions about human nature. Not only are these assumptions viewed as much too narrow to be realistic, but they are also blamed for generating inaccurate or indeterminate predictions about behavior across a wide range of contexts.

Criticisms directed at the assumptions focus both on assumptions about preferences and beliefs. The idea of exclusively self-interested and materialistic humans does not square with the view that people have of themselves. Most people see themselves as driven by preferences that are often altruistic and self-actualizing, preferences that are moreover dependent on the social context in which they are located (Sears and Funk 1990a, 1990b). Furthermore, the assumption that beliefs are based only on observation and logic also seems ludicrous in light of the heuristics, ideologies, and biases that are prevalent in human thought processes (Simon 1985, 1986; March 1978; Tversky and Kahneman 1986; Quattrone and Tversky 1988). Finally, it seems indisputable that people differ from one another in their preferences and in the way they form beliefs.

The typical rejoinder to this type of criticism has always been the argument that unrealistic simplifications are necessary for theory building and that the true test of a theory should be in the usefulness of its predictions (Friedman 1953). Many critics, however, have noted that rational choice theories often lead to indeterminate or inaccurate predictions. In many political choice contexts, it is difficult for conventional rational choice theories to predict how individuals will behave (Kingdon 1993; Douglas and Wildavsky 1982). The largest single class of such choice contexts are those that involve indefinitely repeated strategic interactions among individuals, in which the utility (extent of preference fulfillment) provided by each individual's choice depends on the unobservable actions of the others. In most such interactions, an individual cannot calculate which among a large subset (or often the entire set) of available choices will bring the highest expected utility (Fudenberg and Maskin 1986). Such cases seem to encompass a large proportion of nontrivial political choices made by both elites and masses, and for these conventional rational choice theories can often do little more than predict that outcomes will be chaotic.[4]

Moreover, even when rational choice theory succeeds in making determinate predictions, these predictions have often proven to be inaccurate when set against empirical reality (Etzioni 1988, chap. 4; Mansbridge 1990, chap. 1; Lane 1991, chaps. 17 and 23). Most notable in political science have been various "paradoxes" concerning the seeming irrationality of large-scale collective action. In particular, they focus on two of the most common types of political behavior: voting in elections and participation in large-scale demonstrations or rebellions. Both of these behaviors occur on a regular basis, and indeed they are the central elements of contemporary mass politics. Yet rational choice theories have had a difficult time explaining why they occur at all. In both situations, it appears rational for individuals to remain inactive. Action has costs, a single individual will have only a minuscule effect on the expected political outcome, and the effect of the outcome on the individual will generally not depend on whether she or he participated.

Integrating Culture and Rationality in Explanation

These shortcomings have led many rational choice theorists to defend a weaker, "thinner" version of the approach. This version maintains the assumption that individuals maximize the expected utility of their choices, but it abandons the assumption that preferences are solely selfish and materialistic and/or that beliefs are based solely on observation and logical inference. Altruism and expressive preferences are possible, and heuristics and ideology are admitted into belief formation. Preferences and the processing of information into beliefs may differ among individuals and within an individual over time and can be the result of social processes. Although this frees the rational choice approach from reliance on certain implausible assumptions, it also leaves a hole in its deductive foundations: What accounts for preferences and beliefs, and how are they to be determined in each particular context? Without some specification of preferences and beliefs, thin rational choice theories lose the ability to generate predictions.

Stripped of its "thicker" and empirically questionable assumptions that preferences are selfish and materialistic and that beliefs are derived from observation of empirical reality, rational choice becomes a theory that links preferences and beliefs to behavior without specifying the content of those preferences and beliefs. Given this, it then becomes imperative that the preferences and beliefs be accounted for, particularly the way in which they vary among individuals or within an individual over time. Such variations in individual preferences and beliefs correspond fairly closely to culture as it has been conceptualized by social scientists working within the political culture approach. Culture has usually been seen as a social-psychological variable (Almond 1990, 144–145) comprising an individual's attitudes, which in turn have been formed through social interaction. Furthermore, these attitudes have traditionally been divided into their motivational and cognitive components, that is, preferences and beliefs, along with an evaluative component that translates them into choices between actions (Parsons and Shils 1951, 10–11). Hence, implicitly if not explicitly, the move by rational choice theorists toward a thinner view of rationality has been a move toward bringing culture back into the picture. This in turn means that culture is no longer viewed as the antithesis of rational choice but rather as essential to rational choice analysis of real-world political behavior (North 1981, 1990; Wildavsky 1987a; Kreps 1990; Bates 1990; Almond 1990; Ferejohn 1991; Lane 1992; Johnson 1993).

Along these lines, a small but rapidly growing number of theories integrate culture and rational choice into explanations of political behavior. These theories can be divided into two categories, depending on the effect that culture is seen to have in determining the behavior of rational individuals. The first category focuses broadly on the way culture affects the expected utility of different choices via its role in shaping preferences and causal beliefs. The second focuses more specifically on how culture can coordinate expectations among individuals in situations of strategic interaction, allowing each individual to anticipate how others will act and hence to choose their own optimal action.

Culture and Expected Utility

One of the first prominent theories to apply rational choice theory outside of economics was also notable in assuming a role for culture in preference formation. In

The Economics of Discrimination, Becker (1957) assumes that certain individuals have a "taste for discrimination," a kind of preference for avoiding contact with members of other races. Work along this line has been continued by a number of others (Johnson 1965, 1967; Sowell 1975; Klitgaard 1976; Schelling 1978, chap. 4; Seers 1983). Each of these authors uses discriminatory preferences to explain situations in which rational individuals willingly sacrifice material benefits in order to avoid contact with undesired others, and then explores the effects of different environmental contexts on the extent and/or form of discriminatory behavior.

Another general type of preference related to culture is altruism, whose general effect on rational choice has been investigated by a number of authors (Phelps 1975; Collard 1978; Boulding 1981; Margolis 1982; Moe 1980, chap. 5; Hardin 1982, chap. 7; Taylor 1987, chap. 5). Altruism, in rational choice terms, is the extent to which an individual incorporates the welfare of another individual or group of individuals into his or her own utility. Cooperative behavior, including large-scale collective action, is generally more likely among rational individuals who have developed altruism toward one another than among those who have not. Likewise, conflict is generally more likely among rational individuals who have developed "negative altruism" toward one another—that is, negatively value one another's welfare. Hence, assuming positive or negative altruism within particular groups of individuals seems to bring the predictions of rational choice theory more in line with reality by allowing collective action or conflict sometimes to occur even when it is not in the personal material interest of the participants.

A related type of preference is the desire for approval from particular others. Like positive altruism, the desire for approval may motivate cooperative behavior in cases in which purely materialistic preferences may not. Social pressures may form a kind of "selective incentive" (Olson 1965) that groups can use to elicit cooperative behavior from members when material incentives are lacking. A number of authors have investigated how social approval preferences can be invoked to explain the aforementioned "paradoxical" political behaviors of voting (Silver 1973; Uhlaner 1989a, 1989b) and participation in demonstrations and rebellions (Chong 1991, chap. 3; Opp 1986; 1989, chap. 5) and to investigate the dynamics of such behaviors.

A final type of culture-related preference that may have an effect on political behavior is an acquired intrinsic pleasure or displeasure associated with a particular kind of activity, generally referred to as an "expressive preference." Existing investigations have focused on the effects of a particular group of individuals' associating positive fulfillment with a particular type of collective action. Again, studies in political science have focused primarily on the two paradoxes of voting (Fiorina 1976; Brennan and Lomansky 1985, 1987, 1993; Glazer 1987) and participation in demonstrations and rebellions (Tullock 1971; Silver 1974; Chong 1991, chap. 4), investigating the role of expressive preferences in generating higher levels of participation than would otherwise occur.

Although the introduction of cultural factors into rational choice in political science has centered primarily on preferences, a number of investigations have been made on culturally influenced beliefs and their effects on decisions. One large body of research that investigates this phenomenon among elites is the so-called ideas or epistemic communities literature, which is largely consistent with the thin rational choice approach yet seeks to show through historical analysis how ideologies shared within certain social groups have had effects on policy formation (e.g., Hall 1989; Goldstein and Keohane 1993). The literature relating to the paradoxes of voting and collective action, in contrast, has focused on one particular type of belief: the impact that one's actions have on political outcomes. These writings have generally sought to demonstrate that individuals engaging in collective action may often believe (because of socialization, propaganda, or other factors) that their participation has a greater impact on outcomes than is true in reality (Barzel and Silberberg 1973; Opp 1986; 1989, chap. 8).

All of these preferences and beliefs are cultural in the sense that they tend to vary in type and magnitude across different groups of individuals and can be acquired or lost over time. Furthermore, given that certain types of preferences and beliefs are seen to promote cooperative outcomes and general welfare, it has been argued that it may be in the interest of parents or governments to "invest" in the socialization of individuals into the appropriate culture (Coleman 1987, 1990; Akerlof 1983), and hence that the inculcation of culture itself may be a rational decision.

Clearly preferences and beliefs are interrelated in the determination of expected utility and can often have substitutable or reinforcing effects on behavior. For instance, the belief that one's own welfare is positively related to another person's can have an effect on action equivalent to positive altruism toward that other person. In the latter case, action on behalf of the other person is based on an intrinsic preference, whereas in the former case, a particular belief causes an individual to act as though he or she had such a preference.[5] Likewise, an inflated belief in one's personal importance in contributing toward a political outcome can under certain circumstances make one act as though one valued that outcome more.

Culture and Coordination

The direct effect of culturally induced preferences and beliefs on expected utility is only one way in which such preferences and beliefs can affect action. A more subtle but nonetheless important effect takes place under conditions in which expected utility is no longer a sufficient guide to rational behavior because it cannot be calculated for all alternatives. One common circumstance in which such uncertainty often arises is when individuals interact strategically, that is, when the outcome of a particular action for each individual depends on the actions of others, and when individuals must choose their actions without knowing in advance what the others' actions will be. In such cases, any commonly held belief or preference that points to one set of mutually rational actions over others can facilitate the coordination of action and hence determine equilibrium outcomes. Knowing the nature of such beliefs or preferences can thus allow a theorist to predict actions and outcomes.

Such coordinating beliefs or preferences have been referred to as focal points in the sense that they focus attention on a particular set of mutually rational actions (Schelling 1960). In order for such a belief or preference to determine behavior, it must be commonly held by the various individuals involved, and this commonality must be mutually recognized by each such individual. The latter requirement distinguishes such a preference and belief from those that directly affect calculations of expected utility. This commonality can be seen as cultural in the sense that it will usually arise among a group of individuals who have shared common experiences that have generated similarities in outlooks.[6]

Examples of such cultural coordination have been cited by economists to explain the ability of traders to engage in risky exchanges in the absence of a reliable contract system (Landa 1978, 1994; Greif 1992, 1994). Similar arguments have been applied to account for outcomes in the political arena by a number of authors. John Ferejohn (1991) has discussed how mutual knowledge in Stuart England of social traditions that gave precedence to higher classes, even if such traditions were not internalized, allowed individuals to coordinate who would run for office under conditions in which all sides sought to avoid a direct contest between candidates. Looking at more recent history, Geoffrey Garrett and Barry Weingast (1993) have discussed how the Cassis de Dijon decision of the European Court of Justice, though lacking legal binding power, set a precedent that allowed negotiators for the Single European Act of 1987 to converge their positions around the principle of mutual recognition. More broadly, Russell Hardin (1995, chap. 2) has argued that knowledge of culturally embedded practices allows ethnic groups to coordinate their actions in a way that encourages particularistic collective action.

It should be noted that although the primary emphasis of theoretical investigation has been on the role of focal points in promoting cooperative outcomes, they can under different circumstances promote noncooperative, suboptimal outcomes as well. For instance, George Akerlof (1976) focuses on how high-caste individuals may continue to follow discriminatory practices, even if they do not have discriminatory tastes and these practices lead to collectively inefficient outcomes, because the practices are rational as long as other high-caste individuals are expected to follow them as well. A similar argument can be found in Gerry Mackie's work (1996) on foot binding and infibulation, where he argues that the end of such practices depends on a large number of individuals' simultaneously "defecting" from mutually reinforcing patterns of behavior. In both cases, cultural knowledge of harmful traditions is seen to perpetuate these traditions by coordinating people's expectations about what others will do, and change occurs only when some external shock to the system upsets such expectations.

General Theories of Culture

The theories described in the preceding sections show that cultural analysis can be complementary to the thin rational choice approach. Bringing culture into play allows analysis in which preferences and beliefs are seen to affect behavior in a way that goes beyond the traditional emphases on egoism and logic and hence expands the explanatory range of rational choice theories. Likewise, rational choice assumptions about utility maximization provide a general way of determining how particular cultural preferences and beliefs interact with structure to determine action, and hence facilitate the generation of predictions.

There remains a problem, however. Despite the fruitfulness of this avenue of research, theories that combine culture with rational action face the accusation that specifications of culture amount to no more than post hoc manipulations of variables in order to explain outcomes that would otherwise seem paradoxical. The lack of clear restrictions on the kinds of preference and belief assumptions that can be inserted into a thin rational choice theory makes this accusation relevant. Conceivably, a theorist could observe a certain type of political behavior, then determine what types of preferences and beliefs fit the behavior, label these preferences and beliefs the culture of the individuals involved, and then use this culture to explain the behavior. What is to prevent such surreptitious tautology?

One way of doing so is through a general theory that places limits on the varieties of cultures that can exist and clearly specifies the content of possible cultures.[7] One effort to create such a general theory of culture is the grid-group cultural theory pioneered by anthropologist Mary Douglas and adapted to political science by a number of authors (e.g., Wildavsky 1987a; Thompson, Ellis, and Wildavsky 1990; Coyle and Ellis 1994).

Grid-group cultural theory divides individuals into four major cultural types: individualist, fatalist, hierarchist, and egalitarian. Each of the categories has clear implications for the types of preferences and beliefs that are held by people within them. The theory does more than simply to classify, because it posits that these four types are the only ones that can support viable social institutions, and hence it infers that adaptation pressures will cause virtually all individuals to belong to one of the categories. Furthermore, it assumes that each individual will remain within a single category across the entire range of his or her actions.

The preferences and beliefs associated with each category, though they generate biases that influence behavior, do not cause people to act in an irrational manner. Instead they influence the choices resulting from people's rational decisionmaking and even allow people to make rational decisions under circumstances in which they would otherwise suffer from uncertainty. Rather than arguing for the mutual exclusiveness of culture and rationality, users of grid-group cultural theory argue that cultural biases provide the raw material for rational action in many cases (Chai and Wildavsky forthcoming).

The exact way in which cultural biases affect rationality can be ascertained by briefly examining each of the cultural categories in turn. Fatalists tend to be self-oriented and lacking in altruism. Moreover, they have an extremely pessimistic view of nature, expecting that attempts to improve their lot will result in failure. Reinforcing these beliefs is a deep risk aversion and a strong tendency to discount future rewards. They have an equally pessimistic view of human nature, expecting others to act in an opportunistic and noncooperative way in all cases in which it is not clearly against the others' interest to do so. Because of such expectations, they will not act cooperatively in situations in which the optimality of such cooperation depends on the cooperation of others. In general, they will avoid risks and pursue behaviors that free them from having to depend on others for their own success.

Individualists have a far more optimistic view of nature, expecting the environment to be bountiful and well-providing. They tend to be risk seekers and have long time horizons. Furthermore, though they are not altruistic, they have optimistic beliefs about mutual cooperation under decentralized institutions that promote bidding and bargaining and where cooperation is not clearly a suboptimal strategy. Hence they will seek to create such institutions whenever possible.

Egalitarians, unlike fatalists and individualists, are group oriented and have other-regarding, altruistic preferences. Hence they are likely to cooperate within the groups in which such altruism is shared. However, they prefer distributive outcomes in which all members of a group receive equal shares in all collectively obtained goods. Furthermore, they dislike collective decision mechanisms that allow some individuals to exercise more control over a particular outcome than others. This can only lead to cooperative equilibria if group members desire the same goods and there is some mechanism that allows them to reach a consensus on the means by which to pursue them. This means that egalitarian groups can tolerate only small differences in preferences and beliefs in order to remain stable, and hence they will tend to splinter rather than tolerate heterogeneity.

Hierarchists, like egalitarians, have positive altruism toward fellow group members. However, they are not averse to outcomes in which shares in collectively obtained goods are unequal, and they accept collective decision mechanisms that assign certain members permanent authority over particular classes of outcomes. Hierarchical groups can thus cooperate under a wider range of circumstances than egalitarian groups, but they can only do so as long as their collective decision mechanisms remain effective in obtaining the goods that they seek. When this is no longer the case, hierarchical groups, like egalitarian ones, will tend to splinter.

Of course, grid-group theory is not the only general theory that divides individuals or groups into coherent cultural types and uses the characteristics of these cultures to explain political behavior. Other recent theories of this sort include Daniel Elazar's (1984) division of American cultures into traditional, moralistic, and individualistic types and Alan Fiske's (1991) division of social relationships into four types: communal sharing, authority ranking, equality matching, and market pricing. Another group of related theories draws from nineteenth-century sociological theories of tradition and modernity, linking each possible culture to a different stage in a broader process of development. Prominent theories of this sort in political science include Stephen Chilton's (1988, 1991) division of possible cultures into six successive "ways of relating" and Richard Wilson's analysis of cultures as "compliance ideologies" linked to four different stages of societal development. These theories, like grid-group cultural theory, are more than simple categorizations, because each specifies limits on the types of cultures that are viable and posits that individuals and/or groups will act largely in accordance with a single culture across the entire range of their interactions. The development-oriented cultural theories, in addition, specify sets of structural conditions under which each type of culture will predominate over the others.

None of these theories purports to explain all individual-level variations in preferences and beliefs. Individuals within the same culture may exhibit differences in preferences and beliefs, as long as those differences do not contradict the central cultural biases shared by adherents of that culture. Because these theories do not claim to predict each and every significant aspect of culture or to describe all the processes by which culture is generated, they can to a certain extent be complementary with alternative theories of culture.

The main alternative to these types of cultural theories is endogenous theories of preference and belief formation. These theories, rather than specifying the universe of possible cultural types, describe the dynamic process by which individuals acquire particular preferences and beliefs over time. In economics, the most prominent such theories have been those that describe how past levels of consumption for certain goods can increase or decrease an individual's relative preferences for these goods (Scitovsky 1976; Stigler and Becker 1977; Becker and Murphy 1988). Such theories can be used to examine cultural phenomena such as the development of tastes for food, art, and music. In sociology a number of theories have focused on the ways in which preferences (Homans 1961; Blau 1964; Emerson 1987) and beliefs (Friedkin and Johnsen 1990; Carley 1991) are acquired through reinforcement in repeated bilateral interactions between individuals. Applied within the context of social networks that shape such interactions, these theories may be used to examine the ways in which particular preferences and beliefs diffuse within a group or society. One theory of preference and belief formation that has found a wide variety of applications in the social sciences is psychological dissonance theory, which is based on the idea that individuals adjust preferences and beliefs in order to maintain a specific perception of themselves or of their past actions (some of the most prominent applications outside of psychology are Hirschman 1965; Akerlof and Dickens 1982; Elster 1989, chap. 1; 1993). Elsewhere I have argued that, appropriately specified, a dissonance theory of preference and belief formation can be used to explain a wide range of cultural phenomena (Chai forthcoming).

As this plurality of theories makes clear, there will in the foreseeable future be no single dominant general theory of culture for predicting the preferences and beliefs that inform rational action. It is impossible in this limited space to evaluate each theory individually, but all view culture in a way that is compatible with the assumption of rationality yet provide a richer and more nuanced view of human preferences and beliefs than is supplied in the conventional rational choice approach. Each also specifies what sorts of preferences and beliefs are possible, and thus, combined with the rationality assumption, they can generate a theory that takes cultural differences into account in predicting action while retaining some of the deterministic a priori nature of the conventional rational choice approach.

Ultimately the integration of culture and rational choice will have proved worthwhile only when a general integrative theory is shown to provide determinate and accurate explanations both for phenomena that the conventional theories have been able to explain as well as for phenomena that have generated anomalies. The debate between cultural theorists and rational choice theorists has shown that there are major explanatory gaps in both approaches that need to be filled. While there is no guarantee that a general integrative theory can fill all of those gaps, the explanatory success of midrange integrative theories (such as those on voting and collective action) in addressing aspects of political behavior that would otherwise seem paradoxical indicates the promise that exists in developing and refining a general theory. Likewise, the recent renaissance in theories of culture has provided sets of assumptions upon which such a general theory can be based. A growing consensus about the weaknesses of the existing approaches along with the availability of plausible alternatives comprise two necessary conditions for a paradigm shift. What is now needed is efforts to develop and refine the alternatives into practical tools that can be used to examine the full range of human phenomena.

Notes

1. A related development is appropriation of the "new institutionalism," which has been adapted from theoretical work in sociology. See March and Olsen 1989; Powell and DiMaggio 1991.

2. The debate over culture versus rationality in political science is only part of a larger debate over diametrically opposed views of human nature and methodology that has taken place within all the social science disciplines. See Swedberg 1990 for a short history.

3. An even stronger version of these assumptions assumes that individuals are also able to observe or infer all relevant facts about their environment.

4. An alternative is to argue that an institutional deus ex machina provides the means through which individuals can predict the actions of others, but such an argument is plausible only in a limited number of cases.

5. This distinction has been referred to as one between "immanent" and "instrumental" preferences. See Hechter 1993.

6. The exception may be when recognition of a particular focal point is based on certain characteristics of the interaction itself, though even in this case some prior common knowledge is required so that individuals know which characteristics are the relevant ones to look for. For a discussion of the distinction between "endogenous" and "exogenous" expectations, see Harsanyi and Selten 1988, chapter 10.

7. The other major alternative is to specify a general methodology that allows reliable measurement of preferences and beliefs across a wide range of contexts. For discussion, see Chai forthcoming, chapter 2.

Part Two

Institutions and Culture

Chapter Three

A Cultural Theory of Organizations

DENNIS J. COYLE

What is the point of organization theory? The literature on the development of public and private organizations is populated with studies that have "yielded little more than recitations of dates and names—organizational histories that went little beyond the detail and insight of routine newspaper coverage" (Sproull, Weiner, and Wolf 1978, xii). Excessive emphasis on details and peculiarities can "prove at once so fascinating and so exasperating. . . . There is complexity but not clarity" (Wildavsky 1989, 98). We can study each organization, public and private, large and small, as a unique entity. But to what end? For the study of organization to become organizational theory, there must be learning—that is, it must create knowledge that is transferable.

Theory requires generalization that enables prediction and prescription. "God," Tocqueville said, "stands in no need of general ideas" (1990, 2:13). For us earthly grunts, however, who cannot comprehend everything simultaneously, generalization allows us to simplify the comparison of key attributes. But if everyone's general ideas are unique to oneself, then we have not progressed; we have simply replaced empirical incomparability with theoretical incomprehensibility, creating a scholarly Tower of Babel, and we are back where we started. This can be not only pointless but also annoying; as Tocqueville wryly complained about French intellectualism, "I am informed every morning when I wake that some general and eternal law has just been discovered which I never heard mentioned before" (1990, 2:14). To avoid adding to this cacophony, I will seek to "organize" the disparate field of organization theory by using grid-group theory to integrate concepts, terminology, and exemplary approaches in the existing literature[1] as well as to broaden analysis by bringing in forms of social relations and intellectual orientations often given inadequate attention.

Using a modest number of categories into which organizations and actions can fall, the grid-group approach enables comparison that is comprehensive and critical yet constrained. Yet any theoretical approach must defend itself against the charge that its conceptual framework unreasonably limits or biases analysis. The categories must be exhaustive, or else we may at best end up knowing quite a bit about very little, and at worst—if criticism is only unidirectional—parading advocacy disguised as analysis. Robert Denhardt's (1981) "critical" theory of public organization, for example, seeks to "reveal certain contradictions inherent in hierarchical organizations" (633) in order to equalize power relations and thereby allow expression of "the true needs of individuals" (634), as if egalitarianism had the monopoly on truth, and hierarchy the monopoly on contradictions. Too often, as Todd La Porte (1971) complained, "[a]nalytic concepts are . . . rooted in underlying normative presuppositions held by the theorist" (30). The grid-group approach seeks not so much to eliminate bias as to tame it by making it explicit and comparative. The exhaustive categories, by providing alternative bases for criticism, encourage balance while avoiding the paralysis of relativism (Lockhart and Franzwa 1994). A theory that is comprehensive, comparative, and critical can thereby accommodate the normative function of organization theory or public administration without short-circuiting empirical analysis.

A cultural theory of organizations emphasizes that meaning is constructed through everyday life, that we judge policies and organizations not just in isolation but also for their effects on our ways of life, and that we continually reevaluate our cultural preferences in light of experience. Cultural analysis imputes this evaluative rationality to individuals and organizations. Like rational choice, it "call[s] into question the emphasis on irrationalism that was found in the behavioral models" (Ceaser 1990, 81) yet acknowledges that it is nonsensical to talk of rational choice without social context (Wildavsky 1994a; Zey 1992). A cultural approach does not assume a nation of rationally calculating actors, fully cognizant of their preferences and the alternatives before them. Rather, preference formation is seen as an experiential process in which preferences develop through social interaction. Culture salvages theory by rooting it in experience and elevates empiricism (experience) by making it meaningful.

In the organizational context, these cultural dynamics are displayed in the fundamental act of organizations: decisionmaking. Organizations exist to constrain action in line with knowledge and preferences; simply put, "[o]rganization is bias" (Thompson and Wildavsky 1986, 275), and it is through decisionmaking that an organization reveals its identity, its bias. Of course the institutionalization of norms and rules may also function to eliminate decisionmaking by preprogramming behavior. The work of Herbert Simon (1955, 1956, 1976; March and Simon 1958) on decisionmaking provides a foundation for linking organizational and grid-group theory.[2] One of Simon's most notable contributions was the notion of bounded rationality, the recognition that not every option can or should be considered at every decision point (March 1978). This perspective represented a considerable advance over insistence on "synoptic" rationality—comprehensive consideration of all possibilities—by acknowledging the effects of learning and experience. Our past, as organizations or individuals, structures our present; it makes choice manageable. "The rational individual is, and must be, an organized and institutionalized individual," according to Simon (1976, 102).

Simon emphasized the role of fact and value premises in constraining decisions, and these premises are central to my cultural analysis of organizations. The organization's premises constitute its "physiology," which complements its "anatomy"—the allocation of decisionmaking authority (Simon 1976, 220). We might say that grid-group theory grounds anatomy in physiology in that organizational form may follow from, or at least should be compatible with, decision premises. Where these are inconsistent, dissonance and pathology result. Bounded rationality opens the door to plural rationality, the idea that different forms of social organization "bound" their members with different premises and thus have different standards of rationality (Grauer, Thompson, and Wierzbicki 1985). It is culture, that mix of values, beliefs, and practice, that bounds rationality, and different cultures are compatible with different combinations of fact and value premises.

The Cultural Framework

The cultural theory employed here utilizes an exhaustive but concise typology of social forms built on the identification of "grid" and "group" as the fundamental variables of social life (Thompson, Ellis, and Wildavsky 1990, 5; see also Douglas 1982a; Douglas 1992; Wildavsky 1987a). The degree of group and the degree of grid are the basic constraints that pattern choice and thus create the four basic social forms. Group refers to the extent to which decisions are made or actions are motivated by concern for the welfare of the group, and there is a consequently strong sense of group boundaries. Grid is essentially synonymous with regulation, constraint, or prescription; it measures the degree of compliance with externally defined or preexisting limits on decisions or behavior. A tightly rule- or status-bound social context is highly gridded, for example. Since grid narrows the field of action, in a sense it increases organization. The modern large-scale formal organization may be characterized by a high degree of grid.

In its emphasis on the core variables and foundational types of organization, and in its quest for comprehensiveness and universalism, grid-group cultural theory seeks to transcend simple typology. But the framework can still be usefully compared and integrated with other organizational categories and typologies in the literature, such as those of Amitai Etzioni (1975), Giandomenico Majone (1986), and William Ouchi (1980). Grid and group may seem unusual independent variables from which to derive a typology of organizational forms, but they are related to familiar concepts (Figure 3.1). Group is similar to ends and values, since it is agreement on values, or ultimate ends, that binds the group. In a more

Despotism	Hierarchy
Coercion/alienation (E)	Pure normative/moral (E)
No voice/no exit (H)	Loyalty (voice/no exit) (H)
	Bureaucracy/rules (O)
	Rational (S)
	Bureaucratic/computation (TT)
Libertarianism	**Egalitarianism**
Remuneration calculative (E)	Social normative/moral (E)
Exit/no voice (H)	Voice/exit (H)
Market reciprocity (O)	Clan/common values (O)
Market (M)	Profession (M)
Open (S)	Natural (S)
Anomic inspiration (TT)	Collegial/judgment (TT)
Representative compromise (TT)	

Grid = rules, facts, means, lack of exit

Group = ends, values, voice

Sources
(E)   Etzione 1975
(H)   Hirschman 1970
(M)   Majone 1986
(O)   Ouchi 1980
(S)   Scott 1981
(TT) Thompson and Tuden 1959

FIGURE 3.1   The grid and group of organizations

loosely defined group or organization, it may be process values that bind the group. Rules, or grid, are the formalization of means, or factual premises. Thus Simon's (1976) emphasis on fact and value premises as constraining decisionmaking is compatible with Cultural Theory's emphasis on the foundational nature of grid and group. James D. Thompson and Arthur Tuden (1959) constructed a similar set of typologies of decisionmaking processes and organizational structures based on the degree of agreement on outcome preferences (values) and causation beliefs (facts), and Etzioni (1975) used the terms power (grid) and involvement (group). Another analytic scheme familiar to many social scientists, Albert O. Hirschman's (1970) use of voice and exit, is also closely analogous. As grid increases, as roles become more confining, there is less opportunity for exit, or at least exit is viewed as less legitimate. Voice is most relevant when groups are tightly bound, when members deliberate to reach group positions; in effect, how far one's voice carries defines the group. Together, the grid and group variables define four primary modes of social relations. These are the basic internally consistent organizational forms, essentially what Etzioni (1975) called "congruent types." The recurring attributes of the types described by various theorists suggest that grid-group theory may be on the right track in positing these four ways of organizing.

When value agreement and factual certainty are high, the corresponding organizational form (and culture) is hierarchy. In these cases, group identity and role differentiation are strong, and these variables identify the upper right corner of the cultural model. It is knowledge that provides order; when knowledge is complete, the organization is like a fully analyzable machine (Taylor 1911), held together by standard operating procedure. The classic Weberian bureaucracy, the organizational type that virtually every model incorporates, resides here. Bureaucracy is the more common term, but cultural theorists generally prefer hierarchy because it is at once more precise and more encompassing in that it allows for hierarchical forms other than modern, rational bureaucracy. Hirschman's (1970) analysis has interesting implications here, because if we accept that group is roughly analogous to voice and grid to declining opportunity for exit, then the high-grid, high-group locus is identified with voice without exit—in other words, loyalty, which is Hirschman's third category and an important virtue in hierarchies.

The opposite pole, where self-interest reigns over group identity and there are few constraints on action, is the locus of the libertarian culture,[3] and its preferred organizational form, the market (Ouchi 1980; Majone 1986). Oliver Williamson (1979) showed how a more hierarchical organization might develop from market relations, providing a bridge between these forms. This low-grid, low-group corner is also the home of Thompson and Tuden's anomic/inspiration and representative/compromise types as well (1959).[4] In a climate of such individualized social relations, associations tend to be shifting, instrumental coalitions or networks (Zaleznik 1970). Grid-group theory recognizes that a market itself is a form of organization, since it mediates among conflicting preferences and patterns relations. Actual social entities—businesses, agencies, and voluntary associations, for example—may also be "marketlike" in that their boundaries and internal processes and relations are subject to continual change. Abraham Zaleznik (1970), for example, viewed organizational leadership largely as a market-style competition. This may or may not lead to pathologies, depending on environmental circumstances, as I will discuss later. Conversely, entities within a market may organize hierarchically, essentially hypothesizing about a shared fact and value regimen that will resonate in the larger market, which tests these competing hierarchies.

This cultural theory removes the privileged status of hierarchy, viewing it as just one of the fundamental forms. Giving the market its due as a defining type illuminates the dynamics of organizations lying between these two forms, and I will devote greater attention to the market-to-hierarchy continuum later. But another interesting contribution of the grid-group model is the prominent place it assigns to two additional social forms that usually receive little or no attention. The internal consistency of hierarchy and markets is relatively clear, in that they are either high or low on both measures of social boundedness, grid and group. In contrast, the modes of social relations in the other corners of the typology are low on one social measure, yet high on the other. This can make them difficult to sustain; in one case resort may be made to force, in the other to voluntarism. One culture may be a compelling ideal, the other a harsh reality.

When constraints are few but group consciousness high, "it means the voluntary respect for the concern of others as a principle of action" (Gretschmann 1986, 394). This is the egalitarian or sectarian culture, or roughly what Ouchi (1980) called clan and Klaus Gretschmann (1986) and Friedhart Hegner (1986) called solidarity. Many idealistic movements aspire to this social form, but it can be difficult to sustain over time or on a large scale. The organizational significance of egalitarianism is more clear if we view the ideal forms as pressures or tendencies. Egalitarianism provides an alternative organizational logic that, when distinguished from those of markets and hierarchies, clarifies the analytic waters, particularly the internal structure of organizations and their environmental fit.

When action is highly constrained yet group concern is trampled by self-interest, we find what may be called fatalism, although I prefer to label it despotism, because that accounts for the nature of leadership in such a regime and is consistent with the other basic types (Coyle 1994a, 225). The leader's power under despotism is "exceptional, arbitrary, and without limits in its exercise, except those deriving from his own will," as General Francisco Franco has been described (Alba 1980, 258).[5] Etzioni (1975) similarly characterized this dual nature of repressive leaders and subjugated followers in his "coercion/alienation" model. And in Hirschman's (1970) framework this is where members are deprived of both voice and exit, powerless to change their lot by either transforming the system or going elsewhere. This high-grid, low-group corner of the model is not a widely advocated organizational form, but organizations buffeted by pathologies may tend in this direction, or at least they may be viewed that way by their members.

The hierarchical, egalitarian, and libertarian categories are roughly comparable to Richard Scott's (1981) rational, natural, and open organizations.[6] Grid-group theory provides an explanation of why these three categories are so useful by deriving them from the basic variables of social life. Emphasizing these organizational forms is not intended to imply that organizations must neatly fit into these types, with an uninhabited no-man's-land between them. Such a theory would be hard pressed to account for the reality of diverse and shifting forms and would be particularly inadequate in accounting for organizational change. To suggest that, say, a bureaucratic hierarchy might pull up its stakes and transform itself into a freewheeling market structure is to exaggerate both human rationality and organizational plasticity. The fundamental types may be best thought of as tendencies or pressures rather than operational forms. Other organizational structures may develop as hybrids, and gradual movement from one pole to another through trial-and-error experience more plausibly describes organizational change. "The continuum from market to hierarchy is less like a ruler than a football," Charles Perrow has said (1986, 255). The football analogy may exaggerate the concentration along the midrange, but it is fair to say that the continuum is more a ruler than a barbell. Even supposedly unfettered markets move far enough on the grid and group axes to enforce basic rules against force and fraud, for example. And as long as human perception is flawed and individualized and cooperation and understanding depend in part on the imperfections of language, hierarchy can never be pure. In the case of hybrids, the basic types indicate the kinds of tensions they internalize or the dissonance they will experience.

Organizations and Environments

Drawing attention to the diversity of organizational forms invites a central question of organizational theory: Which form of organization is best? The answer is the social scientist's standard caveat: It all depends. Grid-group theory helps us understand *what* it depends on by pointing to the variety of environments that correspond to the organizational forms. Essentially the same question may be asked empirically rather than normatively by addressing how and why organizations change. In either case it is the match between organization and environment that is the key issue, and grid and group that help illuminate the choices. Attention to environment rescues culture from being reduced to preference, just as culture rescues rationality from methodological individualism (Wildavsky 1994a). "An organizational act is rational," Michael Thompson and Aaron Wildavsky have argued, "if it supports one's organizational culture—one's way of life" (1986, 276). This is an important antidote to theories of universal rationality devoid of social or institutional context (March and Olsen 1984). But if cultural preference can blind us to questions of environmental fit—if we value process over success—then rationality can quickly become pathology (March and Olsen 1988, 341–345).

Important environmental variables (Table 3.1), drawn from the literature of organization theory, are basically variants of grid and group. Hierarchy is best suited to conditions of value agreement and factual certainty, as Martin Landau (Landau and Stout 1979) and Wildavsky (1972) have suggested. For Weber (1947, 339), administration was "the exercise of control on the basis of knowledge," which can be embedded in bureaucratic structure. When we know what to do and how to do it, predefined structure is efficient. Assuming high degrees of agreement and control was essential to Woodrow Wilson's (1887) separation of politics from administration; politics would provide the directives, and a neutral administration would execute them (Goodnow 1900). If, however, politics permeates public organization because agreement on ends is never clear or complete and means are uncertain or have unanticipated consequences, then centralized bureaucracy may seem less like administration without politics and more like politics without authority.

TABLE 3.1   Conditions, Consequences, and Organizational Forms

	Hierarchy	*Egalitarian*	*Market*
Conditions:			
Fact certainty	High	Low	Low
Value agreement	High	High	Low
Flux	Low	Moderate	High
Transaction costs	High	High	Low
Reciprocity	Low	Low	High
Consequences:			
Empirical	Replication, predictability	Constrained discovery	Discovery
Normative	Order	Equality	Liberty

This context is one in which flux or change is low; hierarchies excel at replicating routine tasks, but are ill suited to environmental turbulence. Similarly, Williamson's (1979, 1981) concept of transaction costs helps to explain the process of adapting organization to environment: When transactions become repetitive and predictable, we can economize on costs by internalizing exchange, perhaps initially through contracting and eventually through merger or expansion. Hierarchies do not require a high degree of reciprocity, in the sense of complementary behavior by external agents.

In contrast, markets depend on a higher degree of reciprocity, the willingness of actors to behave in a trustworthy fashion. Otherwise, transaction costs are intolerably high. Markets work best when key information is widely available, reducing transaction costs. They are sensitive to change, so flux is not a problem, nor is low value agreement or factual uncertainty. All that is needed is agreement on some basic process values, allowing actors to pursue their own ends independently. Because markets excel at flexible response to stimuli and do not require a prior definition of roles, uncertainty is not threatening and may actually create opportunity. In other words, they are loosely coupled, whereas hierarchies are tightly coupled (Aldrich 1979, 76; Scott 1981, 50; Weick 1976). Whereas hierarchies codify and institutionalize existing knowledge, markets are superior discovery mechanisms (Hayek 1979, 67), testing hypotheses and creating knowledge. "People may be dumb," libertarians would say, "but markets are always smart" (Wildavsky 1987b, 288).

Egalitarian organization shares one fundamental characteristic with markets—weak grid—and one with hierarchy—strong group—and the environment to which it is appropriate is an amalgam of the environments of the other cultures. Like the market, it is suited to environmental conditions that are variants of low grid, such as a high degree of factual certainty, and like hierarchy, it is suited to conditions that are variants of high group, such as strong value agreement. Discovery is encouraged yet constrained by egalitarian organization, because members may exercise their own judgment, but only within the confines of the group value consensus. Karen Hult and Charles Walcott (1989) have described this as collegial-consensual structure. This distinctive combination of agreement and uncertainty, of freedom and group awareness, is the genesis of "politically correct" thinking and acting, which can be benevolent, indeed essential, within the group but seen as oppressive if imposed on outsiders. The pure hierarchy minimizes choice—and thus the danger of culturally wrong choices—by preprogramming social relations, whereas pure markets put nothing off limits. Only within egalitarianism is there such a striking tension: Experimentation is good, but only within the perceived limitations of the common good.

The transactional circumstances that encourage the formation of hierarchies—high costs and low reciprocity—also encourage the development of egalitarian sects. In other words, internalization of relations promotes decisionmaking efficiency. Both high-group forms of organization are tightly bounded in that their boundaries are clear—they are clearly differentiated from the outside world—but internally they are radically different: Hierarchy is vertical and tight, whereas egalitarianism is flat and loose. Although egalitarianism has similarities to both hierarchy and markets, it is not a hybrid found somewhere between these other two types. Indeed, distinguishing egalitarianism clarifies the path of transformation from market to hierarchy, which would otherwise be cluttered with a hodgepodge of social relations.

In its emphasis on what might be called barefoot theorizing—the development of social relations and preferences through the crucible of experience—cultural analysis points out a capacity critical in organizational success: the ability to gauge the environment accurately. Organizational pathologies can quickly develop if there are disincentives to the communication of accurate information, for example. Shooting the messenger corrupts the organization. But free-flowing communication may not be enough if accurate environmental knowledge is lacking. In organization as in personal life, we muddle along, acting on our best assessments of situations, supplemented by intuition and wishful thinking. We swim in a sea of uncertainty about uncertainty, so to speak, never sure of the accuracy of our perceptions. Cultural theory accepts that there is no "immaculate perception"; rather, we filter information through our cultural blinders. Consciously addressing the effects of those blinders by making them explicit, as the grid-group approach does, can reduce but not eliminate distortion.

Hierarchies may be particularly vulnerable to misperceiving the environment or not recognizing shifting trends (Kaufman 1971), because they do not crave constant feedback, as markets do. Public funding, by removing the threat of extinction that can push even cumbersome private hierarchies to adjust for change or failure, can render governmental bureaucracy especially insensitive. Robert K. Merton (1952) provides the classic discussion of the pathologies that may result when compliance displaces comprehension of an organization's function. Hierarchies may perceive or assume greater certainty or environmental stability than is justified, relishing their procedures and rituals while fading into obscurity or irrelevance. In such cases, rationalization may replace verification, as form becomes rooted in dogma rather than knowledge. If the pretense becomes apparent, dissension may grow, which can be dealt with constructively by "disorganizing"—incorporating market-style discovery mechanisms—or destructively, as leaders resort to despotic-style coercion to maintain their authority and the organizational structure. Aspirations of dominance may drown out environmental sensitivity (Morgan 1990, 176). To flourish, hierarchies may need to take pains to develop environmental feedback mechanisms that less constrained organizational forms might take for granted. Of course environmental signs of peril may be suppressed by elites seeking to preserve their status, and so hierarchies also need to inculcate a loyalty to the organization that dilutes self-interest. Marketlike behavior can germinate its own organizational pathologies. Hierarchies require trust among members, a sense of common mission, and acceptance of the structure (Douglas 1986, 55). Competition within an organization or fighting against the structure, which Zaleznik (1970) generally views as constructive because it stimulates careful thinking about the organization, may be wasteful or even destructive if it erases this institutional knowledge.

Public Administration and Organizational Variety

The pursuit of the public interest may take various organizational forms, depending on our conception of it and on circumstances. Formal public control may not be essential, and markets anchor one end of the most prominent continuum, from hierarchy to markets, for the provision of public goods. Public policy need not presume public organization. The disciplinary lines that allocate bureaucracy to political scientists and markets to economists do engender a more manageable research agenda. But defining away all but the governmental realm suggests that centralized, tax-supported, politically controlled organization is an end in itself for public administration (V. Ostrom 1973, 33–35). Our understanding of bureaucracies and markets as well as of collegial groups and anomic or despotic forms must be integrated at some point, or intellectual illumination becomes delusion. By facilitating comparison of diverse forms, a cultural theory of organizations avoids prematurely narrowing the field of inquiry and cautions against a sharp public-private distinction.

Public administration, or the application of organizational theory to the polity, can then be most usefully thought of as the comparative analysis of social forms and processes for the pursuit of the public interest. Of course this leaves unanswered the very large question of what is the public interest, but grid-group theory at least helps to reveal the nature of the debate. Each of the organizational forms actively defended in political and social life—libertarian markets, egalitarian sects, and hierarchies—promotes different fundamental values—liberty, equality, and order, respectively. Hence it is insufficient to assert that the public interest requires a certain organizational form, a certain pattern of social relations, as if it were a simple means-end equation. The social processes themselves may be an important element of the public interest.

Normative preferences embedded in particular cultures may skew perceptions of the organizational environment. Libertarians will tend to prescribe markets, hierarchists bureaucracies or traditional order, and egalitarians small, consensual groups. Stephen Richardson's (1956) analysis of British and American merchant ships provides a classic example of differential organization under essentially identical circumstances. But grid-group theory weakens its analytic power if it exaggerates the controlling influence of cultural lenses. For example, Wildavsky (1989) showed well how leadership can vary with regime cultures, but he did not so much "unpack situation," which he set out to do, as discount it, by almost exclusively emphasizing the role of cultural values over environmental context. Pluralism does not require functional equivalency; it does not mean that all cultural perspectives "are equally right or wrong" (Douglas 1986, 109) in every situation. Perception may not be immaculate, but neither need it be entirely social. If we can judge only by our culture, then the constrained relativism of grid-group theory is too easily reduced to a scholarly version of that 1960s mantra, "Whatever you're into, man."

Herbert Simon, "with a preoccupation for intra-organizational arrangements," as Vincent Ostrom (1973) noted, similarly "reduced the theoretical impact of his challenge" (47). Although he emphasized the fit between the organization and its premises, Simon paid little heed to the relationship between the premises and the environment and thus could not "establish the relative efficiency of different organizational arrangements" (46). A marriage of cultural and organizational theory should enlighten judgment in at least two ways: by making explicit the relationships between patterns of social relations and normative values, and by further interrogating the relations between forms and environment. If we know, for example, that markets may leave unacceptable risks unregulated or that hierarchies may elevate procedure over accomplishment, we can factor that into our political judgments. By extending the grid-group (or fact-value) framework to environments as well as organizations, we can integrate insights from transaction-cost economics (Williamson 1979, 1981) and better understand why organizations form at all as well as which forms are most appropriate, and when.

A Theory of Disorganizing

Organizational forms are continually tested against the normative preferences of leaders or members and against the hard knocks of reality. Organizations are purposive, although we may not fully understand their derivation or functions. Experience can teach more than we comprehend. If our social or political processes continually produce perverse or surprising results, we may be more amenable to reform. In this way organizations may be like the proverbial mule: stubborn of habit, but attentive if hit over the head enough times. Organizations are hypotheses, and they are continually tested for effectiveness. If their premises of factual certainty (grid) and value agreement (group) are inaccurate, organizations may be pushed through experience or reflection toward a better fit. If devotion to existing premises thwarts adaptation, bounded rationality may, as Vincent Ostrom put it, become "bounded irrationality" (1973, 47).

When both grid and group shift simultaneously, we have movement along the axis from hierarchies to markets. To move outward and upward from markets is to move from informal and ever changing networks to increasingly formal and rigid relations. It is a journey toward organization, in the traditional hierarchical sense. To organize is to constrain increasingly the free-flowing interactions of the market culture, culminating in hierarchical organization, which is the social form that best suits conditions of high value and fact agreement; it is the structural expression of certainty. Grid-group's contribution may perhaps be more aptly termed a theory of organizing, or disorganizing (Weick 1979), than a theory of organization, in that the emphasis is more on alternative forms and the tensions and shifts between them. Organization, like culture, is dynamic, and the continuum from markets to hierarchies, given that these are the most commonly recognized forms, comprehends a large portion of the work being done on organizations.[7]

The movement along this axis from market to hierarchy (Figure 3.2) is not equivalent to a journey from private to public organization; rather, both realms may be "organized" to a varying degree. And so there is a fork in the road: From the perspective of public administration, one path is internal in that a formal public agency is retained (ending in the garbage can), and the other is external, with the pursuit of public welfare entrusted to private actors, with decreasing constraints (ending in anarchy). Though it is fair to say that a low-group, low-grid culture will generally be compatible with a relatively autonomous private sphere, it does not follow that governmental control or administration will be seen as illegitimate. Conversely, a hierarchical culture may have a minimal state, even though it is compatible with expansive bureaucracy. But the cultures will differ greatly in how they "constitute" the state (Coyle 1995). For example, relationships will be more competitive in a market culture, whether in the public or private realm.

At one end of the spectrum lies the classic bureaucratic hierarchy promoted by Progressive Era reformers. Advocates largely assumed the degree of certainty and agreement that would legitimate such centralized, elite control (Wilson 1887; Goodnow 1900). Great faith was placed in the potential of scientific rationality (Taylor 1911; Weber 1946, 1947). Human creations were seen as superior to natural ones not because they are flexible and respond to circumstances, but because, as Lester Ward (1973, 48) wrote in 1893, they "are conceived in advance by the mind, designed with skill for definite purposes, and wrought by the aid of a variety of mechanical principles." In practice, planning and administration could never be as free of politics, as free of dispute over means and ends, as the idealists asserted; an apolitical organization could not be fully realized in a political envi-

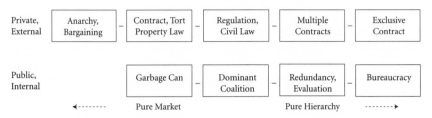

FIGURE 3.2   Degrees of organization

ronment beset by uncertainty and disagreement. But hierarchical advocates often have assailed breaches of rational, centralized control, rather than view the organizational ideal as inappropriate to the task environment.[8]

At the other extreme is anarchic bargaining and competition (Abrahamsson 1993), roughly equivalent to the state of nature that many liberal theorists envisioned prior to civil society. Though anarchy remains an ideal to those who argue that society can flourish without a state,[9] a more pragmatic, if less pure, form of low-grid, low-group organizational culture is the market, in which a common monetary and price system facilitates transactions by allowing comparison through "abstract rules of equivalence" (Hegner 1986). The market legitimates a minimal state designed to protect private property and enforce contracts, providing the security and reliance to allow private action and voluntary exchange to flourish (Nozick 1974). The common-law adjudicatory method of enforcing norms of private ordering represents a step toward hierarchy (Majone 1986, 447), in that judges are constrained by gradually evolving doctrines (grid) and are attentive to the social significance of substantive law (group). Yet it remains a competitive, adversarial process that is responsive to the arguments and needs of the parties and the particular circumstances and tolerates considerable doctrinal diversity and ambiguity.[10]

Although basic procedural constraints may be viewed as legitimate in the libertarian culture, the substantive pursuit of the good life is left in private hands. This "unorganized organization," to use Ahrne's (1990, 138) phrase, may be justified as a means of maximizing liberty, or it may be accepted simply because there is great disagreement or uncertainty regarding the public interest. The public realm may encroach upon this private sphere, either for the selfish interests of those who have captured the government, as public choice analysis would suggest (Buchanan and Tullock 1962; Mitchell and Simmons 1994), or because of popular support for turning private forces to public ends. The latter requires a political process by which shared values or agreement on ends or means can be established, such as elections, litigation, or deliberative processes. The result may be, for example, statutory modification of common-law doctrines of tort, contract, or property or, moving in a higher-grid, higher-group direction, more direct governmental regulation of private activity.

Moving from the "organized" end of the spectrum, several theorists and reformers have attempted either to incorporate some of the virtues of markets into public organization or at least to account for an organizational reality that is often far from the ideal of rational bureaucracy. The work of Landau (1969, 1973b; Landau and Stout 1979) and Wildavsky (1972), for example, may be seen as attempts to bring Weberian bureaucracy more in line with imperfect knowledge of the task environment. Redundancy and formal evaluation are ways to interrogate the unknown in order to discover superior methods and to protect against surprise or failure while still maintaining a large degree of centralized control. Niskanen has advocated explicit competition among bureaus because, he says, though it "may reduce the probability that the expected task is accomplished, . . . it increases the probability that the right task will be accomplished, often in unexpected ways" (1980, 173).

These reforms still generally presuppose substantial shared purpose within each entity. Less organized is the "dominant coalition" model, in which there is continuous jockeying for control of the organization's agenda and structure (Coleman 1975; Cyert and March 1963; Thompson 1967; Zaleznik 1970). There may be little sense of organizational identity and ends apart from an amalgam of coalitional interests; the organization is essentially a bounded market, a setting "in which groups and individuals with varying interests and preferences come together and engage in exchanges" (Pfeffer and Salancik 1978, 26). This middle category, where there is at least fuzzy agreement on goals, some understanding of means, and partial organization, may be the most heavily populated and has been drawing greater attention from scholars (Lincoln 1985). The "garbage can" model (Cohen, March, and Olsen 1972; March and Olsen 1979) is a vivid description of how a veneer of organization may obscure a high degree of disorganization and uncertainty. Increasingly theorists are recognizing the merits of disorganization, because "situations in which decision-makers know neither what to do nor how to do it may be more common than one would suspect" (Hult and Walcott, 1989).

Contracting essentially incorporates a private entity as a subunit of a public organizational structure on a temporary, performance-oriented basis. Public management may be quite detailed through the clauses of the contract, yet not at the cost of long-term flexibility, since at the expiration of the contract the government may choose to not renew the contract or to renegotiate the terms. Modifying an agreement on paper is simpler than restructuring a public entity. As Elinor Ostrom (1986) has pointed out, contracting may be most appropriate where private provision of services is recognized as more efficient, yet public control reduces transaction costs, as in her example of municipal garbage collection. Concurrent multiple contracting is even more "disorganized," encouraging competition and discovery.

At a more macro public level, federalism may be well suited to moderate levels of value agreement and knowledge, as it allows a variety of solutions to economic or social problems to be pursued simultaneously (Landau 1973a). Through monitoring by competing states and the professional policy community, successful approaches can be broadly disseminated (Walker 1969). Of course there is a critical difference between contracting and federalism: Contracting ensures that someone will pick up the garbage, to use the Ostrom example, whereas competing states may choose to forgo a service or program entirely. Many federal programs essentially integrate the two methods by setting national standards but giving states flexibility in implementation; if a state declines entirely, federal regulation preempts its role.[11] Similarly, states may delegate considerable authority to localities, either because they are presumed to be more sensitive to local conditions and thus better able to match policy to environment, or because they are deemed to be the appropriate level for achieving a value consensus. These are applications of the principle of subsidiarity—the devolution of authority to the lowest appropriate level (Mercier 1994).

Although high grid and high group cannot be equated with government, the case for centralized public control may be more persuasive in these circumstances, and the case for privatization stronger when knowledge is low and disagreement high. Bureaucratic reforms, such as creating competition among agencies or introducing zero-based or performance budgeting, can be seen as attempts to accommodate public desires for control or bureaucratic defenses of turf while matching the organization more closely to the task environment. On the private side of the divide, regulation introduces a degree of public control while recognizing the basic liberal inclination to "let a thousand flowers bloom," so to speak, by allowing the private pursuit of individual and social interest. Privatizing does not ensure highly decentralized organization; instead it relies on the market to discover efficient forms and processes. When knowledge is sufficient and there are economies of scale, monopolies or oligopolies may develop. Interestingly, antitrust regulation reflects a public distrust of private monopoly, whereas ostensibly democratic control may legitimate public monopoly. Centralized exclusive control in the public and in the private realms thus suffers from different vices: Private monopolies may be effective but seen as illegitimate, whereas public monopolies may wear the mantle of legitimacy but be ineffective.[12]

Egalitarianism: The Lost Culture of Organization

I began with the road from hierarchy to market because that is where the profession has primarily traveled, when it has traveled at all. Searching the literature for egalitarianism can seem like a "Where's Waldo?" exercise. Organization theory has largely been preoccupied with hierarchical forms and deviations from them. When an alternative to hierarchy has been recognized at all, it has most commonly been the market (Krusselberg 1986; Williamson 1975), and the market-to-hierarchy continuum helps to place these deviations in comparative perspective. Though an accurate mapping of the entire cultural terrain awaits more scholarly attention to organizational hybrids tending toward egalitarianism and even despotism, we can hazard some generalizations.

Markets and hierarchies are vulnerable to the criticism that they may slide toward despotism. In the latter case, this takes place as loyalty and cohesion crumble, perhaps as a result of a changing environment or self-interested leaders, and leadership becomes increasingly authoritarian in order to maintain the existing power relations. A similar fate can befall egalitarian groups. In markets, firms may seek to thwart competition and thus exercise coercive authority by monopolizing information or production or seeking governmental regulation to disadvantage adversaries (Mitchell and Simmons 1994).

Part of the challenge in welcoming egalitarian groups into the church of organization theory may lie in finding them. Egalitarian groups tend to be small or short-lived. Procedures may be continually renegotiated among equals, and the tendency to split is high, since a group rooted in consensus cannot long accommodate dissension as people shift their perspectives (Ellis 1991). The challenge in developing a permanent or large egalitarian organization is to move beyond the small sect without "selling out" the guiding principles of low-grid, high-group organization (Douglas and Wildavsky 1982; Newman 1980). The self-interest of its members may push an egalitarian group in a more individualized direction (lowering group), or toward bureaucratization (increasing grid) through a war of paradigms.[13] But the motivation to overcome the challenge can be strong, as egalitarianism offers an enticing promise of reconciling freedom with community (Iannello 1992; Rothschild and Whitt 1986).

Successful maintenance of egalitarian forms may depend on applying them in appropriate contexts and incorporating them into larger, cultural hybrids to guard against their vulnerabilities. Though Green environmental or protest groups such as the Clamshell Alliance may be earnestly egalitarian in structure, collegial or professional associations may be the most common examples in the larger world of organizations (Hult and Walcott 1989; Majone 1986). For example, a large manufacturing corporation may spin off a semiautonomous research unit with a flattened hierarchy, peopled by creative designers and engineers free to pursue their own ideas, yet sharing the common goal of producing a superior widget. The subunit may exhibit relatively strong value agreement while embracing, indeed being motivated by, empirical uncertainty. As knowledge is discovered, it can be incorporated into the structure and processes of the larger firm. If discovery entails extraordinary costs, resource demands, or hazards, control may be centralized and investigation constrained to a higher degree than might otherwise be optimal. For example, the production of a nuclear bomb during World War II involved a constant tension between the decentralizing imperatives of the pursuit of knowledge and hierarchical centralization necessitated by cost and security concerns.

Egalitarian organization may also develop from a libertarian culture, if awareness of shared interest among parties grows. What Gretschmann (1986) has called solidarity can be based on "homogeneous preferences, common values, . . . the assumption that personal utility functions contain interpersonal arguments, and non-separable production functions" (393)—in other words, a sense that "we're all in it together." The interaction of free individuals can become rewarding in itself; as Gretschmann put it, "In such cases there are not only transaction costs but also *transaction benefits* involved" (1986, 393; emphasis in original). This mutual recognition can lead to a "gentlemanly" market, so to speak, in which competition is muted in the interest of community, without going so far as formally to recognize the group and establish boundaries and consensual decisionmaking. Solidarity is thus a sort of relaxed egalitarianism, tolerating some of the looseness and diversity of market culture. John Rawls (1971) has also derived a variant of egalitarianism from self-interest, by depriving individuals of self-knowledge and assuming high risk aversion. But his just polity is essentially a marriage of hierarchy and egalitarianism, as it justifies the use of state coercion (grid) to advantage the least well-off.

Academic freedom is in many ways a classically egalitarian notion in which a shared quest for knowledge binds the group while individual lines of inquiry are at least ostensibly respected.[14] Yet the creation of knowledge is largely historically based, accumulated over the years much like the development of the common law, and a consequent sense of tradition and discipline introduces a degree of respect for roles into academia. And the need to compete for students and donations pushes universities toward the world of markets, although the professoriate may be organizationally isolated from marketing expectations lest their tender sensibilities be offended.

The public organization route on the market-to-hierarchy continuum may be more egalitarian, as the legitimacy of public organization may hinge on implicit democratic approval. But democracy can take several cultural forms. The Burkean model of representative statesmanship reconciles the populism of democracy with the elitism of hierarchy, especially if there are restrictions on who may vote or hold office. More open, competitive elections bring market individualism into politics, and many public choice scholars would suggest that politics is little more than the pursuit of private ends through public coercion (Mitchell and Simmons 1994). But if politics is viewed as a deliberative process that develops and melds preferences rather than as a battleground for preexisting preferences, then egalitarian democratic institutions and processes, such as town meetings and alternative dispute resolution, may be important mechanisms for legitimating subsequent implementation structures. And since implementation still entails value choices, pushing bureaucracy in a more participatory, egalitarian direction may be appropriate (Spicer 1995, 79; Stewart 1975).

The diversity of organizational forms and of the environments to which they may be suited cautions against assertions that a particular organizational form is superior or more advanced. The cultural theory of organizations developed here roots prescription in an understanding of the fundamental role of group and grid, of facts and values, and of the appropriate matches of organizations and environments that derive from these variables. It does not claim to have found the one best way to organize, but it can recommend forms, depending on context and aspiration. Grid-group theory provides a digestible set of alternative tendencies that organizational "mechanics"—leaders and analysts in the public and private realms—can use to understand and test forms in their environments. Since agreement and certainty can vary widely, having a diversity of organizational forms available seems prudent. And given our imperfect perceptions of environmental factors, there is much to be said for encouraging different structures to operate simultaneously in similar environments to better learn what fits where. Variety may not be requisite, but it's a darn good idea.[15]

The Organizational Future

Modern man may be "organizational man," but that in itself does not tell us much. It may be that a Martian viewing Earth through a social-structure telescope would see a landscape overwhelmed by organization (Simon 1991, 27), but what modes of organization, why, and with what effects? When we look at the variety of organizational forms that grid-group theory illuminates, it can hardly be said that humanity is in the relentless grip of bureaucratic hierarchy (Britain and Cohen 1980, 26). As social values and perceptions shift, so do organizations. The organizational world reflects the resurgence of individualism and egalitarianism that has flavored politics since the 1960s as both public and private entities have pushed to lower hierarchies, broaden participation, and increase flexibility. Technological and economic changes have also done their part, facilitating rapid communication and worldwide markets.

Two contemporary intellectual trends may encourage this tendency to "disorganize." On one hand, new theories of ecological complexity or even chaos growing out of the physical sciences undercut faith that science can comprehend and master the universe.[16] For decades, leading ecologists such as Frederic Clements (1916), Paul Sears (1959), and Eugene Odum (1969, 1971) maintained that nature followed a logical path toward a stable climax state that could be precisely identified and comprehended by science (Worster 1990). By implication, society's hope would largely lie with hierarchy, with its emphasis on preservation, planning, and comprehensive rationality. More recent work, largely by population biologists, portrays nature not as an orderly progression but as a haphazard patchwork in which change is constant, apparently directionless, and often unpredictable (Drury and Nisbet 1973; Gleick 1987; Pickett and White, 1985), suggesting the prudence of maintaining organizations that can quickly detect and effectively respond to surprise rather than eliminate it (see Jantsch 1979; Kiel 1994). Indeed, organizational theorists have borrowed directly from population biology and revisionist evolutionary theory (Aldrich 1979; Hannan and Freeman 1977). "Our world is impossible to pin down, constantly changing and infinitely more interesting than we ever imagined," as Margaret Wheatley (1992, 8) has recently remarked, and the social implications will be the growth of "more fluid, organic structures, even of boundaryless organizations" (13). Increasingly, control defers to management, the art of muddling through with insufficient knowledge (Landau 1979; Lindblom 1959).

On the other hand, postmodernism erodes faith in grand designs and universal forms, trusting little other than perhaps personal narrative (Rosenau 1992). We might say that organization is despotism to the postmodernist (Foucault 1970), who regards constraint as nothing more than assertions of power and is doubtful of human capacities for unity, given the limitations of language and perception. Postmodernism can also heighten fears of irreversible harmful consequences of organization (Bergquist 1993, 209). Ironically, in this age of postmodernism and chaos, as we learn more as a society, we seem to believe less.

Postmodernism shares some of the vices identified at the beginning of this chapter with atheoretical empiricism; as Wildavsky put it, if each situation is treated as discrete, "history would be reduced to narrative; interpretation, to repetition" (1989, 90). Organization theory, or for that matter any branch of the social sciences, requires a degree of modernist optimism that communication and the promotion of knowledge are possible, that we can have interpretation as well as narrative. The grid-group theory of culture may in some small way defend the Enlightenment against postmodernism by accepting that our perceptions and beliefs are to some degree culturally determined or biased but providing a framework by which we may hope to identify and overcome our biases enough to enable social and political life and intellectual enterprise to flourish.

Notes

Like a mosquito buzzing around my ear, this is a project that has refused to go away. It began as a comprehensive examination answer in 1985 and reawoke after several years of slumber when Aaron Wildavsky and I began a joint project on organizations. I have benefited from his incisive comments and our countless conversations about culture and organization. I would like to thank Martin Landau for a stimulating seminar that first sparked my interest in organizational and administrative theory, Richard Ellis for his encouragement to return to the subject, and him and Michael Thompson for their helpful comments.

1. Any brief survey of as vast a field as organization theory cannot do justice to all its nuances, and my coverage here is illustrative, not exhaustive.

2. On using Simon as the foundation on which to build the field of public administration, see Landau 1972, 192–194, 198–202, 209.

3. This orientation is commonly labeled "individualistic" (Thompson, Ellis, and Wildavsky 1990), but I think libertarian is the more apt adjective, as individualism may comprise despotism as well (Coyle 1994a, 222).

4. Thompson and Tuden would place the representative/compromise type in the upper left corner, but there really is no agreement on policy means or facts, only on the legitimate methods for seeking values agreement. Indeed, instrumental compromise between competing interests, rather than forging common interests, is what greases the skids of libertarian social life.

5. Aaron Wildavsky occasionally acknowledged the association of despotism with fatalism, as when he observed that "[u]nder fatalistic regimes, leadership is *despotic*—continuous and total," and cited the Franco example (1989, 100; emphasis in original).

6. Although egalitarianism entails a shared interest in more than the simple survival of the organizational structure that Scott suggests (1981, 22).

7. The particular role of egalitarianism and its absence from this organizational continuum are discussed later.

8. See, for example, the defense of the land planning ideal against the inroads of politicized variances (Rose 1983).

9. The "ordered anarchy" of the Nuer, as described by E. E. Evans-Pritchard (1940), provides a classic example of a viable anarchy. He noted "the lack of government organs, . . . the absence of legal institutions, of developed leadership, and generally, of organized political life" (181).

10. Tocqueville (1990, 1:276) cited reliance on the common law as an important factor in constraining the excessive rationalism of the democratic state.

11. On the constitutionality of federal dictation of state policy choices, see *New York v. United States*, 505 U.S. 144 (1992).

12. Recognizing that large-scale centralized private organization may be efficient if a functioning market enables decentralized consumers and potential competitors to constrain private authority, antitrust theory has shifted its focus from concentration per se toward interference with the market (Williamson 1975).

13. Lee Sproull, Stephen Weiner, and David Wolf (1978) portray the clash of these organizational imperatives in the context of "organizing an anarchy."

14. On the organization of education, see Bess 1984; Cohen and March 1974; and Weick 1976.

15. Elsewhere (Coyle 1994a) I have questioned the argument of many grid-group theorists that variety is requisite, that cultures depend on each other (Thompson, Ellis, and Wildavsky 1990). Depending on circumstances, particular cultural forms may be clearly superior or more likely to survive while others expire, and any form of organization may be sustained in adverse circumstances if its members or partisans are determined enough. Much depends on values: If we crave order, for example, we may embrace rational or organic hierarchies and accept inequality, limits on freedom, and a lower level of material well-being. Conversely, if we favor freedom, we may tolerate a high degree of error, anxiety, and alienation and the destruction of knowledge embodied in tradition.

16. On the significance of different cultural conceptions of the natural environment, see Coyle 1994b; Holling 1979; Thompson 1993; and Thompson, Ellis, and Wildavsky 1990.

Chapter Four

Cultures:
Frameworks, Theories,
and Models

VINCENT OSTROM
ELINOR OSTROM

In this essay we critically reflect on our own efforts to come to terms with the place of cultures, frameworks, theories, and models as these are features of the intellectual enterprise in the social sciences. These topics have been at the core of work by Aaron Wildavsky. We first worked with Aaron as a colleague when Aaron and Vincent were visiting scholars at Resources for the Future in Washington, D.C., during 1963 and 1964. Aaron was working on the theory of public budgeting, and Vincent was working on institutional arrangements for water resource development in California and on the joint development of water resources of the Columbia River by Canada and the United States. Lin was working on public entrepreneurship in groundwater basin development in southern California.

We shared a number of intellectual interests and friends. Aaron had done his graduate work in political science at Yale University. Vincent had become closely associated with Robert Agger at the University of Oregon, who had worked closely with Harold Lasswell while at the Yale Law School. Both Agger and Lasswell were fellows at the Center for Advanced Study in the Behavioral Sciences in the first class of fellows in 1954/55. Vincent became acquainted with Lasswell at that time and was invited to be a fellow during the following year when Robert Dahl and Charles Lindblom also served as fellows. Vincent's preoccupation at that time was with the relationship of culture, science, and politics as reflected in works on historical, comparative, and analytical jurisprudence.

Since then, we pursued our different research programs, which continued to intersect with one another. We exchanged manuscripts and critical commentaries. We all shared intellectual interests that involved collaborative efforts with colleagues in anthropology, economics, law, public administration, and sociology.

Over the course of these many years, the two of us have reached the conclusion that a single, general theory of culture, economics, government, law, or politics is not possible. Identifying common elements in theories of such subjects, however, is possible. Theory, like language, is subject to innovative developments. We cannot anticipate what the character of future innovations is likely to be. Thus we need to work with frameworks that identify the elements to be taken into consideration when constructing theory and building models. If used in the context of comparative analysis, we can build complementary modes of inquiry to extend our knowledge of what can be learned from human experience in diverse cultural traditions. We need not surrender to complete cultural relativism; but we do face difficult problems in coming to terms with the ways that human experience is conceptualized and in working with multiple criteria of performance. These problems are sufficiently difficult that we cannot expect resolution until both scholars and practitioners learn how to communicate and work with one another about patterns of order in human societies.

In our effort to continue in this chapter the type of dialogue that we shared with Aaron, we begin by indicating why we think that a general theory of culture, politics, or public administration is not possible. We then turn to the problem of frameworks, theories, and models. In the third section we turn to what we see as problems with Aaron's "cultural theory." Finally, we offer a commentary on some of the conclusions we have reached about these subjects in our conversations with Aaron.

Why a General Theory Is Not Possible

Walter Eucken's critique of economic theory in *The Foundations of Economics* ([1940] 1951) provides a critical understanding of the problems confronting a general theory in the cultural and social sciences. His critique of a general theory of economics was that a single model, as in the case of the perfectly competitive market, was the source of a great antinomy between theory and studies in economic history. An open, competitive market is of relatively recent origins in human experience. Human experience as hunters and gatherers and with subsistence agriculture represents prior stages of economic development. Rather than conceptualizing economics as applying to stages of development, the study of economics, according to Eucken, needed to apply alike to different types of economies and stages. Principles of economics had to apply to different time and place exigencies. In referring to the differences in command economies and market economies, Eucken argued that diverse functions could be performed in different ways. Planning applied to both command and market economies. The way that such a function was performed would involve different structures and processes in a command as contrasted to a market economy. Comparative analysis offered the opportunity for comparative assessments of performance.

Eucken's work was associated with what the Germans call *Ordnungstheorie*, meaning a theory of order. Different systems of economic orders are possible. Economic orders coexist with other systems of orders, including political orders. Close relationships exist between patterns of economic ordering and patterns of political ordering as well as still other patterns of order. How these patterns of order fit together and complemented one another needed to be worked out and understood. The emphasis on competitive equilibrium in Anglo-American economics gave attention to price theory. The emphasis on information-generating aspects of prices in market economics, by contrast, yielded emphasis on entrepreneurship and innovation in Austrian economics. Different types of economic orders were associated with varying structures and processes implying different patterns of performance.

These generalizations complemented our own concerns with the ways that structures and processes functioned within and among the different units of government in metropolitan areas and among federal and nonfederal systems of government. Different processes of cooperation and competition were being engaged within something that might be characterized as public economies in contrast to market economies. Minimal attention had been given to problems of consumption in market economies, but Kenneth Galbraith's (1952) emphasis on countervailing power suggested that competitive dynamics in public economies could exist in highly federalized systems of governance subject to significant magnitudes of fragmentation of authority relationships and overlapping jurisdictions. How these possibilities were worked out in practice required careful attention in efforts to assess performance in public economies in contrast to market economies.

Wildavsky's pioneering work on implementation of public policy (Pressman and Wildavsky [1973] 1984), for example, would—in Eucken's conception of theory—lead to different theoretical implications if applied to a command and control economy of the Soviet type or a polycentric federal system of governance. The existence of pervasive networks of informers, secret police, and special security forces in the former were not subject to public accountability. A command apparatus functioning under strict discipline and strict secrecy was accompanied by terror and fear. This creates implementation problems quite different from those in a system of order functioning in an open public realm with publicity associated with freedom of speech, press, assembly, and association. In the latter, conflicts over policies are to be expected. Contestations mediated through diverse legislative, executive, and judicial structures to achieve conflict resolution in accordance with norms of justice and fairness yield implementation problems different from those of a command form of political order.

Reliance on different conceptions to constitute patterns of order in human societies implies that different forms of language are being used. Moving to a meta-level to give expression to terms that enable scholars to work with similar elements requires using elements in a framework to elucidate similarities and differences for comparative analysis. If certain prototypical situations such as exchange relationships, teamwork, and rivalry can be specified across societies, then comparative assessment becomes possible. Such modes of analysis are themselves cultural artifacts to be assessed by their contributions to human understanding.

The Place of Frameworks, Theories, and Models

We distinguish four levels of theoretical discourse. The most general level, which is often identified as "theory," is the metatheoretical level. At this level, ontological, philosophical, and epistemological presuppositions are taken into account in setting the most general approach to knowledge. Though the term "theory" is generally applied to these metatheoretical considerations, that use of the term is different from our reference to frameworks, theories, and models. The problem of arraying basic elements to set the frame for deriving theoretical inferences in a general field of inquiry requires recourse to the basic elements that need to be taken into account. If those elements can be specified, the key question at a theoretical level is whether some activating factor, force, or agency can be specified as operating in accordance with principles so as to yield predictable consequences. These tendencies may operate in such a way that regularities occur in patterns of order as well as the transformation achieved by those patterns of order.

Thus we distinguish three levels of theoretical discourse apart from metatheoretical discourse. A *framework* provides a way of looking at a complex set of phenomena. Frameworks help to identify the elements that should be included in the theories that elucidate frameworks as applied to more confined sets of phenomena. A *theory* requires assumptions about motive powers or forces that lead to particular processes and likely outcomes. A theory generates explanations of observed behavior in some realm of the world. A *model* is the most focused level of theoretical discourse. A model of a theory specifies all working parts in the most simplified form so as to assess the implications of very particular assumptions about the working parts of a theory. These terms are recklessly used in much of the social sciences. Highly abstract and general conceptions of broad phenomena may be referred to as a framework, a theory, or a model, depending on the preferences of the particular scholar. We think that a recognition of the nested layers of theoretical discourse helps social scientists to recognize that they can develop very general frameworks of analysis that apply to many different types of social systems, but the necessity of making even more specific assumptions about the particulars of each and every element of analysis as one moves to a theory and potentially to a model restricts the generality of the theoretical discourse. Deduction and inferential reasoning are ways of confining attention.

Ibn Khaldûn (1967), a fourteenth-century Tunisian scholar, for example, proposed that a science of culture could be used as a basis for the critical understanding of historical studies. Ibn Khaldûn elucidated the broad parts of a framework needed to understand the relationship of *people* to the ecological conditions of the *place* in which they live. Culture has meanings associated with the verbs to cultivate, to habituate, and to inhabit. The aspects bearing on inhabiting, cultivating, building, and associating together to sustain life and to keep the tools and conditions used in such processes in good repair are the cultural attributes of life. These are the ways that people relate to place and to one another. These are the aspects of culture in which knowledge and its use are expressed as *intelligibilia*. Sentiments, feelings, and aspirations gain expression as *sensibilia*. These factors combine as *existentia* composed of both the natural and the artifactual features of peoples living in places that form the conditions of human habitation characteristic of human culture/societies (Mahdi 1964).

Ibn Khaldûn envisaged a historical cycle in which the nomadic peoples of the Mediterranean world were unified through political leadership. Those conditions of political dominion encouraged patterns of urbanization associated with the exercise of rulership prerogatives, conditions of peace, and patterns of trade. In the course of succeeding generations, the conditions of urban life relaxed tensions and people became vulnerable to aggression by still other nomadic peoples. This science of culture yielded a political theory marked by the rise and decline of dynasties as persistent patterns occurring in human civilizations of the Mediterranean world.

The work of Alexis de Tocqueville was built on a similar framework. It is as though Tocqueville had relied on Ibn Khaldûn's effort to build a science of culture. In *Democracy in America* ([1835 and 1840] 1945), Tocqueville's primary reference is to Anglo-Americans, though he gives some critical attention to Native Americans, African Americans, and the problems posed by the three races and their relationships with one another. Tocqueville identified the element of *place* with "the peculiar and accidental situation in which Providence has placed the Americans" ([1835] 1945, 1:288). The historical background and the social conditions of Anglo-Americans as the *people* primarily involved helps to frame his analysis. Tocqueville's analysis turns to the way that the *laws* as institutional arrangements and the *manners and customs of the people* shape their patterns of existence in North America by contrast, for example, to the French of Quebec and implicitly to his compatriots in France.

Using such a framework and presuming that the Anglo-Americans as human actors behave in characteristic ways, Tocqueville was able to elucidate how (1) people, (2) place, (3) laws, and (4) manners and customs of the people interact in ways that yield a self-governing society in contrast to state-governed societies. Within such a framework, and postulating "self-interest rightly understood," Tocqueville worked out the theoretical explanations for how a system that he called "decentralized administration" functioned among the states of New England in contrast to a system of centralized bureaucratic administration in France. These two systems had fundamentally different structural characteristics yielding different patterns of process and performance.

Vincent Ostrom, Charles Tiebout, and Robert Warren (1961) drew on a similar framework to conceptualize how multiple units of government in metropolitan areas worked both as a system of governance and as a public economy to have some of the patterns of cooperation, competition, conflict, and conflict resolution characteristic of market economies. A competitive public economy generates a system of public administration different from the one conceptualized by Woodrow Wilson (1887), who proposed that systems of bureaucratic administration apply to all governments alike.

Frameworks can be used to formulate families of theories. Theories, in turn, can be more carefully articulated in families of models. What is called "game theory" is one very general theory of human behavior that is consistent with the types of frameworks used by Ibn Khaldûn and Tocqueville. A particular game-theoretical model, the "Prisoner's Dilemma," has generated an extraordinary investment of research efforts. To fully utilize the power of game theory, one must examine how diverse parameters affect the structure of particular games and the type of behavior adopted.

With the development of experimental methods among economists, political scientists, social psychologists, and sociologists, scholars have developed a large number of highly specified models. Experimentalists derive competing hypotheses and give new attention to the way that variation in the elements of a framework affect the type of resolutions that people achieve while participating in such situations. Elinor Ostrom, Roy Gardner, and James Walker (1994), for example, have overtly used the institutional analysis and development framework to formulate a theory of common-pool resource governance and management. They then developed two types of models: (1) a game-theoretic model of appropriation from a resource, and (2) sets of instructions for running appropriation experiments in a laboratory. They showed that when subjects make decisions in a sparse institutional situation in which no communication is allowed, predictions consistent with finitely repeated noncooperative game theory are empirically supported. The subjects produce a "Tragedy of the Commons" in the laboratory. By contrast, when subjects communicate before each decision round, they are able to agree on joint strategies and then use normative discourse to reduce overuse and to increase joint payoffs. Further, if given an opportunity to covenant with one another and to establish a sanctioning system of their own design, those who agree achieve close to optimal returns with low levels of rule-breaking behavior. In light of testing these alternative models, E. Ostrom, Gardner, and Walker formulated a new theory that better explains observed behavior. Considerable leverage has been gained in the cultural and social sciences by those working with frameworks, theories, and models in ways in which these might apply to prototypical situations applicable to exchange relationships, teamwork, and rivalry.

Culture Theory

Intellectuals like Ibn Khaldûn and Tocqueville worked with frameworks that Ibn Khaldûn referred to as a science of culture and Tocqueville referred to as a science of association. These apply to the constitution of self-governing societies. The possibility of developing other frameworks is not foreclosed in addressing regularities that occur in different human societies. In Mary Douglas's preface to *Natural Symbols*, she argued that "there is a drive to achieve consonance in all of the layers of experience" ([1970] 1982c, vii). We agree. This drive is especially strong among intellectuals. In the introduction to the new edition of *Natural Symbols*, dated May 1982, she alluded to "the project of developing a sociological understanding of culture" ([1970] 1982c, xix). We presume that this project, in part, involves a quest for a *framework* that might yield a sociological understanding of culture.

In developing a matrix from the concepts of "group" and "grid," she was engaged in such a quest. In distinguishing the two, she observed: "To the extent that the family is a bounded unit, contained in a set of rooms, known by a common name sharing a common interest in some property, it is a group, however ephemeral. To the extent that the roles within it are allocated on principles of sex, age and seniority, there is a grid controlling the flow of behavior" ([1970] 1982c, 57). Group attributes can be expressed horizontally by a continuum ranging from a minimum experience of group boundaries toward a maximum concentrating on "group allegiances and on recognizable signs of inclusion and exclusion" ([1970] 1982c, 57). Grid is represented by a vertical continuum that gauges the extent to which one's life is organized in a grid of ego-centered social categories having to do with sex, age, seniority, and other such attributes. Social distinctions are made with reference to such general attributes as age, sex, and so on for sorting out roles in ways of life.

Group and grid are ordering principles in constituting ways of life. If we juxtapose these distinctions to one of the key formulations advanced by Henry Sumner Maine in *Ancient Law*, we see a thesis being advanced that "we may say that the movement of the progressive societies has hitherto been a movement *from Status to Contract*" ([1861] 1864, 168; Maine's emphasis). The term "contract" applies not only to market-exchange relationships but also to diverse patterns of voluntary association, and in Tocqueville's treatment it can be applied to units of government organized in relation to covenantal agreements having the standing of constitutions in creating diverse units of government as essential features in self-governing societies.

Following Maine's thesis, factors of sex, age, and seniority—grid—are ways of ranking people that occurred in customary law among nonliterate peoples relying only on spoken language. Moving to principles of contract in ordering human relationships implies increasing autonomy among individuals both in exchange relationships and in voluntary patterns of association characteristic of elaborate networks of groups engaged in both monetized and nonmonetized relationships with one another. The autonomy of personae (persons, roles, collectivities) having legal standing in associated relationships is marked by increasing tendencies toward equality.

As the domain of supreme authority associated with sovereign states becomes the dominant pattern of organization presuming to establish a single, comprehensive, and uniform code of law, we can also understand how attributes associated with grid rankings receive greater emphasis with increasing demands for equality. Put into such evolutionary contexts, we can understand how variable emphasis on group/grid relationships has substantial significance for human societies. Such a framework could have substantial significance in addressing time-related aspects of human civilization rather than contemporary patterns of order within a given time frame.

In *Cultural Theory*, Michael Thompson, Richard Ellis, and Aaron Wildavsky (1990) used the group/grid matrix formulated by Mary Douglas to construct the matrix represented in Figure 4.1. They presented five vignettes—those of the ununionized weaver, the high-caste Hindu villager, the hermit, the self-made manufacturer, and the communard—that illustrate five types of structural conditions: those of fatalism, hierarchy, autonomy, individualism, and egalitarianism, respectively. These sociocultural arrangements are associated with character types—social beings—identified as fatalists, hierarchists, hermits, individualists, and egalitarians. The thrust of the analysis is concerned with the social construction of human nature.

Here a profoundly important issue is raised about the relationship of sociocultural conditions to the constitution of character types and the relationship of character types represented by what Tocqueville treats as the habits of the heart and mind. The manners and customs of people are expressions of their habits of the heart and mind. The *human construction of social reality* has its counterpart in the *social construction of human nature*. The diachronic character of life with its sequence of generations has its complement in the synchronic character of patterned order in human societies accompanied by "a drive to achieve consonance in all of the layers of experience" (Douglas [1970] 1982c, vii).

Commentary and Conclusions

First, we must express some discomfort with the grid/group distinction. Linguistic communities are bounded, are known by some common name, and share common interests in some properties. Distinctions about rules are allocated by sex, age, and similar attributes among a large portion of the animal kingdom as well as in the species *Homo sapiens*. Whether an ununionized weaver could be a member of the same organization as a "self-made" manufacturer is, for us, an open question. How the dimensions of grid and group are to be related to a zero point in a Cartesian square ranging into positive and negative values is difficult for us to understand.

There are important issues beyond grid and group that are of critical importance to the cultural and social sciences and humanities. These include the way that people and place are put together in relation to patterns of thought; expres-

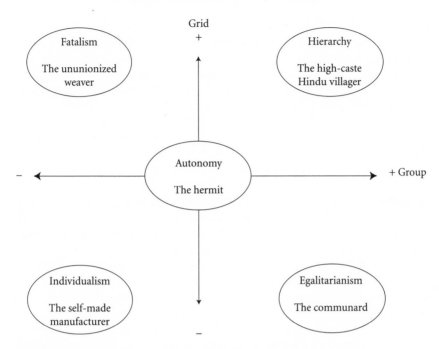

FIGURE 4.1   The five vignettes mapped onto the two dimensions of sociality

sions of sentiments, feelings, and aspirations; and systems of rule-ordered relationships. Peoples and places exist in networks of temporal and spatial relationships, gaining their fit with regard to variabilities that do not exist in neatly ordered parameters or cycles. These represent the doings of human beings who share a sufficiently similar genetic heritage that we as human beings have the potential to use our own resources to understand others. Applying the postulated conditions to the rational actor in perfect competitive markets is not the only way to conceptualize rationality. The calculations associated with reasoning are also associated with rational discourse. Criteria for standards of selection need not be confined to a concept of utility but may include criteria related to fairness, justice, liberty, logical coherence, truth-values, aesthetics, and so on.

Human beings everywhere confront basic puzzles, dilemmas, anomalies, and problems in constituting their relationships with one another. Individuals may seek their own good, but patterns of interaction with one another may realize misery instead. Such possibilities occur among contemporaries in relating to one another in a given time frame. They also occur in the intergenerational character of life as generations succeed one another.

For example, in examining the interactive effect of race to the institution of slavery, Tocqueville recognized that the differential status of masters and slaves generated quite different character structures. Both of these character structures were incompatible with a work ethic reflected in the sense of achievement gained by free labor. The institution of slavery was not compatible with the requirements of a free, self-governing society. The combination of slavery with race created a basic anomaly for Anglo-Americans that Tocqueville could not anticipate being resolved in the foreseeable future, because prejudices and character structures would have their intergenerational effects into the indefinite future.

Tocqueville also recognized that American political institutions were vulnerable to a tyranny of the majority. Majority-vote arrangements allowed for coalitions to be formed to slate candidates and for winning coalitions to control political agendas and override the checks and balances afforded by the constitutional separation of powers. Patterns of normal politics had the potential of overriding constitutional limitations. How to maintain the constitutional basis and the moral foundations of a self-governing society over successive generations was a crucial problem for the viability of American society.

The human construction of social reality received primary attention in the first volume of *Democracy in America*. There attention was given to how the manners and customs of the Anglo-Americans developed a system of order characteristic of a self-governing society on the North American continent and how such a system worked in achieving adaptive potentials under those conditions. The analysis in the second volume addresses the question of whether American society can effectively reproduce itself over succeeding generations into the indefinite future. Tocqueville's preoccupation, then, was with the social construction of human nature—the concern of Thompson, Ellis, and Wildavsky in *Cultural Theory*.

Tocqueville's analysis unfolds in four steps in which he addresses patterns of thought; patterns of sentiments, feelings, and aspirations; and patterns of social relationships. His conclusions were elaborated in book four of volume two. If people act on the basis of "natural" inclinations, American democracy is not viable over successive generations into the indefinite future. If, however, Americans act with reference to the continuing developments of the art and science of association, Tocqueville concluded that American society can remain viable into the indefinite future. Patterns of normal politics would need to be accompanied by reform agendas capable of successfully achieving necessary constitutional modifications and changes through time to assure successful adaptations to a changing world. Tocqueville was saying that it was necessary to give serious attention to "speaking truth to power" as Aaron Wildavsky (1979) would have expressed the problem.

What Aaron had to say in a lifetime of productive scholarship in addressing a theory of public budgeting as a manifestation of normal politics, public policy analysis and the problem of implementation, the patterns of culture, and the social construction of human nature has given him a place of honor and immortality in our own lives. We wrestled with Aaron as Jacob wrestled with his God; and we have become the more enlightened for having engaged in the struggles.

Part Three

Cultural Theories of Change

Chapter Five

Political Culture and Political Change

CHARLES LOCKHART

In a 1985 essay entitled "Change in Political Culture," Aaron Wildavsky suggested that in a world of nearly constant motion, political stability rather than political change is the remarkable phenomenon crying out for explanation (1985a, 95). Stability was rare; change was everywhere. Yet if political stability was the real puzzle, it was political change that drew Wildavsky to Mary Douglas's grid-group typology. Douglas's categories, he believed, could aid in making sense of the "cultural revolution" he saw taking place all around him, particularly the rise of egalitarianism.

Wildavsky's faith in the explanatory power of political culture was, to say the least, unusual among contemporary political scientists, most of whom regard the concept of political culture with skepticism, particularly when the phenomenon to be explained is political change.[1] Culture is frequently conceived as unchanging habits that are passed down from generation to generation without question. When social scientists consider culture at all, it is generally treated as the bulwark of stability and the antithesis of change. Laws, rulers, and institutions may change, but culture remains the same.

Among the most trenchant critiques of cultural explanation is Ronald Rogowski's study of citizen allegiance (1974, 3–17; see also Johnson 1982, 9; Steinmo 1994). Rogowski's argument against cultural explanation of social life rests on a critique of the socialization concept commonly associated with works of the "first wave" of postwar American political culture theory. This conception of "cumulative socialization" has been concisely detailed by Harry Eckstein (1988, 790–791). In this view, early learning—indeed all prior learning—acts as a "filter" through which later learning is passed. What is learned early is deeply rooted in the human psyche and thus resistant to change. Further, this filter aids in the construction of orientations that fit various pieces of learning into larger coherent patterns. In this view, then, culture amounts to established patterns of interpreting and attending to a complex, ambiguous world. Cultures carry inertia, which makes rapid reorientation unlikely (Eckstein 1988, 796; see also Elkins and Simeon 1979).

Articulating a theme echoed recently by others (e.g., March and Olsen 1989), Rogowski doubted that early learning is exceptionally important. He drew on German experience to support his view. What appeared to be high levels of support for the Nazi regime in the late 1930s was widely attributed to long-standing authoritarian cultural orientations among Germans. Yet, despite this cultural predisposition, by the early 1970s the Federal Republic had acquired a quarter century's experience as a successful democracy and appeared to enjoy high levels of popular support. Further, according to Rogowski, this democratic support revealed few intergenerational differences. He concluded, therefore, that cultural explanations of this change are inconsistent with the first wave's emphasis on the importance of early learning, and thus cultural explanations are ad hoc. Rogowski's analysis pitted political culture theories against rational choice theory, which portrays people as adept at adjusting their behavior in such a way as to realize their interests under shifting circumstances.[2]

If Rogowski's charges are accurate, theories of political culture likely hold little promise for the development of a political science interested in understanding change. But how satisfactory is Rogowski's alternative perspective, which tries to explain human choices by ignoring the deeper patterns of beliefs and values that inform these choices? How do people recognize their interests and preferences, particularly against a background of shifting natural and social environmental conditions, if not through culture (Inglehart 1988, 1229)? Rather than starkly pitting inherited beliefs against rationally calculated interests—or values against institutions—a cultural theory of political change must ask how institutions and values as well as interests and beliefs are reciprocally related.

Cultural Change as a Reaction to Surprise

In contrast to the early work on culture that Rogowski criticized, Douglas and Wildavsky's Cultural Theory emphasized lifelong learning. Socialization, Douglas in particular has emphasized, occurs not only in childhood but throughout life. The early cultural anthropologists who posited a tight relationship between child-rearing customs and the formation of national character (e.g., Mead 1953) created, as Douglas noted, "a gloomy view of human adaptability. According to a kind of delayed Calvinist predeterminism, the human personality is adaptive in infancy, but soon set into a hard mold." Such a theoretical stance, Douglas observed, was "helpless in the face of change" (1982a, 185). Grid-group theorists insist that institutions and social relations shape perceptions throughout life. If a bureaucratic functionary decides at the ripe age of forty to become a trader on the futures market, Douglas's framework leads us to predict that new institutional relationships will reshape that person's perceptions in certain predictable ways. By putting the social and the institutional back into the cultural, change can be anticipated and understood.

In *Cultural Theory*, Michael Thompson, Richard Ellis, and Aaron Wildavsky (1990) also emphasized that cultural commitments are integrally connected to experience within the world. Culture acts as a filter through which the world is experienced, and yet at the same time experience with the world shapes one's cultural biases. Thompson et al. argue that through this reciprocal causal flow, people sort themselves into cultures that are distinguished, in part, by rival views of the world. For instance, individualists expect the environment to be bountiful and resilient. Accordingly, "exploiting" the environment carries no pejorative connotation for them. Egalitarians, in contrast, perceive a delicately balanced environment that is likely to be disastrously disrupted by humans' ambitious development projects. Hierarchists believe in a combination of these environments. Theirs is a tolerant/perverse world that can accommodate humans' development projects up to certain limits beyond which further activity threatens disaster. Fatalists think that the environment responds randomly to human activities.

Thompson et al. drew on these culturally specific conceptions of the natural world to introduce the concept of surprise. This innovation enables us to envision a variety of ways in which culture may change (1990, 69–93). When the world no longer works in the manner that one's culture predicts, surprise occurs, followed by doubt and perhaps defection. Consider, for instance, an individualist who anticipates bounty and resilience but who begins to experience failure. Perhaps her Gulf of Maine fishing fleet, once highly productive, returns with progressively smaller catches that eventually produce insufficient income to cover overhead (as a consequence maybe of the collapse of the egalitarian's delicate environment). In this situation our individualist's initial reaction is apt to be surprise: The world is not working the way she expects, but she is likely to persevere for a time. As disappointing experiences occur repeatedly, however, our individualist is likely to begin doubting her initial beliefs. If distressing outcomes persist, she may well alter her beliefs about the way the world works. As she does so, she joins another culture. For instance, if she gradually adopts the view that modern fishing fleets have greater capacity for harvesting than fish have for reproducing, she may become a hierarchist and will likely advocate more extensive national and international regulation of ocean fishing, believing that the resulting expertise-driven policy will reduce extraction below critical boundary levels and allow fish populations to rebound.

Of course surprising experiences can happen to adherents of all cultures, not just individualists. Egalitarians may find themselves in a bountiful environment and consequently fail, at least initially, to prosper as others do, since they will only gradually adjust their perceptions about what the environment allows. Similarly, if fatalists find themselves in an environment in which resources are scarce, they may slowly decide that survival requires sharing limited material resources with their fellows. And hierarchists may find themselves in a random environment in which hierarchy's expertise is of little help in discerning boundaries demarcating perverse from tolerant regions. Their faith in expertise will erode, and they may succumb to a fatalism better suited to this random world (Thompson, Ellis, and Wildavsky 1990, 71–74).

This theory of surprise is not limited to the natural world. It applies equally well to the social world. During the Great Depression, for instance, when there seemed to be only a tenuous relationship between effort and achievement, faith in competitive individualism was undermined and support for alternative modes of organizing social life increased. Some people who had previously held individualistic cultural biases and had thus attributed poverty to a lack of individual initiative now came to recognize that the economic conditions associated with the depression—conditions beyond the control of individual workers—created too few jobs to employ many people who had long histories of self-reliance. Accordingly, these people supported President Franklin D. Roosevelt's efforts to improve economic conditions by increasing the activities of the national government. Similarly, in the film *Salam Bombay* an initially plucky boy is beaten down by the random nature of life on the streets. His original entrepreneurial optimism is gradually transformed into fatalistic resignation because the latter provides a more effective adaptation to the random, hostile environment he encounters (Ellis 1993a, 139).

Thompson et al. (1990, 75–78) showed that familiar examples can be produced for all possible shifts from one culture to another. For instance, the move from fatalist to individualist is the basis for "rags to riches" stories. Individualists become hierarchists through bureaucratization: A successful small business with a single entrepreneurial boss gradually becomes routinized with multiple bosses having distinct job descriptions. Hierarchists may become egalitarians by following the path of the schismatic. The loyalists becomes heretics, or, in a more secular setting, whistleblowers. If, as is likely, the whistleblower is "drummed out of the regiment" and fails to win a substantial settlement, he or she may end up a fatalist, ostracized from high-group support but lacking the entrepreneur's self-confidence. The familiarity of these examples suggests that cultural change is all around us; what is lacking has been a cultural theory that systematically orders such change.

Political Change as Adaptive Problem-Solving

Fundamental changes in cultural orientation *can* happen. Moreover, the concept of surprise seems a potentially fruitful way to understand such change when it does occur. Complete changes in cultural commitment, however, are rare. Indeed, if such dramatic changes in cultural orientation were not rare, one would start to question the value of culture in social explanation. Another possibility is change that occurs as a result of conscious "problem-solving" efforts on the part of adherents of a culture to adapt the institutions that realize their preferred values to shifting circumstances. This is similar to what Eckstein designated as "pattern-maintaining" change (1988, 793–794). In responding to changes in circumstances, adherents of a culture are more likely to adjust their institutions so as to better support their way of life than they are to transfer their allegiance to a rival culture.

During the rapid industrialization of the 1870s, for example, Otto von Bismarck faced increasing socialist agitation among urban workers. This situation raised two prominent issues for Bismarck. First, he was concerned with social order, and particularly with retaining the existing, predominantly hierarchical society. Second, he recognized that industrialization was destroying the economic and social security of many workers (Katzenstein 1987, 171), and he believed that it was his duty, as a leader of the social collective, to respond to the distress of other, less capable, more vulnerable social contributors. Accordingly, Bismarck created a two-pronged strategy of repressing socialist agitation and securing workers from some of the most distressing social hazards (unemployment and medical expenses due to sickness or injury and aging) associated with industrialization. In the process of securing the traditional order of his society, Bismarck, along with his political allies, created new institutions, specifically the social insurance programs of the modern welfare state. Thus dramatic innovations sprouted from the efforts of adherents of a culture to defend their way of life in changing circumstances.

Similarly, in the aftermath of the Meiji Restoration the leaders of thoroughly hierarchical Japan were faced with the dilemma of how to maintain core cultural values in the face of external challenge. The Japanese were well aware that the more technologically advanced European powers were dismembering and occupying China, and the Japanese had begun to have modest experiences with what they referred to as "unequal treaties" themselves. Japanese leaders had long relied on their island status in defending their society with what were, by the mid-nineteenth century, antiquated armaments. They had also maintained institutional integrity by carefully controlling the flow of people and ideas across their frontier, focusing themselves inwardly on their quasi-feudal style of life with little regard for the outside world. This orientation prevented the pollution of the Japanese way of life by unwanted foreign practices. The goal of cultural purity was widely supported, and this orientation attracted advocates even after Japan's "opening" by Western powers.

But the Restoration leaders argued that this long-standing isolationist orientation now endangered Japan by leaving it vulnerable to technologically advanced Western imperialists. In their view, national defense could no longer be achieved by ignoring strange foreign developments. Rather, it now required the innovative step of turning outward and selectively emulating foreign practices. Only through this change in policy, they argued, could Japan acquire military capacities similar to those of the Western societies and save itself from suffering the same fate as China. Though this approach would introduce foreign ideas to Japan, the Japanese would have substantial choice as to which ideas to accept and how to apply them. In contrast, if Japan were conquered by Western imperialists, foreign ideas would be imposed without regard for Japanese preferences. The Restoration elites carried the day and launched Japan on a remarkably ambitious project of societal mobilization and economic development. This effort was closely directed by central state bureaucrats and aimed at acquiring modern technological, industrial, and military capabilities. Here too, then, in the face of threatening new circumstances, the defense of cultural values fostered the creation of new institutions.

In a highly pluralistic society such as the contemporary United States, searches for institutional innovation that maintain central cultural values in altered social circumstances become both more interesting and complex. Under pluralistic conditions people are apt to have socialization agents that represent different cultures. These people may retain sympathies for rival cultures, particularly with respect to different domains of social life (Hochschild 1981; Walzer 1983), thus leading to the development of hybrid cultural biases. Consider, for instance, the situation of a successful attorney who is also a wife and mother. Following a series of academic and professional mentors, she generally applies an individualistic cultural bias toward workplace issues. But, in accordance with themes introduced to her by contemporary feminists, she practices egalitarianism in her home: roughly equal spousal sharing of household responsibilities and participation of the children in family decisions. Our attorney has, then, a hybrid cultural bias that joins individualism and egalitarianism.

Historical contingencies may alter the cross-pressures weighing on such a hybrid bias and contribute to political change in the process. The emergence of the family leave issue, for example, sharpens tensions between the home and the workplace and may prompt our attorney to broaden the application of her egalitarian cultural bias to an aspect of the workplace by endorsing new programs to help working parents at the expense of the firm's economic efficiency. In so doing she does not replace her culture of individualism with a new culture of egalitarianism; rather she shifts marginally the way she applies her two preexisting cultural biases across the domains of social life, lending support to different social policies and institutions in the process.

The contingent issues that prompt such cultural shifts are not easily predicted, of course, but the intrapersonal mechanism that triggers the revised application of particular cultures can be specified. This trigger is appropriately viewed as a shift in relevant analogies that has the effect of relocating a boundary between social categories. Heretofore, for example, our attorney has associated workplace matters with an individualistic efficiency model, and affairs relating to the home with an egalitarian caring model. So long as coworkers are viewed as workers, the efficiency model applies to their activities. But the family leave issue reveals some coworkers as parents and suggests the relevance of applying the caring model. In such a situation, a number of people may begin applying egalitarianism to a matter on which their practice has previously been individualistic. Cumulatively, these marginal shifts in the application of hybrid cultural biases may alter the relative influence of rival cultures and thus prompt institutional change.

Political Change Through Shifting Coalitions: The Case of Early America

In addition to producing people with hybrid cultural biases, conditions of social pluralism frequently foster coalitions between the adherents of different cultures. Moreover, the issues raised by historical contingencies may prompt changes in the character of these coalitions and thus in the political institutions that they build and maintain. The political history of the United States, for instance, may be characterized in terms of oscillation between various multicultural coalitions. Louis Hartz (1955) was correct about the dominant culture of the United States, but he mistook predominance for consensus. Individualists, though predominant, are not hegemonic (Ellis 1993a). Rather, American individualists provide the enduring element within governing coalitions that, at least in the nineteenth century, oscillated in such a way as sometimes to include egalitarians and at other times hierarchists. Thus an additional way in which Cultural Theory can contribute to the explanation of political change is by identifying the attractors and repellents that underlie shifting coalitions among cultures (Thompson, Ellis, and Wildavsky 1990, 86–96). Each culture shares values with its rivals. Individualism and egalitarianism, for example, both value personal autonomy against hierarchical authority; individualism and hierarchy both support social stratification, albeit for different reasons; and egalitarianism and hierarchy each exhibit direct concern for the health of the social collectivity. These shared values provide a basis for coalitions, but each of these cultures also remains at odds with its rivals over crucial beliefs and values. Coalitions thus tend to be temporary.

In the colonial United States, to pursue the American example, widespread social stratification was supported with both hierarchical and individualistic justifications (Bailyn 1967, 302–303). But by the mid-1760s increasing English regulation of the American colonies (e.g., the Stamp Act) began to foster opposition to some forms of stratification from individualists such as Samuel Langdon as well as egalitarians such as Thomas Paine. Colonial Americans had grown accustomed to the benign neglect with which Britain had generally viewed the colonies before it had incurred the expenses of the French and Indian War, and had thus developed expectations that they were to govern their own social lives. The imposition of new British regulations triggered individualists to question these British actions and eventually to join egalitarians in condemning British institutions as high-handed and thoroughly corrupt. The result was an antiauthority coalition of individualist and egalitarian cultures reacting against distant, indifferent hierarchical authorities. In addition to leading an ill-managed but successful revolution, this antiauthority coalition formed new governing institutions in several of the resulting states that emphasized local control through an active citizenry operating legislatures with limited powers.

Individualists, however, also value the acquisition and development of material resources and thus support sufficient state power to secure these objectives. In these concerns individualists share less with egalitarians than with hierarchists. In the decade following the Revolution a series of events (most especially, Shays's rebellion) alarmed many, though hardly all, individualists. Fears of "desperate debtors" (as Alexander Hamilton referred to Shays in Federalist No. 6) using egalitarian state legislatures to attack property provided the trigger for a coalition between individualism and hierarchy. The preceding individualistic-egalitarian (I-E) coalition had so undermined social stratification (Wood 1993) that propertied interests felt endangered, and increasing numbers of individualists thought that government should serve less to represent ordinary people than to filter out their crasser influences (Ellis 1993a, 63–67). ("I-E" denotes a coalition between individualists and egalitarians in which individualists are the dominant partners. Reversing the letters [E-I] would denote a coalition in which egalitarians dominated over their individualistic partners.) The constitutional convention of 1787 illustrates the movement of these individualists back toward a coalition with hierarchists such as Alexander Hamilton and Gouverneur Morris (Ellis and Wildavsky 1989, 24–31). This Federalist coalition built a substantially more centralized, powerful, and active national government than had existed under the Articles of Confederation.

If a desire for stable rules to support property led many individualists to ally with hierarchists in the 1780s, the 1790s saw many of those same individualists swing away from the individualist-hierarchical (I-H) Federalist coalition that had secured the Constitution. Individualists became alienated by the Federalist party's practices of economic favoritism and exclusion—franchises, concessions, charters—and its glorification of centralized authority and gravitated once again toward an alliance with egalitarians. This shift reached a crucial juncture in the election of 1800 that brought the Republican victory of Thomas Jefferson and the resurgence of an I-E coalition. The trigger in this instance lies in the very success of the preceding I-H coalition's efforts to stratify society through various forms of favoritism. The Jeffersonian coalition was not as ambitious in destroying the Federalist state as many of its supporters had hoped, and Jeffersonian antiauthority principles were actually relaxed for a time after 1812, but a countervailing (I-H) coalition was not able to regain control. The cultural coalition of the Jeffersonian period was reasserted with a vengeance by Andrew Jackson's presidency (1829–1837), which marked a high point in terms of antistatist collaboration between individualists and egalitarians (Ellis and Wildavsky 1989, 37–112).

James Madison, as Ellis and Wildavsky (1989, 221–222) have shown, was an individualist whom we can follow as a bellwether of the coalition dynamics of the period. Madison was counted among the revolutionary forces of the 1770s. But he quickly realized the limitations of the Articles of Confederation and became—along with Hamilton—a leading figure in the Federalist movement. Thereafter, he shifted into the Republican ranks, and his presidency—at least until the shattering experiences of the War of 1812—tried to keep the Jeffersonian cultural coalition together. Madison's strategic shifts provide a classic instance of the pattern-maintaining, adaptive change analyzed in the previous section. As an individualist

Madison was committed to a range of individual rights and liberties: security of personal property, right to self-government, equality before the law, religious freedom, and so on. At different historical junctures different cultures threatened one or more of these liberties. In order to preserve various individual rights against these shifting threats, Madison formed coalitions with different cultures. So when the British Empire increased the regulation of its North American colonies, Madison joined with egalitarians in fighting this attack on self-government. But when these same egalitarians began to threaten property rights, Madison joined with Hamilton and other hierarchists seeking to create new state institutions that would more effectively secure personal property. And when Hamilton and his allies persisted in public policy procedures that favored some people over others, Madison returned again to a coalition with egalitarians that supported his individualistic conception of human equality.

Instances of shifting coalitions stem from events that are difficult to predict, but as in the case of hybrid cultural biases, we can specify a trigger mechanism. Under threat from hierarchical authority, individualists will seek out egalitarian allies who can help safeguard their commitment to smaller, less intrusive government. All such coalitions and the institutions they create are vulnerable to dissolution, since there remain many issues on which egalitarians and individualists do not agree, such as how much inequality in income and power is legitimate. As the hierarchical threat recedes, the inherent differences between egalitarian and individualists will become manifest and the coalition will start to pull apart. With their eyes now on the leveling tendencies of the egalitarian, individualists will begin to cast around for hierarchical coalition partners willing to build governing institutions that can provide order and security for property. There is no final equilibrium point; change is inherent in the different competencies and biases of different cultures.

Explaining Change in Germany

Returning now to the case of the Federal Republic of Germany, which Rogowski (1974) used so effectively to discredit cultural explanation, provides further opportunity for applying the concepts of hybrid cultural biases and shifting cultural coalitions to the explanation of political change. The remarkably rapid transformation in Germany from a predominantly hierarchical to a preeminently individualistic society (Dahrendorf 1967; Grendstad 1990) poses a fundamental challenge to cultural explanations.

To understand cultural change in Germany requires that we recognize that there was no single national culture or national character in Germany. German society, like all other large-scale societies, was "multicultural." Although hierarchy was clearly predominant, the cultures of egalitarianism and individualism were reasonably well developed by the end of the imperial period. Egalitarianism, for instance, provided the basis for an opposition workers' socialist movement, and individualism appeared, most noticeably, among entrepreneurs who had long been the constrained lesser partners in the ruling H-I "blood and iron" coalition. These low-grid cultures were somewhat discredited by their association with the social turbulence and economic difficulties of the Weimar period. The strongly hierarchical Nazis took advantage of the discrediting of alternative cultures and solidified their mass support by reestablishing social stability and economic prosperity (central virtues for hierarchists and individualists, respectively). By leading Germany to the brink of destruction in World War II, the Nazis discredited hierarchical appeals. Moreover, the war left the German regions that initially formed the Federal Republic dominated by Western societies that worked selectively with German elites to build individualistic institutions.

Thus historical contingencies—the disrepute that the policies of the Nazi hierarchy had produced and the unusual openness to external influence created by Germany's wartime destruction—interacted with the presence of a significant indigenous individualistic culture to facilitate a reversal in the relative influence of the partners in the long-standing German governing coalition of hierarchy and individualism. German individualists were encouraged and emboldened by their Western allies and set about constructing individualistic institutions: a competitive, representative political system and a form of market capitalism. Meanwhile, German hierarchists frequently found that their preferred values and institutions were discouraged by the West. During the formal occupation, a coalition of Western and German individualists dominated western Germany, reshaping its institutions in accordance with their values. As the Federal Republic acquired autonomy, it became increasingly clear that indigenous German individualists had replaced hierarchists as the preeminent partners in the governing coalition.[3]

Rogowski argues that a paucity of generational differences in citizen support for this new coalition and its institutions precludes a cultural explanation of this transformation (1974, 9). Others have since provided extensive evidence of intergenerational change. Kendall L. Baker, Russell J. Dalton, and Kai Hildebrandt have employed one of the measures that Gabriel Almond and Sidney Verba (1963) developed as an index of democratic allegiance—participation in political discussion—to reveal these intergenerational differences (Baker, Dalton, and Hildebrandt 1981, chap. 2, esp. 45–52; see also Pulzer 1989). They divided contemporary citizens of the Federal Republic into five generations (1981, 13) and then showed that although participation in political discussion increases for all generations between 1953 and 1972, there are also sharp and growing intergenerational differences. Engaging in political discussion is much more common among later generations (1981, 47), and these differences stand up under analysis involving the sorts of controls (i.e., for education, class, sex, and so on—the usual suspects) that Rogowski required (1981, 50). Clearly the changing character of political institutions shaped citizens in new ways. But institutional change occurred because newly dominant individualistic elites required, and over time constructed, different institutions in order to realize their distinctive values.

Even given the limitations of the data available in the mid-1970s, Rogowski overlooked matters such as the capacity of total defeat in total war—entailing high levels of homelessness, joblessness, death and disability among family and friends, and so on—to shake an adult's confidence in existing beliefs. If following a particular pattern of social relations leads people to such hideous experiences, some—especially those with hybrid cultural biases—may apply a different culture, at least in certain domains of social life. Particularly during the republic's early decades, then, it is reasonable to interpret the growing support for individualistic institutions (Conradt 1978, 49; 1980; Dalton 1989, 100–104) as the combined result of cultural shifts among older people, particularly those with hybrid cultural biases, and increasing proportions of individualistic and egalitarian cultural biases among younger people socialized under the markedly different institutional circumstances of the Federal Republic (Rohrschneider 1994).

Cultural Theory thus offers a means for interpreting German society's responses to shifting events from the late 1930s to the early 1970s that does not force culturalists into strained, unconvincing improvisation. First, with respect to intercultural coalition dynamics, Cultural Theory focuses on an externally prompted and encouraged transposition of the two cultures forming Germany's long-standing dominant coalition. In the immediate postwar period, historical contingencies greatly facilitated the efforts of individualists in western Germany and hindered their hierarchical counterparts. Rather than relying on a process about which Rogowski is understandably skeptical (an entire society of hierarchists rapidly reorienting and adopting individualism), the initial transformation of the Federal Republic was accomplished by emboldened indigenous individualists replacing hierarchists in numerous positions throughout the governing coalition. Thus what had once been an H-I coalition became an I-H coalition. Over time the new institutions that this coalition constructed socialized increasing proportions of the Federal Republic's population to accept individualism (Rohrschneider 1994).

Second, with respect to people with hybrid cultural biases, the historical contingencies of the early postwar period encouraged H-I and I-H hybrids in the western regions of Germany to apply their individualistic biases across more political and economic domains of life. These historical contingencies provided considerable scope for realizing individualistic ambitions and more limited avenues for achieving hierarchical aspirations. More significant, from the standpoint of using culture to explain political change, over time these contingencies triggered shifts in relevant analogies. Hierarchy became increasingly associated with the German defeat and the stagnant, punitive East. Individualism, in contrast, became progressively associated with growing prosperity and the ascendant, constructively interventionist West (e.g., the Marshall Plan). Under these circumstances there was a growing tendency among West Germans with hybrid (particularly I-H or H-I) cultural biases to apply their individualistic biases across more of the public domain.

Explaining the Growth of Government

I conclude by revisiting U.S. political history, a history that is sometimes thought to defy Wagner's law: The influential late-nineteenth-century German economist Adolf Wagner argued, as many others have since, that among societies experiencing economic development, rates of governmental growth inevitably exceed rates of economic development (Larkey, Stolp, and Winer 1981). Wagner attributed these high rates of growth in government to a broad range of factors, including: frictions generated by increasingly dense urban living; escalating legal complexities produced by the specialization of labor; increasing importance of public goods such as education that are difficult for individual entrepreneurs to provide; and continuing efforts to counter social hazards associated with the business cycle such as unemployment. In "The Logic of Public Sector Growth," Wildavsky (1985b) rejected the idea that these economic and technological factors necessitated public sector growth. For example, Wildavsky pointed out that increasingly dense urban living also facilitated greater economies of scale in the provision of a variety of public services. Wagner and his followers, Wildavsky argued, were imputing an "unspecified, ever-present but powerful logic of industrialization that ineluctably tends but in a single direction" (1985b, 234). Political development, Wildavsky countered, can go in many directions depending on one's cultural bias. Growth in government was not an inevitable outgrowth of economic growth but rather the result of widespread hierarchical and, less important, egalitarian cultural preferences among political elites who wanted the larger, more active governments that economic growth made possible.

Wildavsky pointed to the greater influence of individualistic preferences in the United States to explain the tendency of U.S. public sector growth to lag behind that of the most advanced European societies throughout this century. If the United States were dominated solely by individualists, as Hartz suggested (1955), then we might expect government to grow at a pace slower than that of the economy as individualistic elites clung to their preferences for modest, less active governments. But American political history defies Hartz's theory as well, since it includes periods of rapid government growth as well as retrenchment.

U.S. state development exhibits three distinct historical patterns. The first can be likened to a pendulum swinging back and forth between periods of government retrenchment and development. As discussed earlier, these swings are exemplified by the weak central government orientation predominant in the immediate post-Revolutionary period, the Federalist effort during the 1790s to construct a larger, more active government based on the new constitution, and the zeal that the Jacksonians brought to reducing the size of government in the 1930s. Government size and activity levels grew again in response to the Civil War. But the balance of the nineteenth century exhibits a second pattern in which strong individualistic influence kept government development at modest levels even while economic development was proceeding at a rapid pace. A third pattern begins to develop in the twentieth century. Here the more hierarchical Progressives increased the capacities and—less dramatically—the activities of the national government. Subsequently a broad coalition took advantage of the Great Depression and World War II to build a national government more closely resembling those of other advanced societies.

Overall, then, the U.S. national government has undergone periods of obvious growth (e.g., the 1790s and the bulk of the twentieth century), a lengthy period of modest growth (e.g., the post–Civil War nineteenth century), and periods of retrenchment (e.g., the 1780s and 1830s). Lest we think that retrenchment is a phenomenon of the distant past, we should keep in mind that in the mid-1990s the individualist-dominated Republican House of Representatives has been busily at work producing legislative initiatives that would dramatically trim the size and scope of the federal government.

In contrast to Wagner and Hartz, rational choice theorists are not committed to a single characterization of change in government size (Green and Shapiro 1994). According to rational choice theorists, if people whose self-interest requires government growth (e.g., government contractors, social program recipients) are collectively more influential than those whose self-interest is served by government retrenchment (e.g., private entrepreneurs, taxpayers' associations), then government will grow. If the reverse is true, then public budgets and activities will shrink (see also Peltzman 1980). Hence rational choice theory is able to accommodate a political history in which periods of state-bashing and state-building alternate. But rational choice is a theory of preference implementation rather than preference formation, and thus it does not help us to understand how people come to see state activities as being for or against their interests, nor why people sharing preferences for a particular direction of change in the size of government might be more influential at one juncture and less at another.

Cultural Theory, in contrast, is a theory of preference formation, and it draws on a broader range of life-guiding principles than the hedonistic, egoistic conception of interest that is employed in most examples of rational choice theory. Accordingly, Cultural Theory provides a basis for explaining why particular people want to increase or decrease the size of government. Moreover, its conception of societies as composed of multiple cultures alerts us to the possibility of shifting cultural coalitions. The changing character of these coalitions helps to explain, for example, why American state groups grow during some periods and experience retrenchment in others. Cultural Theory is thus better able to explain the shifting course of American political development than Wagner, Hartz, or rational choice theory.

Notes

I want to thank Richard Ellis for his help on this chapter.

1. This topic hardly monopolizes the reservations of contemporary political scientists with respect to the explanatory power of the culture concept. Some focus on what they see

as the conceptual vagueness of political culture theories (Dittmer 1977; see also Shweder 1991). Others (Lijphart 1984; LaPalombara 1987) emphasize peculiarities of the first wave of postwar American cultural analysis (Almond 1956; Almond and Coleman 1960; Almond and Verba 1963; Pye and Verba 1965; Almond and Powell 1966). Almond's studies in particular are criticized for a conservative, system-maintenance bias and for making the United States an implicit model of political development. Still others (Lowi 1984; Berliner 1988) view culture as insubstantial and residual. Scholars holding this view are thus often skeptical of causal linkages between culture and its alleged consequences (Orloff and Skocpol 1984) and origins (Hall 1986, 34). From this perspective institutions are more basic to political life than culture (March and Olsen 1989; Coleman 1990). For a useful review of various reservations about cultural explanation, see Lane 1992.

2. Richard Shweder (1991, 269–312) also articulates a view skeptical of Eckstein's conception of socialization. However, Shweder evinces equal skepticism of Rogowski's rational choice perspective, indeed of all except highly context-specific orientations (1991, 103–108).

3. As Stephen Padgett (1989, 125) has shown, egalitarians have become more influential since the late 1960s, and varying cultural coalitions dominate predictable policy areas: Corporatist issues involve the Christian Democratic Union (CDU) and the Social Democratic Party (SPD) in a loose H-E coalition, market issues involve the CDU and the Free Democratic Party (FDP) in a loose I-H coalition, and individual rights issues involve the SPD and FDP in a loose E-I coalition.

Chapter Six

A Proposed Fragmentation of the Theory of Cultural Change

ARTHUR L. STINCHCOMBE

In 1954 I was in a training school in an army hospital in San Antonio. I went out on the town one Saturday night with a black army friend. We went into a local YMCA to ask directions, and my friend went off to use the toilet. The night clerk at the Y advised me that down here in the South black and white people did not go out together the way they did, perhaps, where I came from. As far as I could tell, this was offered with an air of sincere advice, to help me stay out of trouble. I thanked him with as good grace as I could manage and went on about my business with my friend. I think it is clear that no employee of the Y would give such advice anywhere in the country today, and that if I met it now I would not think of thanking someone for trying to help me. We have moved a long way, especially in the South, since 1954.

Surveys conducted since the 1950s document the substantial cultural change that has occurred during this period. Some National Opinion Research Center (NORC) colleagues and I (Stinchcombe et al. 1974) sought causes for changes in values about crime and punishment in objective social conditions—in crime rates, racial segregation, education, urbanization, and suburbanization. None of these worked very well to explain punitive values; they worked a bit better on gun control.

Social changes would not explain changes in crime values if the values were consensual universals rather than clashes of interest. But we do not know how to theorize about relatively rapid changes in consensual universals. We think that consensus has to stay where it is, having no clashing interests to drive it anywhere;

when we find a consensus that has nothing to drive it and yet it goes somewhere, we are mystified.

Other measures of culture were strongly related to evaluations of crime. The strongest of these was that hunters were much more opposed to gun control than nonhunters—hunters were and are disproportionately rural, western or southern, and Protestant, all of which are also associated with attitudes on gun control. But clearly, being a hunter is participating in a hunting culture rather than a measure of one's social position. Similarly, general punitiveness was related to general moral and cultural conservatism. We believe what we do about capital punishment or gun control because we are embedded in subcultures. Gerhard Lenski (1961) likewise showed that different religious cultures in the United States were as powerful as social class in explaining values. The holding of one cultural value explains the holding of others.

But differences over a decade or two are about as big as the biggest cross-sectional differences, except for hunting culture's relation to gun control. From 1965 to 1978 the percentage wanting the courts to be harsher with criminals increased about 30 percent. Approval of capital punishment *decreased* by 20 percent from 1936 to the 1960s, and then from the 1960s to the 1970s *increased* again by about 20 percent.

Religion has to do with values, so we are not surprised to find a 20 percent difference among religions in answers to survey questions on fundamental values. But to have the whole culture move as far as the distance from Jewish to Protestant or Unitarian to Catholic over a decade or two surprises us. Large shifts in central American values, unexplained by social structural shifts, simply escape us.

Values measured by questions on virginity, abortion, civil liberty, equal rights for women, civil rights for oppressed races, socialized medicine for the old, have driven major institutional changes in legal and administrative rights and in cohabitation arrangements over the last half century. Some changes went in the liberal direction, some conservative. Shifts in culture explain changes in politics and family life. But we have few explanations of the cultural changes.

In *The Changing American Voter*, Norman Nie, Sidney Verba, and John R. Petrocik (1979) showed that people's choice of parties to represent their interests in politics also shifted radically over a couple of decades. People were much less likely to think that one of the political parties continuously represents their interests in the late 1970s than in the 1950s (43–73, 83). Philip Converse (1964, 1969, 1976) argued that what we considered normal increasing partisan loyalty with age in the 1950s no longer applied in the 1970s—nowadays many people retain "independent" partisan identification on into middle age. The partisan alignments of political subcultures in the United States have also changed drastically over the course of two or three decades, so that V. O. Key and Alexander Heard's *Southern Politics* (1949), for example, no longer describes Southern allegiances. We have thus witnessed changes in attachment to partisan politics over a few years that are of the same order of magnitude as the differences between social groups, and the relations among subcultures themselves in partisan attachments have shifts that are of the same order of magnitude as changes in the whole electorate (Nie, Verba, and Petrocik 1979, 110–155).

The principal means we have of understanding this theoretical vacuum is not a theory but a calculation device: cohort analysis. Much cultural change consists of young people learning something different in their socialization from what their elders believe. There is a variable relation between the culture of the young and the culture of the old. Recent general "cultural" liberalization has disproportionately characterized the young, moral conservatism the old (but for more recent data showing a decline in cohort effects, see DiMaggio, Evans, and Bryson 1995). Independent partisan identification is found disproportionately among the young. Once young cohorts had learned to be culturally liberal or to be independent voters, they tended to stay that way as they aged. Cohort calculations do indeed clarify matters, if correctly done (Converse [1976] has shown that they often are not). But these cohort calculations do not constitute a theory about why young voters in the 1950s learned the partisan attachments that their parents would have wanted to teach them, but young voters in the 1960s did not, and instead learned to be independent.

Nie, Verba, and Petrocik's (1979, 174–209) study of changing electoral behavior did more than to perform calculations. They argued (in part) that people learned their political values from elections, from the issue differences between candidates, and from the issues the candidates agree on. As parties came to be more dominated by ideological activists, with the candidacies of Barry Goldwater, George McGovern, and Ronald Reagan, elections no longer induced the political traditionalism of family partisan attachment. Parents in the 1950s could teach their children their own partisan identifications because Dwight Eisenhower was not teaching much about politics. By waging an ideological contest, McGovern and Goldwater taught the new electorate to analyze politics as issues. Historical events have a teaching impact on the public as a whole, and especially on those with less to unlearn, as Karl Mannheim ([1928] 1952) taught us.

Paul Lazarsfeld and Wagner Thielens (1958, 131–191; see also Feldman and Newcomb 1969, vol. 2, Table 2D, 19–14, for politics, and Table 2E, 25–32, for religion) have suggested that the general liberal drift (on social issues if not on economic issues) may be a result of the schools' no longer being in the control of the average elder. Instead they have come under the control of cosmopolitans, particularly the "secular humanist" cosmopolitans on liberal arts college faculties (Ladd and Lipset [1975, 9–167] show the cultural liberalism of social science professors). The young learn something different from their elders because school boards no longer fire liberal teachers, nor do distinguished colleges or universities fire liberal professors (see also Stinchcombe 1982). If schools select people with distinctive values as well as distinctive knowledge (against profit, for civil liberty, thinking of poetry and spreadsheets as merely different forms of knowledge, believing in natural selection), then they will tend to teach the young that distinctiveness. This will produce differences in values and behavior between the young who go to college (and to a smaller degree those who go to elementary and secondary schools) and the old.

These mechanisms, however, give no general explanation of why they work one way at one time, another way at another. Why should party militants not have presented Goldwaters and McGoverns rather than Eisenhowers in the 1950s? Why should liberal arts colleges in the early nineteenth century in the United States have had fraternities that were morally and culturally more liberal than their faculties (Rudolph 1956, 101–117, 129), whereas today fraternities are more conservative? Urbanization and industrialization move slowly, whereas attitudes and voting patterns change by large magnitudes in short time spans. Social-structural explanations therefore work badly in explaining this sort of rapid change in basic values and basic institutional commitments.

We must instead start to look at shifts in the relationship between the values of the institutions of the young (schools and colleges, Boy Scouts, singles' bars, rock or rap concerts, Planned Parenthood or college health services, etc.) versus the average opinion of middle-aged people. This relationship is likely to account for cohort effects. And we need to know a lot more about how current events such as elections fit differently into the lives of people who are just learning about politics than into the lives of those who have learned all they want to know about it.

But culture is not only the values we hold. It is also the words, images, and myths we learn to think with. The more flexible a language or a body of myths is, the more different sorts of activities can be praised or blamed with it. Thus structures for *calling on values* by using commonly understood value symbols and their associations can sometimes be applied quickly to new areas, creating substantial changes in values in an area *precisely because* they have a stable meaning. The meaning of, say, the presidency can change rapidly because we have many different symbols to praise and blame presidents with. It is easy to change symbols, but difficult to change the meaning of a symbol.

Six Ways to Be Great

Luc Boltanski and Laurent Thévenot (1991) have written a wonderful study of six systems of cultural recognition of greatness that they call "worlds." They argued that continuing cultural structures are always present and studied arguments that devotees of these structures use against the others.

Prayer or poetry (and hence saints and poets) get their greatness from *inspiration* (they are in the "world of inspiration"). Grand gestures showing inspiration or genius create the kind of greatness recognized in such a world. *Productivity* worlds, in contrast, require efficient routines to make valuable objects; quantitative people use spreadsheets to determine what objects should be routinely and efficiently made with what resources. People urging the inspiration road to greatness attack the routine, the praise of abstract numbers and expertise, the materialism of objects as goals, of the industrial world whose greatness is productivity; engineers are suspicious of prayer and poetry as ways to get things done (Boltanski and Thévenot 1991, 302–303, 330).

"Rather than being celebrated because they occupy positions of prestige, [*celebrities*] occupy positions of prestige because they are celebrated" (Mills 1956, 74). They think that what makes political leaders valuable is their news value, their style. In contrast, members of the core of a political party (the "*civic world*" of power) think that steady loyal service to group goals and responsible use of power make politicians into statesmen. But both the civic and the celebrity cultural structures stay in place, so that there are people who would prefer Calvin Coolidge the Silent to Ronald Reagan, whose public image depended on the sound bite; Coolidge and Reagan appealed to different cultural worlds on behalf of the same political party. Such enduring cultural substructures are a device of stability. As politics becomes entertainment and inside dopester news, there is a ready-made celebrity cultural system to praise people for doing it, and another civic cultural system to criticize them for carrying it too far because people become great by serving collective values.

But such stable cultural substructures can be a sextuple of cultural powers, in waiting for a series of potential cultural revolutions. Reagan was trained in the movie industry to be a sort of president for which an apprenticeship to Coolidge would not have prepared him. We have a cultural substructure defending "public relations" as central to politics and business and religion, thus extending the celebrity world to these as well. Presidents' greatness can then be in either the celebrity or the civil world.

Similarly, the older "rating and dating game," in which teenagers of the opposite sex were rated by popularity (celebrity on a local scene), coexisted with a system that praised adult mothers and fathers for giving their children "a good start in life," a *decent* world. Contraception and abortion then made it possible to extend rating and dating well into adulthood, because it is children that bring out the culture of responsibility to descendants. Couples living together, without children in prospect, have more affairs than couples married with children, providing them with a continuing indicator of popularity in a rating game (though "dating" is no longer descriptive). Thus a cultural shift to more premarital sex can make use of ready-made popularity systems, discovering greatness through promiscuity in the culture of *Cosmopolitan* or *Playboy,* substituting for more chaste indicators to praise popularity. Married people are still praised for paying the mortgage and saving for college tuition.

Solid social structures often make social change easier. Parliaments make changing laws easier. Market makers produce liquidity in the stock market so that both prices and ownership of business can change quickly. Computer cash registers reporting by wire to *Billboard* allow the list of the top 100 albums to be more volatile than it was when less accurate survey results were used (Anand and Peterson 1995). Social change often depends on the solidity of social routines.

Solid cultural structures of productivity likewise enable spreadsheet descriptions of manufacturing operations, facilitating change by dropping failed models; those of celebrity enable "the greatest democracy in the world" to be reduced to sound bites; those of inspiration enable the inspired poetry of the King James version of the Bible to become the cultural backbone of a fundamentalist home-schooling movement in the world of descent (Stevens 1996). The availability of alternative ways to praise famous men enables any particular social structure to change its culture easily and quickly; changed praise will still be understood because it uses symbols that have been used before. With solid structures of cultural meaning, *Cosmopolitan* can grow while *Good Housekeeping* declines, Newt Gingrich can become Abraham Lincoln's political heir, and wealth rather than wisdom or religious inspiration can qualify one for the boards of universities.

Edward O. Lauman et al. (1994) call a population with an average of about five sex partners in a lifetime, "a most monogamous people"; Queen Victoria would not be amused.[1] But the definition of "monogamous" may evolve in Queen Victoria's direction if the HIV virus evolves so as to be as transmissible as gonorrhea. Such irregular cycles with different and erratic causes may not look like "cultural change" in the epochal sense. But the culture that applies to early adulthood is now a mix of adolescent popularity systems and adult sexuality, without much change in either families or high schools. Both cultural structures, celebrity and descent, remain stable, while the boundary between them moves every few years. This can constitute rapid cultural change, or stability except for details, depending on whether one is Queen Victoria or a modern twenty-year-old.

Culture, Nature, and Change

My father, a construction craftsman, used to talk about "the innate perversity of inanimate objects." When we think of "nature," we usually mean things that go their own way without responsiveness to our will, that are innately perverse. Material artifacts are shaped by culture; they are useful to the archaeologist precisely because after being shaped they went their own way and preserved the record of cultural shaping by depositing it in "nature."

I present these commonplaces to introduce the argument that the rapidity of "cultural change" is partly a linguistic illusion caused by calling things that do not change "nature," or "natural," or "the environment." Thus the cultural product in which I live was cultured into approximately its current form (named 1710 Asbury) about ninety years ago. Francis Asbury and John Wesley (Wesley is the next street west), both Methodist bishops, were bigger figures in Evanston, Illinois—the home of the United Methodist Church—at that time than now. My "environment," then, has more Methodist bishops in it than modern culture does. But of course in 1905 there was no actual Wesley in Methodist Evanston, but only a cultural object worthy of naming streets after. Knowledge of Methodism is built into the symbolic archaeology of Evanston, not into its current culture. Archaeology (even in its Lévi-Strauss [1955] 1965 or its Foucault [1969] 1972 form) would not exist if many things that "go their own way" were not ultimately cultural. But I would not be called a cultural consumer of Methodist bishops. As social theorists we often make the opposite assumption; Talcott Parsons (e.g., 1959) often wrote as if much of American culture were due to Wesley, partly because his hero, Max Weber, visited the United States when it was.

When we theorize about culture, we talk as if it were basically a part of nature, "exterior and constraining" (Durkheim [1895] 1966, 1–13). But when we *study* culture empirically, we tend to use *Billboard* as a source (Anand and Peterson 1995). The argument that culture changes rapidly, then, is partly an illusion. It applies to the parts of culture we study (public opinion, trends in court decisions, the content of popular songs, fashions, or social movement ideologies), but not to the parts we theorize about ("exterior and constraining," or "basic American values"). Our empirical work then shows culture rapidly changing, because that is what we think of as interesting factually, not "natural." Our theories are about the unchanging residual that makes it part of the "nature" of American society. Empirical studies lose sight of street names preserving a cultural deposit of a split in the Anglican Church. The theoretical side misses cultural change, whereas the empirical side gives us few facts about cultural stability.

Where culture itself is the basic cause of the thingness of things, as in families or corporations or money, then the things themselves can change rapidly; their going immutably their own way is an illusion. People talk of "the bottom line" of money in the accounts of a business as if it were still made of gold, a hard reality. The argument for the gold standard was based on the causal unity of gold, not easily changed by moth and rust but also not by culture (Carruthers and Babb 1996). Inflation, the cultural determination of the value of money, is in part the result of the fact that the bottom line is no longer in specie. Thus culturally changeable objects, which we *think of* as things that go their own way regardless, make changes in the bottom line by change in culture invisible.

The illusion of cultural change because of inattention to stable parts of the culture is especially found in cumulative culture, such as science. Elementary physics textbooks are fairly stable over time. It is not at all unreasonable to use Richard Feynman's introductory textbook (Feynman, Leighton, and Sands 1963–1966) to introduce physics today. But the physics in *Scientific American* is constantly changing and never reproduces an old textbook. In introductory geometry, Euclid would recognize many of the proofs, but no proof recognizable to Euclid would appear in a mathematics journal.

Here we see social structures within science differentiated by how fast their culture changes. At the frontiers of science the timing of questions for research is central, and the core active questions change rapidly. As soon as something is found out, it need not be found out again, except to verify it and to learn the technique. It drifts from journals into textbooks. Research laboratories have changing products more like the fashion garment industry, and elementary classes have stable products like the gray goods industry.

This means that the *same* body of culture changes at different rates in different locations, and where we study the culture determines what level of stability we find. Different disciplines have different gradients of change rates from frontier to elementary. Elementary sociology responds to shifts in research fashions (Cole 1994) much more rapidly than elementary physics to the latest speculations on the clumping of galaxies. So one easily imagines that the elementary physics textbook is a description of "nature," whereas elementary sociology looks more like "culture." But physics on the frontier of knowledge changes more rapidly than elementary sociology.

Thus both cultural change and cultural stability are partly illusions; it all depends on where one looks. Street names preserve the importance of Methodism while Evanston professors living on those streets teach secular humanism. Looking at either alone misrepresents change.

Changed Form, Same Substance

Perhaps the most general change in cultural form is increased (or occasionally decreased) formalization, routinization, or rationalization. I mean several things by formalization.

1. The cultural form is detached from many other influences, as an "algorithm," so that it can run on automatically with only a few highly specified inputs and outputs, as when simple algebra is used to compute the value of $y = x^2$ whether x is atoms or suns; one need know little about either atoms or suns to compute the algorithm.
2. Formalized culture is attached to social action in only a few places, its "inputs" and "outputs." Formalized culture governs "routines" rather than "life"; the extreme of formalized culture describes "machines" governed by their own laws without human intervention.
3. Only a few aspects of an object created by (or used in) a routine or algorithm are relevant to it; the formalization of gold into coins ("franking") makes only their denomination relevant. Where gold coins but not bills are appropriate gifts for musicians (as was true in Venezuela in 1965), this use of money is not so formalized as to make gold and bills interchangeable.
4. Consequently much of the history and peculiarity of the world is formally irrelevant; in an appellate court the "facts" formalized and defined as sufficient by a lower court are normally taken as given, and the court does not look behind the facts, though it may examine their sufficiency.
5. Some aspects of a cultural system are more rapidly formalized than others; musical notation is more formalized than tunes, and jurisdiction of courts is more formalized than courts' interpretation of contracts.

6. Usually formalization is itself created by formal processes; custom becomes law by formal legislation. Formalization feeds on itself; a formal formalization apparatus creates formality.

Formalization then detaches a bit of the substance in culture from the rest. Form is *not* contradictory to that part of the substance "allowed into" its inputs and "relevant to" its outputs. But it excludes all other substance. In polynomials in algebra, but not in life, only variations in the value of x influence the value of y. In cost accounting, but not on the factory floor, only things that have costs affect the value of the output.

Formalization, then, is a move of abstraction of bits of substance from everything else the culture might say. If the abstraction is wrong, the routine governed by formalized culture will have variable and unpredictable outputs, will be "out of control." Thus if one abstracts from race in California schools, one gets overrepresentation of Asians and underrepresentation of blacks at Berkeley. It is hard to convince blacks that such abstraction is just, or Asians that racial quotas (another abstraction) would be better. Earlier Jews had the problem of Asians, and Italians the problem of blacks, and neither of them liked it either.

Since formalization depends on successful abstraction, it results in two extreme forms of cultural change, which I will call "perpetual vain abstraction" and "growth of black boxes." The law of evidence in Anglo-American law is a good case of perpetual vain abstraction, and the mechanics of rigid bodies in the nineteenth century is a good case of growth of black boxes (Latour 1987, esp. chap. 3, 103–144).[2]

The Law of Evidence and Perpetual Vain Abstraction

The law of evidence in English and American law (most legal systems do not have it) is mainly directed at keeping juries from making mistakes in inference that judges and lawyers fear or hope they will make (Rothstein 1981, 6–11; Thayer [1896] 1969; but see Morgan 1956, 106–140). One trouble is that juries will make sensible but unconstitutional assessments, as when they want to put a bad guy in jail even when he has not been proved guilty of the crime charged.

But putting a democratic assembly of sworn "peers" into the role of correctly abstracting legally relevant facts generates many judge and lawyer hypotheses about possible jury errors. Counsel may be tempted to show that the victim of a rape is a "bad girl," so male citizens might have "innocently" misinterpreted her degree of consent. The historical stream of judge guesses about potential jury errors generates new potential misuses of evidence that require remedy in the law. So compilations of the law of evidence such as John Henry Wigmore's (1940) already spanned five volumes in 1923 but reached ten by 1940. More and more substance had to be abstracted by amateurs to create legal facts (i.e., abstractions of the "natural facts"), which kept on creating opportunities for error by juries, or by professional witnesses, or by appeals to bigotry. And such growing causes of error required growing formalization of the law to prevent new mistakes. Codifications of that law are themselves not sufficiently formal, but what textbooks will say is that they evidently left the previous law standing (Rothstein 1981, 69, 71–72), or that the judge has "considerable discretion" and that "only a blatantly egregious ruling will be overturned by the appellate court" (Rothstein 1981, 11–12).

This shows that the form of the formality in the law of evidence has changed since the days of Jeremy Bentham's tirades against it (Twining 1990, 39–41). Bentham complained of rigid rules about what evidence could be admitted, which evidence was "best," what facts could not be challenged because they had already been decided (res judicata), and so on. Now most rules about evidence specify restricted conditions under which judges are allowed to take control and use their discretion. Discretion over evidence usually resides with the contending parties in Anglo-American law; this provision is a core element of an "adversary" system of law. Formalizing criteria of division of discretion between judges and counsel then substitutes for the older formal regulation of the substance of evidence. For example, the right of criminal defendants to defend themselves by attacking the reputations of witnesses is usually weighed more heavily than the similar right of parties in civil cases. The weighing of the cost of allowing protected slander versus the rights of the parties is up to the judge, within wide limits. This judicial discretion can often be supported with cases, because judges in appellate courts have understood the distinction between criminal defense and civil disputes in the past.

But the formal discretion to give criminal defendants more breaks and civil parties less is now less specified in rigid rules as it was in Bentham's day and is more specified as formal jurisdiction of a judge to admit or exclude some kinds of reputational evidence by "weighing" harm versus probative value. Arbitrary damage to reputations is an injustice too, but the balance between that injustice and the injustice of a criminal conviction of an innocent person is different from the balance between it and civil damages. Jurisdictional rules are ordinarily highly formal, from the right of signature over corporate checking accounts to the exact location of the jurisdiction between admiralty courts and domestic civil courts at the docks in the harbor. When the jurisdiction over who decides what evidence should be admitted passes from opposing counsel to the judge, the conditions of the judge's discretion are highly formalized, and after that particular use of judge discretion, counsel resume their normal discretion.

Among varieties of jurisdictional law, however, discretion over evidence occurs in a constantly changing system of interaction about constantly changing flows of evidence, professional and scientific knowledge, legal complexities of transactions, and consequently changes in what "legal facts" really are and how they can best be established. So the formalization of jurisdiction over discretion about admission or weighing of evidence is perpetual vain abstraction, because we always need more formalization to handle new potential jury error.

Perpetual vain abstraction also has characterized the accounting and administrative regulations of scientists by their university, on behalf of the National Science Foundation (NSF) or other grantors. Those scientists to whom the agencies want to give money are always doing new things (otherwise they would not be worth giving money to). Those things change in the middle of the grant as preliminary experiments suggest a new line of inquiry. But to make scientists accountable, grantors want to know what they are going to do, what they have in fact done, why it costs so much, and how they can prove that it was worth that much. Scientists' work is as hard to govern by rules as jury deliberation. So the complexity of the administrative office for research and contracts on campus has to grow constantly for a constant number of scientists, as grantors constantly invent new abstractions to cram the scientific substance (still to be invented) into.

Growth of Black Boxes

The opposite of trying vainly to formalize a shifting flow of substance is formalization so successful that we can forget the substance almost all the time. To understand routinization of new scientific knowledge into black boxes or machines (Latour 1987; Collins 1994a), it is useful to contrast the mechanics of rigid bodies in the nineteenth century with social anthropology in the twentieth century (sociology would do as well, but the argument is longer; see Cole 1994). It is clear that rigid bodies (steel roller bearings, gears, crowbars, camshafts, and the like) usually bear constant physical relationships to one another.[3] A wide variety of mechanical processes can be built into reliable machines, representing blueprints accurately in a real mechanism, with specified machining tolerances, specifications in the purchase orders for motors, and so on. Once a mechanical process has been built into formalized pieces of the culture of machine design, only engineers need know what is there in order to design better machines, and machinists need to know how to create material machines that mirror the formalized culture of design. The design is then an algorithm, and the operation of the machine is a routine governed automatically by the algorithm.

These machines then can be fed into laboratory or industrial procedure as "black boxes" and can be bought on the market or produced in laboratory machine shops with little scientist input. They then can be combined into mechanical systems to study new physical or chemical phenomena, without having to think, for example, about how the telescope follows the sun or how the motor turns the fan in the wind tunnel.

But in anthropology the phenomena are constantly changing, as, for example, when the Shona move into Harare, study in English-language secondary schools, buy condoms (or do not but could), and treat their sewage rather than leaving it near the path to the maize field. One cannot therefore draw a blueprint of a Shona culture machine, producing the appropriate cultural products and actions, and build and operate its real-world equivalent to help one study, say, "cultural contact" under controlled conditions. Thus there are almost no black boxes in anthropology that we do not have to study any more because we already know all that is inside them. The flow of new substance into anthropology is as great as in the jury room, but anthropology has not committed itself to formalize control of all the inputs, so it does not quite produce a Wigmore on evidence (1940). Nineteenth-century mechanics becomes dull, "mere" engineering, whereas twentieth-century anthropology becomes a source of historical archives on the passing of Shona culture.

A Differentiated Sociology of Formalization of Culture

The main point of this section is that one changes culture by formalizing it. Some formalizing processes are doomed to failure, as when juries continue to make inferences that lawyers and judges do not like, and the NSF (fortunately) fails to make scientists do research by the numbers.

Other processes bury culture in black boxes that we only need to look into if we want greater precision or more reliability in well-understood real-world representations of dead algorithms. No one has to know the sine of an angle in a machine, because if it is ever needed a computer or a reference book will know it, and anyway its inclined-plane effect is built into the blueprint. That sine value is part of a black box, to be opened only by an engineer, and then only if necessary.

In addition, some black boxes simply bury part of a culture that we do not need at present. A composer can enter middle C and forget everything essential from nineteenth-century physics that goes into designing a pitch pipe, or why organs or other instruments with purer tones are more likely to sound funny in our modern tuning system than are pianos or harpsichords. People are paid to formalize things so that we can forget them.

Anything serious, modern people will try to abstract and formalize. When they fail at formalizing something serious, they formalize it anyway, as the law of evidence or NSF administrative regulation shows. Frank Knight, a University of Chicago economist, said: "If we cannot measure a thing, go ahead and measure it anyway" (Merton, Sills, and Stigler, 1984, 324)—a perfect summary of the generalization about formalization applied to science. Seriousness leads to the abstractions in the law of evidence, NSF administrative regulation, and scientific methodology. But in the nature of the case, juries and scientists generate substance that will not fit the abstraction, so generate perpetual vain abstraction with a few black boxes that may actually stay black and closed.

When we try to isolate a bit of culture to formalize and routinize it, we change the culture. Formalized culture has the purpose of being insensitive to context, except for a few relevant inputs and outputs. A successful algorithm or machine can be a part that runs on, doing its thing regardless of context in a larger system.

But detaching a formalized abstraction from its context is a problematic achievement. Perpetual vain formalization has ungovernable sources of new context built in, like the jury in Anglo-American justice or scientists in NSF grants. It therefore creates over time a great mushy mass of formality that can never quite grasp its substance.

Building a successful black box such as a design for a diesel engine, tedious as that successful formalization of the design may be, creates a different form of cultural change. The successfully formalized engine design disappears from everyday cultural life, though the machine is present everywhere, because very few people ever have to think about it.

Why Fragment Theory?

I argue here that if cultural phenomena are in fact fragmented, a unified theory fails to provide guidance for what research to do next. If one thinks that culture is all one thing, that it is unified as a cause of behavior, or that it is a consensus that we have always had, then one has too unified a theoretical apparatus to grasp it. Niels Bohr once defined physics as the conviction that a simple and unified explanation of nature is possible. Insofar as we have taken our definition of the scientific task from physics and applied it to culture, we have sapped our theory of interest. I have fragmented the theory of cultural change by example to give an idea of a toolbox of theoretical mechanisms rather than a sorry scheme of things entire.

The mechanisms of the first section of this essay are those in which young people learn things different from what their elders would have taught them. Schools, elections, and gradual cosmopolitanization are social structures that could teach the young what most of their seniors do not believe. These learning mechanisms usually produce differences among cohorts, periods, and age groups in rates of cultural change and hence in what they believe at a given time.

The second section is a generalization to cultural structures of what Noam Chomsky (1969, 9–24) called the *generativity* of grammar. A stable structure of language can make it easy to say an infinite number of sentences never before said. Boltanski and Thévenot (1991) described six such cultural substructures. The solidity of these cultural substructures makes each easily transferable to phenomena previously governed by another cultural substructure, as when the cultural substructure of celebrity as a way of being great, first thoroughly developed in Hollywood, was imported into civic life by movie star political candidates.

The third section breaks particular areas of culture into rapidly changing "frontier" parts, such as research physics, and more stable parts, such as the physics in the elementary textbook. One can find whatever level of cultural change one wants by choosing to study research frontiers rather than elementary classrooms. With a theory of culture as a unified thing, one wonders why the rate of rebuilding instructional laboratories is much slower than research laboratories, or why Asbury will still be a street name in Evanston when everyone has forgotten that it was once a dry (i.e., alcohol-free) town partly in Asbury's honor.

The final section is about culture change by *formalization* of culture. Culture as well as social organization is formalized—devoted to specialized purposes, turned into algorithms, written into computer programs, arranged into dictionaries, codified by bar association committees, or drawn into blueprints. But sometimes formalization can never end, as I argued in the case of the law of evidence. In other cases formalization ends so finally that it can be put into a black box and nearly forgotten while "culture" is reorganized around the inputs and outputs of the algorithms.

In sum, the idea that the social structure changes and then culture adapts to it is not the principal way that culture changes. Probably the less culture is connected to social structure, the freer it is to change rapidly. Musical fashions change even faster than cosmology, whereas physics tightly connected to objects of daily life can be taught to children by parents who cannot see what rap music or the big bang is all about. And the structure of culture we use to praise famous men changes at a glacial pace, though whether we praise them as presidents or as movie stars may change with an election.

Notes

1. Actually this phrase was used in the description of the results of a pilot study done at NORC using the General Social Survey. The nearest sober analogy to this elegant alliteration in Lauman et al. is on pp. 546–547. The estimate of five sex partners per lifetime is an inference based on male reports for younger cohorts' cumulative sex partners by age forty (p. 198, graphed on p. 202). Women have considerably fewer heterosexual sex partners than men, which Queen Victoria would like even if she could not explain it.

2. Latour's point is different from mine, but it also supports my point here. At the end of Latour's diesel story, we may no longer have a clear inventor, but we have a black-box machine that can pull our trains without our knowing how the fuel is mixed with air.

3. Variables that determine whether nineteenth-century mechanics apply without substantial complication include rigidity, low wear and breakage, low stickiness, not being embedded in viscous fluids, low friction, absence of shock waves, and the like. Only if enough boundary conditions hold can one bury mechanical theory in black boxes.

Part Four

Risk and Culture

Chapter Seven

The Depoliticization of Risk

MARY DOUGLAS

Politics is foremost in the international and national debates about risks, whether they concern risk to the environment, regulation to control risk, or implementation of the laws. But in the accompanying academic discussion politics and justice have very little formal place. This is a complaint against the academics about how political issues are sometimes ignored or muffled in academic work, sometimes espoused unwittingly, and sometimes treated with no concern for objectivity. There are two cleavages within the academic field of risk analysis. First, there is a conflict about nothing less than the nature of reality. Second, at the next level, the conflict is about how the first should be studied. My purpose in writing about these conflicts in academia is to try to reconcile contrary positions.

In 1992 the Royal Society issued a report entitled *Risk: Analysis, Perception, and Management.* It was an updating of a Royal Society report of a decade earlier, *Risk Analysis* (1983), which had drawn criticism for saying practically nothing about risk perception and management. The 1992 report, unlike its predecessor, was not issued as a report *of* the Society but rather as a report of the work of the study group chaired by Sir Frederick Warner in the form of six independent chapters each attributed to its subchairman. The preface indicated that this saved editing and delay in publication. The preface also suggested delicately that this dissociating device was not merely intended to serve greater speed and punctuality. Controversial issues were raised, especially in chapters 5 and 6, which dealt with risk perception and risk management. Evidently the scientists reporting on engineering risk,

---

I wish to thank the Political Economy Research Centre at the University of Sheffield for the opportunity to present an early version of this paper in their seminar series, February 17, 1994.

toxicology, and epidemiology had been able to reach general agreement. But difficulties arose in dealing with the ambiguities of the so-called social sciences.

Sir Frederick, in a later article in *Science and Public Affairs* (Warner 1992), said quite frankly that the trouble had been caused by the social scientists. It was partly a disagreement between them and the natural scientists on what is real about risk, and partly a disagreement among the social scientists themselves on method. Joining a dispute between psychologists and anthropologists, and taking sides unabashedly, Sir Frederick praised the solid work of psychologists; he particularly commended the careful sampling and psychometric analysis that had identified factors in risk perception, such as the "dread factor," and had developed a theory about the "social amplification of risk." But these honest souls "had reckoned," he said, "without the anthropologists who dismiss their contributions." He evidently counted the psychometric crowd among the true scientists when at the end of his article he deplored the political isolation of scientists and complained that in Parliament scientists have little influence when pitted against fifty Members from the London School of Economics.

To explain what the dispute was about, let me quote Professor Brian Wynne on the intrinsic difficulties of being understood at all. Citing Kierkegaard, he said, "We reconstruct the meanings offered to us by others into forms that correspond with our fundamental identities; in the process, the original meanings are transformed, or perhaps we should say violated. Kierkegaard wrote with great power about the tragedy, not just that we are confined to distorting each others' meanings, but more that we are confined to pretending that it is otherwise" (Wynne 1992, 275–276). Wynne went on to describe his own experience as participant observer of the 1977 Windscale Public Enquiry into a planned oxide fuels reprocessing facility at the Sellafield nuclear complex (Wynne 1982). In his 1982 book he had "examined the way that the dominant rationality silently and systematically deleted my questions about institutional commitment, behavior and trustworthiness, as if they had nothing to do with the risk. This same rationality constructed the decision issue as one of objective discovery rather than social commitment, and hence also constructed the opponents and their concerns as factually wrong or irrational" (1992, 278).

This is how the issue of reality comes up. Wynne also quoted Harry Otway and Philip Pahner (1976) for suggesting that risk definitions as framed by experts were taken by the experts to be more real than the definitions of lay people. Beyond the issues of measurement and quantification of risks and risk perceptions were more basic questions about which dimensions of experience should be recognized and which should be denied validity. The feeling that reality is how the experts define it, and that alternative definitions are irrational and possibly subversive, and even based on bad faith, is the issue that disturbed the meetings of the Royal Society study groups. Sir Frederick's constituency wanted to stay with a reality defined by the experts. Why they felt this to be safer has probably to do with politics, as I shall try to show later. That is the first cleavage.

In October 1992 the Foundation for Science and Technology and the Royal Society held a joint meeting to launch the report. Complete decorum reigned until near end, when a psychologist got up from the floor and reproached the Royal Society report for giving undue space to radical views. When he asked that the term "social construction of risk" be eliminated from the discussion, shouting, clapping, and hissing broke out and the meeting was adjourned.

First let me agree quickly that the term "social construction of risk" has been a source of confusion. Somehow the engineers and some others understand it as a denial of the reality of the risks. But the emphasis is on the word "social" as distinct from "individual construction of risk." Once we get past the expert's perception and try to assess the wider perception of the nonexpert public, we can choose to focus attention on individuals confronting and defining risk on their own, or we can take a collective view. This is where the cleavage on method appears.

All knowledge and everything we talk about is collectively constructed. Language is no private invention. Words are a collective product, and so are meanings. There could not be risks, illnesses, dangers, or any reality, knowledge of which is not constructed. It might be better if the word "social construal" were used instead of "construction," because all evidence has to be construed. Construal, being an act of interpretation, does not imply impugning of reality. But I myself protest on behalf of the anthropologists that the Royal Society report granted much too much space to the psychometric approach to risk perception. I welcome this opportunity to tell serious social scientists what is wrong with the psychometric approach, with its biased sampling and alleged "discovery" of psychological factors attached to particular risks, scientistic pretensions, and claims to objectivity.

Theories of Risk Perception

In what follows, without trying to make an exhaustive survey, I will introduce four approaches to risk perception. The first (psychometric) and the second (social amplification) try to avoid analyzing a political dimension, with varied success. The objectives of the third are connected with achieving justice, and it does not pretend to be apolitical. The fourth grasps the political nettle and aims to incorporate political opposition as part of the analysis as well as part of what is being studied.

Psychometric and Rational Actor Models

This is the approach that completely bypasses political factors and pays no attention to them whatever. Paul Slovic (1992) narrates how in 1970 he and another graduate student in the psychology department of Stanford University were asked by Gilbert White about their research into risk taking and probabilistic judgments for simple gambles. White wondered whether they could throw light on human response to natural hazards such as floods or earthquakes. They realized that their field had been defined too narrowly to tell much about risk taking outside the laboratory, and they forthwith redirected their methods to studying what they came to call "cognitive processes and societal risk taking."

At that time the dominant paradigm had been launched by an engineer, Chauncy Starr (1969), who argued that acceptable risks are accepted risks; if the public accepts a risk, it is acceptable. From that assumption his program was to remind the lay public who were agitating against the risk of exposure to nuclear radiation that they accepted greater risks every day for far less benefit: an hour's sunbathing, a daily glass of cola, crossing the road. Against this approach, the psychologists developed questionnaires to ask the public directly about their perceptions of risk-benefit trade-offs and continued work on the technical and statistical problems entailed.

The underlying objectives of this psychometric program are those of cognitive science: to identify universal principles of the human mind. This high level of abstraction effectively removes the inquiry from the dust and turmoil of politics. The team of Amos Tversky and Daniel Kahneman (1981) writes with wit and elegance unusual in the social sciences; they uncover quizzical paradoxes and curious anomalies in human behavior that challenge the rational actor model of economics and political philosophy. This paradigm has given rise to so much experimentation as to deserve the title of "normal science" in the field of risk research, which means a large investment has been made in its assumptions and procedures.

The excellent summary of this approach given in chapter 5 of the Royal Society's 1992 report is no doubt oversimplified. But even from the original essays the layperson is no wiser as to why people take risks about living in floodplains or on earthquake faults or near nuclear power stations. The outcomes of the research say little about big decisions. There is a rude question that it is embarrassing to put to such a civilized set of people about their urbane procedures. Why have these seemingly trite discoveries been made the basis of worldwide research programs on the perception of risk?

It is true that they help to explain various divergences between official statistics and public beliefs. For example, a type of event will tend to be judged more probable to the extent that instances of it are readily available in the memory; questionnaires showed that deaths from the most vivid causes are thought to be the most frequent (Lichtenstein et al. 1978). "Vivid" catches and holds attention while "dull" passes into background. Other examples helped to develop what became known as the "availability heuristic." This is not denying that laypeople are rational; not at all: just that they have other things on their mind when they listen to the experts. But what does vividness consist in? How does one thing become more available than another?

The overall objective of the psychometric project is to build up gradually a model of individual cognitive response to risk. However, several features of the research design could be improved. Certain criticisms are commonly made: one against the small size of the samples, one against the reliance on subjective responses, and another against the whole procedure of deriving axioms from laboratory questionnaires. I will add a few more. The respondents are chosen and the questions designed as if nothing in their previous lives or personal experience would make a difference to their response to risks and probabilities; this is a rejection of the reciprocal influence between culture and personal beliefs.

Again—and this is another aspect of the neglect of the cultural dimension—individual answers are correlated to individual risks. Both the respondents and the risks are decontextualized for the sake of a universalizable theory of mind. Again, and perhaps the most serious criticism, the respondents are faced with a limited list of risks that the researchers have defined. But life is full of risks; at every step we are dogged by risky decisions, and life without risk is not worth living (Fried 1970). What guarantees that the spectrum of selected risks gives a fair view of the life choices an individual has to weigh?

If we were being offered a theory of cognition that explained how some events become salient and others backgrounded, it would be very interesting indeed. But a lot of backgrounding and foregrounding has been done in advance, so that implicitly the respondents' answers are being measured against a common idea of what is a salient risk. The common idea is local to our own culture and so does not say anything about the "human" cognitive process. What has developed is a local theory of psychological meanings attached to separate items called risks or hazards.

Certain risks have associated with them "dread," uncontrollability, involuntariness of exposure, and inequitable distribution of risk bearing. Within this paradigm there is no research, as far as I know, on how the dread factor arises, and it sounds much like saying that certain events are feared because the dread factor is associated with them. The focus is on the free-floating events and apparently free-floating psychological meanings. All over the world where this paradigm holds sway, field researchers are practicing normal science, looking for the dread factor, joyously finding it as predicted, and paying no systematic attention to the processes by which the meanings become attached.

Everyone in the risk perception business agrees that the mind's perceiving involves active organizing of the experience by the subject. But in spite of accepting a post-Kantian view of the perceptual process, the research design of the psychometric approach ignores the subject's development of perceptual lenses. The emphasis is on the impact of "risks" on the mind, like the impact of sense impressions on the retina in seventeenth-century optics. Though they follow with fascination the laboratory subject actively distorting a situation that has supposedly only one right answer, the explanations of what the respondent has done to turn a question around are intended to illustrate universal cognitive tendencies implicitly founded in the human biological heritage. To be frank about my own bias, I cannot take seriously a theory of risk perception that has eliminated cultural factors. When people knowingly take risks, they are not alone; the bigger the risk, the more likely they are to consult among their family and friends and go to experts. Deciding to take a risk is generally a cooperative matter, and this makes the results of questionnaires on the psychometric model implausible as clues to how people think about risks.

Social Amplification

Ten years ago when I tried to do a literature review of how the social sciences approached the question of risk acceptability I found practically nothing. I felt that reviewing the literature on a silence was like walking round a hole in the ground. Since then, several new approaches have developed. The social amplification approach tries to supplement some of the deficiencies in the psychometric paradigm. It very properly starts by studying the funnel of social experiences through which the prospect of hazards is filtered to individuals; it is primarily concerned with how social and cultural processes intensify or attenuate perceptions of risk. The key words are "signals," transmitted through a variety of "social amplification stations." Examples of such "stations" cited are groups of scientists, government agencies, activist groups, and so on. The social amplification approach aims to account for the differential interpretations placed on hazardous events.

This sounds like a promising program, but for three drawbacks. The first is that it enters the arena of politics unconsciously, with a political bias apparently hidden from its practitioners. Though it claims to be explaining how some hazards come to be played down and others played up by the social filtering mechanisms, the title gives a true idea of the central concern, which is how hazards come to be *amplified*. In other words, without apology or recognition, the research is directed to explaining how things seem to be more dangerous than they really are. In the context of technological risk this is a barely disguised political bias. Though the research does turn its attention to risks that are taken voluntarily and to risks that are apparent to others but not to the chief actors, this seems to be done with the intention of meeting the criticism of lack of balance. A systematic approach would absolutely need to develop a theory of selection. To account for how some risks are selected for attention would mean keeping in mind the concomitant neglect (or "attenuation") of other dangers.

Second, the whole concept of amplification suggests a focus on what the real hazard truly is (that is, unamplified), and how the public tends to get a false (amplified) view of it. This is an unconscious and naive realism. It would be safer to admit some indeterminacy about the expert reading of evidence as well as indeterminacy in what the public observes. Brian Wynne (1989) has made famous a case of sheep farmers' being more knowledgeable about the effects of nuclear radiation than the scientists.

Third, the idea of signals and signal stations needs to be thoroughly worked out. At present it is at the stage of arm-waving. Signals and signal stations come close to a sociological version of salience. But again, the trouble is that salience is supposed to be the same for everyone. The term suggests that in any culture some objects, places, persons, or words attract attention, acting as points of reference and producing conspicuous solutions to questions that might otherwise be flooded with ambiguity. Thomas Schelling's (1960) idea about salience is in the air again and being reintroduced in epistemology, economics, and organization theory. It certainly deserves a good run in studying risk perception under the guise of "signal stations." The question about risk perception then would be how salience is bestowed, which is parallel to the previous question about the "availability heuristic." This is where the possibility of reconciling the rifts between the social scientists on risk perception should be possible.

Frankly Political Arguments

It is impossible for readers not to know about the host of political writings warning of risks foisted on the people by unscrupulous industrialists and politicians, about risks being minimized, denied, concealed. A lot of it is intended for journalism. This is where the whole new field of risk analysis started. First there was the public protest, then government and industry called for advice about why the public was so outraged, and then the academic study of risk perception developed somewhat along the lines I have indicated, producing what is now a vast bibliography and including many different types of inquiry.

For our purposes here it will be enough to cite one book that directly addresses questions of justice. Kristin Shrader-Frechette's *Risk and Rationality* (1991) aims to provide a philosophically respectable position on risk. I use it here because the author specifically attacks *Risk and Culture* (Douglas and Wildavsky 1982). Shrader-Frechette pits her own frankly populist standpoint against two allegedly antipopulist theories of risk. In her vocabulary "populist" means taking public complaints seriously and giving credit to the people's fears about rising morbidity and death rates due to technology. It means democratic principles and legislation designed to respond to bottom-up claims. "Antipopulist" in this vocabulary indicates the enemy of the people. In the context of risk the enemy dismisses popular fears of technology as baseless and gives esoteric and suspect reasons for supporting a coalition of government and industry against pollution control and workplace dangers. Shrader-Frechette indicts two approaches to risk: One is the naive positivism of engineers and scientists for whom a fact is a fact and has nothing to do with values (echoes of the Royal Society's engineers); the other is the grid-group cultural theory espoused by myself and a handful of colleagues. Shrader-Frechette writes passionately in defense of the people's risk aversion, too lightly dismissed by politically biased antipopulists. Risk theory does indeed tend to be muddied by political debating strategies; risk is inevitably politicized, since major values are at stake; employment, poverty, lives, and regions laid waste; budgets emptied; and timetables overturned. I sympathize with the scorn Shrader-

Frechette pours on the attempts of professional risk analysts to evade the political aspects of their science, and I offer qualified support for her proposals for improving current methods of risk assessment.

The main positive idea is that risk-cost-benefit analysis could be improved by ethical weighting techniques; alternative analyses should be done to take account of different ethical assumptions; and "expert opinions" should be weighted according to their past performance. As a defender of the people Shrader-Frechette wishes to end arbitrariness in risk decisions and hopes that improved analysis will curb back-scratching, payoffs, bribes, and ignorance. She wants to find ways of improving cost-benefit analysis by incorporating ethical and political biases. Starting from a political standpoint, she wants to depoliticize the issues, so as to provide an opening for populist views. In a review of this book I said:

> It is probably true that risk-cost-benefit analysis as practiced fails to take account of egalitarian values, social obligations and rights of individuals. And ethical weighting will certainly open the field to a new kind of democratic debate. Passionate interest in carcinogens in parts to the million will be shifted to passionate interest in complex principles of ethical weighting. This would probably restore the prestige of science, for it is widely remarked that science when used to arbitrate in politics loses its authority. If the political strains are transferred to the scrutiny of ethical weighting systems, environmentalists may discover that the populist view is not necessarily in support of what seems to be obviously good and right. Eventually the focus will be directed to cultural differences, and to political disagreement. This is where cultural theory comes in, for it starts by mapping the political and ethical differences engaged beneath the surface of any argument about risks (Douglas 1993, 485).

At this point I am ready to introduce grid-group cultural theory as a fourth type of approach that has a method of incorporating the political debate in its analysis.

"Culture" as Type of Bias or "Culture" as Dialogue

Considerable misunderstanding of the methods and objectives of grid-group cultural theory has arisen from its critics' rewriting of the terminology. In the theory a typology of cultures is derived from cultural biases; but overhasty readers take the elements of the typology to be culture "groups." It is easy to be scathing about whether communities divide into hierarchical groups, egalitarian groups, individualist groups: They do not, and no one ever said they do. A cultural bias is a point of view, with its own framing assumptions and readily available solutions for standardized problems. Scattered persons not in any group at all may share a similar cultural bias. It is a question of a way of life, and the way of life depends heavily on the way of earning a living and on the social relations that are entailed. A common culture is a source for salient reference points and heuristics and so is complementary to some of the aforementioned approaches to risk. But note also the adversarial element: Each culture in this analysis is thought to be strongly in competition with its alternatives.

Because I need to avoid giving the impression of a culture as a sharply defined group of people, I would like to try presenting culture as a dialogue. This is like joining a powerful movement in the social sciences to turn action into speech and text, and I should say firmly where it is different: I am not taking the Habermasian view of the ideal society as dialogue, because I am not emphasizing possible harmony, but the contrary. The aspect of the cultural dialogue that needs to be understood is accountability. Think of culture as essentially a dialogue that allocates praise and blame. Then focus particularly on the blame.

Intercultural dialogue is inherently agonistic; the outcome will at any one point be a victory for one and defeat for another of the contestants; the contest is about the form of the life to be led in common. That is why blaming is so central. Every accident and mishap affords the members of the dialogue an opportunity to call one another to account. Somebody dies, someone is blamed; someone is injured, someone is blamed. Blaming ranges the universe, with all its benefits and hazards, on one side or another. Under this optic it is implausible that risks be perceived except through the accountability that they activate. The blaming process is normal cultural activity, and we have to examine the dangers that are around as made more salient by the handles they provide for blaming. That salience depends on accountability opens the study of cognitive salience to politics.

Each culture is founded on a distinctive institutional base, which gives it interests to protect, and its own conventional way of doing things. Consequently each culture allocates blame to different sectors, and they vary according to the amount of blaming that they tolerate. In this perspective the risk signals for which the social amplification researchers are looking would be features of the systems of accountability in each cultural type.

I can shorten the introduction to the theory of culture that I wrote with the late Aaron Wildavsky (Douglas and Wildavsky 1982) by summarizing four kinds of competing dialogues about risk in any industrial society. The basic discriminator is the attitude to power and authority: There are two ways of exerting power, one bureaucratic and hierarchical, and the other by bargaining and exchanging; there are two ways of resisting the influence from these bases, one by active criticism, and the other by withdrawal. The four cultural types that are thus distinguished (you can call them hierarchy, market, critical activist, and isolate) are always in flux, always open to conversion to one of the other positions. The competition is generally overt and highly political. This comes closer to the dynamic model presented by Steve Rayner (1992) and to Michael Thompson's (1992, 1996) insistence that cultures are always counterpoised against one another, than the more static versions I have usually offered. Here is a thumbnail sketch of the three types engaged in political debate:

1. One is based on government and administration, anchored in an established hierarchy, reductionist in reasoning style, and professionally concerned for measurability. It requires objective bases for comparison that can be used to justify the decisions it makes. It takes a longer view than the

others, and this may give it a coolness about accepting disaster. The hier-archists, in their struggle to create analytic operational formulae, tend to prefer a risk research vocabulary that can be formalized without being politicized. Control of information is so important for maintaining their hegemony that they may well be accused of attenuating risks, making them sound less serious than the other quarters of the public believe.

2. Another type is based on the market, individualist in ethics, pragmatic in style of reasoning; it casts suspicion on grand theories; it tends to be incre-mentalist in politics, positivist in sociology, and behaviorist in psychologi-cal theory. It takes such a short view of the future that again it tends to be less tender about the misfortunes of others. Market representatives who want market forces left free to make the world safer by advanced technol-ogy would like the language of risk to be contained within technical meanings. For example, the Royal Society risk report of 1983 discussed toxicity, engineering, and epidemiology as technical problems. These peo-ple will be much more interested in showing how normally acceptable risks are amplified by social processes, and they may be accused of mini-mizing risks.

3. The third, in opposition to the established hierarchy and to the market, is essentially a radical political discourse; it is the conscience of the commu-nity, reformist in objectives and holistic in modes of reasoning; it is the source of the scorn routinely poured on the bureaucratic concerns of the first type and on the materialist goals of the second type. The radical crit-ics, with liberation and radical political change as their program, find the context of risk a convenient arena for their part of the dialogue. They are much more interested in showing that risks have been concealed and the public misled. They are accused by the others of amplifying dangers, and perhaps with reason.

Thus we have three sources of risk signals, and we would expect at any one time a three-sided policy struggle and from one of the corners a hegemonic discourse dominating the rest.

When we have identified three kinds of cultural signal stations, we should be at-tending carefully to the favorite words that come to the fore in each culture and how the choice of themes is calculated to draw together the defenders of a cultural type against its opponents. As the debate unfolds, temporary coalitions emerge between members of the three opposing discourses. Common points of reference and some common vocabulary are necessary, however deep the divergence between objec-tives. Just as transgression became the salient point of reference for blaming for dis-aster in the Bible, and sin in the history of Christianity, in our secular, scientific world, risk has become the convenient, conspicuous blame term that all parties con-nive to promote. Steve Rayner (1992) has argued that recently a hegemonic dis-course has emerged: International concern about the environment is led by the radical critics, and the language and assumptions of the debate are dominated by those from the radical corner. The keystone of the conversational edifice is "risk."

It is difficult to recommend this cultural theory to someone who would really like a social science pure of politics. Its central idea is that any community is engaged in a heavy debate about its own governance. Whatever the scale, whether an African village of a few hundred people, a major bureaucracy, industrial units, or the organized professions, politics always lurks. Insofar as a group of people is worthy of the name of community, blaming goes on as part of the normal political process. By identifying three institutional bases and one neutral position for the isolates, and recognizing four dialogues about nature, danger, risk, and responsibility, we can go a long way toward incorporating arguments about politics in the analysis. Ideally this will provide a stronger kind of objectivity than one sought by avoiding politics altogether. And it will be much more revealing about the debate on risk than any questionnaire that homogenizes the cultural element.

Objectivity and the Exclusion of Politics

By shunning politics the risk analysis profession has won prestige, but in the long term it puts itself in danger of nullity. If the political dimension is there, it is not safe to evade it; the only thing to do is to confront it and include the political dialogue in your theory.

It has been observed that the psychometric research was originally funded by industry and government at a time of heated national controversy about nuclear power. I have heard it whispered that the researchers receiving grants would be expected to justify the experts and that a result that showed the public's fears of risk to be irrational would have been very acceptable. One member of the team has thought it necessary to deny that anything of this kind was either intended or demonstrated. But more plausibly, in such conditions it would have been dangerous to say anything that could be politically construed, and in practice there is practically nothing that is safe from that attack, as I know from the reviews of *Risk and Culture.* The safe course is to go all out for purity. My personal explanation of the success of this peculiar moment in the history of ideas is precisely that by the rigorous search for universal cognitive laws the profession achieved this pure status, above-and-beyond politics. Research along psychometric lines gave to a newly emergent profession the halo of objectivity.

In a secular society claims to this sort of objectivity are like claims to speak for God in an earlier time. If ever there was such a thing as pure research, this is it. To be able to exhibit purity on the subject of risk is a remarkable achievement, for the risks are prominent and the funds for studying risk perception forthcoming just because the debate is highly political. However elegant its formulae may be, and however useful for charting the basic conditions of the human cognition, the pure scholasticism of the psychometric approach as at present pursued disables it from relevance to risk perception.

If we were invited to make a coalition between grid-group cultural theory and psychometrics, it would be like going to heaven. Given such an invitation we would try to be practical and ask the high priests of the cult to apply its laboratory questionnaires to subjects drawn from well-identified opposed cultural types. Not only would this afford a real test of their theorizing, but also it would have the advantage of relating it to risk perception. If we were to collaborate with social amplification research, we would help them to identify the cultural equivalent of "risk stations," and so they would learn to hear the different messages about risks that emanate respectively from each. If we had an option to collaborate in Shrader-Frechette's program to improve cost-benefit analysis by incorporating ethical weighting, we would ask for different cultural weightings to be included in the exercise.

"Risk" in the present-day international and national political debates is a rhetorical strategy, a convention for allowing conversations to seem to proceed even while attacking. We can conclude this brief survey by noting that the idea of risk bids fair to dominate the scenario for political science and that those universities that leave it out of their curriculum may themselves be left high and dry. Note that this strong risk aversion of academics, which leads them to exclude the main factor from the research that is their very bread and butter, is an Anglo-Saxon bias. In France risk has already started to provide a new vocabulary for questions of justice and justification (Duclos 1989, 1991; Boltanski and Thévenot 1991; Laufer 1993). In Germany Ulrich Beck (1986) has made the first stab at rewriting all of political science in terms of vulnerability to risk. You can expect the French to be more political and philosophical; you can suppose readily that the politicization of risk has gone further in Germany thanks to the militant Greens; and I suppose you can expect the Anglo-Saxons to be more bureaucratic and hence to seek remoteness from the fracas and to restrict their interests to what can be measured precisely.

Everyone agrees that "humans do not perceive the world with pristine eyes, but through perceptual lenses such as the family, friends, superordinates and fellow workers" (Renn 1991). This being so, my claims are that the central problem for risk research is to know more about the lenses, and that this objective places risk assessment squarely in the departments of political culture and political economy.

Chapter Eight

What's Special About Cancer?

HOWARD MARGOLIS

Though I barely knew Aaron Wildavsky, on two occasions when I could use his help in the important matter of earning a living, he promptly offered it. One of these was in finding support for a study of expert versus lay conflicts of risk intuition, which was later published as *Dealing with Risk* (Margolis 1996). But what I want to discuss here is an intellectual debt, also connected with that book.

Several years ago I published an account of just what it is that shifts in the course of Thomas Kuhn's famous paradigm shifts (Margolis 1993). What turns out to be characteristic of the most striking cases (Darwin, Copernicus, Lavoisier, among others) is that the crucial step—what the famous discoverer saw that many others had missed—amounted to seeing what was "hidden in plain sight." This held in the sense that for some time before the discovery was finally made (in two of the cases, including the Copernican, for a very long time), anyone competent to make the discovery at all had been within easy reach of it but nevertheless missed seeing it. What made the discovery hard was not some forbidding logical gap, too broad to be crossed by an ordinary mind, but some widely shared cognitive barrier that made it hard to see what in hindsight was in plain sight for anyone who could look. What made the discoverer exceptional was a knack for seeing what others could have seen but somehow were blind to.

Wildavsky managed a striking feat of that sort on the much discussed puzzle of expert/lay conflicts of risk intuition, modest on the scale of Copernicus or Darwin, but remarkable enough nevertheless. Recalling Wildavsky's insight will lead us into a question that seems to me worth more discussion than it has received: Why does cancer play a role in these expert/lay conflicts that seems extraordinary even after allowing for cancer's prominence as a major source of mortality? What is special about cancer? The usual answer is that there is a special dread of cancer as a particularly unpleasant sort of deadly disease. But introspection and casual inquiry lead me to expect that for many of us, a disabling stroke sounds at least as bad as cancer, and it is also common, but it somehow fails to generate the special dread that cancer is said to evoke. So there is a question that may need a better answer.

The Usual View

The prevailing account of expert versus lay risk conflicts says that experts focus on a very narrow range of consequences, but ordinary people have a much richer sense of what is involved in choices about risk. And that is why experts may feel comfortable with a level of precautions that seems wholly inadequate to ordinary people. In this view experts are entrenched in the habits of mind that go with assessing risks in terms of quantifiable danger. But ordinary citizens care a great deal about qualitative aspects of risk, such as voluntariness and how far authorities responsible for managing the risk have earned their trust, and about risk to future generations. A considerable list of these qualitative aspects of risk has come to be part of the usual story of why expert and lay intuitions so often conflict. The catalog of qualitative features of risk is compiled by discovering correlations between lay perceptions of various risks and lay ratings on various dimensions when asked to think about a particular risk. A common interpretation of this work is that it reveals an alternative rationality underlying lay intuition that is different from, but just as reasonable as, what the experts can offer.

Wildavsky was unsympathetic to that claim, and he was far from alone in that. But his response took a different turn from many others' who also found the "alternative rationality" view unpalatable. Most of those who regretted this usual story as a normatively sound account of lay risk perception still accepted it as an accurate account. Wildavsky, however, saw an aspect of the claimed special lay sensitivity to qualitative dimensions of risk that, once clearly noticed, seems so jarring as to put the whole story in question.

Table 8.1 provides a particularly thorough but otherwise quite typical inventory of these psychometric dimensions. Unless you are another Wildavsky, you can look at this list for a long time and not notice what is so profoundly odd about it. And what is odd is that even a listing of psychometric dimensions as exhaustive as this one (nineteen in all) finds no room for what could be expected to be the primary determinant of perceived risk not only for experts but for the rest of us as well. Nowhere on the list is there any explicit concern with some measure of how many people are likely to suffer if the risk is neglected.

Sometimes the qualitative dimensions (most obviously "catastrophic potential") could at least overlap quantitative concern. Across an array of such dimensions, perceptions of how big a danger is at issue could be captured by responses to a series of dimensions (such as catastrophic potential), each correlated with quantitative risk. Conceivably—even presumably—so. Yet it remains remarkable how indirect the concern with actual damage is, to the point at which it is not even clear that it is there but instead must be conjectured.

TABLE 8.1 Psychometric Risk Dimensions

Factor	Conditions Associated with Increased Public Concern	Conditions Associated with Decreased Public Concern
1. Catastrophic potential	Fatalities and injuries grouped in time and space	Fatalities scattered and random
2. Familiarity	Unfamiliar	Familiar
3. Understanding	Mechanisms or process not understood	Mechanisms or process understood
4. Uncertainty	Risks scientifically unknown or uncertain	Risks known to science
5. Controllability (personal)	Uncontrollable	Controllable
6. Voluntariness of exposure	Involuntary	Voluntary
7. Effects on children	Children specifically at risk	Children not specifically at risk
8. Effects manifestation	Delayed effects	Immediate effects
9. Effects on future generations	Risk to future generations	No risk to future generations
10. Victim identity	Identifiable victims	Statistical victims
11. Dread	Effects dreaded	Effects not dreaded
12. Trust in institutions	Lack of trust in responsible institutions	Trust in responsible institutions
13. Media attention	Much media attention	Little media attention
14. Accident history	Major and sometimes minor accidents	No major or minor accidents
15. Equity	Inequitable distribution of risks and benefits	Equitable distribution of risks and benefits
16. Benefits	Unclear benefits	Clear benefits
17. Reversibility	Effects irreversible	Effects reversible
18. Personal stake	Individual personally at risk	Individual not personally at risk
19. Origin	Caused by human actions or failures	Caused by acts of nature or God

Source: Margolis 1996, 28.

In general the psychometric surveys find that the various dimensions that correlate with lay concern are themselves highly intercorrelated (Fischhoff et al., 1978). Consequently there is ambiguity in the weights that should be assigned to particular dimensions. To simplify only a bit, the usual statistical procedures resolve that ambiguity by some variant of minimizing the number of variables needed to reach some intensity of overall correlation. This yields a "rich get richer" tendency. If X and Y are themselves correlated, but the effect of X (when Y is left out of the regression) is bigger than that of Y (when X is left out), then X is likely to be given its own (apparent) effect *plus* as much of Y as can be captured by their pairwise correlation. Another variable also stronger than Y would soak up some of whatever is left, and so on. When the computer printout emerges, Y may be squeezed out of any significant effect at all, even if there actually is a distinct Y effect. But actual danger would not be squeezed out of statistical significance if it were a really strong effect. Rather, some of the qualitative features would tend to be absorbed into quantitative danger rather than the reverse.[1] Wildavsky and remarkably few others really saw this significant oddity of the psychometric work, even though it is right there, "hidden in plain sight."

The reason the absence of a clear connection between lay perceived risk and actuarial risk goes unnoticed is probably that when we look at a list like that of Table 8.1, we take it as too obvious to need explicit mention that people making judgments about risk care about how far there would be danger in ignoring that risk. We then wrongly suppose that the situation is like that shown by the solid lines in Figure 8.1. (Eventually the dashed lines in the figure will come into the story, but not yet.) In this view, a person's sense of danger would be contingent on quantitative measures but modulated by qualitative aspects such as those listed in Table 8.1. Thus the usual story, translated into the framework of Figure 8.1, is that experts are narrowly focused on what they can quantify (the box in the upper left), but ordinary people care, and care strongly, about the qualitative features as well (the box in the upper right). Depending on your social and political outlook, this either shows that ordinary people have different and perhaps better intuitions than technocrats (and, especially in a democracy, ought to be listened to), or that popular sentiment can be a highly fallible guide to what is in the public interest (and so, like the popular inclination to repeal various items of the Bill of Rights, perhaps the weight of those lay risk intuitions ought to be tempered by a process not too directly exposed to popular sentiments.)

The availability of these contrasting readings of what to make of the usual account allows not only people who take a sympathetic view of lay perceptions but also most of those who do not live with the psychometric story—the former, of course, much more happily. Wildavsky seems to have been the first to take seriously what the psychometric reports literally are saying, which is that how much danger is really at risk is not merely modulated (in lay responses) by qualitative considerations, but also that qualitative aspects of risk dominate lay perception to the point that how much danger is really there can be treated as irrelevant. But that

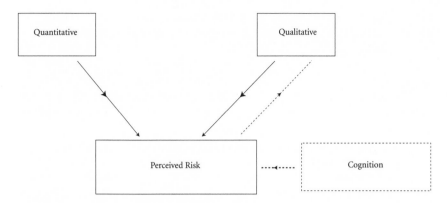

FIGURE 8.1   What governs perceived risk

is odd enough to consider whether some entirely different account—even an account that itself seems decidedly odd at first sight—might in fact be more sound.

In collaboration with Mary Douglas, Wildavsky worked out a cultural account of risk (Douglas and Wildavsky 1982) in which what risks people worry about reflects cultural propensities that indeed can be independent of what danger actually goes with accepting a risk. What prompts visceral concern, in this view, might have little to do with quantitative measures of danger even if (when directly asked for a definition) ordinary citizens, not just experts, respond mainly in quantitative terms.[2]

How plausible might that cultural account be, where quantitative risk is taken to be unimportant for defining what risks people actually care strongly about? The first point to notice is that no one who thinks about the matter can really doubt that most (indeed, by far most) of what we think we know is what we sense that "everyone knows." But then what cultural theorists call the social construction of knowledge (how what "everyone knows" comes about) would surely include the social construction of knowledge of what *subtle* dangers warrant intense concern. That must be an essential part of an account of risk perception, even though the language invites quarrels.[3] And yet even a cultural theorist presumably would allow that the social processes that account for widely shared beliefs must be grounded in how cognition works in individuals.

In *Dealing with Risk,* I followed Wildavsky in taking seriously the puzzle of apparent lay indifference to quantitative appraisal of danger. But the result was a primarily cognitive (rather than sociological or cultural) account, which I want to extend through some additional discussion of the special salience of cancer risks. In a generous review Mary Douglas (forthcoming) suggested that the cognitive account can be seen as complementary to rather than alternative to the cultural account. I certainly would not reject that. But in the cultural account itself, in any modern society there would be competing views favoring as well as discouraging attention to quantitative aspects of risk: favoring hierarchical or market tastes (each in this context sympathetic to a balancing of costs and benefits, hence intrinsically leaning toward quantitative assessment) as well as egalitarian sentiments suspicious or downright antagonistic to that sort of experts' calculus. Why quantitative considerations can play a large role in some contexts and be widely ignored in others, within the same society, turns most plausibly on individual cognitive propensities that allow social contagion to support leaving things to the experts in some contexts and suspicion of experts in others. The balance of the discussion here proceeds from that possibility.

Suppose that lay concern does not in fact give (much) greater weight to qualitative dimensions than experts would give. Surveys designed to find out how much people care about qualitative as opposed to quantitative considerations are consistent with this possibility, rarely showing a difference of as much as a factor of two between how much typical individuals value lives saved across different risks—say, between cancer and noncancer risks.[4] But if the very large gap between expert and lay intuitions cannot be accounted for by a special lay sensitivity to qualitative aspects of risk, then what prompts the divergence would have to lie *outside* the psychometric list: There must be something essential to understanding the psychometric results in that as yet unspecified box on the right side of Figure 8.1. For the subtle risks that are characteristic of expert/lay conflicts, something about how cognition works not yet considered would govern the sense of visceral risk, which in turn would prompt elevated responses to items on the psychometric list. In such cases (not in general) the causal arrow would easily go from perceived risk backward to responses along the psychometric dimensions, rather than from qualitative features of risk forward to perceptions of risk.

Hence this view proposes that the psychometric list might not in fact reveal how lay qualitative perceptions cause lay perceptions of risk, but rather how lay risk perceptions prompt the qualitative responses. Taking seriously that possibility of cause/effect ambiguities for the qualitative dimensions is really all that is needed to start an account in which psychometric responses indeed ride free of any clear correlation with actuarial risk. Critical here is the point that expert/lay controversies are almost always about risks statistically very much smaller than risks we ordinarily attend to at all. If we ordinarily took note of all risks that could be classified as greater than the Environmental Protection Agency's (EPA) one-in-a-million standard, then we would have time to do nothing else all day long than to take note of the risks we were running. A decided peculiarity of sharp expert/lay controversy, therefore, is that it is almost always associated with risks so remote (statistically) that ordinarily they would not prompt any sense of visceral risk at all.

But it is in just that sort of case that it would be most difficult for cues necessarily acquired mostly from everyday experience to function in their ordinarily reliable way: It is in just that context that cues that ordinarily signal danger might be irrelevant to any actual danger, or that cues that ordinarily signal security might do so in circumstances in which the actual danger (on a social scale) is large enough to prompt strong concern if that danger were recognized. Hence it is also for just such risks—that is, for statistically very subtle risks—that it would most easily happen that perceived risk—the visceral sense of risk that is really at issue here—could show little connection with risk as judged by experts. That would give us what seems to me a far more plausible explanation of expert/lay conflict than supposing that "kills few" versus "kills a lot" or something of that nature were important only for experts and of so little interest to the rest of us that you have to fish, or wish, to find any lay concern about how big a risk is at issue in the psychometric correlations.

Suppose (to take the most obvious examples) that nuclear waste prompts visceral concern far beyond what expert judgment would seem to warrant, but traffic fatalities do not. This would push toward an exaggerated (relative to expert assessments) sense of actuarial risk about nuclear waste danger relative to traffic danger. But even after that exaggeration people are still ordinarily aware that traffic fatalities are a very much larger absolute hazard. Correlating responses across many such items (the psychometric procedure) might then swamp any particular correlation between danger in its usual sense and perceived risk by the stronger correlations between the subjective (hence more pliable) qualitative dimensions and perceived risk. And it does not help much to restrict the attempt to find correlations to just the sorts of cases in which expert/lay conflicts are most common—that is, to cases involving radiation and chemicals. Even with this restriction, effects of actuarial risk on lay perception of risk are slim, as a leading proponent of the psychometric view (Slovic 1992) has himself pointed out.

An Alternative View

So now consider the possibility that lay perceived risk (for these very-low-probability cases) may be really governed by neither the qualitative nor the quantitative inputs of Figure 8.1 but instead by something not yet discussed (something that would fill in the dotted input box of Figure 8.1). Then the causal arrow linking perceptions of both qualitative and quantitative features of risk may go backward: from perceived risk back to what on the psychometric account are causes, as suggested by the dotted connections in Figure 8.1.[5]

In that account psychometric responses reflect perceived risk rather than explain it. And if causality in fact runs backward (to what has usually been assumed), then the responses of participants in the surveys that provide the data for the psychometric correlations would be substantially arbitrary. A person would be merely picking out a sort of portfolio of worrisome aspects of a target risk that seems to fit with the intensity of their perception of this risk. If you sense a risk as worrisome, then your responses to whatever dimensions of risk are offered would certainly be biased upward by that worry, and the converse would hold if you are not particularly worried about a risk. The more strongly this risk prompts worries, the stronger that bias would tend to be. So if we compared two individuals identical except that one was inclined to worry about risk X and the other was not, and we arbitrarily selected one risk dimension from the nineteen listed in Table 8.1, then we could expect to see the worried individual rank that arbitrarily chosen dimension in a more worried way than the relaxed individual. If we happen to pick "voluntariness," for example, the risk would seem less voluntary to the worried individual; if we happened to pick "benefits," there would seem to be lower benefit to the worried individual; and so on. That is what I mean by suggesting reverse causation. For the subtle risks at issue here, in this view, the worry (or absence of worry) comes first and shades the response on the risk dimensions, rather than responses on the risk dimensions coming first and then governing the overall perception of how much to worry. And if this were so, then such surveys would necessarily reveal correlations between the psychometric dimensions offered and the perceived risk, even in the most extreme (and implausible) case in which there was no causal relation whatsoever.

This brief sketch might reasonably strike a reader as an unlikely story. But I think it is in fact the most nearly correct story. In *Dealing with Risk* I tried to spell it out in enough detail and with enough review of the psychological literature that supports it to make it a very plausible story. And I then used case materials to test its implications and to reach what I think is a reasonably convincing story.

That story turns on the interacting roles of what I call the three Fs: fungibility, framing, and fairness, but with fungibility—in particular *missing* fungibility—most fundamental. Framing in the sense used here depends on whether taking precautions is seen as a way of avoiding a loss, or as a way of making a gain: We are ordinarily much more willing to incur costs to avoid a possible loss than to make an equivalent possible gain. Fairness depends on whether the party who will have to pay the costs is perceived as being to blame for the risk. But emphatically most important for the cases that are the focus of expert/lay conflicts is the possibility of missing fungibility. Fungibility is missing when individuals are alert to the danger in a situation but not to the opportunity, or alert to opportunity but not to danger.

If we are noticing only one side of the ordinarily inevitable competition between opportunity and danger, there is nothing to balance: Either danger or opportunity alone is all that seems at issue, and we always prefer less of the first and more of the second. Hence there is nothing to trade off, weigh, or assess. Then danger (or opportunity for the opposite case) is not fungible: Accepting a bit more risk buys us nothing (or, for the opposite case, giving up a bit of opportunity buys us nothing). But realistically, in almost every case some balance between caution and boldness is needed to make a prudent choice. Both kinds of missed fungibility occur (where opportunity is neglected and where danger is neglected). But it is the former that overwhelmingly predominates in the case of environmental controversies.

When fungibility is missing, perceptions of framing and fairness, rather than being independent factors, usually fall in train with perceptions relating to fungibility. Hence the presence or absence of fungibility becomes the key issue. As with the reversed causation claim, this risk matrix account is worked out in detail in *Dealing with Risk*, but here I only review and elaborate on one particular aspect of it, which turns on the specially salient role that everyone notices is played by concern over cancer.

The Special Role of Cancer

Consider a fractionally microscopic risk of cancer as opposed to a risk of misspending a tiny fraction of some large budget—say $1 million of the Department of Energy (DOE) budget. Human judgment is pervasively marked by anchor-and-adjust effects. Far more than we consciously notice, we are somehow cued into a "ballpark," and then we adjust from there. When no good cues to the right ballpark are available, we are remarkably apt to use whatever does happen to be available. Amos Tversky and Daniel Kahneman (1981) demonstrated large effects on estimates of the population of unfamiliar foreign countries by spinning a carnival wheel in front of the groups of college students making the estimate: The groups clearly anchored on whatever number showed up on the wheel. Many other experiments have confirmed such effects, and much public opinion research has shown that recently salient news items can have huge effects when they have little competition in providing the anchor for public responses.

In the context we are considering, even one chance in a million of a cancer gives us something to anchor on: some single individual with cancer. I expect that every reader will be able to feel the tug of this anchor but that virtually no reader has any such immediate intuitive sense of what is lost by DOE wasting $1 million of its budget. It is not that, if challenged, you could not come up with something. But the cancer danger is something with an immediate intuitive bite, whereas the opportunity forgone by inefficiently spending $1 million of the DOE budget has almost no bite at all. Perhaps that is because if we were readily prompted to think of alternative uses of resources, it would easily be burdensome, since we are making choices about using resources all the time. Life is easier because we mostly just do the usual thing without thinking about alternatives. And perhaps it would be uncomfortable to be too readily prompted to second thoughts, so that anytime you spend $5 for something you could easily get along without, you are easily reminded that you could have given that $5 to a charity that would provide a decent meal to a hungry child.

Yet where there is an easily visualized anchor for fractionally tiny misuse of resources, it can win attention. Most American readers will be aware of the Air Force's $500 hammer, though this is already from another decade. More recently, a House of Representatives banking scandal that in fact cost taxpayers nothing played an important role in the big Republican victory in the 1994 congressional elections. But in each of these cases ordinary people had a ready anchor for a sense that something outrageous had occurred: Everyone knows that a hammer should not cost $500 and that ordinary people cannot write checks for money they do not have in the bank. So it is not that dollar costs do not win our attention. It is that dollar costs do not win our attention unless they are substantial relative to some familiar anchor (the price of a hammer, writing bad checks). But deaths, and for the various reasons discussed next, cancer deaths especially, readily prompt our attention.

Once a matter has got our attention, the powerful human propensity to seek causes comes into play. What amounts to socially shared scapegoats is a universal feature of human cultures, though we use a different word when the cognitive propensity that accounts for scapegoating takes a form we see as sensible. Then we talk of the admirable human characteristics of curiosity, restless searching for truth, willingness to proceed on the basis of bold speculation. So we might say (or not, contingent on a taste for provocation) that science is scapegoating subjected to discipline. A scientist looks for the guilty party (what is causing this odd thing that has caught my attention), and then pursues a hunch with the intensity of a seventeenth-century seeker of witches.

We are not in fact more amply supplied today than were our ancestors with what we see as believable accounts of what causes disease. But now it is clear (from the brute fact of huge increases in longevity, and elimination of whole categories of disease) that the persistent belief in reasons for misfortune that humans have always exhibited has finally reached some convincing connection with what actually causes some of these misfortunes.

"Everyone knows" that germs cause certain diseases, parasites others, and that with age people (like automobiles and furniture) tend to become worn out. If we set aside accidents and war (which, however, would not contravene the argument sketched next), then two of the three current major killers, heart and circulation diseases, are readily assimilated into our well-entrenched sense that as things get old they wear out. What is left as a predominant life-threatening category without an intuitive explanation is cancer.

Cancer somehow invades otherwise healthy organs of the bodies, and then insidiously spreads to other parts of the body until a person is killed. That leaves us feeling the need to identify something, especially something blamable, that might be causing this terrible thing. But an expert-level discussion of what causes cancer is extremely complicated (there are multiple stages, many contributing factors from a variety of sources, yielding many different kinds of cancer). Even with all the complications the story is still far from complete. Hence there is a special readiness to believe that some simple hidden cause of cancer has been found. And if this is given moral force—if that hidden cause provides a culprit—then the power to seize attention becomes very potent indeed.

Dread as an Explanation

How much can be accounted for by a special dread of cancer? And then how much by an especially great dread of cancer caused by radiation, which is invisible and therefore cannot easily be guarded against? But this dread explanation of what causes some risks to be treated with concern that goes far beyond their actuarial significance warrants at least a bit of suspicion. Does it really explain why a risk is especially feared to say that it is a dreaded risk? Would Molière have something to say about that?

It is certainly true that given the salience of cancer (as a very big contributor to mortality), and given its peculiar properties, then *so long as fungibility can be easily missed,* cancer has a powerful potential to trigger special concern. And that concern can quickly come to be guarded by powerful social and emotional commitments. All that seems required is that a risk of cancer, however small, become linked, however weakly, with a candidate for a guilty party. Some risks are indeed dreaded, however naive it may be to suppose that saying a risk is dreaded explains why it is dreaded. But now dreadedness derives from rather than accounts for the way the risk is perceived.

This inverted form of dread is more discriminating or at least more specialized than suggested by the usual talk of dread of cancer or even of dread of invisible radiation that can cause cancer. Few people exhibit any special dread or ordinarily even any special interest in cancer caused by radiation if the source is medical x-rays, or radioactive detectors in smoke alarms, or cosmic rays in airplanes or on a high-altitude vacation. What all these have in common is that anyone can see that preventing exposure to radiation by giving up these things would also entail giving up something we would like to have. There is fungibility here between what we have to gain from more caution and what we would have to give up by more caution.

Consider the instructive case of risk of lung cancer from exposure to indoor radon. Despite EPA efforts the public has never shown great concern with the threat of indoor radon, though exactly what EPA has tried to warn the public about is cancer that might be caused by invisible radiation from radon gas in homes. But if there is an unusually high concentration of radon gas in your house, it is coming from the ground beneath your house. Who is the culprit? Apparently God is the culprit, and God cannot be sued. Therefore the cost of doing something about radon—even the cost of finding out how much radon is there by ordering a test—is not a cost that can entirely escape your attention, since you will have to pay it yourself. So here there is no accountable culprit. And you then cannot miss fungibility: awareness that caution might entail costs. So dread of cancer caused by invisible radiation, under these conditions, turns out (as that is reflected by press coverage, environmental activism, and so on) to be no longer very consequential.

But change the situation a bit. Suppose it is not your home but a home you are considering buying? At this point, for many people, dread enters. But now also fungibility has been lost, since testing for radon is ordinarily (in many places now, by law) a cost to the seller. The point here, of course, is not that the test is not worth the cost, but that dread commonly enters when a person's alertness to the cost of taking precautions slips off-screen. That would not apply to readers who in fact have had their own houses tested for radon. But for many people, even many people as intelligent and well informed as readers of this book are likely to be, the point will apply, so that they can experience firsthand dread arising as a reflection of whether the context—here merely a verbal context—is one that prompts fungibility or not. But in ordinary language, it sounds absurd to say that I dread the risk of cancer from radon radiation, but only if someone else is going to pay the cost of taking precautions against it.

So it sometimes turns out to be easy, we can observe, to generate dread, and then moral outrage—that "they" are leaving "us" exposed to deadly radon, provided there is a "them" to be blamed—which is precisely what has sometimes happened with respect to the decidedly small component of radon that can come from drinking water. If there is an external entity that can be taken as responsible, fungibility is likely to disappear. The process then readily yields a powerful moral sense that something wrong is going on. And moral wrongdoing is not to be explained away by accountants and economists talking about cost-effectiveness. Nor would it be right to let such a matter be easily forgotten (so if there is someone moved to remind you, you will be open to such reminders, not annoyed or bored, or dismissive of scaremongering).

Finally, although the discussion has focused on what is special about cancer, familiarity with a series of such episodes opens the door to anchor-and-adjust effects for other subtle risks that in one way or another can be perceived as "looking like" the cancer cases. Subtle threats, when fungibility is missed and a culprit is available, become a familiar pattern of response, which becomes the anchor for response to parallel subtle threats not necessarily involving cancer—again with the essential proviso that fungibility is missed.

Of course we do not ordinarily see our intuitions as working in the way I have been sketching. Rather, we just see what we see, and if challenged we ordinarily think of reasons why what we see is the reasonable thing to see. Causal reasoning to support challenged intuitions is something we can all produce with remarkable fluency. And in fact when our intuitions are dealing with familiar judgments, not subtle or exotic judgments, intuitions are almost always reliable, and hence there is an advantage to ordinarily acting on them with confidence and to dismissing merely verbal counters. That sets in place habits that maintain confidence at a high level even when the basis of an intuition is badly flawed and weak, so long as nothing from direct experience conflicts with it. How strong such effects are is difficult to appreciate.

How Intuition Works

Dealing with Risk exploits a simple puzzle ("chips"[6]) that usually prompts a very confident intuition that happens to be flatly wrong. With that exemplar, I try to engage a reader in a demonstration of how stubbornly intuitions can resist mere logic. The difficulty of challenging a clear intuition is very much greater than we would suppose until confronted with a sharp demonstration of how far even intelligent and sophisticated people (you and me, for example) are vulnerable to powerful convictions about things that very simple arguments show to be logically wrong. But conviction commonly yields only reluctantly when challenged by simple counterarguments, even in the "chips" puzzle, where none of the complexity, social pressures, or moral commitment that characterize real situations are present at all.

Effects particularly important for the discussion here develop from the weakness of unaided intuition with respect to probabilities much smaller than those that prompt attention in ordinary life. We see "twoness" effects that transport a suspicion that exposure to X can cause cancer to a powerful intuition that even a microscopic exposure to X might well be causing cancer and indeed ought to be treated as if it did cause cancer ("better safe than sorry").

But given a high enough dose to a vulnerable enough test animal, a great many substances (natural as readily as manmade) can yield an association with cancer (Ames and Gold 1990). Hence there are many opportunities indeed to believe that substances are around that can cause cancer. And if the substance is there because of some human activity, there is also a candidate for culprit. Further, the extended anchor-and-adjust process discussed a moment ago can support great concern even when the risk of cancer is exceedingly small, and sometimes even when the harm at issue is not directly cancer at all.

It is easy to point to other much-publicized examples of beliefs that take sturdy hold on the basis of weak evidence, morally buffered by a candidate for culprit. Characteristically, belief then cannot easily be dislodged when much better evidence turns out to be inconsistent with the original claims—e.g., that Bendectin (a medicine for morning sickness) causes birth defects; that breast implants disrupt immune function; that Agent Orange caused manifold disabilities in U.S. and Australian veterans of the Vietnam War.

These have all been conspicuous noncancer concerns. But birth defects would have a mix of qualities that might rival cancer in readiness to prompt scapegoating. Bendectin, additionally, got a special start from parallels with the history of thalidomide, in which a drug administered to pregnant women did indeed cause severe birth defects. Agent Orange enlists sympathy for draftees in an unpopular war. Hence, in one way or another, all these cases can look enough like the cancer context to provide the anchor for very firm anchor-and-adjust assessments of where blame is due. And all are supported by a particular intense activist incentive, since all provide victims (and their lawyers) with a substantial stake in that belief. As this is written, Gulf War syndrome is the focus of very active controversy, this time not involving an unpopular war, but now with the Agent Orange extension of the usual pattern to guide popular intuition.

"Do No Harm"

The main remedial proposal in *Dealing with Risk* (the "do no harm" proposal) turns on the possibility of engaging everyday intuition about a fair *process* to balance every day but in this context perhaps severely misjudged intuitions about a fair *judgment*. In the argument reviewed here, problems of that sort arise when fungibility is missed. Hence cases in which "do no harm" would play a substantial role would be just those cases in which lay intuition turns out to have been blind to features of a situation that lay intuition itself would judge relevant if noticed. A partial remedy might be an explicit component of a risk decision process that asks that *if a proposal is justified by an intent to save lives, then there ought to be reasonable confidence that the proposal would in fact be more likely to save lives than to cost lives.*[7]

This is a very modest proposal. Most citizens would suppose that this is already what we do. Indeed, the most fundamental point about implementation of this proposal is that it be framed in a way that fits comfortably with commonsense intuitions about how a fair process ought to work. Nevertheless, taking a "do no harm" requirement seriously entails something very different from the compounding of cautious assumptions, focused single-mindedly on just one target effect, that routinely is taken to be adequate risk assessment. The "do no harm" standard is intended to appeal to the everyday intuition that it would be unfair to impose regulations in the name of protecting health and safety that are not in fact based on reasonable confidence that they are more likely to save people than to kill people. If built securely into a risk assessment process, that modest standard would put something on the table when single-minded "better safe than sorry" intuitions are contingent on not noticing that some things intended to make us safer may in fact leave us sorrier.

The problem, recall, turns on the enhancement through anchor-and-adjust processes of the danger side of the almost inevitable tension between danger and opportunity. That leads to wholly one-sided intuitions, however, *only* when accompanied by invisibility of opportunity forgone. That invisibility occurs when opportunity sacrificed lacks a cognitively significant anchor, as illustrated earlier with possible misallocation of DOE spending. Challenging intuitions prompted by that unbalanced sensitivity is very difficult. Mere evidence and argument are unpromising alone, since without well-motivated effort, we are unlikely to see much sense in a logical argument that goes against a clear intuition. We much more easily believe that there must be something wrong with the argument than that there is something wrong with our clearly held intuition. Even a modest degree of openness becomes likely only if the door to doubting our present intuition has been opened by a clearly contrary intuition (so we notice that both cannot be right).

Concern about a fair process does not have the ready bite that concern about a fair result does—even if, as required here, the process is specifically framed to fit comfortably with commonsense intuitions about fairness. Thus "do no harm" is not likely to be effective unless mandated by courts or legislators (such that the obligation to take that kind of assessment seriously cannot be easily evaded), though in some circumstances, perhaps even administrative rules might prove workable. But if formally in place, "do no harm" might make a considerable difference in how often we can make social risk choices that will look sensible rather than bizarre to our grandchildren. This is a perspective that was of lively concern to Wildavsky, so that the kind of net risk assessment required for "do no harm" received his emphatic attention (e.g., Wildavsky 1988d). What is novel in the proposal here is only that a widely noticed point is framed in a way intended to appeal not only to everyday intuitions about efficiency but also to everyday intuitions about fairness.

Notes

This chapter has profited from advice from the editors and from Jonathan Baron, Cass Sunstein, John Bailar, and Karl Dake. And I owe a debt to Mary Douglas for providing the opportunity to write it.

1. Alternatively, the analysis might invoke theoretical or commonsense considerations (in this case both) to make a variable the first to be considered by the regression routine, or to report this "forced" result as well as the result of simply letting the routine run. The forced result, given a well-argued justification, has considerable merit compared to the more usual procedure of effectively ceding control of the analysis to the mindless number crunching of the computer program.

2. Anyone who asks people to say what they think about risk finds that what is explicitly associated with risk is primarily the threat of actual danger. And just as with the experts, if asked to define danger, the rest of us will talk about a sense that concerns both the magnitude of possible damage and how likely it is that such damage would occur. But it is common in survey work to obtain very different responses, depending on how questions are framed. In the psychometric work people are not directly asked about how they define risk but instead are prompted to respond to their visceral sense of various risks along various candidate features of risk. (See the discussion of visceral versus actuarial senses of risk in Margolis 1996, chapter 2.) A question then arises about which kind of response should most influence policy choices: the visceral responses of ordinary citizens that show up in the psychometric surveys or the responses of those same citizens when directly asked to define risk—or even the roughly similar (to the direct question) typical responses people give if asked how much more should be spent to save a life from one sort of risk as against another. Median responses (see note 4) tend to stay close to unity and, in sharp contrast to what is implied by many regulatory standards responding to public concern, rarely stray beyond a factor of two of actuarial risk. See Wibecke 1994. A detailed survey and analysis of these matters is in Jenni forthcoming.

3. In ordinary language, a constructed or negotiated result is a result deliberately worked out. But as Marx famously remarked, men make history but not as they intend, and the same goes for beliefs, only more so. So talk of knowledge as constructed, or negotiated, turns what should be an important but uncontroversial insight about the social character of knowledge into an amorphous beast that wants to gobble up far more than it reasonably ought to be fed.

4. A minority of subjects, however, report far more extreme positions. Work on what Jonathan Baron (1996) and his collaborators call "protected values" is relevant here. An effect that Baron has repeatedly found is that, with respect to acts that his subjects deem morally outrageous, there is commonly a marked reluctance to allow—and for some sub-

jects a firm denial—that quantitative considerations are relevant at all. A fraction of respondents in the "how much" surveys mentioned in note 2 also exhibit such incommensurability, as if destroying half as many people (or dolphins, or species) is not seen as any better than killing twice as many. Apparently, even the smaller outrage is as bad as it is possible to be, so more harm is not any worse. But no one is likely to really believe that. (Someone who did might then see Oskar Schindler's saving of a minute fraction of holocaust victims as worthless: The situation was just as bad whether he acted or not.) So what does it mean if I deny that twice as much harm is worse than half as much? What we are seeing is perhaps a person's report on a visceral response. Dollars come in nicely quantitative units. A person can notice the difference between $15.52 and $14.98. But disgust and outrage do not come in any such units.

5. In Figure 8.1 I have left out a reverse connection from perceived risk back to perceived quantitative effects, reflecting the earlier discussion of why this relation, though it must be present, fails to show itself in the psychometric work.

6. Suppose three white poker chips are in a cup: one with a blue dot on each side, another with a red dot on each side, and the third with a blue dot on one side and a red dot on the other. Without looking you pick one chip and lay it on the table. This turns out to show a red dot on the up side. What is the chance that there is also a red dot on the down side? Overwhelmingly, the response is 1/2. And ordinarily people feel very confident about that. The correct answer is 2/3.

7. This is a variant of an idea considered in various forms by many others. See Graham and Wiener 1995; Warren and Marchant 1993; Viscusi 1994; and many earlier, less extensively elaborated proposals, such as Lave 1981 and Wildavsky 1988d.

Part Five

Culture and the Environment: Empirical Studies

Chapter Nine

Cultural Theory, Postmaterialism, and Environmental Attitudes

GUNNAR GRENDSTAD
PER SELLE

Too often researchers avoid comparing theories, proceeding as if their own theory was the only source of enlightenment. Pitting rival theories against one another enables the researcher not only to assess a theory's relative explanatory power but also to evaluate better the validity of its basic assumptions and theoretical coherence. If nothing else, comparison provides a valuable antidote to the perfectionist impulse that demands a theory that explains everything. A theory should be judged not against an impossible standard of perfection but, as Aaron Wildavsky was fond of saying, by how well it performs in comparison with rival theories. "How's your husband, Mrs. Cohen?" he used to recount. "Compared to whom?" replies the good lady.

In this chapter we juxtapose two theories of political culture: the theory of postmaterialism developed by Ronald Inglehart (1971, 1977, 1979, 1990) and the "Cultural Theory" developed by Mary Douglas, Aaron Wildavsky, and others (Douglas 1982a, 1982b; Wildavsky 1987a; Thompson, Ellis, and Wildavsky 1990). Since its inception in the early 1970s, Inglehart's concept of postmaterialism has undergone extensive cross-national empirical testing. Douglas and Wildavsky's Cultural Theory, in contrast, has only recently been the subject of systematic survey research. In this chapter we consider both Cultural Theory and postmaterialist theory using a 1993 Norwegian national survey of environmental attitudes.

Comparing Postmaterialism and Cultural Theory

Postmaterialism, as Inglehart conceives it, is a new value system that gained importance in Western industrialized countries after World War II. It reflects the postwar generation's movement away from materialist values such as political order and economic stability, and toward postmaterialist values such as political participation and an increased public voice in government decisions. Cultural Theory posits that the cultures of fatalism, individualism, egalitarianism, and hierarchy have recurred throughout history, although the relative strength of each culture within a society changes across time and space. Wildavsky (1991d), in particular, has emphasized the importance of the rise of egalitarianism in the postwar West. Inglehart and Wildavsky have both used their theories to make sense of the rise of the "New Left," the "New Social Movements," and the "New Politics" as well as environmentalism.

The theory of postmaterialism, as formulated by Inglehart, rests upon two conjoined hypotheses. First, the "scarcity hypothesis" states that individuals tend to place a high priority on whatever is in short supply. Second, the "socialization hypothesis" claims that individuals tend to retain a given set of value priorities throughout adult life once this set has been established in their formative years. To these hypotheses, Inglehart adds Abraham Maslow's (1954) hierarchy of needs, in which physiological needs precede higher-order needs, so as to provide his theory with the *direction* of value change. The formative experience of economic and political security, Inglehart argues, tends to promote the adoption of postmaterialist values in adult life.

Materialism incorporates preferences for a stable economy that will yield material prosperity, and for a safe political system that will sustain law and order. Postmaterialism broadly encompasses self-actualization, self-esteem, esthetics, intellectual needs, and a "greater emphasis on social solidarity" (Inglehart 1987, 1292). Postmaterialism redefines women's role in the society from that of complementing to that of competing with men's positions. It also entails greater political participation in new social movements, especially environmental movements.

Both Inglehart and Wildavsky aspire to building a generalizable theory that transcends particular societies, and both of their theories also emphasize value conflicts within a society. Both postmaterialist theory and Cultural Theory reject the assumption that there is only one political culture within a given society. Both theories work at a sufficiently high level of abstraction that they can be used as a basis for cross-national studies as well as for comparative work within nations. Indeed, Inglehart's sociopsychological theory of postmaterialism has perhaps been the most innovative empirical approach used in large-scale comparative research since the wane of structural-functionalism in the 1960s.

Despite these similarities, though, the two theories differ markedly both in the scholarly traditions out of which they emerge and in the theoretical structures in which they are embedded. Each theory differs radically in its treatment of institutions and cognition. Moreover, Cultural Theory is typological, whereas Inglehart's postmaterialist theory is not. Cultural change is emphasized in both theories, but they differ profoundly on the causes of change and the pervasiveness of change. Table 9.1 summarizes some of the similarities and differences between the two theories, which we explore in greater depth in the subsequent discussion.

Theoretical Traditions

Inglehart's conception of political culture builds upon the rich "civic culture" tradition of the 1960s (Almond and Verba 1963). This sociopsychological theory emphasizes political culture as subjective political competence, that is, as "attitudes, beliefs and feelings about politics current in a nation at a given time" (Almond and Powell 1978, 25). The "civic culture" tradition, however, was also rooted in the structural-functionalism that was prevalent in the 1950s and 1960s. The structural-functionalism of the "civic culture" tradition was evident in the way "political culture" was used as the intermediate level connecting structure and action. The decline of Parsonian functionalism in the 1960s and the consequent deemphasizing of structural models propelled sociocultural theory toward the sort of "micro models" typified by postmaterialist theory.

Inglehart anchored his theory in the "Michigan school" of voting behavior, which made the individual the unit of analysis. In so doing, Inglehart created a theory that could be readily tested through systematic survey research. Testability came at a price, however, for postmaterialism neglected the institutions, structures, and traditions that shape individual consciousness.

Cultural Theory rests upon the micro wing of Durkheimian anthropology (Wuthnow et al. 1984; Collins 1994b). This tradition emphasizes how institutions affect individuals' thought and action, thereby rejecting methodological individualism (Wildavsky 1991c; Wildavsky 1994a). Yet a theory's unit of analysis becomes ambiguous when the individuals are embedded in institutions. Such theories, therefore, are not easily tested by surveys. Thus, when we operationalize Cultural Theory using survey responses, the individual in a sense becomes a disaggregated institutional proxy.

Cultural Theory rehabilitates functionalism, although functions are associated not with entire societies, as they usually were during the 1950s, but rather with institutions and subcultures within societies. Functionalism posits a dynamic and self-stabilizing system that, in the absence of external shocks, feeds on itself to create an equilibrium. When functions are associated with different ways of life within a society, Cultural Theory can be viewed as an institutional theory of multiple equilibria in which different cultural contexts have opposing effects on the action of the individual (Grendstad and Selle 1995). Cultural Theory aims to integrate individuals and institutions, although different theorists have interpreted this integration differently.[1]

The theory of postmaterialism has, apart from macroeconomic considerations, no institutional references. Since it is based on the assumption of a "universal" process in which materialism irreversibly leads to postmaterialism as economic

TABLE 9.1   Postmaterialism and Cultural Theory: A Collation

	Postmaterialism	Cultural Theory
Theoretical Structure	Taxonomic classification	Typological from dimensions
Theory's coverage	Universal and postwar	Universal and ahistoric
Political culture	Attitudes, beliefs, and feelings	Mutually supporting social relations and biases as way of life
Major goal	Analyze postwar value shift	Match biases and social relations
Academic traditions	"Michigan school" of voting behavior; Weberian	The Micro wing of Durkheimian anthropology
Developmental	Yes	No
Comparison	Central	Central
Conflicts	New and central between materialists and post-materialists	Enduring and central between ways of life
Concept of functionalism	Rejected	Cultural functionalism
Microfoundations	Social psychology	Cognition
Concept of culture	Attitudes, beliefs, and feelings	Cognition and way of life
Institutions	Nonexistent	Central
Unit of analysis	Individual	Individual in context
Analytical fallacy	Institutional neglect	Vertical conflation
Decisions	Central	Central
Cognition	Internalized values, norms, attitudes	i) Habits and routines ii) Decisional calculations
Cultural Change	Central; one-dimensional	Central; multidimensional
Primary cause of cultural change	Economic	Surprise
Values imprinted	Formative years	Continuous
Subsequent individual value change	None	Extensive
Societal change	Generational replacement	Waxing and waning ways of life
Methodological Constraints	Item ranking corresponding to dual-outcome decision-making	Item rating corresponding to multidimensionality of biases
Methodological flaw	Misclassification of "materialists"	Unclassified individuals
Status of Environmentalism	Internalized	Co-opted

security increases, the theory is in no need of institutional accounts. Postmaterialism's isolation of the individual thereby becomes a means for separating structures and values. This not only echoes the wane of functionalism in the 1960s, but it also links postmaterialism with the notions of a postmodern society consisting of disconnected spheres (Lyotard 1984). In part, the "postmodern" move away from the ambitions of coherence implies that different societal spheres are disintegrating (Bell 1976). Unlike the neoconservatives, however, who fear a "new mass man" because of the lack of integrating institutions, Inglehart offers a more optimistic future by relying for integration on Maslow's hierarchy of needs.

Microfoundations

Postmaterialism is a theory of socialization. The values internalized by the individual during the formative years provide value stability in the adult years. The institutions in which an individual spends his adult life are thus treated as relatively insignificant. Cultural Theory, in contrast, downplays the individual's formative socialization in favor of the formative power of institutions to shape values and beliefs throughout a person's life. Because of its attention to the intervening role of institutions, Cultural Theory leads us to anticipate more changes in an adult's basic values than does Inglehart's theory, which predicts a high degree of individual value stability stemming from formative socialization.

Recently Inglehart (1987, 1990, 1994) has begun to modify his theory's socialization assumptions in significant ways, complementing Maslow's hierarchy of needs with a theory of diminishing marginal utility (DMU). DMU states that anything being added to something that is appreciated provides less additional value (or utility) than what has been added previously. For example, hiring an additional policeman adds less security to your neighborhood than did the preceding officer. Diminishing marginal returns enables the theory to account not only for movement from materialism to postmaterialism but also for a reverse flow from postmaterialism to materialism. Unfortunately, Inglehart neglects this second option and only uses the economic argument of diminishing utility to buttress his argument of a materialist exodus (Abramson and Inglehart 1995, 121, 129). Whether fully admitted or not, DMU nevertheless provides the theory of postmaterialism with more flexibility, and perhaps longevity as well.

Cultural change is central to both theories, although they treat change in fundamentally different ways. The theory of postmaterialism is founded on the observation of a cultural shift in postwar Western societies from materialist values to postmaterialist values. Inglehart's argument, bountifully supported by empirical data (Abramson and Inglehart 1995), is that societal value change has occurred primarily in one direction: from materialism to postmaterialism. If there were to be a severe economic downturn, Inglehart's theory would lead us to expect movement back toward materialism, at least among the young who would be socialized under these new, more adverse economic conditions. By contrast, Cultural Theory's idea of change is more indeterminate and allows for a greater number of possible individual-level changes. Cultural Theory envisions two-way traffic at the individual level between all four cultures, thus generating a total of twelve possible micro-level changes (Thompson 1992; also Thompson, Ellis, and Wildavsky 1990).

The theory of postmaterialism identifies the economy as fundamental for cultural change. "One of the most important sources of cultural variation," Inglehart claims, "is a given society's level of economic development" (1990, 31). The cultural shift from materialist to postmaterialist priorities is described as a "universal process" that "should occur in any country that moves from conditions of economic insecurity to relative security" (Inglehart and Abramson 1994, 347). Yet at the same time Inglehart says that the value imprints in the formative years are subject to "certain circumstances"; they "depend . . . on the relationship between one's values and the setting in which one lives" (Inglehart 1979, 310–311). Another term for "circumstance" and "setting" is "institution"—that is, how school systems, welfare systems, and party systems affect whether postmaterialist values will crystallize or not. In these passages we see a risk that the theory of postmaterialism may invoke institutions in an ad hoc fashion when its predictions fail. Postmaterialism may jeopardize its theoretical foundations if the theory resigns the "universal application" of postmaterialism to contingent contexts. Consequently, the present version of the theory still depends too much on retrodictive empirical knowledge, which perhaps stems from its being an inductive theory.

For Cultural Theory the role of the economy is marginal. The theory identifies two factors for continuous individual value change. One element points to the bounded rationality (i.e., cultural bias) of institutionally embedded individuals. The other points out that life itself may defy our expectations. These two elements combine to explain cultural change in an as yet rudimentary theory of surprise. Surprise is the accumulated gap between expectations and observations. Because the theory of surprise jettisons determinism, Cultural Theory does not predict who becomes a fatalist, an individualist, an egalitarian, or a hierarchist, though it does predict the sorts of defections that will tend to occur as a result of certain sorts of surprises (Thompson 1992).

Methodological Constraints

In survey research, we can distinguish between ranking and rating procedures. Which format is chosen is obviously important, since there is abundant evidence that the format in which questions are posed can strongly affect survey responses (see Inglehart 1994, 291). The ranking method, which Inglehart's theory uses, forces the respondent to rank order several choices, all of which may be desirable. The aim is to identify the values that are most important to the respondent. The rating procedure, on the other hand, allows the respondent to agree or disagree with each statement, usually on a five- or seven-point Likert scale, in order to measure intensity of feeling. The rating procedure opens up the possibility that the respondent may simultaneously express disagreement and agreement with statements that on their face seem to call for a congruent response, or succumb to what survey researchers call an "acquiescence bias," that is, tend to agree with each item. These response patterns, particularly the acquiescence bias, can produce positive correlations between statements that are in fact spurious or meaningless. The rating procedure, however, has the advantage of allowing the researcher to measure multiple value dimensions.

Those researchers who have tried to test Cultural Theory using survey research have opted for the rating method, because it yields multiple dimensions corresponding to the four cultural biases. However, since individuals are scored on each dimension, the procedure may not always consistently classify individuals as fatalists, individualists, egalitarians, or hierarchists. A respondent who is prone to acquiesce to every statement may score high on all four cultural biases, while another, more contrarian respondent could have low scores on all four biases.

Inglehart's ranking method presents respondents with two materialist and two postmaterialist statements. The respondent is asked to identify a first and a second priority and is classified on the basis of how he or she prioritized materialist ("Fight rising prices" and "Maintain order in the nation") and postmaterialist values ("Give people more say in government decisions" and "Protect freedom of speech").

The most cogent critique of Inglehart's methodology has come from Flanagan (1982, 1987), who argues that the concept of postmaterialism is a misnomer and should be replaced by the concept of libertarianism. Flanagan contends not only that the term "libertarianism" captures Inglehart's ideas of postmaterialism more precisely but also that one of the measures of materialism is distinctly *non*material. Though the "Fight rising prices" item clearly measures materialist concerns, the other, "Maintain order in the nation," would seem to measure authoritarianism rather than economic materialism. Adherents of the New Right, Flanagan suggests, might give top priority to the authoritarian option. They may reject both postmaterialism and materialism yet select the materialist item as their second priority because they are less opposed to it than to the postmaterialist values. Because the ranking method allows the researcher only to gauge how a respondent feels about values relative to one another, the method may obscure respondents' attitudes toward certain values. Inglehart's method has no way of distinguishing between the authoritarian adherent of the New Right who is also a thorough economic materialist and the authoritarian New Rightist who despises materialism but despises it less than postmaterialist values.

Flanagan maintains that although Inglehart's theory generates a reliable picture of the antiauthoritarian postmaterialists (the "New Left"), it conflates authoritarians and materialists (i.e., "New Right," "Old Right," and "Old Left"). Inglehart's items, Flanagan (1987) argues, will therefore always overestimate the number of materialists (and underestimate the number of *non*materialists) in a population. Indeed one might add that the whole idea of a New Right would seem to be anomalous in a theory that reserves "law and order" concerns for a supposedly diminishing materialist culture.

Testing Cultural Theory and Postmaterialism

Since the beginning of the 1970s environmentalism has gained momentum in Western politics through expanding governmental agencies, a growth in voluntary environmental organizations, and an increased public concern for the many faces of pollution. Environmentalism, which we define as a cluster of attitudes accenting environmental threats and prioritizing the preservation of nature over economic growth and technological progress, is central to both Cultural Theory and Inglehart's postmaterialist theory.

Industrial society is intimately connected to the concept that Inglehart labels materialism. Industrial society, according to Inglehart, passed a critical stage of material prosperity in the late 1960s: The postwar generation took economic security for granted and developed postmaterialist values. At the same time, however, industrial society generated pollution levels that increasingly worried and then mobilized parts of the public. Proenvironmental attitudes thus penetrated conventional politics at the same time that postmaterialists rejected the very materialist basis that had helped to generate the pollution.

Despite the congruence between environmentalism and postmaterialism, environmentalism was not an integral part of the postmaterialist concept at the inception of the theory. In his original presentation of the theory, Inglehart only briefly mentioned in a footnote that he suspected that behind the increasing concerns over pollution and the environment was a postmaterialist "sensitivity to the esthetic defects of industrial society" (1971, 1012 n. 31). A decade later, however, Inglehart was placing environmentalism at the ideological core of postmaterialism. He now explained that postmaterialists "furnish the ideologues and core support for the environmental, zero-growth and anti-nuclear movements" (1981, 880). More recently still, Inglehart has suggested that environmentalism is not just a postmaterialist issue (1990, 259), but that environmental values are centrally implicated in the categories themselves: "When environmentalism raises questions of environmental quality versus economic growth, it pits Materialist priorities squarely against Postmaterialist ones" (267). Green politics is now generally considered "the archetypical example of postmaterial politics" (Dalton 1994, xiii).

In contrast, environmentalism seems much more loosely connected to the concept of egalitarianism. Equality of condition or strong group solidarity would seem to have no logical or necessary connection to a commitment to environmental preservation. Yet environmentalism has been central to the empirical application of Cultural Theory (Douglas and Wildavsky 1982; Schwarz and Thompson 1990; Wildavsky 1991d). Two features have been hypothesized as critical in generating environmental commitment and attitudes among egalitarians. First, the precarious social life that results from having little in the way of authority to prevent individuals from leaving the group compels the adherents of an egalitarian culture to point to risks on the outside to sustain the vulnerable inside (Douglas and Wildavsky 1982). Second, egalitarians are drawn to an environmental agenda because of their conceptions of natural resources as nonrenewable and rapidly depleting (Thompson, Ellis, and Wildavsky 1990, 62) and of nature as fragile, a "terribly unforgiving place [where] the least jolt may trigger its complete collapse" (Thompson, Ellis, and Wildavsky 1990, 5).

Because individualists believe nature to be resilient, they tend to downplay environmental threats, believing that nature will bounce back and fearing that environmental scares will be used to enhance centralized control and undermine their preferred life of bidding and bargain. Hierarchical adherents believe environmental problems can be managed by experts who know the difference between what is dangerous and what is safe. Up to a point, they believe, nature is resilient, but beyond that it can be fragile. And only the managers and experts can tell us just where that point is. Fatalists see nature as capricious. One can neither predict, plan for, nor learn from its disasters. Some get lucky and avoid nature's wrath, others are swallowed up by it (Thompson, Ellis, and Wildavsky 1990, 26–29; Schwarz and Thompson 1990; Thompson 1996a).

The Hypotheses

From these theories we derive a number of hypotheses, which we then attempt to test. First, we expect egalitarianism to correlate strongly with postmaterialism, because these concepts converge theoretically on political participation and social solidarity, and empirically on New Left politics and new social movements. Egalitarianism should also correlate strongly and negatively with materialism, since these concepts diverge on the role of authority and the need for economic growth.[2]

We expect individualism to correlate moderately with materialism, because these concepts converge on the issue of economic growth. Our expectation is not unambiguous, however, because individualism also points in the direction of democratic values such as free speech and a responsive government, which Inglehart uses to measure postmaterialism.

Adherents of hierarchy and materialism accept tradition and authority, disregard political participation, and repudiate the new social movements. We therefore expect hierarchy to correlate strongly with materialism.

The theory of postmaterialism is silent on the subject of those inactive individuals at the fringes of society, but we nonetheless hypothesize that that the worldview of fatalism will incline its adherents more toward support for authority and the material yields of a growing economy than toward the self-actualizing needs and social solidarity of postmaterialism.

We also expect environmentalism to correlate positively with egalitarianism and negatively with hierarchy, individualism, and fatalism. Inglehart's postmaterialist index should correlate the strongest with environmentalism. We base this prediction not only on Inglehart's own claim that his index relates to "questions of environmental quality versus economic growth" (1990, 267), but also on the fact that our environmental measures pose an explicit trade-off between environmental values and economic values and thus on their face should be closely related to the materialist item of "Fight rising prices."

Measuring Cultures

In the spring of 1993, the International Social Science Programme (ISSP) carried out a survey of public attitudes toward the environment. The Norwegian part of the survey ("Values, Nature, and Environmentalism") included 1,414 respondents. The international survey contained questions designed to measure materialist and postmaterialist priorities, but only the Norwegian survey also included questions measuring cultural bias. Table 9.2 shows the wording and coding of the five predictors we use in this study: fatalism, individualism, egalitarianism, hierarchy, and materialism-postmaterialism.

Two statements were used to measure each of the four cultural biases.[3] The fatalist items measure external efficacy and attitudes toward cooperation; the individualist items measure support for equal opportunity and accumulation of property; the egalitarian items measure commitment to equalizing resources; and the hierarchy items measure support for authority and respect for the past.

In order to increase the validity of the measures of cultural bias, we summed the two questions to create a two-item scale. Table 9.2 shows the descriptive statistics for the four cultures. A perfectly uniform distribution of a variable would yield a mean of 3. Thus the means listed in Table 9.2 indicate a national bias toward individualism and egalitarianism and a rejection of hierarchy and fatalism. Egalitarianism has the highest standard deviation, which suggests that it is the most contested of the four biases.

We constructed the materialism-postmaterialism index by recoding the respondents' first and second priorities in two materialist (M1 and M2) and two postmaterialist (P1 and P2) statements. If the respondent preferred a materialist option as both first and second priorities, we assigned him or her the value 1 (Strong materialist) on the index. If the respondent chose materialism as the first priority and postmaterialism as the second, we assigned the value 2 (Weak materialist). If the respondent opted for postmaterialism as the first priority and materialism as the second, we assigned the value 3 (Weak postmaterialist). If postmaterialism was the first and second priority, the respondent was assigned the value 4 (Strong postmaterialist).

When we treat the materialist-postmaterialist index as a metric as opposed to a discrete variable (see Table 9.2), the mean of the index (2.25) indicates that the Norwegian population is more materialist than postmaterialist (since a uniform distribution would give a mean of 2.5). The sample consists of 20 percent "strong materialists" and 10 percent "strong postmaterialists," and the remaining 70 percent mix the two priorities. Given Norway's successful postwar economic record, which should provide fertile ground for postmaterialist values, these figures are surprisingly low and are below the West European average.[4]

A strength of these measures is that none of them refers to environmentalism. The cultural measures tap attitudes toward economic equality, authority, tradition, and cooperation, and the materialism-postmaterialism measure probes economic security and law and order (the materialist component) and individual ex-

TABLE 9.2   Measuring Cultural Theory and Materialism-Postmaterialism

	Mean	Standard Deviation	N
Fatalism:	2.64	0.86	1,342
Cooperation with others rarely works.			
It seems that whomever you vote for, things go on pretty much the same.			
Individualism:	3.44	0.93	1,267
Everyone should have an equal chance to succeed and fail without government interference.			
If people have the vision and ability to acquire property, they ought to be allowed to enjoy it.			
Egalitarianism:	3.79	1.04	1,302
What this world needs is a fairness revolution to make the distribution of goods more equal.			
I support a tax shift so that the burden falls more heavily on corporations and people with large incomes.			
Hierarchy:	2.72	0.99	1,198
One of the problems with people today is that they challenge authority too often.			
The best way to provide for future generations is to preserve our customs and heritage.			
Materialism-Postmaterialism:	2.25	0.89	1,239

A   Which one thing do you think should be Norway's highest priority, the most important thing it should do?

B   Which one thing do you think should be the next highest priority, the second most important thing it should do?

M1   Maintain order in the nation
P1   Give people more say in government decisions
M2   Fight rising prices
P2   Protect freedom of speech
        Can't choose

		Frequency of Postmaterialism Index		
		N	Percent	Valid Percent
Strong materialist	1	250	18	20
Weak materialist	2	556	39	45
Weak postmaterialist	3	308	22	25
Strong postmaterialist	4	125	9	10
Missing		175	12	

Each of the eight variables of Culture Theory runs on a five-point scale from "strongly disagree" (1) to "strongly agree" (5). The variables used in this chapter are based on a pairwise adding of the two variables pertaining to each culture; each of the four sums was divided by 2 and their decimals truncated in order to restore the original five-point scale. This allows a just comparison with the materialism-postmaterialism four-point scale indicator. Data source: "Values, Nature, and Environmentalism," Norwegian Social Science Data Services, 1993.

pression and political participation (the postmaterialist component). Thus we can be confident that the dependent and independent variables are measuring genuinely distinct phenomena.

The Results

We first report the correlations between the cultural variables themselves (Table 9.3). Postmaterialism is correlated negatively with fatalism (Pearson's $r = -.15$), individualism ($-.17$), and hierarchy ($-.24$). In other words, materialism is positively related to fatalism, individualism, and hierarchy. Postmaterialism is correlated positively with egalitarianism (.12). These results confirm the *direction* of our hypotheses, but the *strength* of the correlations are sometimes markedly less than we expected. The moderate correlation between hierarchy and materialism, though stronger than any of the other three relationships, is still weaker than the theoretical affinity between the concepts led us to predict. Even more striking, egalitarianism is correlated only weakly at best with postmaterialism, which is sharply at variance with our expectation of a strong positive correlation between the two variables.

Among the cultural bias variables, hierarchy and fatalism are the most closely associated (.28). Fatalism's idea of individual futility and hierarchy's idea of authority and tradition seem to combine among the "lowerarchs," those who find themselves at the receiving end of the command line. Individualism is correlated moderately with fatalism (.19) and hierarchy (.18). Egalitarianism is correlated with neither hierarchy (.02) nor fatalism (.05). The negative correlation between individualism's equal opportunity and egalitarianism's equality of results ($-.21$) supports the claim that the major conflict in modern societies is between egalitarianism and individualism (Ellis 1993b).

Our findings also lend some support to Flanagan's contention that Inglehart's materialist item "Maintain order in the nation" measures authoritarian preferences (Panel B in Table 9.3). The strongest correlation between any of the cultural biases and materialist items is that between the authoritarian "Maintain order" item and hierarchy (.18). Fatalism (.11) and individualism (.13) are weakly correlated with this item. On the materialist item "Fight rising prices," none of the cultural bias items showed any significant relationship.

The question we now wish to explore is how strongly related these cultural measures are to environmentalism. We are particularly interested in pitting postmaterialism against egalitarianism to see which of the two quite independent concepts better predicts environmental attitudes.

From the 1993 survey, we used twenty-nine variables that measure environmental attitudes. To generalize the information in these twenty-nine variables, we ran factor analyses (see Appendix). We kept the first principal component as a catchall dimension and labeled it "Environmentalism." Almost all of the variables loaded on this catchall dimension (factor E in Appendix). We also kept eight subdimensions (factors 1–8 in Appendix). The first factor pulled together various "environ-

TABLE 9.3   Cultural Theory and Materialism-Postmaterialism: Relationships Between Indicators (Panel A) and First Priority "Materialist" Items (Panel B)

	Fatalism	Individualism	Egalitarianism	Hierarchy
Panel A				
Individualism	.19			
Egalitarianism	.05	−.21		
Hierarchy	.28	.18	.02	
Materialism-Postmaterialism	−.15	−.17	.12	−.24
Panel B				
First priority				
Maintain order in the nation	.11	.13	−.05	.18
Fight rising prices	.02	.02	−.07	.02

All measures are Pearson's *r* correlation coefficient. Correlations exceeding .10 are two-tailed significant at the .05 level (n = 982). Data source: "Values, Nature, and Environmentalism," Norwegian Social Science Data Services, 1993.

mental dangers" perceived to harm the environment. The second factor, "no recourse," tapped the uneasy relationship between modern life and pristine nature. The third measures individual "willingness to pay" for the protection of the environment. The fourth shows a preference for "economic growth and progress." The fifth brings together questions on "environmental behavior." The sixth measures "animal rights," the seventh taps "passionate vegetarianism," and the final factor is the belief that nature is a struggle for the "survival of the fittest."

By regressing the nine dimensions of environmentalism on the five independent cultural variables, we are able to ascertain how well fatalism, individualism, egalitarianism, hierarchy, and postmaterialism explain the variation in environmental attitudes generally (represented by the catchall dimension E) as well as the various subdimensions of environmental attitudes that we have identified (dimensions 1–8). Table 9.4 reports the results of these analyses.

Egalitarianism and postmaterialism are both associated with the general dimension of environmental attitudes (E). But egalitarianism explains far more of the variation in environmental attitudes than does postmaterialism. Hierarchy and individualism are negatively associated with general environmental attitudes. That is, hierarchical values of authority and tradition and individualistic values of opportunity and property incline people to be less favorably disposed toward environmental values. Fatalism has no relationship at all to this dimension.

If we look only at factor 4, which measures attitudes to economic growth and progress, egalitarianism loses its strong predictive power. This loss may stem from the absence of a trade-off between economy and environmentalism in some of these items. The absence of a trade-off allows materialists, hierarchists, and individualists unambiguously to endorse growth and progress. Indeed, the growth and progress index is remarkably strongly related to hierarchy.[5] Materialism,

TABLE 9.4 Cultural Theory, Postmaterialism, and Subdimensions of Environmental Attitudes: Correlations and Beta Coefficients

		Environmentalism E	Economic growth and progress 4	No Recourse 2	Environmental dangers 1	Willingness to pay 3	Survival of the fittest 8	Passionate vegetarianism 7	Environmental behavior 5	Animal rights 6	R^2
Egalitarianism	r_{xy}	.39	-.14	.24	.21	.16	-.10	.12	.13	.03	
	β	.35	-.07	.22	.18	.14	-.08	.12	.13	.06	.30
Hierarchy	r_{xy}	-.17	.43	.18	-.11	-.09	.02	.13	.00	-.03	
	β	-.12	.34	.14	-.12	-.02	-.04	.13	.01	-.05	.22
Fatalism	r_{xy}	.00	.29	.31	.09	-.16	.16	.08	.00	.01	
	β	.06	.16	.28	.13	-.13	.15	.05	-.01	.00	.19
Individualism	r_{xy}	-.22	.28	-.03	-.08	-.17	.15	.00	-.01	.10	
	β	-.12	.17	-.05	-.05	-.10	.11	.01	.02	.12	12
Materialism-Postmaterialism	r_{xy}	.19	-.25	.00	.08	.11	-.04	.03	.02	-.03	
	β	.11	-.12	.04	.04	.05	.00	.05	.01	-.03	.06
	R^2	.20	.28	.17	.07	.07	.05	.04	.02	.02	

The eight environmental subdimensions (across) are listed in descending order according to their explained variance (in percent). The predictors (down) are sorted in descending order according to their explanatory capacity; we obtain this score by multiplying the correlation coefficient by the beta coefficient and summarizing these product terms across all nine dependent variables (Knoke and Bohrnstedt 1994). Correlation coefficients (r_{xy}) are significant at the .05 level when exceeding |.10|; the regression coefficients (β) are significant at the .05 level when exceeding |.10| (N = 446). Data source: "Values, Nature, and Environmentalism," Norwegian Social Science Data Services, 1993.

however, falls considerably short of hierarchy in predicting this dimension. This is a surprising observation, since materialism, which is partly measured by the "Fight rising prices" item, ought to be better correlated with items that so directly tap attitudes toward economic growth.

Fatalism, egalitarianism, and to a lesser extent hierarchy are associated with the "no recourse" dimension (2), which probes whether modern life irreversibly harms pristine nature. The notion of no recourse fits well with the capricious worldview held by the adherents of fatalism. The finding of a relationship with egalitarianism is consistent with our hypothesis that egalitarians would tend to see nature as terribly fragile and prone to irreversible harms. Individualism and postmaterialism are not correlated with this dimension.

Bearing out our original hypothesis, egalitarianism is also positively correlated with the "environmental dangers" dimension (1). None of the other variables shows much relationship to this dimension, although hierarchy is very slightly inversely related and fatalism shows a slight positive relationship.

On "willingness to pay" to protect the environment (3), only egalitarians and to a lesser extent postmaterialists show positive correlations. Individualists, not surprisingly, are unwilling to pay. The most interesting finding here is that although fatalists, like egalitarians, feel that modern life does terrible harm to nature, they are as unwilling as individualists to pay to protect the environment. Spending money, fatalists evidently believe, is a waste of time and effort: What happens happens and there's not much we can do about it.

The other four, more marginal subdimensions do not seem to be strongly related to any of the cultural measures, although egalitarians are somewhat more likely to report environmental behaviors (5) and to be passionate vegetarians (7), and fatalists and individualists tend to view nature as the survival of the fittest (8).

Table 9.4 summarizes the success of the five independent variables across the nine environmental dimensions. Overall the five variables best explain the dimension of economic growth and progress (4), perhaps because this dimension most directly engages the terms of mainstream political debate today. Although egalitarianism is only moderately related to this specific dimension, it is clearly the most powerful variable across all nine dimensions. This supports the claims of Cultural Theory about the connection between egalitarianism and environmentalism. Hierarchy proved to be a much stronger predictor of environmental attitudes than we expected or than Cultural Theory predicts. The analysis also indicates that adherents of fatalism, however marginalized, do help us to explain environmental attitudes. Individualism proved to be a much less powerful predictor of environmental attitudes than we expected, although on narrowly economic issues the category did have explanatory power.

The biggest surprise is that the materialism-postmaterialism index proved to be the weakest of the five predictors. Our results suggest that either Inglehart is wrong about the relationship between postmaterialist values and environmentalism, or that his measures of postmaterialism and materialism are inadequate.

Conclusions

In this chapter we have critically compared the theory of postmaterialism and Cultural Theory and empirically tested their explanations of environmental values and beliefs. The empirical test has shown that Cultural Theory does surprisingly well in accounting for environmental attitudes, particularly in comparison to the theory of postmaterialism, which accounts for next to nothing in environmental values and beliefs. These results suggest that future survey researchers would do well to include items measuring cultural bias so that the theory can be more fully tested, both in the environmental domain and in other policy domains.

Notes

We thank Hilmar Rommetvedt, Jo Saglie, Kaare Strom, Mike Thompson, and especially Richard Ellis for comments. The Norwegian Science Data Services (NSD) provided the data we used in this chapter, but the NSD is not responsible for our analysis or interpretation of the data.

1. Several debates exist within Cultural Theory. One debate concerns whether the grid and group dimensions constitute an analytic scheme or heuristic device only (Douglas 1982b), or whether these dimensions are part of a larger theory of social patterns (Thompson 1984, 1996a; Schwarz and Thompson 1990). Another debate centers on coherence and the relationship between determinism and volunteerism, and divides between those who understand explanations in terms of organizations (Rayner 1992) and those who rely on attributes of socialized individuals (Dake and Wildavsky 1990; Johnson 1991). Related to this is the dispute as to whether the individual self remains culturally coherent across diverse cultural contexts (Douglas 1982a) or whether the multiple self adapts to different cultural contexts (Schwarz and Thompson 1990; Rayner 1992).

2. In the following, we consider Inglehart's two concepts as opposing poles on the same dimension; a positive correlation with postmaterialism thereby implies a negative correlation with materialism, and vice versa.

3. We adapted these questions from the "Cultural Biases Questionnaires" developed by Karl Dake, Survey Research Center, University of California at Berkeley.

4. In the early 1980s there were 8 percent strong postmaterialists and 31 to 36 percent strong materialists in Norway (Jenssen and Listhaug 1988, 156; see also Lafferty and Knutsen 1985; Knutsen 1986). The Norwegian 1993 figures in Table 9.2 are still below the aggregated (unweighted) 13 percent strong postmaterialists versus 26 percent strong materialists in other West European countries: West Germany 21 versus 24 percent, Netherlands 16 versus 23 percent, Italy 13 versus 25 percent, Ireland 13 versus 26 percent, Great Britain 10 versus 25 percent, and Northern Ireland 5 versus 37 percent.

5. If we remove the one item in this factor that lacks face validity ("Human beings should respect nature because it was created by God"), the relationship with hierarchy, although diminished somewhat, remains strong.

Appendix: Environmentalism and Its Subdimensions: Factor Analyses

	E	1	2	3	4	5	6	7	8
1 Environmental Dangers:									
Air pollution caused by industry is dangerous for the environment	.55	.74	.11	.09	−.09	.00	.15	−.05	.10
Pollution of Norway's rivers, lakes, and streams is dangerous for the environment	.45	.73	−.00	−.05	−.01	.13	.11	−.03	.09
Pesticides and chemicals used in farming are dangerous for the environment	.52	.71	.08	.09	.02	.15	−.05	.08	−.05
Nuclear power stations are dangerous for the environment	.50	.55	.30	.17	−.04	−.06	−.08	.11	−.21
A rise in the world's temperature caused by the "greenhouse effect" is dangerous for the environment	.51	.54	.00	.15	−.24	.06	.03	.17	.25
Air pollution caused by cars is dangerous for the environment	.58	.49	.22	.18	−.21	.14	.15	−.14	−.22
2 No Recourse:									
Economic growth always harms the environment	.46	.05	.71	.25	−.15	.07	−.13	−.01	.05
Almost everything we do in modern life harms the environment	.47	.18	.69	.10	−.13	.02	.11	−.06	.01
Any change humans cause in nature—no matter how scientific—is likely to make things worse	.37	.16	.69	−.15	−.10	.08	.16	.11	.08
Overall, modern science does more harm than good	.23	.01	.65	−.07	.12	.02	.08	.31	.16
Nature would be at peace/harmony if only human beings would leave it alone	.32	.16	.54	.06	.12	.02	.18	.02	.15
It is too difficult for someone like me to do much about the environment	−.16	−.22	.36	−.20	.08	−.10	−.08	.08	.15
3 Willingness to Pay:									
How willing would you be to pay much higher prices in order to protect the environment?	.63	.15	.03	.83	−.06	.17	.08	.04	.09
How willing would you be to pay much higher taxes in order to protect the environment?	.56	.06	−.01	.81	−.12	.18	−.02	.05	−.04
How willing would you be to accept cuts in your standard of living in order to protect the environment?	.64	.11	.10	.76	−.16	.20	.09	.04	−.03

(continues)

Appendix: Environmentalism and Its Subdimensions: Factor Analyses (*continued*)

	E	1	2	3	4	5	6	7	8
4 Economic Growth and Progress:									
In order to protect the environment, Norway needs economic growth	-.30	.04	-.16	-.14	**.69**	-.00	.17	.00	.13
Modern science will solve our environmental problems with little change to our way of life	-.38	-.10	-.03	.00	**.68**	-.23	-.08	.02	.01
People worry too much about human progress harming the environment	-.50	-.27	-.04	-.33	**.58**	.05	.05	-.01	.06
We worry too much about the future of the environment and not enough about prices and jobs today	-.47	-.18	.13	-.49	**.57**	.10	-.06	.01	-.02
Human beings should respect nature because it was created by God	.06	.00	.31	.06	**.45**	.10	-.08	.29	-.26
5 Environmental Behavior:									
I do what is right for the environment, even when it costs more money or takes more time	.40	-.00	.09	.29	.14	**.68**	.10	.03	.01
How often do you make a special effort to sort glass or metal or plastic or paper and so on for recycling?	.32	.07	.03	.10	-.06	**.68**	-.12	-.08	-.10
How often do you cut back on driving a car for environmental reasons?	.49	.18	.00	.10	-.21	**.66**	.10	.13	-.01
How often do you make a special effort to buy fruits and vegetables grown without pesticides or chemicals?	.40	.18	-.01	.09	.06	**.53**	.17	.42	.10
6 Animal Rights:									
It is right to use animals for medical testing if it might save human lives	-.28	-.09	-.04	-.04	.09	-.00	**.81**	-.11	.13
Animals should have the same moral rights that human beings do	.32	.09	.24	.10	.16	.11	**.74**	.00	.10
7 Passionate Vegetarianism:									
How often do you refuse to eat meat for moral or environmental reasons?	.19	-.04	-.00	.11	-.05	.10	-.02	**.74**	-.02
We believe too often in science, and not enough in feelings and faith	.19	.09	.29	-.06	.11	-.03	.13	**.65**	.02
8 Survival of the Fittest:									
Nature is really a fierce struggle for survival of the fittest	.05	.06	.18	.02	.09	-.05	-.05	-.01	**.84**

The first factor (*E*), italicized, is the single unrotated factor which accounts for 17.6 percent of the variance, principal component. For the factors 1–8, principal component loadings account for 56.8 percent of common variance, varimax rotation (N = 538). Boldface indicates primary loadings. "Values, Nature, and Environmentalism," Norwegian Social Science Data Services, 1993.

Chapter Ten

Seeing Green: Cultural Biases and Environmental Preferences

RICHARD J. ELLIS
FRED THOMPSON

It is often said that environmentalism transcends political ideology, that it is neither left nor right. In 1987 Dave Foreman (1992, 8), then leader of Earth First!, told people, "We aren't in the political spectrum. . . . We aren't left, we aren't right. . . . We aren't even playing that game." The German Greens, when they entered the Bundestag, insisted that they be seated in the center rather than to the left of the Democratic Socialists (Paehlke 1989, 177). "Neither Left nor Right, we are out in front" is a standard mantra within the environmental movement across the industrial world (Dalton 1994, 122).

This view that environmentalism is "inherently neither left nor right" has been cogently argued by political scientist Robert Paehlke, in his much praised book, *Environmentalism and the Future of Progressive Politics* (1989, 177). Paehlke suggests that we need to draw "a distinction between the 'distributive' politics of the traditional political spectrum and environmental politics" (178). Distributive politics, as Paehlke defines it, "is concerned with distribution and redistribution of the products and other intended benefits of economic activity." The ethical debate in this sphere is "carried out in terms of equity." Environmentalism, according to Paehlke, offers a totally separate discourse and represents an ideology that is altogether apart from the conventional left-right continuum (7). Environmental politics, Paehlke explains, "competes with the whole distributional agenda" (189). Since "there is . . . no necessary relationship between one's position on environmental issues and one's position on distributional issues" (189), Paehlke argues that to map the contemporary ideological spectrum properly, one needs at least two dimensions. The first is the familiar left-right dimension that is based on distributive economic concerns; the second is a completely independent dimension that runs from proenvironmentalism to antienvironmentalism (190, also 178; cf. Cotgrove 1982, 112; and Milbrath 1984, 24).

An alternative hypothesis is that environmentalism is rooted in much the same egalitarian and even anticapitalist impulse as the old left politics. In this reading, environmentalists are closet socialists, or as Peter Beckman has it, watermelons— green on the outside and red on the inside (Holmes 1991, 48; also Simon 1995, 20). A more sophisticated version of this thesis is offered by Aaron Wildavsky and his various collaborators (Douglas and Wildavsky 1982; Dake and Wildavsky 1990; Wildavsky 1991d), who argue that environmentalism is part and parcel of the egalitarian impulse to rein in the acquisitive entrepreneur and limit the inequalities that entrepreneurial activities inevitably create.

Wildavsky argues that environmental activists construct their policy preferences so as to bolster their preferred social relationships, which he identifies as egalitarian. Perceptions about environmental risks and dangers are, in this view, embedded in cultural orientations and are not merely a function of the level of information about the safety of particular technologies or policies, nor a product of generalized psychological predispositions such as risk acceptance or aversion. Environmental activists are concerned about the greenhouse effect or deforestation not only because they are concerned about Mother Nature but because they desire to transform how human beings live with one another in an egalitarian direction. To accept the environmentalists' view that nature is fragile and that the slightest misstep may result in cataclysmic consequences for the human species is also to justify a politics that would dramatically curtail the competitive individualist way of life. The debate about nature, then, is also fundamentally a contest over cultures.

In making the case for the connection between egalitarianism and environmentalism, Wildavsky has pointed to a variety of egalitarian statements made by environmental activists (1991d, 74–81). And certainly one could multiply instances of such statements many times over. Living in an ecologically sustainable way, says ecology activist Lorna Salzman, "opens up the possibility of an egalitarian society, whereas industrial society rules it out" (Sale 1986, 33). Conversely, Sheldon Kamieniecki and his colleagues (Kamieniecki, Coleman, and Vos 1995, 26) tell us that "the likelihood that sustainability will be achieved . . . may depend on the extent to which it is able to foster redistribution." More systematic data are required, however, to test whether egalitarianism and environmental commitment are as closely related as Wildavsky maintains.

But Is It True?

To test the Wildavsky and Paehlke hypotheses, we carried out several surveys. Respondents were offered a series of statements designed to tap cultural biases as well as environmental attitudes and beliefs and were asked for each to indicate their position on a seven-point Likert scale: strongly disagree (-3), disagree (-2), somewhat disagree (-1), neither agree nor disagree (0), somewhat agree ($+1$), agree ($+2$), strongly agree ($+3$). The first and primary survey, "Nature and Society" (NATSOC1), went to the northwest memberships of three environmental groups: Audubon Society (n = 215), the Sierra Club (n = 202), and the Earth Island Institute (n = 290). We also sent the same survey to a small group of leaders and activists in the latter two groups (n = 33 and n = 29, respectively), although we draw on the leadership survey only sparingly in this chapter. The Audubon Society and the Sierra Club are well known, established, mainstream environmental groups. The Earth Island Institute, founded by David Brower in the early 1980s, is an avowedly "nonmainstream" environmental organization that self-consciously defines itself as working at the intersection of social justice and ecology issues. Unless otherwise indicated, the correlations reported in this paper refer to the NATSOC1 survey administered to the *memberships* (i.e., not the leaderships) of these three groups. For comparative purposes, we also administered a third survey (NATSOC2), a much shortened version of NATSOC1, to a random sample of residents in largely rural Yamhill County, Oregon, and in Salem, Oregon's capital city (n = 377). Finally, we also draw on Dan Metz's (1995–1996) survey (which included a number of the same items as NATSOC1) of members of the Voluntary Human Extinction Movement (VHEMT) (n = 219), a small fringe group in the Northwest that is committed to persuading people to cease having children. Thirty-six percent of VHEMT members indicated that they were also members of Earth First! (n = 79), probably the most well-known radical environmental group in the United States. The response rates for each of these samples ranged from 50 to 60 percent.[1]

We begin our test of the Wildavsky and Paehlke theses by examining the correlation between egalitarian or distributive concerns on the one hand and environmental commitment on the other. We measure egalitarianism by a scale constructed from three statements (Cronbach's alpha = .77 in both NATSOC1 and NATSOC2[2]): (1) "The world would be a more peaceful place if its wealth were divided more equally among nations"; (2) "We need to dramatically reduce inequalities between the rich and the poor, whites and people of color, and men and women"; and (3) "What our country needs is a fairness revolution to make the distribution of goods more equal." Environmentalism can be measured in a number of different ways, but we begin with a simple, single statement, "We are spending too little money on improving and protecting the environment." If Paehlke is correct that environmentalism constitutes a relatively autonomous sphere of ideas, there should be at best a weak correlation between this single statement and egalitarianism. If Wildavsky is correct, the correlation should be strong. Among our environmentalists in NATSOC1, we find a robust correlation of .36 between the three-item egalitarian scale and support for environmental spending. In other words, those environmental group members who are concerned about inequality are substantially more likely to favor greater spending on environmental protection.

Perhaps, though, this is too narrow a rendering of what Paehlke means by environmentalism. In an effort to capture the spirit of the environmental sensibility that Paehlke discusses we created a ten-item scale (alpha = .83) in NATSOC1 that was modeled on the "New Environmental Paradigm" (NEP) pioneered by Riley Dunlap and Kent Van Liere (1978) and used by Lester Milbrath (1984) and others. The central aspects of NEP, as laid out by Dunlap and Van Liere and by Milbrath are antianthropocentrism, a belief that there are limits to growth, a view of nature as fragile, an awareness of the imminent possibility of ecological catastrophe, and a belief in the need for a basic transformation in the way we live our lives (Dunlap et al. 1992, 4, 6; Milbrath 1984, 44–48). Our ten-item scale of ecological consciousness (ECOCON) included such statements as "If things continue on their present course, we will soon experience a major ecological catastrophe," "Humans are no more important than any other species," and "No wild place will be safe from us until we reconsider our devout belief that economic growth is always good" (see Appendix for a complete list of the ten items used in our index). Were Paehlke correct, we would expect to find a weak correlation between ECOCON and egalitarian ideology. What we find is that egalitarianism, as measured by our three-item scale, is strongly correlated ($r = .39$) with ECOCON. That is, those environmental group members who are more strongly committed to an ecological worldview also tend to be more egalitarian on redistributive issues.[3]

The relationship between egalitarianism and environmentalism is even more impressive if we turn to our sample of the general public in Salem and in Yamhill County.[4] Egalitarianism (measured by the same three-item scale as in NATSOC1) is strongly related to *each* of the ten environmental statements we offered to the general public. Indeed, as Table 10.1 shows, each of the three egalitarian items taken separately correlates significantly, and usually strongly, with each of the ten environmental questions. Commitment to reducing inequalities, Table 10.1 clearly shows, is powerfully related to a wide range of environmental perceptions and beliefs.

Even if we measure ideology along the conventional liberal-conservative axis, Paehlke's thesis does not fare particularly well. Among environmental group members, there is a correlation of .29 between adherence to ECOCON and one's self-designation in terms of liberalism and conservatism, and a .24 correlation between party identification and adherence to ECOCON. On the environmental spending question, the relationship with ideology and party identification was stronger still: .36 and .34, respectively, in NATSOC1, and .39 and .37 in NATSOC2 (cf. Dunlap et al. 1992, 10; and Guth et al. 1995, esp. 372).

The importance of conventional measures of political ideology and party identification in accounting for environmental attitudes undermines Paehlke's thesis, but what about Wildavsky's? After all, if ideology accounts for environmental attitudes, why introduce the concept of cultural bias or egalitarianism? To test whether egalitarianism really adds to our understanding of environmentalism we ran egalitarianism and liberal-conservative self-identification head-to-head in re-

TABLE 10.1   Correlations Between Egalitarianism and Environmentalism in NATSOC2

	Egalitarian Index	More Peaceful	Reduce Inequalities	Fairness Revolution
1. If things continue on their present course, we will soon experience a major ecological catastrophe.	.51	.29	.54	.41
2. The problems of the environment are not as bad as most people think.	−.32	−.18	−.39	−.21
3. The oceans are gradually dying from oil pollution and dumping of waste.	.51	.34	.49	.43
4. We are fast using up the world's natural resources.	.51	.33	.51	.42
5. People worry too much about human progress harming the environment.	−.32	−.27	−.34	−.17[a]
6. On many environmental questions, the stakes are simply too high to leave issues to the normal processes of political bargaining and compromise.	.41	.26	.42	.33
7. Environmental protection may be a just course for society even if the course is taken undemocratically.	.41	.31	.39	.31
8. We are spending too little money on improving and protecting the environment.	.47	.37	.48	.31
9. Humans are no more important than any other species.	.36	.26	.33	.29
10. We would be better off if we dramatically reduced the number of people on this earth.	.20	.18	.15[a]	.17[a]

[a] Significant at $p < .01$. All other correlations significant at $p < .001$.

gression equations. In both NATSOC1 and NATSOC2, egalitarianism consistently explains far more variance in environmental attitudes than do conventional measures of political ideology. In NATSOC1, egalitarianism (standardized regression coefficient $\beta = .35$) does far better at accounting for ECOCON than does liberal-conservative self-designation ($\beta = .17$). The regression coefficients for egalitarianism were significant at less than the .001 level on almost 60 percent of the thirty-four environmental items and at less than the .05 level on almost three-quarters of the items, whereas ideology reached the .001 level of significance on only 20 percent of the items and the .05 level on 35 percent. Similarly, in NATSOC2, egalitarianism was significant at less than the .001 level on eight of the eleven items and at less than the .05 level on all but one (the only item on which egalitarianism failed to reach this level of significance was an item that measured attitudes to science and technology and did not specifically mention the environment). In contrast, ideological self-designation was significant at less than the .001 level on fewer than one-fifth of the items and at less than the .05 level on just over one-half. Cultural bias, it seems, sorts out the environmental debate in ways that conventional measures of ideology and partisanship do not.

What about attitudes to the market? Is Wildavsky correct that the new environmental impulse is at bottom the old anticapitalist impulse, the same war by other means? To answer that question we devised a three-item scale (alpha = .65 in NATSOC1 and .64 in NATSOC2) tapping support for what Wildavsky calls competitive individualism or market individualism. The three statements were: (1) "Competitive markets are almost always the best way to supply people with the things they need"; (2) "Society would be better off if there was much less government regulation of business"; and (3) "People who are successful in business have a right to enjoy their wealth as they see fit." The correlation between support for competitive individualism and environmental commitment shows much the same pattern we unearthed in our investigation of egalitarianism. Support for environmental spending was inversely correlated ($-.36$ in NATSOC1 and $-.37$ in NATSOC2) with support for competitive individualism. The more supportive one is of market capitalism, in other words, the less supportive one tends to be of spending to protect the environment. Among environmental group members there was also an inverse correlation ($-.34$) between support for competitive individualism and adherence to ECOCON.[5]

Among environmental group members, market individualism seems to have roughly the same importance as egalitarianism in accounting for environmental attitudes. If market individualism and egalitarianism are placed into the same regression equation, together with Wildavsky's third category of hierarchy (alpha = .75 in NATSOC1 and .64 in NATSOC2; see Appendix for the items used), we find that egalitarianism and market individualism have equal explanatory weight ($\beta = .25$) in accounting for support for environmental spending. Similarly, in explaining ECOCON both egalitarianism ($\beta = .29$) and market individualism ($\beta = -.25$) have standardized regression coefficients that are significant at less than the .001 level (Table 10.2). NATSOC2 shows an even stronger explanatory role for egalitarianism, although a relatively less important one for market individualism. On the environmental spending question, the standardized regression coefficient for egalitarianism is .39, compared to only $-.17$ for market individualism. In an eight-item ENVIRO scale (alpha = .90; see Appendix for the items used)[6] the coefficient is .49 for egalitarianism and $-.20$ for individualism.

The explanatory power of egalitarianism and market individualism is more impressive still when we pit these two variables as well as hierarchy against the standard demographic variables (age, income, gender, and education), party identification, and political ideology. In both NATSOC1 and NATSOC2, as Table 10.3 documents, egalitarianism and market individualism easily outdistance these other variables in accounting for environmental attitudes. Knowing age, gender, education, income, party identification, and to a lesser extent ideology typically

TABLE 10.2   Standardized Regression Coefficients by Cultural Bias and Ideology

	Egalitarianism vs. Ideology	Egalitarianism vs. Individualism and Hierarchy
NATSOC 1		
ECOCON	Egalitarianism .35[a]	Egalitarianism .29[a]
	Ideology .11[c]	Individualism −.25[a]
		Hierarchy .10[c]
Spending on Environment	Ideology .24[a]	Egalitarianism .25[a]
	Egalitarianism .23[a]	Individualism −.25[a]
		Hierarchy .05
NATSOC 2		
CONCERN	Egalitarianism .47[a]	Egalitarianism .49[a]
	Ideology .21[a]	Individualism −.20[a]
		Hierarchy −.11[c]
Spending on Environment	Egalitarianism .41[a]	Egalitarianism .39[a]
	Ideology .19[a]	Individualism −.17[b]
		Hierarchy −.11[c]

[a] $p < .001$
[b] $p < .01$
[c] $p < .05$
For ideology a positive coefficient means that liberals are more likely to agree.

adds relatively little to our understanding of environmental attitudes that is not already contained in the cultural bias variables, especially egalitarianism but also market individualism. Our findings, in sum, suggest that if we want to explain variations in environmental preferences and concerns, we will do better by asking people about their worldviews and beliefs, particularly their attitudes toward equality and markets, rather than their demographic traits or even their position on the liberal-conservative continuum (cf. Van Liere and Dunlap 1980, 194; Guth et al. 1995, 373, 376).

NEP and Deep Ecology: Liberating or Illiberal?

Dunlap and Van Liere's (1984) research on the impact of the "Dominant Social Paradigm" (DSP) on environmental attitudes leaves us well prepared for the finding that attitudes toward the market and private property are importantly connected to environmental concerns. Our findings would seem to lend further support to those who argue that the nation's environmental commitment has been impeded by traditional capitalist values like laissez-faire, limited government, and private property (Dunlap and Van Liere 1978, 10; 1984), and that only if such values are jettisoned will a new ecological consciousness flourish.

TABLE 10.3   Standardized Regression Coefficients by Cultural Bias, Ideology, Party Identification, and Demographic Traits

	NATSOC 1		NATSOC 2	
	ECOCON	Spending on Environment	ENVIRO	Spending on Environment
Egalitarianism	.30[a]	.16[b]	.29[a]	.26[a]
	(.39)	(.36)	(.57)	(.47)
Individualism	−.20[a]	−.19[b]	−.28[a]	−.24[b]
	(−.34)	(−.36)	(−.44)	(−.37)
Hierarchy	.14[b]	.07	−.07	−.05
	(−.09)	(−.13)	(−.15)	(−.13)
Ideology	.13[c]	.14[c]	.12	.11
	(.29)	(.36)	(.42)	(.39)
Party	−.08	.07	.12	.11
	(.24)	(.34)	(.43)	(.37)
Age	−.03	−.04	.06	.06
	(−.08)	(−.10)	(−.02)	(−.03)
Education	−.03	.05	−.04	−.01
	(−.02)	(.10)	(.07)	(.09)
Sex	−.05	.03	.00	.08
	(−.06)	(.00)	(−.19)	(−.08)
Income	−.04	.03	−.03	.03
	(−.13)	(−.04)	(−.02)	(.07)
Multiple R	.46	.44	.66	.56
R^2, All variables	.21	.19	.43	.32
R^2, Egal & Ind only	.18	.17	.37	.25
R^2, Egal only	.15	.13	.30	.22

[a] $p < .001$
[b] $p < .01$
[c] $p < .05$

Bivariate correlations are in parentheses immediately underneath the regression coefficients. For ideology, party identification, and sex, a positive coefficient means that liberals, Democrats, and men are more likely to agree.

But our evidence also suggests some qualifications and cautions that have not hitherto been noted by empirical researchers in this area. The tone of this literature is too often wholly uncritical of what is seen as an emerging and even liberating ecological consciousness. Lester Milbrath (1984), for instance, describes those who accept the NEP as an enlightened "vanguard," whereas those who adhere to the DSP are the benighted "rearguard." Less brazen but not dissimilar is the position of Dunlap and Van Liere, who see the new ecological consciousness of NEP as the hope of the future (1978, 17) and the "antiecological" DSP (10) as the source of our inability to improve the environment or aggressively remedy problems of environmental degradation (see also Catton and Dunlap 1980).

Our results reveal a darker side to the new ecological consciousness that has previously gone unmeasured if not unnoticed. Those environmentalists who scored high in the new ecological consciousness, as measured by our ten-item ECOCON scale, were also extremely likely to embrace antidemocratic, illiberal, or antipolitical statements about environmental issues. There was a very large correlation (r = .50) between our ECOCON index and an "Illiberalism" index (alpha = .77) made up of the following four statements: (1) "If we are to save the environment, we will have to give up the exercise of certain basic rights we now enjoy"; (2) "On many environmental questions, the stakes are simply too high to leave issues to the normal process of political bargaining and compromise"; (3) "Environmental protection may be a just course for society even if that course is taken undemocratically"; and (4) "We are morally obligated to resort to whatever means necessary in order to defend the earth from destruction."[7] These results should give us pause before we automatically assume that a higher "ecological consciousness," at least as it is conceptualized by Milbrath, Dunlap, and others, is always a good thing. The ecological vanguard may, like other vanguards before it, be prepared to act in the name of others (plants, animals, the ecosystem) while using antidemocratic or illiberal means.

The same caution, not incidentally, should be accorded to the philosophy or sensibility known as "deep ecology."[8] Its proponents make large, even extravagant claims. Deep ecology, we are told, reflects a higher level of consciousness (Wuerthner 1985; also Manes 1990). Bill Devall, one of its most prominent exponents, suggests that "the role of deep ecology in contemporary society is liberating, transforming, questing. There is Utopia in deep ecology, a Utopia based not on man's continued and intensified conquest or domination of nonhuman nature but based on a questing for self-realization" (Devall 1980, 322). The correlations we found in NATSOC1 between Illiberalism and each of the two statements we used to tap deep ecology ("Humans are no more important than any other species" [r = .23] and "Human happiness and human reproduction are less important than a healthy planet" [r = .40]) indicate a darker side to this supposedly liberating consciousness.[9]

Of particular interest is the finding (Table 10.4) that among environmentalists there was no correlation at all between egalitarianism and Illiberalism. This is particularly striking since we have already seen that egalitarians tended to be substantially more alarmist about the state of the environment and more likely to subscribe to basic tenets of the new ecological consciousness. Since both alarm about the state of the environment and the new ecological consciousness more broadly are strongly related to Illiberalism in NATSOC1, it suggests that egalitarian values may carry with them an inoculation against the more antidemocratic or illiberal temptations of environmental commitment. We hesitate to push this interpretation too far, however, as VHEMT and NATSOC2 yielded starkly different results. In VHEMT there was a modest correlation (r = .25) between egalitarianism and Illiberalism, perhaps suggesting that at the radical edges the egalitarian

TABLE 10.4   Correlations Between Illiberalism and Egalitarianism

	NATSOC1	NATSOC2	VHEMT
Illiberalism Index	.05	.46[a]	.26[a]
	(−.06)	(.16[b])	(.16[c])
	(−.16[a])		(.03)
1. If we are to save the environment, we will have to give up the exercise of certain basic rights we now enjoy.	.03	−	.07
	(−.04)		(.05)
	(−.11[b])		(−.02)
2. On many environmental questions, the stakes are simply too high to leave issues to the normal process of political bargaining and compromise.	.07	.41[a]	.29[a]
	(−.06)	(.11[c])	(.17[b])
	(−.12[a])		(.05)
3. Environmental protection may be taken just course for society even if that course is taken undemocratically.	.02	.41[a]	−
	(−.07)	(.18[b])	
	(−.16[a])		
4. We are normally obligated to resort to whatever means necessary in order to defend the earth from destruction.	.05	−	.23[a]
	(−.04)		(.16[c])
	(−.12[b])		(.05)

[a]$p < .001$
[b]$p < .01$
[c]$p < .05$

Bivariate correlations are listed first. Underneath in parentheses are standardized regression coefficients, first controlling for level of environmental concern, and then, underneath that, controlling for ECOCON. Level of environmental concern in NATSOC1 and NATSOC2 is measured by three items: "Oceans dying," "Ecological catastrophe," and "World's natural resources." In VHEMT environmental concern is measured by "Oceans dying" and the statement, "There are likely to be serious and disruptive shortages of essential raw materials if things go on as they are." In the VHEMT survey the egalitarian index is made up of only two items, "Fairness revolution" and "Peaceful place."

inoculation against illiberalism starts to wear off. NATSOC2, meanwhile, found a very strong correlation of .49 between Illiberalism (measured by only two items, "Stakes Too High," and "Just Course") and egalitarianism. The strength of this relationship is due largely to the much higher levels of environmental concern among Salem-Yamhill egalitarians, although, as Table 10.4 shows, after controlling for environmental concern the relationship between Illiberalism and egalitarianism remains statistically significant.[10]

Other Correlates of Egalitarianism

What else can our data tell us about the validity of Wildavsky's cultural thesis? In *Cultural Theory*, Wildavsky and his coauthors hypothesize that egalitarians typically construct a view of human beings as being born good but corrupted by institutions. This optimistic view of human nature, they argue, is essential to sustaining egalitarian commitment, for without it egalitarians would find it difficult to sustain their ideal of a noncoercive community of equals. Were "an egalitarian to become persuaded that human nature is irretrievably bad, he could hardly resist hierarchical arguments for increasing institutional restraints upon individuals, or deny the individualists' claim that there was no sense in trying to remake human nature" (Thompson, Ellis, and Wildavsky 1990, 34). To give up on a certain construction of human nature as essentially good would be to give up on the egalitarian faith in a world remade and a people reformed.

Though the logic of this argument is appealing, no systematic survey evidence has been produced to support the claim. To test the hypothesized relationship between egalitarianism and views of human nature, we created a scale (alpha = .68) based on two statements in NATSOC1: (1) "Human beings are basically good but are corrupted by institutions," and (2) "If we could only get back to nature, people's natural goodness would emerge." We found a robust correlation ($r = .32$) between this rosy view of human nature and our three-item measure of egalitarianism, supporting the Wildavsky hypothesis.

Another aspect of Wildavsky's cultural thesis is that egalitarians are prone to view nature as fragile. Egalitarians construct a view of nature as "a terrifyingly unforgiving place [in which] the least jolt may trigger its complete collapse" (Thompson, Ellis, and Wildavsky 1990, 27). This myth of nature justifies those who would prefer to live in small, tight-knit, decentralized communities that tread lightly on the earth. By the same token, it helps to undermine competitive individualism, because if people come to believe that nature is terribly fragile it becomes difficult to sustain the continuous trial-and-error process that is the essence of the self-regulating way of life, since any mistake could cause irreparable damage.

The statements in NATSOC1 that best capture this alarmist conception of nature are: (1) "If things continue on their present course, we will soon experience a major ecological catastrophe"; (2) "Unrelenting exploitation of nature has driven us to the brink of ecological collapse"; and (3) "The oceans are gradually dying from oil pollution and dumping of waste." Using these three statements as a measure of the myth of nature as fragile (alpha = .80), we found a correlation with egalitarianism of .30. In NATSOC2 only the first and third statements were used, but the correlation between a scale made up of these two statements (alpha = .83) and egalitarianism was an even more impressive .51. Again the Wildavsky hypothesis gains strong support.

Another hypothesized correlate of egalitarianism is distrust of technology. In *Risk and Culture*, Douglas and Wildavsky (1982) argue that increasing concerns about the dangers of technology could be attributed to a rise in egalitarianism (or what they then called sectarianism). If this is so, we should find a substantial correlation between attitudes to technology and egalitarianism. We created an antitechnology index (alpha = .69) from three statements in NATSOC1: (1) "Science and technology are a major cause of the destruction of the natural world"; (2) "The bad effects of technology outweigh its advantages"; and (3) "Science and technology provide the human race with its best hope for the future." Although there was a positive correlation between this antitechnology index and egalitarianism, the relationship was not strong ($r = .25$). Even less impressive, the correlations between the three individual egalitarianism items and the three technology items ranged from a low of .10 to a high of .24 (Table 10.5). More supportive was the VHEMT survey, in which there was a strong correlation (.34) with egalitarianism, especially for the statement, "We are in danger of letting technology run away with us." Egalitarians, Table 10.5 suggests, are consistently more likely to distrust science and technology, but the relationship is not nearly as strong as Douglas and Wildavsky lead us to expect.[11] Indeed, in NATSOC2 the relationship between egalitarianism and technology disappeared altogether on the one technology item that we used.

In evaluating the explanatory power of Wildavsky's concept of egalitarianism it helps again to compare it with the performance of the standard demographic variables as well as party identification and political ideology. As Table 10.6 shows, egalitarianism outperforms each of these other variables, even in the case of technology. For each of the three indexes (human nature, nature as fragile, and antitechnology), egalitarianism has the largest bivariate correlation and the largest standardized regression coefficient. In short, whatever egalitarianism's weaknesses, it far outperforms the standard sociopolitical variables researchers tend to use, all of which, including political ideology, fare poorly in explaining variations in attitudes to nature, human nature, and technology.

Worlds Apart

The individual-level correlations between cultural biases and environmental attitudes are generally supportive of Wildavsky's thesis, but a fuller test of that thesis requires also comparing the mean levels of support among environmentalists and the general public. It will come as no great surprise to learn that members of environmental groups are more concerned about environmental problems than is the general public; that concern, after all, is presumably what led these individuals to join an environmental group in the first place. Nor should it surprise us that members of more radical environmental groups such as Earth First! and the Earth Island Institute show higher levels of ecological awareness and commitment than do members of more mainstream groups such as the Sierra Club and Audubon (see Ellis and Thompson 1996 for documentation). Less obvious is the question of whether the cultural biases of the general public differ significantly from the cultural biases of environmentalists, as Wildavsky predicts.

As the summary presented in Table 10.7 indicates, the cultural biases of the general public and environmentalists do indeed diverge sharply, with the general public consistently less egalitarian and more supportive of both hierarchy and market individualism than members of any of the environmental groups, including the more moderate Audubon Society. Particularly dramatic is the cultural

TABLE 10.5 Correlations Between Egalitarianism and Attitudes Toward Technology

	Anti-technology Index		Science and technology provide the human race with its best hope for the future			The bad effects of technology outweigh its advantages[a]		Science and technology are a major cause of the destruction of the natural world	We are in danger of letting technology run away with us
	NATSOC1	VHEMT	NATSOC1	NATSOC2	VHEMT	NATSOC1	VHEMT	NATSOC1	VHEMT
Egalitarianism Index									
The world would be a more peaceful place if its wealth were divided more equally among nations.	$.25^b$	$.28^b$	$-.17^b$	$.06$	$-.14^d$	$.22^b$	$.22^c$	$.21^b$	$.34^b$
	$.24^b$	$.19^c$	$-.19^b$	$.09$	$-.06$	$.21^b$	$.15^d$	$.17^b$	$.29^c$
We need to dramatically reduce inequalities between the rich and the poor, whites and people of color, and men and women.	$.15^b$	—	$-.10^c$	$.01$		$.12^c$	—	$.14^b$	—
What our country needs is a fairness revolution to make the distribution of goods more equal.	$.22^b$	$.30^b$	$-.12^c$	$.06$	$-.18^c$	$.24^b$	$.24^b$	$.19^b$	$.32^b$

[a] The wording in the VHEMT survey is "The good effects of technology outweigh its bad effects." (Scoring has been reversed.)
[b] $p < .001$
[c] $p < .01$
[d] $p < .05$

TABLE 10.6   Ideological and Demographic Correlates of Views of Human Nature,
Nature, and Technology in NATSOC1

	Human Nature	Fragile Nature	Antitechnology
Egalitarianism	.32	.30	.25
	(.25[a])	(.26[a])	(.26[a])
Ideology	.17	.20	.12
	(.11[c])	(.08)	(.09)
Party ID	.04	.18	.06
	(−.16[b])	(−.01)	(−.12[c])
Income	−.14	−.16	−.20
	(−.02)	(−.09)	(−.12[c])
Sex	−.03	−.09	−.03
	(−.06)	(.09[c])	(−.04)
Age	−.13	−.05	−.02
	(−.07)	(−.02)	(.01)
Education	−.13	−.05	−.12
	(−.16[b])	(−.02)	(−.07)

[a]$p < .001$
[b]$p < .01$
[c]$p < .05$

Bivariate correlations are listed first, and standardized regression coefficients are immediately underneath in parentheses.

chasm separating the Salem-Yamhill public from the Sierra Club leadership and the members and leaders of the Earth Island Institute.

One way of illustrating the cultural gap separating environmentalists from the general public is to compare the two populations' percentages of "pure egalitarians," which we have operationalized as those whose mean egalitarian score is greater than zero and whose mean individualism and hierarchy scores are less than or equal to zero. Among the Salem-Yamhill public only 5 percent qualify as pure egalitarians, whereas close to one-half of the environmental group members (not counting the leaders) score as pure egalitarians. The differences among the environmentalists are equally revealing of cultural differences. Almost two-thirds of Earth Island Institute members are pure egalitarians, compared to about 30 percent of Audubon Society members and 42 percent of Sierra Club members. More than 70 percent of Sierra Club leaders, however, count as pure egalitarians, as do an extraordinary 89 percent of Earth Island Institute leaders. By far the largest segment of the Salem-Yamhill public (37 percent) adheres to an individualist-hierarchical hybrid cultural bias—that is, they have positive scores on individualism and hierarchy while having egalitarian scores that are less than or equal to zero. Although 16 percent of Audubon members share this hybrid cultural bias, only a small handful of the other environmentalists do (4 percent of Earth Is-

TABLE 10.7   Cultural Bias

		Salem and Yamhill	Audubon Society	Sierra Club	Earth Island	Sierra Leaders	Earth Island Leaders
Egalitarianism	Mean	−.13	.46	.59	1.27	.73	1.86
	% Agree	44	55	59	73	61	84
Individualism	Mean	.91	−.11	−.56	−1.14	−1.14	−1.38
	% Agree	65	43	31	21	23	19
Hierarchy	Mean	.78	.17	−.55	−.89	−.84	−1.61
	% Agree	65	49	30	25	25	11

landers, 3 percent of Sierra Club members, none of the Earth Island Institute leaders, and 6 percent of Sierra Club leaders).

Culturally speaking, these environmentalists and the public are "worlds apart."

The Future of Environmental Politics

Egalitarianism, to recapitulate the central finding of this chapter, is very much at the heart of today's environmental movement. This relationship holds not just at the individual level but at the group level as well. Members of Earth First! and the Earth Island Institute, both strongly egalitarian groups, are much more supportive of a broad range of environmental statements than are members of the substantially less egalitarian Audubon Society and the Sierra Club (see Ellis and Thompson 1996). Our results, then, confirm Wildavsky's central thesis and show that the idea that environmentalism is an autonomous ideology separate from distributional questions is mistaken.

Yet if Paehlke's thesis is empirically untenable in the contemporary United States, he is right that "historically, no particular ideology has had a monopoly on environmental thinking" (1990, 190). Anna Bramwell (1989) shows the connection in Europe between ecology and right-wing, even fascist, movements. And in America at the turn of the century, the conservation movement was strongly associated, at least at the elite level, with Progressive conservatism (Hays 1957). Throughout the first half of the twentieth century in the United States, environmental policies often drew nearly as much support from Republican Party elites as from the Democratic Party. In other times and places, then, environmentalism has seemed to be much closer to the autonomous ideology conceived by Paehlke.

If it is true, as Paehlke says, that logically and even historically "environmental values can point in several political directions" (1990, 19), the question becomes, What is different about today? The short answer is that environmentalism has become enmeshed in a culture war between individualists and egalitarians. For competitive individualists, environmentalism is seen as a Trojan horse used by egalitarians to cripple markets and restrict the use of private property. For egalitarians, unregulated markets are the source of both unconscionable inequalities and environmental destruction. Environmentalism and egalitarianism are so strongly connected today because both the old distributive politics and the new environmental politics pivot around the same institutions and questions, especially the desirability of self-regulating, capitalist markets.

Must it be this way? Is there any prospect of uncoupling environmentalism from the divisive battles over equality and capitalism? This is the normative project that drives Paehlke's insistence on "the ideological autonomy of environmental ideas" (1990, 197).[13] To be effective, Paehlke argues, environmentalism must "stand alone; it must become an autonomous political ideology in its own right" (193). Paehlke seeks "to develop a 'third way' able to defuse the ideological duality of the contemporary world" (5). We agree that the current level of ideological polarization is undesirable, and we sympathize with Paehlke's aims. Uncoupling environmentalism from partisan politics would certainly help to make environmental policymaking less fractious. Removing nature from the contest over culture—that is, the debate over how human beings will live with each other—would surely make it easier to reach political agreement on many environmental questions. Disagreements would, of course, persist, but those differences would revolve more around facts than around values. But we are not optimistic. Environmentalism, far from offering an autonomous third way, has become perhaps the most contentious battleground in the continuing culture wars between individualists and egalitarians. We see no reason to expect this to change anytime soon, particularly since the political parties are increasingly polarized along this cultural fault line (Miller and Jennings 1986; Wildavsky 1991d, 46–62; Wildavsky 1992).[13] For better or for worse, the contemporary debate over how we should relate to nature will continue to be inextricably tied up with the cultural contest over how we should live with each other.

Appendix: Items Used in Scales

A. ECOCON (NATSOC1)

1. If things continue on their present course, we will soon experience a major ecological catastrophe.

2. What human beings are currently doing to nature can be fairly characterized as an "ecoholocaust."

3. Humans are no more important than any other species.

4. We would be better off if we dramatically reduced the number of people on this earth.

5. No wild place will be safe from us until we reconsider our devout belief that economic growth is always good.

6. We can only save the planet by radically transforming our social lives with each other.

7. Unrelenting exploitation of nature has driven us to the brink of ecological collapse.

8. We have reduced natural beauty to postcard prettiness, just another commodity for our consumption.

9. Human happiness and human reproduction are less important than a healthy planet.

10. The oceans are gradually dying of oil pollution and dumping of waste.

B. ENVIRO (NATSOC2)

1. If things continue on their present course, we will soon experience a major ecological catastrophe.

2. The problems of the environment are not as bad as most people think.

3. The oceans are gradually dying from oil pollution and dumping of waste.

4. We are fast using up the world's natural resources.

5. People worry too much about human progress harming the environment.

6. On many environmental questions, the stakes are simply too high to leave issues to the normal process of political bargaining and compromise.

7. Environmental protection may be a just course for society even if that course is taken undemocratically.

8. We are spending too little money on improving and protecting the environment.

C. Egalitarianism (NATSOC1 and NATSOC2)

1. The world would be a more peaceful place if its wealth were divided more equally among nations.

2. We need to dramatically reduce inequalities between the rich and the poor, whites and people of color, and men and women.

3. What our country needs is a fairness revolution to make the distribution of goods more equal.

D. Competitive Individualism (NATSOC1 and NATSOC2)

1. Competitive markets are almost always the best way to supply people with the things they need.

2. Society would be better off if there was much less government regulation of business.

3. People who are successful in business have a right to enjoy their wealth as they see fit.

E. Hierarchy (NATSOC1 and NATSOC2)

1. One of the problems with people today is that they challenge authority too often.

2. Society works best when people strictly obey all rules and regulations.

3. Respect for authority is one of the most important things that children should learn.

F. Human Nature (NATSOC1)

1. Human beings are basically good but are corrupted by institutions.

2. If we could only get back to nature, people's natural goodness would emerge.

G. Nature as Fragile (NATSOC1 only; NATSOC2 used two-item scale made up of only items 1 and 3)

1. If things continue on their present course, we will soon experience a major ecological catastrophe.

2. Unrelenting exploitation of nature has driven us to the brink of ecological collapse.

3. The oceans are gradually dying from oil pollution and dumping of waste.

H. Antitechnology Index (NATSOC1)

1. Science and technology are a major cause of the destruction of the natural world.

2. The bad effects of technology outweigh its advantages.

3. Science and technology provide the human race with its best hope for the future.

I. Illiberalism (NATSOC1; NATSOC2 used two-item scale made up of items 2 and 3)

1. If we are to save the environment, we will have to give up the exercise of certain basic rights we now enjoy.

2. On many environmental questions, the stakes are simply too high to leave issues to the normal process of political bargaining and compromise.

3. Environmental protection may be a just course for society even if that course is taken undemocratically.

4. We are morally obligated to resort to whatever means necessary in order to defend the earth from destruction.

Notes

An earlier version of this chapter was presented to the Western Political Science Association meetings in San Francisco in March 1996. The research for this chapter was made possible by the financial assistance of the Canadian Donner Foundation. The research assistance of Shirley Thomas, Steve Anderson, Morgan Allen, and Brian Shipley has been invaluable. We thank Robert Bartlett, Joe Bowersox, Phil Brick, Jim Friedrich, Gunnar Grendstad, Samuel Hays, Bill Stanbury, and Nathan Teske for their helpful comments and tough criticisms of earlier versions of this chapter. We are also indebted to Dan Metz for allowing us to use results from his survey of the Voluntary Human Extinction Movement and to Mary Houghteling of the Earth Island Institute, whose invaluable assistance went well beyond the call of duty. Also unfailingly helpful were Bob Frenkel and Lisa Morrison of the Sierra Club.

1. More detailed information about the sampling methodology, the response rates, and the nature of each group or population may be found in Appendix A of Ellis and Thompson 1996 and in Metz 1995–1996.

2. Cronbach's alpha is a basic measure of internal consistency between the variables; the higher the value the greater the internal consistency.

3. The same strong relationship ($r = .41$) between environmental consciousness and egalitarianism (measured by a two-item scale made up of the "Fairness Revolution" and "More Peaceful Place" items) held in the VHEMT survey. In VHEMT the index of ecological consciousness was constructed from ten items, only two of which—"We can only save the planet . . ." and "The oceans are gradually dying . . ."—were the same as in the NATSOC survey. Three of the items replicated items used by Dunlap and Van Liere (1978, 13; also Milbrath 1984, 103–104) in their original NEP scale: "The balance of nature is very delicate and easily upset," "Humans must live in harmony with nature in order to survive," and "There are limits to growth beyond which our industrialized society cannot expand." The other five items were "Population levels are growing to beyond what the world can support" (Cotgrove 1982, 127), "There are likely to be serious and disruptive shortages of essential raw materials if things go on as they are," "Industrial societies provide a high level of well-being for most people who live in them" (Milbrath 1984, 103), "The problems of the environment are not as bad as so-called experts have told people" (Dake and Thompson 1992, 46), and "All living organisms deserve to be treated equally." The alpha value for this ten-item scale was .78.

4. That the correlations between egalitarianism and environmentalism are substantially stronger among the mass public than among environmental members is largely an artifact of the far greater variation on environmental items among Salem-Yamhill residents than among environmental members.

5. The correlation between ECOCON and competitive individualism (measured by the same three questions as in NATSOC1) was stronger still in the VHEMT survey (−.40).

6. Of the ten items listed in Table 10.1, items 9 and 10 were not used in this scale because of their relatively low item-to-total correlations (.43 and .28 respectively); including either item lowered the alpha value. Adding these two variables into the scale actually strengthens the relationship with egalitarianism.

7. In the VHEMT survey, there was also a large correlation between ECOCON and Illiberalism (.58). The Illiberalism index in VHEMT was measured by the same statements as in NATSOC1 except that one statement ("Environmental protection may be a just course . . .") was not included.

8. On the relationship between egalitarianism and deep ecology, our findings are mixed. Among Salem-Yamhill residents, we found a strong correlation (.35) between egalitarianism and the statement, "Humans are no more important than any other species." Although both critics and proponents sometimes portray deep ecology as unconcerned with human relationships, the evidence from NATSOC2 suggests that deep ecology (the attempt to equalize humans and other biological creatures) is tied up with the attempt to reduce differences among people. Deep ecology, on this evidence, would seem to be at least in part, as Roderick Nash (1989) argues, the egalitarian impulse extended to all living species. But the evidence from NATSOC1 suggests a much weaker connection. Among environmentalists the correlation between "Humans are no more important . . ." and egalitarianism was small ($r = .16$), and even that weak relationship washed out when controlling for demographic variables. On the other deep ecology item, "Human happiness and human reproduction are less important than a healthy planet," the correlation was weaker still ($r = .10$). The waters become even murkier when one looks at the VHEMT survey, which found a .22 correlation between the deep ecology principle, "All living organisms deserve to be treated equally," and a two-item egalitarian index ("Fairness Revolution" and "More Peaceful Place"), but a much stronger correlation of .32 when one used a three-item egalitarian index that also included the question, "We should seek to eliminate all forms of inequality, hierarchy, and domination." The best one can say on the basis of this mixed evidence is that egalitarians seem somewhat more inclined to support deep ecology, but only modestly so.

9. In VHEMT, which used a different statement to measure deep ecology—"All living organisms deserve to be treated equally"—there was a .42 correlation with Illiberalism.

10. In accounting for Illiberalism in NATSOC1, the most important cultural bias variable by far was hierarchy. Environmentalists who scored high on the hierarchy scale were more likely ($r = .28$) to believe that "If we are to save the environment, we will have to give up the exercise of certain basic rights we now enjoy." Controlling for ECOCON the β coefficient for hierarchy was boosted to .31 ($p < .001$). The correlation between hierarchy and the four-item Illiberalism scale was .19; controlling for ECOCON yielded a β coefficient of .24 ($p < .001$).

11. The relationships between competitive individualism and attitudes to technology were also a mixed bag. In NATSOC1 there was a weak inverse correlation (−.20) between support for competitive individualism and antitechnology feelings, and only on the "best hope" item was there any substantial correlation (.27). In NATSOC2 the relationship between individualism and the "best hope" item was anemic ($r = .13$). The results were starkly different in VHEMT, however. Here there was a strong correlation ($r = .49$) between attitudes to technology and support for competitive individualism. Moreover, each of the three technology items used in VHEMT had correlations with individualism that ranged from .38 to .41.

12. At other times, however, Paehlke seems more interested in making environmentalism the basis for a revitalized, progressive politics of the "moderate left" (1989, 6). In this mode he is less interested in establishing environmentalism's ideological autonomy than he is in creating the basis for an alliance between environmentalism and the left. These two quite different projects coexist uneasily within his book.

13. Partisan differences in environmental voting have existed for at least several decades, but the earlier differences were nowhere near as great as they are today. In 1995 the League of Conservation Voters (LCV) assigned Democrats in Congress (House and Senate) an 83 percent score on the basis of their voting on environmental issues, compared to only 13 percent for Republicans (http://www.lcv.org/lcv95). In 1994 the Democratic score was 70 percent and the Republican score 24 percent (http://www.lcv.org/lcv94/Summary.html). In contrast, using the same LCV scores, Henry Kenski and Margaret Kenski (1980) found that between 1973 and 1978, Democrats averaged about 58 percent and Republicans 34 percent, while Calvert (1989) found that between 1981 and 1984 Democrats averaged 66 percent and Republicans 32 percent. The gap between Republicans and Democrats in LCV scores, then, has grown from 24 percent in the mid-1970s, to 34 percent in the early 1980s, to 46 percent in 1994, before ballooning to an unprecedented 70 percent in 1995.

Part Six

Cultural Theory and Practical Policies

Chapter Eleven

Applying Cultural Theories to Practical Problems

ROBERT KLITGAARD

One day in the spring of 1989, Aaron Wildavsky took me for a walk in Berkeley, or perhaps better put, an intellectual forced march. I was then beginning to work on how to apply cultural concepts to policymaking and management. After reading many of his papers and the manuscript of *Cultural Theory* (Thompson, Ellis, and Wildavsky 1990), I visited Aaron to find out his views. His response: "Let's take a walk."

We hit the pavement. Aaron strode along with his hands clasped at the small of his back in the style of a Spanish nobleman, but this similarity could mislead. This was no leisurely promenade around the *zócalo*. Aaron walked fast and talked even faster, and I smiled as I tried to keep pace. His accents and diction were the antithesis of a Castilian's. Think instead of a New York boxer, who happened to be a genius.

En route Aaron discoursed on the fourfold Douglas/Wildavsky typology. It was undergoing some changes of nomenclature. What is now called the "egalitarian way of life" was then termed "sectarian." There was the uncertain prospect of a fifth way of life, sitting hermitlike above the fray, where many intellectuals would like to be, but probably not Aaron Wildavsky. He talked about how the theory enabled one to make interesting predictions about what sorts of people feared what sorts of environmental risks. It was fascinating.

When a moment presented itself, I posed my problem. Are there culture-by-policy interactions, and if so, how should they be taken into account?[1] That is, if you imagine some desirable outcome depends on a bunch of policy variables, as learning does on the quantity and quality of schooling, do cultural variables also matter? Does the impact of different policy choices depend on aspects of the sociocultural setting? If so, could policymakers and managers and citizens themselves make better policy choices by understanding the interactions?

Aaron suddenly stopped, a complete halt in midblock. My braking was less prompt, and I had to step back to where he had frozen. He was looking straight ahead. He stood there for what seemed like a minute but must only have been a few seconds. Not knowing Aaron very well at the time, I didn't know what this behavior could signify. The appearance in his field of vision of a distant and surprising animal or antique car? A health problem? Had my lingo of culture-by-policy interactions perhaps triggered an allergic reaction?

Finally Aaron looked over at me. "Very interesting," he said, drawing out both words. "Tell me that again." And he resumed walking. So did I, lurching to catch up. I repeated my questions. We reached a street corner. Aaron froze again. Another pause. Then he said, "Very interesting. Let's turn back the other way and continue talking about it."

It was a topic to which we returned in subsequent conversations and correspondence. Some of Aaron's work touched on it obliquely. For example, he wrote papers about how his Cultural Theory could explain scholars' differing reactions to policy analytical concepts, such as the Prisoners' Dilemma. At my instigation he was invited in 1992 to a World Bank conference on culture and development, where he speculated that a "cultural audit" in Africa would be a baseline from which culture-by-policy interactions might be discovered (Wildavsky 1994b). But (to my knowledge) he never pushed the question "so what for policy?" as hard as he might have wanted to. If we had a good cultural theory, how could we use it to solve problems better? I like to think that had he been with us now, it is one of the areas on which his remarkable mind might already have shed new light.

My own thinking has edged forward a bit—alas, not at a Wildavskian pace— but I too have not yet pounced on the big "so what." I find myself still stalking the issue, in the fashion of one of the predators of Africa, my new home. The reasons for my lack of action, and perhaps also for Aaron's, are the subject of this paper.

The Potential Importance of Applying Cultural Theories

Africa was the original inspiration of my interest in the practical uses of cultural theories. Africa's problems, as well as the wave of democratic and free-market reforms now sweeping the world, are bringing the cultural dimensions of development and change to the forefront. After the announced changes of policies, we see slow implementation and slow progress in many countries. One possible reason is that policies, political processes, and management systems interact with cultural variables. For practical applications we would like to know how and how much, and under what conditions.

To find out, we must transcend some tired debates. Yes, we know that policies and systems adapt to culture and cultures to them, that policies can change cultures, that cultures have their own dynamic of change, that valuations of developmental ends and means are themselves shaped by culture. We also know that these issues are not binary, that necessary or sufficient cultural conditions are not in the cards. And so it is time to move beyond prefatory remarks and get down to questions of degree. What have we learned about the positive and negative outcomes of various processes and policies under various cultural and other conditions—with what probabilities and at what costs?

Unfortunately, theoretical research on culture rarely touches the practice of economic and political development. We are all familiar with arguments of this kind: "Project X or policy Y failed because it did not take the local culture into account." Economists in particular are accused of making assumptions, based on something called the West or perhaps the North, that are inconsistent with indigenous ways of life. But if one asks, "Isn't development about change? How *should* one take cultural diversity into account? What alternative assumptions *should* be made?" one tends to get a shrug of the shoulders in response. Polly Hill's anthropological critique of economics is typical in saying: "Just as an art critic seldom gives artists practical advice on how to improve their work, so it would seem the height of arrogance for an anthropologist like myself to make practical suggestions on working methods or subject matter to economists. Nothing like that is to be found here" (1986, xi).

The metaphor of the arts is telling, for I find that much of modern anthropology and sociology has departed from the scientific agenda set down by its founding fathers and mothers. In the 1920s Marcel Mauss could write that the ultimate goal of sociology was to help to chart the course of societies, help them to evaluate choices, humbly but helpfully to add sociological knowledge to the debate. In 1952 Margaret Mead led a team of authors sponsored by the United Nations Educational, Scientific, and Cultural Organization (UNESCO) in a study trying to apply anthropology to the problems of development (Mead 1954); two years later Georges Balandier wrote two volumes on anthropology applied to the current problems of Africa (Balandier 1954–1955). But this objective has been eclipsed by another, more humanities-oriented goal—one that is more critical in the deconstructionist sense. Worried by the involvement of their scientific predecessors in the colonial enterprise (which by the mid-1950s was of course the enemy), troubled by commingling with concepts of culture and race (which Nazism had discredited as useful analytical devices), imbued by a relativist agenda, perhaps now self-consciously combined with the seeking of one's own self through the ethnographic encounter—with all this in mind, a new wave of anthropologists shifted the *problématique* of anthropology. Culture, they said, is not static, ahistorical, or uniform; it is multiple, defined at the edges and in conflict, complex yet holistic. "We" not only cannot judge another culture, but also we should question our abilities even to apprehend it. The encounter between the Self and the Other took central stage. The early anthropologists' concerns with scientific description of *le fait social total* and analysis of functional relationships in primitive societies were undercut by skeptical critiques of such "constructions" of reality. The new preoccupation was with the contested nature of scientific (or pseudoscientific) authority as well as of colonial authority; and it was implied that somehow the two must be linked.

In this process, practical questions were submerged. Yes, the anthropologist could call for the preservation of local cultures—at least, until a new generation of feminist anthropologists asked whether sexual subjugation and genital mutilation were simply to be waved aside, indeed defended, in the name of cultural survival. (Abuses of human rights posed similar problems.) But "development" was always placed in quotation marks, always the subject of prior analysis but seldom of practical, constructive, empirically driven research.

Meanwhile, in the backwaters of anthropology and sociology have arisen applied subfields. When one analyzes the cases of success claimed for these fields, one tends to find not the application of scientific models of culture, not the specification of culture-by-policy interactions, not even what Roger Bastide (1971) thought might be applied anthropology's contribution to science—the chance to test and develop scientific theories under conditions of planned change. Instead, one finds what might be called the ability to listen to what the poor say their problems are, what they know and do not know about the solutions, and what they think they need. Maurice Bloch puts it this way: "Anthropology is of as much use in practical problems as almost any other social science, and no more important than common sense and the ability to listen to people. . . . I am still hoping that there will be some successful applied anthropology" (Houtman 1988, 19).

Why have anthropology and other fields that study culture made such meager practical contributions? This is a question that has been driving my own recent forays into anthropology. I think I have discovered several reasons:

- what might be called "cultural differences" within academia, between theorists and those interested in practical applications, between anthropologists and economists, and more generally between humanists and scientists;
- the sheer scientific difficulty of specifying the ways that cultures and policy choices interact;
- a limited and I believe misguided notion of policy analysis, where project ideas magically materialize and cultural knowledge should be taken into account, usually through a study, in the design of projects and in their evaluation—a notion that perpetuates the myth of planning;
- and a fear of misuse, that taking culture into account will lead to oversimplification, discrimination, and sins of commission even more damaging than the sins of omission that occur by not "taking culture into account" (Klitgaard 1994, 1995).

In this essay, imagining I am speaking with Aaron Wildavsky, I want to ask him about the last factor—a fear that taking culture into account will cause more harm than good. Might this not be a threat to all cultural theories, including his?

Some Metaphorical Equations

Let us begin by noting how complex are the relationships between sociocultural settings and practical choices. For starters, our evaluation of various states of the world depends on our culture. In the jargon of economics, the social utility function is culturally conditioned. Second, and again using the economic metaphor, the production function is also culturally conditioned, or at least this is the hypothesis. For example, thinking abstractly, how much "development" occurs as a result of the adoption of a particular policy depends not only on the society's economic situation and political institutions but also on its sociocultural setting. A policy may work in one culture and fail in another. Third, the sociocultural setting is not stagnant. It changes as a result of changing economic conditions, for example, and indeed perhaps as a result of policy choices aimed at "development."

We have, metaphorically, a complicated set of simultaneous equations, in which "culture" enters in three ways. It shapes the utility function; in other words, it determines in part what a society will aspire to or desire. It conditions the production function (various kinds of them) for desired goods and services of many kinds, ranging from education to economic growth to artistic activities. And culture itself changes, meaning that as we try to estimate culture's impact and its interactions with policy choices, we are estimating a moving, dynamic, indeed living "variable." Culture is not static but subject to change. Some of these changes are planned, many are unplanned. Some can be avoided or slowed or speeded; others cannot. Many interesting questions again are empirical.

Imagine we had God's help and for a given society at a particular time could specify these complicated simultaneous equations and their dynamics. In other words, suppose we were divinely gifted social scientists. How could we then use this wonderful cultural theory to make decisions? The economist's answer is to maximize utility. That is, one would allocate resources and choose policies in order to maximize social utility given cultural conditions. We would maximize the value added of various choices given the moderating effects of the sociocultural setting and taking into account how our choices in turn would affect the sociocultural setting over time.

What If We Had a Perfect Cultural Theory?

We do not have such divine models, of course. And yet in the remainder of this chapter I want to pretend that we do, in order to raise what seem to me vexing questions about the practical application of cultural theories. Our ignorance is not, for now, the issue that I wish to address; it is the matter of the use of even perfect cultural knowledge were we to possess it. Consider some examples.

Existing Cultural Arrangements Promote
Inefficiency and Injustice

The following case is cited by anthropologist T. Scarlett Epstein as an example of "the necessity of taking local cultural arrangements into account." Officials of the Agricultural Department in Karnataka, India, tried to introduce local farmers to a new tool for weeding. It was a wonderful labor saver, yet the farmers refused to use it. This apparently irrational behavior was, Epstein explains, understandable in terms of "traditional relationships." Most peasant farmers in Karnataka have traditional relationships with Untouchables (Harijans), which obliges them to provide at least a minimum level of subsistence to their Harijan clients. If the peasant farmer employed fewer of his clients, he would still have to give them in charity almost as much as he might save in wages. Therefore even a weeding hook, which is a small, cheap, and easily employed implement that saves a considerable amount of labor, is rejected by Wangala farmers. They are not irrational or conservative in this matter. On the contrary, they know full well what it is like when their clients squat outside the house begging for food, broadcasting the farmer's meanness to the whole village (1988, 27).

What implications follow from an understanding of this feature of the local culture? Should those arrangements be accepted as they are? Or should they be subverted, unsettled, set in a process of change? Epstein does not explain; she just criticizes the project for not "taking culture into account."

Consider another example. A study of health centers in the Kisli district of Kenya in the 1970s "revealed that inadequate attention had been paid to sociocultural factors." Women were interested in information about child spacing, but their husbands and mothers-in-law often opposed any efforts to limit births. Their opposition was based on many reasons, among them the belief that "after death, people enter the spirit world and hover over their living family members to protect them and provide guidance." "One of the main conclusions drawn from this study," notes a recent UNESCO document, "was that in view of the strong value orientation in support of children and the control husbands still exercise over such matters, family planning programmes should not target only women of child bearing age, but also husbands and older women, particularly mothers-in-law" (UNESCO 1991, 11).

But like "taking culture into account," "targeting" remains vague. Once one has the conclusion of the study, what does one do with it? Is attitude change at stake here? Or simply the hope that if we pay attention to husbands and mothers-in-law, we will not invest in fruitless attempts at change?

The dilemma is quite general. Consider a psychological analogy. Does one "accept" a personality as one finds it, no matter what? Or under some conditions (which?), does one try to induce change in a desired direction (whose desired direction?)? How does the answer depend on the age (child versus youth versus adult)? On the costs of doing so? Are love and solidarity essential for such involvement?

Listening to Which People, When?

Jonathan Rigg emphasizes the implications of rapid change:

> The problem is that village life and the aspirations of villagers in Thailand, and in all developing countries, are fundamentally different from those that existed as recently as 20 years ago. The bases upon which traditional village life and livelihood were founded are arguably incompatible with the modern, commercial world. With this in mind, drawing upon populist conceptions of rural life (even faithfully), and incorporating them into rural development strategies, may well be a blind alley with little to offer rural people who rarely (rightly or wrongly) wish to return to "the good old days" (1991, 204).

Rigg also points out that existing village institutions often do not allow "the people" to make effective choices about their future. Rigg attributes the failure of rural development in Thailand to a culturally inappropriate Western model of collegial egalitarian participation, which clashes with "hierarchical and paternalistic" village societies in Thailand. As a result, in supposedly participatory programs, "projects are very rarely assessed in a democratic fashion, and the opinions and desires of individuals and cliques are extremely influential" (1991, 202–203).

Suppose he is right in a particular case. What happens if the local cultural group, far from being the village democracy and egalitarian society Westerners tend to romanticize, is hierarchical, dictatorial, sexist, and unjust? Does one rely on its given "culturally appropriate" mechanisms for decision? Does one try to introduce change? Does one support or aid only the local cultures that are deemed appropriate, leaving the rest to fend for themselves? On what facts do the answers depend?

Again, the issues are quite general. Long ago, Albert O. Hirschman identified a centerpiece in the art of project design—the choice and the balancing of "trait-taking" and "trait-making." The former took local attributes as given and built projects around them. The advantage was realism; the disadvantage, fatalism. Wasn't taking the existing situation as given in effect giving up on change? "Trait-making," in contrast, made the change of underlying attributes one of the goals of the project. The danger here is sheer failure, that the traits will not change; and to this will be added, predictably, the charge that one is insensitive to local realities. Hirschman pointed out that the dilemma was fundamental and inescapable (1962, chap. 4).

> The dilemma of project design is then the following: if the project is planned, built, and operated on the basis of certain negative attributes of the status quo, taking them for granted, as inevitable and unchangeable, it may miss important opportunities for effecting positive changes in these attributes—on the contrary, it may even confirm

and strengthen them. The achievements of the project would then be far below what they might have been and the net result could even be negative from the point of view of some "social progress function." The project planners will stand convicted as men without imagination who do not really believe in change and perhaps do not desire it. If, on the other hand, success in the construction and operation of the project is made to hinge on a prior or concurrent or subsequent change in some of the attributes of backwardness, then the project's fate becomes a wager; if the wager is lost, so that the needed change does not occur and the project's success is thereby jeopardized, the project planners will be accused of ignoring local circumstances, traditions, and sociopolitical structure and of incorrigible naivete and lack of realism in general (1962, 130–131).

The general version of this problem is that of static and dynamic comparative advantage, in a system with its own dynamic of change from causes outside our scope of intervention. Consider, for example, the debate over protectionism, which has raised similar issues. Should a country act as though its current comparative advantage—say, in raw materials—were permanent and build its economic strategy on its endowments and abilities as they stand? Or should it try to *develop* a comparative advantage, in effect changing its endowments and abilities through investments, the restriction of imports, and other means?

Cultural change is, understandably, a touchy subject. In the literature I have found plenty of pronouncements about the importance of respecting culture, but little about when and how to change various aspects of it. Might we hope for a detailed analysis of cultural change, one that would go beyond polemics and polar solutions? There are many possibilities here. One cannot solve the dilemma of appropriate change and science's contribution to it through moral argument alone. Roger Bastide notes:

> Certain governments, more concerned with avoiding traumas, may be opposed to changes that are too radical and would upset traditional structures and may prefer reforms that are slow and localized. Others, more concerned with rapid progress, may want profound mutations. Ethics has nothing to do with this, unless this conservatism or this "mutationism," instead of serving the general interests of the people, only profits a small group of the privileged (1971, 39; my translation).

In Bastide's experience, it is the French and Western anthropologists who emphasize slow change, whereas anthropologists from the developing countries themselves prefer more rapid breaks with the past. Indeed, to the latter the former's preference for incrementalism may seem itself a form of colonialism.

> Curious thing: White anthropology is often more concerned with this relativity of civilizations, stressing the discovery of indigenous solutions, than are local politics or the anthropology of people of color. It appears perhaps to these latter parties, who have studied at Western universities, that the ethnologist, in underlining the importance of cultural diversities and the necessity of respecting them, remains a "colonialist" or a "neocolonialist," desirous of slowing down progress more than of accelerating it, in this way maintaining the superiority of the White world and the dependence of the emancipated ex-colonies (Bastide 1971, 42).

It is a Western cultural trait nowadays—at least, among most of those who study culture—to assume that a certain mode of cultural change is appropriate: that it be democratic, participatory, slow, built on local institutions and leaders, and, if possible, guided by an anthropologist.

> Finding [local elites to serve as change agents] is not sufficient. Planned acculturation as conceived by Westerners cannot really be authoritarian—it follows a democratic model. And so much so that it never considers the "machinery" of development to be the most important thing, but the enthusiasm of the community. It therefore endeavors to create mixed teams, composed of traditional elements (members of the old community) and new elements (labor organizers, former students, social workers), to give them all a team spirit, and to forge from these disparate elements a dynamic whole. It will be these teams that elaborate inside themselves the techniques of change, who adapt old beliefs to the traits of the new culture, and reciprocally. But one should not proceed too ambitiously at the outset. The method generally adopted is that of "pilot projects": the change to be realized by these teams is small-scale and in a single community [which participates democratically]. The team, though democratically organized, is nonetheless directed, or at least guided, by an ethnographer, because it is necessary to know the structure of a culture before any manipulation of it (Bastide 1971, 68).

Hirschman was right—one cannot escape criticism no matter what one's choice. If one opts for changing cultural traits, one may be accused of colonialism, even if one is a member of the culture in question; and so, Bastide reminds us, may the same accusation arise when one calls for preserving the cultural manifestations that now exist.

A Local Culture Needs a "Change of Mentality"

The scientist Thomas Risley Odhiambo, a Kenyan and a Luo, founder of the International Centre of Insect Physiology and Ecology, has argued that Africa needs to embrace the scientific method in order to get beyond the "colonial interlude." In an article in *Science* (1967), Odhiambo asked whether "there may be something in the cultural attitude and social philosophy that may discourage a tradition in science." His answer was that there was.

"It is my view that the African's monistic (one world) view of nature has proved an impediment to his becoming a natural scientist. . . . In this African philosophy there is no sharp distinction between the subjective and objective worlds," whereas the existence of such a distinction in Europe led to the development of science. The European worldview is static and dualistic, but the African worldview is dynamic and unitary. "As for the African, his monism has deprived him of the choice between either science or mysticism; instead, he has concentrated his intellectual powers in devising a vastly intricate social and communalistic system." Odhiambo concluded that "science, in the modern sense, has no firm foundations in African society." The solution, he argued, was a change of "cultural attitude and social philosophy." Spurning the idea of a different science for Africa or a different yardstick of excellence, Odhiambo said that one had to "reach the basic root of the problem, his monistic world view, and modify it in a manner in which he can begin to regard Nature apart from himself and other beings."

In an interview some twenty years later with science writer Thomas A. Bass, Odhiambo explained that this modification had to create a kind of cultural schizophrenia.

"This African way of thinking is synthetic, rather than analytical. Its truths are arrived at by an additive process that makes them ever more complex and multi-faceted. The analytical approach, on the other hand, is reductive. It ends up with a partial truth that is easier to explain for its being an approximation. Unless the African can learn to use analytical tools better, even against his own instincts—indeed, in this case, become schizophrenic about it—then I have a feeling we're not going to get very far. I myself am schizophrenic. I believe that analytical tools are very powerful and that we should use them. When I'm thinking science, I think analytically. But I don't bring these methods into my general life. There I leave them out."

"Schizophrenia can be a risky condition," Bass commented.

"The Japanese have practiced it very successfully," Odhiambo replied. "They have their culture. They have their technology. It can be done, but one has to think about it deliberately and say, 'These are my compartments. I will not be muddled about it. I will have my scientific life and my cultural life, and I will not live one inside the other.' . . . My own feeling is that if Africa can rationalize its strengths and incorporate science into its culture, we will have a very powerful instrument. Instinctively I am relying more on science than most African thinkers, who are counting on change in the geopolitical situation. I may be totally wrong, but that's my instinct" (Bass 1990, 57–59).

Should one treat Odhiambo's hypothesis—that Africans lack a scientific mentality (meaning perhaps an abstract reasoning tradition?)—as one to be studied and documented, or as one to be rejected as too dangerous? Is the implication that this can be rapidly changed, or simply "taken into account" as a fact of (current) life? Are "mentalities" whole, or is the metaphor of schizophrenia a valid basis on which to proceed? Can one pick and choose the pieces of a culture that one wants? How? Would our answers to these questions change depending on the facts of particular cases?

Cultural Groups Benefit Differentially from a Policy or Project

A group of anthropologists, authors of a review of social soundness analysis in the U.S. Agency for International Development, cites an example of the need to take local culture into account. "In Indonesia, private sector support programs must take account of the issue of indigenous Indonesians vis-à-vis ethnic Chinese [who are also Indonesian citizens]. This is a highly charged and important social issue that, like many, is context-specific" (Gow et al. 1989, 18). What might taking this into account entail? Supporting ethnically discriminatory policies to countervail the distributional implications of privatization? Changing the emphasis on privatization because it affects groups differently? The authors do not elaborate.

In general, if one cultural group stands to benefit from a policy or project more than another, how should this be taken into account? In Togo, CARE's studies of village groups have identified objective factors that predict the degree to which a group is ready for a self-help project or not. How should such information be used? Should only those with the highest probability of success be given help? Or only those with the lowest? On what factual questions do such decisions depend?

The issue is again quite general. It pertains to the optimal allocation of resources given differential returns and given a concern for the distributional equity of outcomes. (The argument can be made in dynamic as well as static terms.)

The Possible Misuse of Training for Cultural Sensitivity

Some call for the training of practitioners in cultural knowledge—this, for example, was Bronislaw Malinowski's recommendation for how anthropology should be applied. But when such training has taken place—as in education in the United States—it has not been free of criticism. Several accusations have been made. Introducing cultural differences as "explanations" for poor performance by minority groups may lead prospective teachers to brand minorities as problem students, even to blame them for not learning. "Anthropology," writes one critic, "has given education students a new and somewhat more sophisticated set of rationalizations for giving up" (Kleinfeld 1983, 284). It is predictable that anthropology and other cultural subjects will be incompletely, perhaps poorly, taught in professional schools or training courses and poorly assimilated by future professionals; given this, say the critics, cultural categories may parade as fixed categories.

There is another line of criticism. Since anthropology teaches that each culture is different, "teachers will not know in advance which patterns of interaction will be prevalent in their students' communities, and which of those lead to learning difficulties"—at least, not without a detailed ethnographic study of each locality, which is clearly infeasible, as it "requires intense observation, by a trained observer, over an extended period of time" (Zeuli and Floden 1987, 6). With the needed knowledge unavailable, teachers may fall back on cultural stereotypes, which may only make matters worse. What to do?

Scientific Misunderstanding

Suppose we devised "good" measures in the statistical sense for a few "cultural" variables (perhaps such variables as ascriptive-achievement, group-individual, tight versus loose locus of control, religion, and matriarchal-patriarchal). Suppose that we combined these variables in a model that turned out to predict, imperfectly but "significantly," certain behavior of interest. And suppose that we showed that such variables had significant predictive power apart from economic variables pertaining to price, quantity, quality, and so forth. The model would be imperfect in the sense that it would make predictive mistakes. But one could win money betting on it.

Even so, might such a model lead to unfortunate scientific results? With regard to culture, does it not somehow *miss the point* to say that one has developed a model with some cultural "variables" that can help to predict various outcomes? Does this wording, this approach, not do violence to what a culture is? To what understanding a culture might be? To the kind of inquiry that cultural studies should represent?

By failing to air these questions and discuss them openly, both sides of the debate tend to fall back on stoppers and extreme solutions: "Only my way of looking at the subject and my means of studying it make sense. You don't understand what a culture is, or what a science is."

Confronting the Dangers and Misunderstandings

What are these questions really asking? They are helping us to go beyond the bromides of "We should take the sociocultural setting into account" and "We should be culturally sensitive." We tend not to think hard enough about what "taking culture into account" and "cultural sensitivity" might mean and entail. By imagining that we had a perfect "cultural theory" we can imagine what perfect "cultural sensitivity" might involve, and it turns out that the answer is not obvious. The six worries I have just examined all make more problematic the task of "taking culture into account."

I believe that as we follow Aaron Wildavsky's example and push forward our scientific understanding of sociocultural settings, we have simultaneously to grapple with these dilemmas of application. The agenda is both scientific and what we might call ethical. When and how can people adapt policies, processes, and systems to existing cultures? When and how can people intentionally change, or preserve, various aspects of culture? And if we could ever understand these processes, how would we, how should we, take them into account?

I wonder what Aaron would say.

Notes

1. The term "interaction" means that mathematically the effect of X on Y depends on Z as well, as in $Y = \alpha_0 + \alpha_1 X + \alpha_2 Y + \alpha_3(XZ)$, where the αs are constants. For example, in psychometrics one speaks of aptitude-by-treatment interactions, where the effectiveness of a pedagogical technique depends on a student's characteristics, such as anxiety and level of conventionally measured intelligence. Much of the literature on culture posits culture-by-policy interactions without using the mathematical metaphor or countenancing the complexities of specifying and measuring interaction effects.

Chapter Twelve

Rewriting the Precepts of Policy Analysis

MICHAEL THOMPSON

Just a week or two after *Cultural Theory* (Thompson, Ellis, and Wildavsky 1990) had been published, I was trotting along beside Aaron Wildavsky on one of his famous walks around Berkeley. "About our next book," he said suddenly. "What do you mean, 'our *next* book'?" I replied. "Haven't we just said everything that we have to say in *Cultural Theory*?" "No, no," said Aaron, "I'm not talking about Cultural Theory! I'm talking about rewriting the precepts of policy analysis." Aaron had the better of me there. Being the founder of the world's first graduate school of public policy, he at least knew *something* about policy analysis, and I even had to wait until I got back to the Survey Research Center before I could look up "precept" in the dictionary.

"Moral instruction," the dictionary said, or "Rule or guide, especially for behavior." The first meaning rang a bell—something to do with that line from William Blake that became so popular with graffiti artists during the 1960s: "The tigers of wrath are wiser than the horses of instruction." I rather fancied being a tiger of wrath, and tearing all those hyperrational weighers of costs and benefits limb from limb, but suspected that this might not be what Aaron had in mind. And then there was the small problem (as far as I was concerned) that, if you are going to rewrite a set of precepts, it helps to know what they are. So we never got it written, which is a great pity, but at least I can record that this is where Aaron was intent on going, and perhaps I can help to keep up the momentum of the work that is assembled in this volume by sketching what I now see to be the essentials of our "next book."

What follows, therefore, is the synopsis for that book—a little introduction by way of a "real-life" story, a contrasting of the conventional approach to the sorts of policy challenges that are raised by this story with the approach that Cultural

Theory allows us to take, and then six fairly tigerish and wrathful rewritings of the current precepts, each little more than a "bullet point" but destined to become an entire chapter in the *magnum opus*. And, finally, an example is presented in which these rewritten precepts are brought to bear on a pressing policy problem: the handling of hazardous wastes.

Queer Goings-on Around the Baltic[1]

The Swedes already have very clean power stations, but they want to make them even cleaner. The money they propose to spend will certainly make a small reduction in Sweden's polluting emissions, but the same money spent on improving the power stations of its filthy neighbor across the Baltic—Poland—would make an *enormous* difference to Sweden's environment. Indeed, according to a 1989 report by the Swedish Energy Administration, if the Swedes were to spend the money in Egypt they would do better than if they spent it on themselves.

This little story suggests that the policy path toward a healthy Baltic Sea is far from smooth, and it raises a host of awkward questions for the policy analyst.

1. Should we see Egypt as a Baltic nation?
2. If Egypt is a Baltic nation do we, perhaps, need to see Poland as a Mediterranean nation? Alternatively, we could speak of the Balto-Mediterranean Sea, but then there would be the tricky business of deciding where it is located.
3. The Swedish voters, especially at a time of recession, are unlikely to warm to the proposal that their taxes be spent in Poland. But the pill could be sweetened by insisting that all the contracts for the work in Poland be placed with Swedish companies. But (assuming that in these days of "late capitalism" you can tell whether a company *is* Swedish) would that be fair to companies in other countries—companies that could probably do the work much more cheaply? And would that disregard for fair competition be fair to the Swedish voters and taxpayers?
4. In view of these confusions over fairness and competition, should all these Swedish-Polish-Egyptian transactions be seen as trade or as aid?
5. What about the "moral hazards"? There are no incentives here for Poland or Egypt to clean up their act. Quite the opposite: The dirtier they make themselves, the more aid they can expect.
6. Might the whole tangled web make more sense if we looked at it not from the perspectives of the nation-states, but from the points of view of the enclosed coastal seas—the Baltic, the Mediterranean and, presumably, quite a few others? Of course, the seas do not *have* points of view, but we can pretend that they have, and that they prefer to be free from substances like titanium dioxide, and that they are happiest when there are lots of fishes swimming around inside them. In other words, we could agree to

treat these common property resources (as they are now called) as the "primary actors," and then we could decide where the money should be spent—Sweden, Poland, Egypt, or wherever—so that the seas themselves got the greatest improvement per currency unit (this approach, much elaborated, is now called "joint implementation"). But then what about national sovereignty? Countries that have grave doubts over surrendering a few powers to the European Union are hardly likely to jump at the suggestion that they should hand the whole lot over to a watery waste that cannot even tell us what it wants.

7. All of these questions assume, as does most policy analysis, that environmental improvement *costs money*, but, as Aaron's colleague in the risk business, John Adams, is always pointing out, it need not.

"There are expensive ways by which a fat person can lose weight—health farms, exercise machines, liposuction—but walking or cycling to work and eating less are likely to be more effective and actually *save* money" (Adams 1993, 259). This is the neglected consumption-reducing option, in which all those expensive and fattening cream buns that you have gone without are translated straight into money in your pocket.

And, behind this neglected option, there lies a neglected definition of what the problem *is* and a neglected definition of what the solution *is*. All those bilateral transfers of funds and all those ingenious retrofittings of power stations, this neglected argument runs, may just be a way of perpetuating grossly inappropriate lines of technological development. Perhaps governments and firms are the problem, not the solution. Could it be that the biggest improvement in environmental quality will come from the grassroots—from major shifts in consumer preferences as citizens come to trust activist groups, such as Greenpeace, more than government ministers and advertising agencies?

How, Then, Do We Sort Out This Mess?

One plausible answer to the "trade or aid" question—an answer that also copes with the moral hazard business—is that the transfers to Poland begin as aid but, as they continue, they be converted into trade. The argument here is that Poland, thanks to its years of communist central planning, now has such an outmoded technological base that it really is in no position to compete with Western market economies. The aid transfers, therefore, should continue until that disadvantage has disappeared. At that moment the playing field will be level and trade—fair trade between roughly equal partners—should begin.

This argument draws on the familiar institutional distinction between *markets* (the competing players merrily bidding and bargaining with one another) and *hierarchies* (the benign authorities who ensure that the conditions needed for the playing of this trading game are in place) and there is much good sense in it. The trouble, however, is that, since neither markets nor hierarchies are in the business of reducing our intake of cream buns (except in wartime when the cream, by some strange alchemy, is converted into guns), this cannot be the whole story. Indeed, the hierarchies-and-markets framework is deficient on two important counts. First, it is an incomplete typology. Second, it does not take explicit account of the very different convictions as to how the world is (and people are) that each of these arrangements for the conduct of social transactions induces in the individuals who constitute those arrangements.

In other words, the conventional typology is *insufficiently variegated* and it ignores the *social construction of nature* (physical and human). This, of course, is the argument that we set out at some length in *Cultural Theory*, along with the important observation that change, in the sort of two-dimensional world that the markets-and-hierarchies approach gives us, is extraordinarily uninteresting: If you're knocked out of markets you'll end up in hierarchies, and if you're knocked out of hierarchies you'll end up in markets . . . end of story. So the conventional approach is deficient on a third count too: It's *boring* (Figure 12.1).

I will not go into these three deficiencies here, because that is what *Cultural Theory* is all about. The import, so far as policy analysis is concerned, is that the Cultural Theory approach allows us not to neglect the currently neglected definitions of the problem and the solution: the *egalitarian's* definitions. And, for good measure, it allows us to recognize the *fatalist's* position, a vital ingredient in any robust policy.

De-neglecting the Egalitarians and the Fatalists

It is the egalitarians—the Greenpeaces and Earth First!s of this world—who are the cream bun rejecters. As their dumping of tons of nonreturnable bottles on the steps of the headquarters of multinational companies suggests, they are not entirely convinced that market forces will solve all our environmental ills. And their T-shirt emblazoned with the rhetorical question "Who Saved the Whales: Greenpeace or the Royal Society?" similarly confirms their less-than-total trust in the hierarchical institutions of the modern state. So here is a distinct and undoubtedly influential institutional category that is uncompromisingly opposed to both markets and hierarchies—the only institutional forms that conventional analysis recognizes.

Fatalists, for their part, are a sort of black hole into which disappears everything that is produced by the other three quadrants but not wanted by them. John Carman (1992), an archaeologist, has called fatalists "dumpees," a neologism that nicely captures the way in which those who find themselves on the outside of all three organized solidarities—markets, hierarchies, and egalitarian groups—cope with that situation: cheerfully guzzling whatever good things happen to come their way and stoically enduring the bad. Fatalists lose little sleep over things like

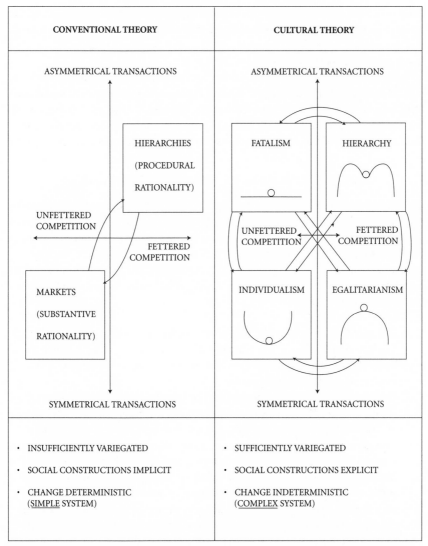

FIGURE 12.1   Conventional and Cultural Theory approaches: The key differences

ozone holes that may or may not be opening up above them. After all, if the holes are there what can they do about them? "Why bother?" is the fatalist's not unreasonable response to the policy issues that so exercise those who are not fatalists. However, it would be a mistake to conclude from this that fatalists are irrelevant to the policy debate. Fatalists are the great "risk absorbers" (acceptance and rejection do not come into it) without whom none of the actors who *are* engaged in the debate could get their policies to work. Just as rubbish—that which has no value—is vital to the viability of that from which it is excluded (the dynamic process by which value is formed and transformed), so fatalists are indispensable to the deciding of policy (Thompson 1979). And they are indispensable to that process precisely because they take no part in it.

With conventional and Cultural Theory approaches contrasted in this way—insufficient to sufficient variegation, tacit to explicit recognition of the social constructions of nature, and boring to interesting change—we can set about deducing what will be entailed in switching from the former to the latter. The message, essentially, is that most of the policy analysis we know and love has reached a dead end.

The End of the Road for Newtonian Policymaking

The science that supplies us with the facts that enable us to define the problems—such as those that we perceive as afflicting the Baltic and the Mediterranean—is in considerable disarray. The argument (recently summarized in a number of readable books on chaos and complexity[2]) is that the science on which we have depended has missed all the squiggly bits and, unfortunately, it is the squiggly bits that matter. Esoteric though this may sound, it has some far-reaching implications for the policy analyst.

1. The intrinsic complexity of ecosystems *and* social systems renders them fundamentally different from noncomplex systems—systems in which the linear cause-and-effect relationships between their components render them *predictable* and *manageable*.
2. Traditional policymaking is appropriate only to noncomplex systems. It involves establishing the facts, weighing up the probable costs and benefits of various possible interventions, and moving from there to the right answer. But in setting out to manage things like the Baltic and Mediterranean Seas, we have put ourselves far beyond the reach of this "Newtonian" approach—the approach in which we find the right answer by the single-minded pursuit of a single rationality. In coming to grips not just with ecological and social systems but also with their interactions, we have placed ourselves, whether we like it or not, in a world of complexity, multiple rationalities, chaos, sensitivity to initial conditions, nonlinearities, and intrinsic unpredictability. And in then reaching, uncritically, for our familiar Newtonian tools—neoclassical economics in particular, but also things like probabilistic risk assessment and the "realist" approach to international relations—we are committing ourselves to a most unwise path. We are aspiring to *manage the unmanageable.*
3. What, then, is the wise path? The first essential is a thoroughgoing rejection of Newtonian policymaking and of the tools on which it relies. Then, with all that garbage cleared out of the way, we can set about constructing a new, post-Newtonian approach and identifying the sorts of tools that would be appropriate to it.

4. These tools, of course, are all around us: In Cultural Theory we have notions such as decisionmaking under contradictory certitudes, myths of nature, visions of the future, ideas of fairness, the theory of surprise, clumsy institutions, and indicators of technological inflexibility; and in plurality-based methods, we have such notions as artificial life modeling and scenario-planning that are readily harnessable to Cultural Theory.[3]

Putting this non-Newtonian tool kit together, therefore, is a straightforward enough task (though it does require us to learn how to use these tools and to devise ways of making them more effective); it is the laying down of the present tools that is the hard part. It is with a view to lessening these difficulties that I offer the following precepts.

Precepts for Policy in a Complex World

1. The design and redesign of institutions so as to nurture *trust* has to be the primary focus.
2. Do not try to predict the unpredictable. If the system is *complex* use "the other tool-kit," not cost-benefit analysis, probabilistic risk assessment, general equilibrium modeling, and so on.
3. "Normal science for public policy"—first establishing the hard science facts, then bringing in the soft science to assess the impacts, acceptability, and so on—is a nonstarter. Begin instead with the *contending social framings* of problem and solution.
4. Ditch the realist framework (the assumption that it is all down to nation-states). Instead, always address *three audiences:* governments, businesses, and activist groups (though do not forget the fatalists). *All* the policy opportunities are in their interactions.
5. The criterion of economic efficiency does not respect widely held *ideas of fairness,* and they are what matter if you want robust policies—policies that nurture rather than squander trust.
6. Finally, it all comes back to *technology as a social and cultural process:* how to minimize inflexibility (technology assessment, that is, without prediction).

For those who find a half page of precepts too cumbersome I can offer a single-sentence superprecept, one that the trainee policy analyst could usefully spend his first semester embroidering in cross-stitch, and then framing, so that when he finally qualifies, he can hang it proudly on his office wall.

> IF YOU'RE HAVING TO ASK WHO'S RIGHT
> (WORSE STILL, IF YOU ALREADY *KNOW*
> WHO'S RIGHT) YOU'RE WRONG!

This superprecept inculcates the first essential: *reflexivity*. Reflexivity, though difficult to achieve in practice, is simplicity itself in theory: the self-conscious examination of the assumptions that underlie any analytical approach. An example would be the unquestioned assumption that environmental improvement costs money. Such an assumption, we have already seen, excludes those who do not share it—the egalitarians—from the policy process. Or, to be precise, it excludes them from one stage in that process—policy selection. They wing their way in, with a vengeance, at the next stage—implementation—as has recently happened with Greenpeace's helicopter-borne intervention that prevented the burial at sea of the Brent Spar oil storage structure.

Handcrafted objects, as any antique dealer will tell you, are more valuable if they come in pairs, which means that the diligent trainee policy analyst will put in a few extra hours, each evening, embroidering another superprecept, one that adds a modicum of *humility* to the reflexivity that has been inculcated by its mate.

> YOU CAN ONLY INTERVENE CONSTRUCTIVELY
> AT THOSE POINTS WHERE CONSTRUCTIVE
> INTERVENTION IS POSSIBLE

What this means is that total control—the ideal of the policymaker, guided by sound policy analysis, pulling the appropriate levers, and bringing us all smoothly to the New Jerusalem—is simply unattainable. If it were attainable then the solution that was agreed on between the market actor (Shell) and the hierarchical actor (the British government) would have come to pass, and the Brent Spar would now be moldering in its watery grave. It is not. It is sitting bolt-upright in a Norwegian fjord—a large and expensive reminder that the whole line of technological development that it embodies is no longer viable.

As it happens, this is not too much of a problem, because that line of technological development has now been superseded by a much more flexible line—one that, being based on seabed installations linked to oil production vessels on the surface, has done away with the need for vast structures like the Brent Spar.[4] The process, therefore, is an erratic and never-ending interplay between actors from all three solidarities—markets, hierarchies, and egalitarian groups—and, during the Brent Spar episode, it has been the markets (with their technological innovations) and the egalitarian groups (with their well-targeted criticisms) that have been making all the running. The hierarchy—the British government and its unreflexive policy analysts—has been left with egg on its face; it intervened at a point in the process where constructive intervention was not possible.

Of course, if the market actors had not been sufficiently innovative, and there had been no alternative line of technological development to shift to, then all three "active" solidarities would have found themselves taking a backseat to fatalism. Something along these lines has now happened in those parts of the former

Soviet Union that are saddled with seventy years' worth of centrally planned technology, a Mafia-dominated private sector, and precious little by way of constructive egalitarian criticism. Trust, in these unfortunate enclaves, has gone seriously into reverse, and the happy day when they will have a responsive citizenry interacting constructively with reflexive policymaking is probably a long way off.

Listing the new precepts (and superprecepts) in this way helps to make clear how very different policy in a complex world is from the sort of policy we have long been used to. But of course fine words, as the saying goes, butter no parsnips; what is needed now is a real-world example: a demonstration of these rewritten precepts in action.

Reflexivity and Humility Among the Hazardous Wastes

Lawrence Summers's (1992) famous World Bank memorandum—urging that the rich countries export their hazardous wastes to the poor countries—is based on the impeccable logic of economic efficiency: Both donors and recipients, once the agreed compensation has been paid, will be better off than if the deal had not gone ahead. So should a rich country, such as Austria, opt for that solution? Joanne Linnerooth-Bayer has designed a survey questionnaire that, among other things, tests the popularity of this Summers option.[5] She presented the option in such a way that those who did not go along with it would actually be letting innocent babies die:

> [I]t seems certain that all of the technically-feasible communities will resist having the facility. Yet a neighboring country, with large-scale environmental problems and few resources for dealing with them, has offered to host the facility for compensation (it can use this compensation to deal with serious problems like improving its air and water quality, thereby reducing, for example, its rate of cancer in children). Should this offer be accepted?

Almost 90 percent of Austrians—a remarkably high figure in survey work—said no. People, they felt, should take responsibility for their own messes—an egalitarian sentiment—and off-loading them onto neighboring countries seriously transgresses this principle.

This does not mean that their hazardous waste is unsiteable (in the way that the Brent Spar became unsiteable), but it does mean that it is not siteable *outside* of Austria. So the remaining questions in her survey focused on the two well-known ways of siting *within* a nation: "top-down" expert assessment of technically suitable locations (the hierarchical preference) and the "voluntary" (or market-based) approach in which a community agrees to take the facility in exchange for compensation (the individualist preference). Trust in the state authorities is evidently still quite strong in Austria, and more than 50 percent of those surveyed felt that this top-down process was fair. Just under 50 percent also felt that the "voluntary" process was fair. So the real outrage—the sense of unfairness that would have Austrians taking to the streets—is reserved for the Summers option—

the option that the conventional policy analyst, applying the criterion of economic efficiency, would recommend.

Conventional policy analysts of course will argue that fairness, unlike economic efficiency, is a value-laden concept and therefore has no place in the dispassionate business that they are engaged in. But they deceive themselves. Embedded in the notion of economic efficiency is one idea of fairness: the individualist's idea that those who put most in should get most out. There is nothing neutral or dispassionate about the criterion of economic efficiency, and to insist otherwise is to act in a deeply political and (so far as the policy analyst is concerned) unprofessional way. So this simple typology of ideas of fairness, together with the equally simple survey instrument by which it is rendered operational, extricates us from the unreflexive (and unprofessional) slough in which the conventional policy analyst is mired. It also demonstrates one of the precepts in action: the rejection of the normal-science approach with its imposition of a singular assessment of the risks involved, and its replacement with the contending social framings of those risks.

Now, armed with this information as to what the good people of Austria see as fair and unfair, we can begin to tailor a clumsy (but robust and consent-rich) way of doing things, a way that includes elements from all three possible solutions.[6]

> First, the explicit ruling out of hazardous waste transfers across Austria's borders.
> Second, a clear (and clearly communicated) reliance on the process of expert technical assessment for the selection of the site.
> Third, the establishment of a process of negotiation for arriving at some ex post facto compensation for the community chosen to host the facility.
> Fourth, the linking of these three to an explicit commitment to reducing the production of hazardous wastes, thereby reducing the future community burden. (This of course establishes a link between two hitherto separate domains: siting policy and technology policy.)

And, indeed, this is pretty much what is now in place in Austria. No solidarity, we should note, has it all its own way—the egalitarians would like the waste localized all the way back to the consumers and producers; the hierarchists would like to be in control of everything; and the individualists would like the compensation to be *ex ante*—but each gets a lot more than nothing. This clumsy institution does more than just nurture trust and consent; it is also a *learning system* that is set up in such a way that it can learn from each of the three ways of knowing that are built into it. If we monitor its progress we can soon discover where it needs modifying: strengthening one component here, refocusing another somewhere else, changing the scale level of a third, and so on.

Even so, the facility may still turn out to be unsiteable, but at least this attention to robustness and learning (the design and redesign of institutions precept) lessens the likelihood that unsiteability is merely the consequence of an institutionally ham-handed and insufficiently reflexive process. And even if the facility *is* unsiteable, the link that has been established with the domain of technology policy provides us with a way of changing failure into success. The "null option" (not putting the facility anywhere), this link shows us, is often not null at all. Far from always being a failure, unsiteability can be just what we need to find a new, and better, way forward.

Making a Silk Purse Out of the Sow's Ear of Unsiteability[7]

One of the drawbacks of the seemingly oh-so-efficient solution proposed by Summers is this: If the rich countries can fairly effortlessly get rid of the unwanted waste-streams from their production processes, then they will never receive any signals that would lead them to search for, and switch to, cleaner (and ultimately more efficient) lines of technological development. An example would be the new, ecological, process for wastewater treatment[8] that has been developed by John Todd and his company, Ocean Arks, and that is currently being backed (in the form of demonstration projects) by venture capital. If successful (and this is a big "if") this technology should sweep away the present biological and chemical technology (filter-beds, activated sludges, oxygenation, and so on) in a Schumpeterian "gale of destruction."

This, at any rate, is what is expected to happen if technological evolution is a simple process—a process that is, in principle, predictable. In this view, new technological developments (John Todd's "ecological machines," for instance) will always be popping up (like mutations in the process of biological evolution), and the market can be relied on to put these new developments into competition with one another and with the established technology, thereby quickly revealing their relative efficiencies. Changes at the margin will then ensure that the most efficient alternative prospers and that the less efficient die out (a state of affairs that is depicted by the heavier of the two curves in Figure 12.2). But technical change is not simple; it is complex. It cannot be relied on always to find its way down a single optimal path, which means that its future states are not predictable. This is a serious blow both to neoclassical economists (who see technology as looking after itself, provided we do not intervene in the operation of the market) and to technology assessors (who aim to steer technology in a socially desirable direction by predicting its consequences and deciding whether we should avoid them). How do we extricate ourselves from that wreckage?

We now know, thanks largely to the work of Brian Arthur (1989), that technology, even in a market system that is not being interfered with, does not automatically find its way to the most efficient of the alternatives that are at any time available. We can find ourselves "locked in" to a less efficient alternative, in which case it will take what ecologists call an "optimal perturbation" to get us to the more ef-

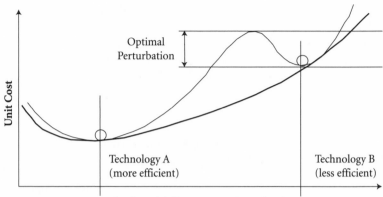

FIGURE 12.2   Jumping from one technology to a more efficient one

ficient one (a state of affairs that is depicted by the lighter curve in Figure 12.2).
So the neoclassicists are wrong. We *do* need to intervene in the market; we *do* need
technology assessment. But the technology assessors, too, are wrong, because they
are committed to predicting technology's consequences, and that is simply not
possible. What *is* possible, however, is for us to intervene so as to lessen the extent
of the "lock-ins": to reduce *technological inflexibility*. If we switch the focus of
technology assessment from anticipation to inflexibility reduction, then we will
have the basis for the sort of intervention we need: the sort of intervention appropriate to a complex system of which we ourselves are part (which brings us to the
precept about technology as a social and cultural process).

With the focus changed in this way, unsiteability now becomes a clear indicator
of inflexibility—of deep "lock-in"—and it is this property that allows us to make
the constructive connection between siting policy and technology policy. Hierarchists, individualists, and egalitarians all have an interest in lock-in. Hierarchists
want to step in and take control so as to bring us all to a socially more sustainable
path; individualists want to profit by delivering the optimal perturbations and in-
vesting in the new technologies that will then sweep away the old; and egalitarians
want to show us that we are living way beyond the limits when we needn't be.

What this means, in practical policy terms, is that government advisers, venture
capitalists, and environmental activists—the "three audiences" in the realism-
rejecting precept—should all be monitoring the siting obstacles that our established technologies are running into, and they should constantly be assessing
those obstacles in terms of the notions of fairness that are held by their fellow
citizens—notions that are so easily, and so inexpensively, revealed by the sorts of
survey instruments that Joanne Linnerooth-Bayer has devised for Austrians and
their hazardous wastes. Only when these signals say, "Jump to another line of

technological development," and there turns out to be no alternative line to jump to, is the null option really null. Only then does fatalism take over the driver's seat.

Conclusion

Which side, I wonder, would Aaron have taken in this dust-up between the horses of instruction (who want to factor in the relevant cultural variables to their established, Newtonian ways of doing things) and the tigers of wrath (who want to demolish those established ways and replace them with an entirely different, non-Newtonian approach)? Aaron certainly believed that culture matters, and he was also convinced that when it comes to understanding *how* culture matters, Cultural Theory is, as he put it, the only game in town. Siding with the tigers of wrath means, above all, taking complexity seriously, that is, taking seriously the proposition that social life is a self-organizing disequilibrium system that never settles down to some stable configuration. It means recognizing, as one reviewer of *Cultural Theory* (Schwartz 1991, 765) put it, that

> each way of life, unchecked, undermines itself. Individualism would mean chaos without hierarchical authority to enforce contracts and repel enemies. To get work done and settle disputes the egalitarian order needs hierarchy, too. Hierarchists, in turn, would be stagnant without the creative energy of individualism, uncohesive without the binding force of equality, unstable without the passivity and acquiescence of fatalism. Dominant and subordinate ways of life thus exist in alliance yet this relationship is fragile, constantly shifting, constantly generating a societal environment conducive to change.

That Aaron was "thinking complex" long before he came across Cultural Theory is evident from his attachment to the word "curvilinear" (Wildavsky 1981). A curvilinear relationship operates, to begin with, by giving you more and more of what you want, but if you continue to apply that policy, it will go into reverse and start giving you the opposite of what you want. Cultural Theory provides an explanation for curvilinearity: The reversal happens at the point at which the contention between solidarities gives way to dependency. Incrementalism, for instance, is a way of framing policy around which individualists and hierarchists can readily unite, but like the criterion of economic efficiency, it excludes the egalitarians: You cannot be incremental if you do not have agreement on what is fair and unfair. So incrementalism worked well, and it went on working well, until it had strengthened individualism and hierarchy to the point at which that alliance desperately needed what it had so energetically excluded: fatalism and egalitarianism. Curvilinearity then ensured that the United States got both, with a vengeance: a great fatalistic swath of nonvoters and the dramatic rise of what Aaron called radical egalitarianism.[9]

If you take this broad view of what has been happening since the 1960s, then one thing is obvious: Culture *does* matter. And if you then take the Cultural Theory view of *how* culture matters, you begin to see how things might have been done differently: Policymakers, if only their analysts had equipped themselves with the reflexivity and modesty that Cultural Theory makes possible, could have seen it coming. That, at any rate, is how it appears to the horses of instruction. But for the tigers of wrath this unconstructive upwelling of fatalism and egalitarianism was not something that just *came;* the policymakers, aided and abetted by the policy analysts, *brought* it. That is why the precepts of policy analysis have to be rewritten and not just revised.

Notes

1. This section is based on Thompson and Trisoglio 1997.

2. Gleick 1987 is a particularly good account of the development of chaos theory, though it fails to mention (perhaps because it did not happen in the United States) the pioneering work in catastrophe theory, of which chaos theory is the direct descendent. Zeeman 1977 would make good that omission. A more recent, and quite racy, account of what has been happening to chaos theory is Waldrop 1992.

3. Some of these are explained in Thompson, Ellis, and Wildavsky 1990, the remainder in Thompson and Trisoglio 1997 and Thompson forthcoming.

4. These innovations have come about, in large part, in response to the challenges of exploiting the oil beneath the deeper and stormier Atlantic Ocean. Greenpeace, accordingly, has now refocused its criticism on the unsustainability (because of global warming from fossil-fuel use) of that move from the North Sea to the Atlantic.

5. Her results, and the typology of ideas of fairness that underlies her questionnaire, are set out in Linnerooth-Bayer and Fitzgerald 1996.

6. Lawrence Summers's solution, as it stands, is simply the market-based solution expanded to the global level. The inverse of his solution—localize waste all the way to the point at which each producer and consumer is responsible for the waste they generate—is, however, quite distinct from both the market-based and top-down solutions: It keeps waste out of the marketplace and it works from the bottom up.

7. This section draws on Thompson 1996b.

8. Sewage works, though not in the same league as hazardous waste facilities, are certainly LULUs (Locally Unwanted Land Uses) and are often difficult to site.

9. It was the rise of fatalism and egalitarianism, coupled with the weakening of the self-subverted alliance of individualism and hierarchy, that was unconstructive, not fatalism and egalitarianism per se. Aaron's view of what was happening in the United States was overly influenced by what he saw happening on the Berkeley campus, and he too readily projected that view across onto Europe, where (as the example of the Austrians and their hazardous wastes shows) the interactions of the solidarities are, in general, quite constructive.

References

Abrahamsson, Bengt. 1993. "The Anarchistic Ideal: The Desire for Nonorganization." In *Why Organizations? How and Why People Organize.* Newbury Park, CA: Sage Publications.

Abramson, Paul, and Ronald Inglehart. 1995. *Value Change in Global Perspective.* Ann Arbor: University of Michigan Press.

Adams, John. 1993. "The Emperor's Old Clothes: The Curious Comeback of Cost-Benefit Analysis." *Environmental Values* 2:247–60.

Ahrne, Goran. 1990. *Agency and Organization: Towards an Organizational Theory of Society.* Newbury Park, CA: Sage Publications.

Akerlof, George A. 1976. "The Economics of Caste and of the Rat Race and Other Woeful Tales." *Quarterly Journal of Economics* 90:599–617.

_____. 1983. "Loyalty Filters." *American Economic Review* 73:54–63.

Akerlof, George A., and William T. Dickens. 1982. "The Economic Consequences of Cognitive Dissonance." *American Economic Review* 72:307–19.

Alba, Carlos R. 1980. "The Organization of Authoritarian Leadership: Franco's Spain." In *Presidents and Prime Ministers,* ed. Richard Rose and Ezra Suleiman. Washington, DC: American Enterprise Institute.

Aldrich, Howard E. 1979. *Organizations and Environments.* Englewood Cliffs, NJ: Prentice-Hall.

Almond, Gabriel A. 1956. "Comparative Political Systems." *Journal of Politics* 18:391–409.

_____. 1960. "Introduction: A Functional Approach to Comparative Politics." In *The Politics of the Developing Areas,* ed. Gabriel A. Almond and James S. Coleman. Princeton: Princeton University Press.

_____. 1965. "A Developmental Approach to Political Systems." *World Politics* 17:183–214.

_____. 1990. "Rational Choice Theory and the Social Sciences." In *A Discipline Divided: Schools and Sects in Political Science.* Newbury Park, CA: Sage Publications.

Almond, Gabriel A., and James S. Coleman, eds. 1960. *The Politics of the Developing Areas.* Princeton: Princeton University Press.

Almond, Gabriel A., and G. Bingham Powell. 1966. *Comparative Politics: A Developmental Approach.* Boston: Little, Brown and Company.

_____. 1978. "Political Culture." In *Comparative Politics: System, Process, and Policy,* ed. Gabriel A. Almond and G. Bingham Powell. 2d ed. Boston: Little, Brown and Company.

Almond, Gabriel A., and Sidney Verba. 1963. *The Civic Culture: Political Attitudes and Democracy in Five Nations.* Boston: Little, Brown and Company.

Almond, Gabriel A., and Sidney Verba, eds. 1980. *The Civic Culture Revisited.* Boston: Little, Brown and Company.

Alt, James, and Kenneth Shepsle, eds. 1990. *Perspectives on Positive Political Economy.* Cambridge: Cambridge University Press.

Ames, Bruce, and Lois Gold. 1990. "Nature's Chemicals and Synthetic Chemicals: Comparative Toxicology." *Proceedings of the National Academy of Sciences* 87:7777–81.

Anand, Narasimhan, and Richard A. Peterson. 1995. "When Market Information Constitutes Fields: The Music Industry Case." Typescript. Vanderbilt University.

Arrow, Kenneth J. 1951. *Social Choice and Individual Values.* New York: John Wiley and Sons.

Arthur, W. Brian. 1989. "Competing Technologies, Increasing Returns, and Lock-in by Historical Events: The Dynamics of Allocation Under Increasing Returns." *Economic Journal* 99:116–31.

Bailyn, Bernard. 1967. *The Ideological Origins of the American Revolution.* Cambridge, MA: The Belknap Press of Harvard University Press.

Baker, Kendall L., Russell J. Dalton, and Kai Hildebrandt. 1981. *Germany Transformed: Political Culture and the New Politics.* Cambridge, MA: Harvard University Press.

Balandier, Georges. 1954–1955. *L'anthropologie appliquée aux problèmes des pays sous-développés.* 2 vols. Prepared for a course at the Institut d'Etudes Politiques, University of Paris. Paris: Les Cours de Droit.

Banfield, Edward C. 1958. *The Moral Basis of a Backward Society.* New York: Free Press.

Barnes, Samuel, and Max Kaase, eds. 1979. *Political Action: Mass Participation in Five Western Democracies.* Beverly Hills, CA: Sage Publications.

Baron, Jonathan. 1966. "Protected Values." Paper prepared for delivery to the Society for Judgment and Decision-Making, Chicago.

Barry, Brian. 1970. *Sociologists, Economists, and Democracy.* London: Collier-Macmillan.

Barth, Fredrik. 1966. "Models of Social Organization." Occasional Papers of the Royal Anthropological Institute, No. 23.

Barzel, Yoram, and Eugene Silberberg. 1973. "Is the Act of Voting Rational?" *Public Choice* 16:51–58.

Bass, Thomas A. 1990. *Camping with the Prince and Other Tales of Science in Africa.* Boston: Houghton Mifflin.

Bastide, Roger. 1971. *Anthropologie appliquée.* Paris: Payot.

Bates, Robert. 1990. "Macropolitical Economy in the Field of Development." In *Perspectives on Positive Political Economy,* ed. James Alt and Kenneth Shepsle. Cambridge: Cambridge University Press.

Beck, Ulrich. 1986. *Die Risikogesellschaft.* Frankfurt am Main: Surkamp. Translated as *The Risk Society* (New York: Sage, 1992).

Becker, Gary S. 1957. *The Economics of Discrimination.* Chicago: University of Chicago Press.
_____. 1976. "Introduction." In *The Economic Approach to Human Behavior,* ed. Gary S. Becker. Chicago: University of Chicago Press.

Becker, Gary S., and Kevin M. Murphy. 1988. "A Theory of Rational Addiction." *Journal of Political Economy* 96:675–700.

Bell, Daniel. 1976. *The Cultural Contradictions of Capitalism.* New York: Basic Books.

Bergquist, William. 1993. *The Postmodern Organization: Mastering the Art of Irreversible Change.* San Francisco: Jossey-Bass.

Berl, Janet, Richard D. McKelvey, and Mark Winer. 1976. "An Experimental Test of the Core in a Simple N-Person Cooperative Nonsidepayment Game." *Journal of Conflict Resolution* 20:453–79.

Berliner, Joseph S. 1988. "The Comparison of Social Welfare Systems." In *State and Welfare USA/USSR: Contemporary Theory and Practice,* ed. Gail W. Lapidus and Guy E. Swanson. Berkeley: Institute of International Studies, University of California.

Bess, James L., ed. 1984. *College and University Organization: Insights from the Behavioral Sciences.* New York: New York University Press.

Black, Duncan. 1958. *The Theory of Committees and Elections.* Cambridge: Cambridge University Press.

Blau, Peter M. 1964. *Exchange and Power in Social Life.* New York: John Wiley and Sons.

Boltanski, Luc, and Laurent Thévenot. 1991. *De la justification: Les économies de la grandeur.* Paris: Gallimard.

Boulding, Kenneth E. 1981. *A Preface to Grants Economics: The Economy of Love and Fear.* New York: Praeger Publishers.

Bramwell, Anna. 1989. *Ecology in the Twentieth Century: A History.* New Haven: Yale University Press.

Brennan, Geoffrey, and Loren F. Lomansky. 1985. "The Impartial Spectator Goes to Washington: Toward a Smithian Theory of Electoral Behavior." *Economics and Philosophy* 1:189–211.

———. 1987. "The Logic of Electoral Preference." *Economics and Philosophy* 3:131–38.

———. 1993. *Democracy and Decision: The Pure Theory of Electoral Preference.* Cambridge: Cambridge University Press.

Britain, Gerald M., and Ronald Cohen. 1980. "Toward an Anthropology of Formal Organizations." In *Hierarchy and Society: Anthropological Perspectives on Bureaucracy,* ed. Gerald M. Britain and Ronald Cohen. Philadelphia: Institute for the Study of Human Lives.

Brown, Robert. 1963. *Explanation in Social Science.* Chicago: Aldine.

Buchanan, James M., and Gordon Tullock. 1962. *The Calculus of Consent: Logical Foundations of Constitutional Democracy.* Ann Arbor: University of Michigan Press.

Calvert, Jerry W. 1989. "Party Politics and Environmental Policy." In *Environmental Politics and Policy: Theories and Evidence,* ed. James P. Lester. Durham, NC: Duke University Press.

Campbell, Angus, Philip Converse, Warren Miller, and Donald Stokes. 1960. *The American Voter.* New York: John Wiley and Sons.

Campbell, Angus, Gerald Gurin, and Warren Miller. 1954. *The Voter Decides.* Evanston, IL: Row, Peterson, and Company.

Campbell, Donald T. 1950. "The Indirect Assessment of Social Attitudes." *Psychological Bulletin* 47:15–38.

Campbell, Donald T., and Donald W. Fiske. 1959. "Convergent and Discriminant Validation by the Multitrait-Multimethod Matrix." *Psychological Bulletin* 56:81–105.

Carley, Kathleen. 1991. "A Theory of Group Stability." *American Sociological Review* 56:331–54.

Carman, John. 1992. "Inverted World: Cultural Theory and Valuing Things from the Past." Typescript. University of Cambridge.

Carruthers, Bruce G., and Sarah Babb. 1996. "The Color of Money and the Nature of Value: Greenbacks and Gold in Postbellum America." *American Journal of Sociology* 101:1556–91.

Catton, William R. Jr., and Riley E. Dunlap. 1980. "A New Ecological Paradigm for Postexuberant Sociology." *American Behavioral Scientist* 24:15–47.

Ceaser, James W. 1990. *Liberal Democracy and Political Science.* Baltimore: Johns Hopkins University Press.

Chai, Sun-Ki. Forthcoming. *Choosing an Identity: A General Model of Preference and Belief Formation and Its Application to Comparative Development.* Ann Arbor: University of Michigan Press.

Chai, Sun-Ki, and Aaron Wildavsky. 1994. "Culture, Rationality, and Violence." In *Politics, Policy, and Culture: Applications of Cultural Theory,* ed. Dennis J. Coyle and Richard J. Ellis. Boulder: Westview Press.

_____. Forthcoming. "Cultural Change, Party Ideology, and Voting Stability." In *Cultural Theory and Social Science: Aaron Wildavsky on Economics, Philosophy, and Rational Choice,* ed. Sun-Ki Chai and Brendon Swedlow. New Brunswick, NJ: Transaction Press.

Chilton, Stephen. 1988. *Defining Political Development.* Boulder: Lynne Rienner Publishers.

_____. 1991. *Grounding Political Development.* Boulder: Lynne Rienner Publishers.

Chomsky, Noam. 1969. *Topics in the Theory of Generative Grammar.* The Hague: Mouton.

Chong, Dennis. 1991. *Collective Action and the Civil Rights Movement.* Chicago: University of Chicago Press.

Clements, Frederic. 1916. *Plant Succession.* Washington, DC: Carnegie Institution.

Cohen, Gerald. 1978. *Karl Marx's Theory of History: A Defense.* Princeton: Princeton University Press.

Cohen, Michael D., and James G. March. 1974. "Leadership in an Organized Anarchy." In *Leadership and Ambiguity: The American College President,* ed. Michael D. Cohen and James G. March. New York: McGraw-Hill.

Cohen, Michael D., James G. March, and Johan P. Olsen. 1972. "A Garbage Can Model of Organizational Choice." *Administrative Science Quarterly* 17:1–25.

Cole, Stephen. 1994. "Why Sociology Doesn't Make Progress Like the Natural Sciences." *Sociological Forum* 9:133–54.

Coleman, James S. 1975. "Social Structure and a Theory of Action." In *Approaches to the Study of Social Structure,* ed. Peter M. Blau. New York: Free Press.

_____. 1986. "Social Theory, Social Research, and a Theory of Action." *American Journal of Sociology* 91:1309–35.

_____. 1987. "Norms as Social Capital." In *Economic Imperialism: The Economics Approach Applied Outside the Field of Economics,* ed. Gerard Radnitzky and Peter Bernholz. New York: Paragon House.

_____. 1990. *Foundations of Social Theory.* Cambridge, MA: Harvard University Press.

Collard, David. 1978. *Altruism and Economy: A Study in Non-selfish Economics.* New York: Oxford University Press.

Collins, Randall. 1994a. "Why the Social Sciences Won't Become High-Consensus, Rapid-Discovery Science." *Sociological Forum* 9:155–77.

_____. 1994b. *Four Sociological Traditions.* Oxford: Oxford University Press.

Conradt, David P. 1978. *The German Polity.* London: Longman.

_____. 1980. "Changing German Political Culture." In *The Civic Culture Revisited,* ed. Gabriel A. Almond and Sidney Verba. Boston: Little, Brown and Company.

Converse, Philip. 1964. "The Nature of Belief Systems in Mass Publics." In *Ideology and Discontent,* ed. David E. Apter. Glencoe, IL: Free Press.

_____. 1969. "Of Time and Partisan Stability." *Comparative Political Studies* 2:139–71.

_____. 1976. *The Dynamics of Party Support: Cohort-Analyzing Party Identification.* Beverly Hills, CA: Sage Publications.

Cook, Karen S., and Margaret Levi, eds. 1990. *The Limits of Rationality.* Chicago: University of Chicago Press.

Cornell, Stephen, and Joseph P. Kalt. 1993. "Culture and Self-government: American Indian Reservations." In *Cultural Assessments* (report on a workshop sponsored by the Rockefeller Foundation with support from the World Bank). New York.

Cotgrove, Stephen. 1982. *Catastrophe or Cornucopia: The Environment, Politics, and the Future.* Chichester: John Wiley and Sons.

Covello, Vincent. 1991. "Risk Comparisons and Risk Communication." In *Communicating Risks to the Public,* ed. Roger E. Kasperson and Pieter Stallen. Dordecht: Kluwer.

Coyle, Dennis J. 1994a. "The Theory That Would Be King." In *Politics, Policy, and Culture: Applications of Cultural Theory,* ed. Dennis J. Coyle and Richard J. Ellis. Boulder: Westview Press.

_____. 1994b. "'This Land Is Your Land, This Land Is My Land': Cultural Conflict in Environmental and Land Use Regulation." In *Politics, Policy, and Culture: Applications of Cultural Theory,* ed. Dennis J. Coyle and Richard J. Ellis. Boulder: Westview Press.

_____. 1995. "Constitutional Cultures and Political Interpretation." Typescript. Catholic University.

Coyle, Dennis J., and Richard J. Ellis, eds. 1994. *Politics, Policy, and Culture: Applications of Cultural Theory.* Boulder: Westview Press.

Cyert, Richard M., and James G. March. 1963. *A Behavioral Theory of the Firm.* Englewood Cliffs, NJ: Prentice-Hall.

Dahrendorf, Ralf. 1967. *Society and Democracy in Germany.* Garden City, NY: Doubleday.

Dake, Karl, and Michael Thompson. 1992. "Making Cultural Theory Operational for Unilever." Unilever Market Research Group, Report No. 6, 2d Series.

_____. 1993. "The Meanings of Sustainable Development: Household Strategies for Managing Needs and Resources." In *Human Ecology: Crossing Boundaries,* ed. S. D. Wright, T. Dietz, R. Borden, G. Young, and G. Guagnano. Fort Collins, CO: The Society for Human Ecology.

Dake, Karl, and Aaron Wildavsky. 1990. "Theories of Risk Perception: Who Fears What and Why?" *Daedalus* 119:41–60.

Dalton, Russell J. 1989. "The German Voter." In *Developments in West German Politics,* ed. Gordon Smith, William E. Paterson, and Peter H. Merkl. Durham, NC: Duke University Press.

_____. 1994. *The Green Rainbow: Environmental Groups in Western Europe.* New Haven: Yale University Press.

Dalton, Russell, Scott Flanagan, and Paul Allen Beck. 1984. *Electoral Change in Advanced Industrial Democracies: Realignment or Dealignment?* Princeton: Princeton University Press.

Denhardt, Robert A. 1981. "Toward a Critical Theory of Public Organization." *Public Administration Review* 41:628–34.

Devall, Bill. 1980. "The Deep Ecology Movement." *Natural Resources Journal* 20:299–322.

Diamond, Larry, ed. 1993. *Political Culture and Democracy in Developing Countries.* Boulder: Lynne Rienner Publishers.

DiMaggio, Paul, John Evans, and Bethany Bryson. 1995. "Have Americans' Social Attitudes Become More Polarized?" Typescript. Princeton University.

Dittmer, Lowell. 1977. "Political Culture and Political Symbolism: Toward a Theoretical Synthesis." *World Politics* 29:552–83.

Douglas, Mary. 1970. *Natural Symbols: Explorations in Cosmology.* London: Barrie and Rockliff.

_____. 1975. "Environments at Risk." In Douglas, *Implicit Meanings: Essays in Anthropology.* London: Routledge.

_____. 1982a. "Cultural Bias." In *In the Active Voice,* ed. Mary Douglas. London: Routledge & Kegan Paul.

_____. 1982b. "Introduction to Grid/Group Analysis." In *Essays in the Sociology of Perception,* ed. Mary Douglas. London: Routledge.

_____. [1970] 1982c. *Natural Symbols: Explorations in Cosmology.* New York: Pantheon.

_____. 1986. *How Institutions Think.* Syracuse, NY: Syracuse University Press.

_____. 1992. *Risk and Blame: Essays in Cultural Theory.* New York: Routledge.

_____. 1993. Review of *Risk and Rationality: Philosophical Foundations for Populist Reforms,* by Kristin Shrader-Frechette. *American Political Science Review* 87:485.

_____. Forthcoming. Review of *Dealing with Risk,* by Howard Margolis. *Journal of Public Policy.*

Douglas, Mary, and Aaron Wildavsky. 1982. *Risk and Culture: An Essay on the Selection of Technological and Environmental Dangers.* Berkeley: University of California Press.

Downing, Theodore E., and Gilbert Kushner, eds. 1989. *Human Rights and Anthropology.* Cambridge, MA: Cultural Survival, Inc.

Downs, Anthony. 1957. *An Economic Theory of Democracy.* New York: Harper & Row.

Drury, William H., and Ian C.T. Nisbet. 1973. "Succession." *Journal of the Arnold Arboretum* 54:331–68.

Dryzek, John S. 1987. *Rational Ecology: Environment and Political Economy.* Oxford: Basil Blackwell.

Duclos, Dennis. 1989. *La peur et le savoir: La société face à la science, la technique, et leurs dangers.* Paris: La Découverte.

_____. 1991. *Les industriels et les risques pour l'environnement.* Paris: Harmattan.

Dunlap, Riley E., and Kent D. Van Liere. 1978. "The 'New Environmental Paradigm.'" *Journal of Environmental Education* 9:10–19.

_____. 1984. "Commitment to the Dominant Social Paradigm and Concern for Environmental Quality." *Social Science Quarterly* 65:1013–28.

Dunlap, Riley E., Kent D. Van Liere, Angela Mertig, William R. Catton Jr., and Robert E. Howell. 1992. "Measuring Endorsement of an Ecological Worldview: A Revised NEP Scale." Paper presented at the Sixth Meeting of the Society for Human Ecology, at Snowbird, UT.

During, Simon, ed. 1993. *The Cultural Studies Reader.* London: Routledge.

Durkheim, Emile. 1951. *Suicide: A Study in Sociology.* Glencoe, IL: Free Press.

_____. 1965. *Montesquieu and Rousseau: Forerunners of Sociology.* Ann Arbor: University of Michigan Press.

_____. [1895] 1966. *Rules of Sociological Method.* Translated by George E.G. Catlin. Glencoe, IL: Free Press.

Easton, David. 1953. *The Political System: An Inquiry into the State of Political Science.* New York: Alfred A. Knopf.

_____. 1957. "An Approach to the Analysis of Political Systems." *World Politics* 9:383–400.

_____. 1965. *A Systems Analysis of Political Life.* New York: John Wiley and Sons.

Eckstein, Harry. 1966. *Division and Cohesion in Democracy: A Study of Norway.* Princeton: Princeton University Press.

_____. 1967. "Norwegian Democracy in Comparative Perspective." *Tidsskrift for samfunnsforskning* 6:305–21.

_____. 1988. "A Culturalist Theory of Political Change." *American Political Science Review* 82:789–804.

_____. 1992. *Regarding Politics: Essays on Political Theory, Stability, and Change.* Berkeley: University of California Press.

_____. 1996. "Culture as a Foundation Concept for the Social Sciences." *Journal of Theoretical Politics* 8:471–97.

Eckstein, Harry, and Ted Robert Gurr. 1975. *Patterns of Authority: A Structural Basis for Political Inquiry.* New York: John Wiley and Sons.

Einstein, Albert. 1920. *Relativity, the Special and General Theory: A Popular Exposition.* London: Methuen.

Elazar, Daniel J. 1984. *American Federalism: A View from the States.* 3d ed. New York: Harper & Row.

Elkins, David J., and Richard E.B. Simeon. 1979. "A Cause in Search of Its Effect, or What Does Political Culture Explain?" *Comparative Politics* 11:127–45.

Ellis, Richard J. 1991. "Explaining the Occurrence of Charismatic Leadership in Organizations." *Journal of Theoretical Politics* 3:305–19.

_____. 1993a. *American Political Cultures.* New York: Oxford University Press.

_____. 1993b. "The Case for Cultural Theory: Reply to Friedman." *Critical Review* 7:81–128.

Ellis, Richard J., and Fred Thompson. 1996. "The Culture Wars by Other Means: Environmental Attitudes and Cultural Biases in the Northwest." Paper presented at the annual meeting of the Western Political Science Association, San Francisco.

Ellis, Richard, and Aaron Wildavsky. 1989. *Dilemmas of Presidential Leadership: From Washington Through Lincoln.* New Brunswick, NJ: Transaction Publishers.

Elster, Jon. 1985. *Making Sense of Marx.* Cambridge: Cambridge University Press.

_____. 1989. *Solomonic Judgements: Studies in the Limitations of Rationality.* Cambridge: Cambridge University Press.

_____. 1993. *Political Psychology.* Cambridge: Cambridge University Press.

Emerson, Richard. 1987. "Towards a Theory of Value in Social Exchange." In *Social Exchange Theory,* ed. Karen S. Cook. Newbury Park, CA: Sage Publications.

Epstein, T. Scarlett. 1988. *A Manual for Culturally-Adapted Market Research (CMR) in the Development Process.* Bexhill-on-Sea, England: RWAL Publications.

Etzioni, Amitai. 1975. *A Comparative Analysis of Complex Organizations.* New York: Free Press.

_____. 1988. *The Moral Dimension: Toward a New Economics.* New York: Free Press.

Eucken, Walter. [1940] 1951. *The Foundations of Economics.* Chicago: University of Chicago Press.

Evans-Pritchard, E. E. 1940. *The Nuer: A Description of the Modes of Livelihood and Political Institutions of a Nilotic People.* New York: Oxford University Press.

Fantasia, Rick, and Eric L. Hirsch. 1995. "Culture and Rebellion: The Appropriation and Transformation of the Veil in the Algerian Revolution." In *Social Movements and Culture,* ed. Hank Johnston and Bert Klandermans. Minneapolis: University of Minnesota Press.

Fedderson, Timothy J. 1992. "A Voting Model Implying Duverger's Law and Positive Turnout." *American Journal of Political Science* 36:939–62.

Feldman, Kenneth, and Theodore Newcomb. 1969. *The Impact of College on Students.* 2 vols. San Francisco: Jossey-Bass.

Ferejohn, John. 1991. "Rationality and Interpretation: Parliamentary Elections in Early Stuart England." In *The Economic Approach to Politics: A Critical Reassessment of the Theory of Rational Action,* ed. Kristen Renwick Monroe. New York: HarperCollins.

Ferejohn, John, and Morris P. Fiorina. 1975. "Closeness Counts Only in Horseshoes and Dancing." *American Political Science Review* 69:920–25.

Feynman, Richard P., Robert B. Leighton, and Matthew Sands. 1963–1966. *The Feynman Lectures on Physics.* 3 vols. Reading, MA: Addison-Wesley.

Fiorina, Morris P. 1976. "The Voting Decision: Instrumental and Expressive Aspects." *Journal of Politics* 38:390–413.

Fiorina, Morris P., and Charles R. Plott. 1978. "Committee Decisions Under Majority Rule." *American Political Science Review* 72:575–98.

Fischhoff, Baruch, Paul Slovic, Sarah Lichtenstein, Stephen Read, and Barbara Combs. 1978. "How Safe Is Safe Enough? A Psychometric Study of Attitudes Towards Technological Risks and Benefits." *Policy Sciences* 9:127–52.

Fiske, Alan. 1991. *Structures of Social Life: The Four Elementary Forms of Human Relations.* New York: Free Press.

Flanagan, Scott C. 1982. "Changing Values in Advanced Industrial Societies: Inglehart's Silent Revolution from the Perspective of Japanese Findings." *Comparative Political Studies* 14:99–128.

———. 1987. "Value Change in Industrial Societies." *American Political Science Review* 81:1303–19.

Foreman, Dave. 1992. "'We Aren't a Debating Society.'" *Earth First! Journal* 12:8, 13.

Foucault, Michel. 1970. *The Order of Things: An Archeology of the Human Sciences.* New York: Pantheon Books.

———. [1969] 1972. *The Archaeology of Knowledge.* Translated by A. M. Sheridan Smith. London: Tavistock.

Franklin, Mark N., and Wolfgang Rüdig. 1995. "On the Durability of Green Politics: Evidence from the 1989 European Election Study." *Comparative Political Studies* 28:409–39.

Fried, Charles. 1970. *An Anatomy of Values: Problems of Personal and Social Choice.* Cambridge, MA: Harvard University Press.

Friedkin, Noah E., and Eugene C. Johnsen. 1990. "Social Influence and Opinions." *Journal of Mathematical Sociology* 15:193–205.

Friedman, Debra, and Michael Hechter. 1990. "The Comparative Advantages of Rational Choice Theory." In *Frontiers of Social Theory,* ed. George Ritzer. New York: Columbia University Press.

Friedman, Jeffrey. 1991. "Accounting for Political Preferences: Cultural Theory vs. Cultural History." *Critical Review* 5:325–51.

Friedman, Milton. 1953. "The Methodology of Positive Economics." In *Essays in Positive Economics.* Chicago: University of Chicago Press.

Fudenberg, Drew, and Eric Maskin. 1986. "The Folk Theorem in Repeated Games with Discounting or with Incomplete Information." *Econometrica* 54:533–54.

Galbraith, Jay. 1973. *Designing Complex Organizations.* Reading, MA: Addison-Wesley.

Galbraith, John Kenneth. 1952. *American Capitalism: The Concept of Countervailing Power.* Boston: Houghton Mifflin.

Garrett, Geoffrey, and Barry R. Weingast. 1993. "Ideas, Interests, and Institutions: Constructing the European Community's Internal Market." In *Ideas and Foreign Policy: Beliefs, Institutions, and Political Change,* ed. Judith Goldstein and Robert O. Keohane. Ithaca: Cornell University Press.

Geertz, Clifford. 1973. *The Interpretation of Cultures.* New York: Basic Books.

Gibbins, John R. 1989. *Contemporary Political Culture: Politics in a Postmodern Age.* London: Sage Publications.

Glazer, Amihai. 1987. "A New Theory of Voting: Why Vote When Millions of Others Do?" *Theory and Decision* 22:257–70.

Gleick, James. 1987. *Chaos: Making a New Science.* New York: Viking-Penguin.

Goldstein, Judith, and Robert O. Keohane, eds. 1993. *Ideas and Foreign Policy: Beliefs, Institutions, and Political Change.* Ithaca: Cornell University Press.

Goodnow, Frank J. 1900. *Politics and Administration: A Study in Government.* New York: Russell and Russell.

Gow, David, Christine Haugen, Alan Hoben, Michael Painter, Jerry VanSant, and Barbara Wyckoff-Baird. 1989. *Social Analysis for the Nineties: Case Studies and Proposed Guidelines.* Bethesda, MD: Development Alternatives, Inc.

Graham, John, and Jon Wiener. 1995. *Risks Versus Risk.* Cambridge, MA: Harvard University Press.

Grauer, M., M. Thompson, and A. P. Wierzbicki, eds. 1985. *Plural Rationality and Interactive Decision Processes: Lecture Notes in Economic and Mathematical Systems.* Berlin: Springer-Verlag.

Gray, John. 1987. "The Economic Approach: Its Prospects and Limitations." In *Economic Imperialism: The Economic Approach Applied Outside the Field of Economics,* ed. Gerard Radnitzky and Peter Bernholz. New York: Paragon House.

Green, Donald P., and Ian Shapiro. 1993. "Pathologies of Rational Choice Theory: A Critique of Applications in Political Science." Working Paper No. 1043, Institution for Social and Policy Studies. New Haven: Yale University Press.

———. 1994. *Pathologies of Rational Choice Theory: A Critique of Applications in Political Science.* New Haven: Yale University Press.

Greif, Avner. 1992. "Institutions and International Trade: Lessons from the Commercial Revolution." *American Economic Review* 82:128–33.

———. 1994. "Cultural Beliefs and the Organization of Society: A Historical and Theoretical Reflection on Collectivist and Individualist Societies." *Journal of Political Economy* 102:912–50.

Grendstad, Gunnar. 1990. "Europe by Cultures: An Exploration in Grid-Group Analysis." Master's thesis, University of Bergen, Norway.

Grendstad, Gunnar, and Per Selle. 1995. "Cultural Theory and the New Institutionalism." *Journal of Theoretical Politics* 7:5–27.

Gretschmann, Klaus. 1986. "Solidarity and Markets." In *Guidance, Control, and Evaluation in the Public Sector,* ed. Franz-Xaver Kaufman, Giandomenico Majone, and Vincent Ostrom. New York: W. de Gruyter.

Gross, Jonathan L., and Steve Rayner. 1985. *Measuring Culture: A Paradigm for the Analysis of Social Organization.* New York: Columbia University Press.

Guth, James L., John C. Green, Lyman A. Kellstedt, and Corwin E. Smidt. 1995. "Faith and the Environment: Religious Beliefs and Attitudes on Environmental Policy." *American Journal of Political Science* 39:364–82.

Hall, Peter A. 1986. *Governing the Economy: The Politics of State Intervention in Britain and France.* New York: Oxford University Press.

Hall, Peter A., ed. 1989. *The Political Power of Economic Ideas: Keynesianism Across Nations.* Princeton: Princeton University Press.

Hannan, Michael, and John Freeman. 1977. "The Population Ecology of Organizations." *American Journal of Sociology* 82:929–64.

Hardin, Russell. 1982. *Collective Action.* Baltimore: Johns Hopkins University Press.

_____. 1995. *One for All: The Logic of Group Conflict.* Princeton: Princeton University Press.

Harsanyi, John. 1969. "Rational Choice Models of Political Behavior vs. Functionalist and Conformist Theories." *World Politics* 21:513–38.

Harsanyi, John, and Reinhard Selten. 1988. *A General Theory of Equilibrium Selection in Games.* Cambridge, MA: MIT Press.

Hartz, Louis. 1955. *The Liberal Tradition in America: An Interpretation of American Political Thought Since the Revolution.* New York: Harcourt Brace.

Hayek, Friedrich. 1979. *The Political Order of a Free People.* Chicago: University of Chicago Press.

Hays, Samuel P. 1968. *Conservation and the Gospel of Efficiency.* Cambridge, MA: Harvard University Press.

Hechter, Michael. 1993. "Should Values Be Written out of the Social Scientist's Lexicon?" *Sociological Theory* 10:214–30.

Hegner, Friedhart. 1986. "Solidarity and Hierarchy: Institutional Arrangements for the Co-ordination of Actions." In *Guidance, Control, and Evaluation in the Public Sector,* ed. Franz-Xaver Kaufman, Giandomenico Majone, and Vincent Ostrom. New York: W. de Gruyter.

Heiner, Robert. 1983. "The Origin of Predictable Behavior." *American Economic Review* 73:560–95.

Hempel, Carl G. 1965. *Aspects of Scientific Explanation.* New York: Free Press.

_____. 1966. *Philosophy of Natural Science.* Englewood Cliffs, NJ: Prentice-Hall.

Hill, Polly. 1986. *Development Economics on Trial: The Anthropological Case for a Prosecution.* Cambridge: Cambridge University Press.

Hirschman, Albert O. 1962. *Development Projects Observed.* Washington, DC: Brookings Institution.

_____. 1965. "Obstacles to Development: A Classification and a Quasi–Vanishing Act." *Economic Development and Cultural Change* 13:385–93.

_____. 1970. *Exit, Voice, and Loyalty: Responses to Decline in Firms, Organizations, and States.* Cambridge, MA: Harvard University Press.

_____. 1982. *Shifting Involvements: Private Interest and Public Action.* Princeton: Princeton University Press.

Hirshleifer, Jack. 1985. "The Expanding Domain of Economics." *American Economic Review* 75:53–68.

Hochschild, Jennifer L. 1981. *What's Fair? American Beliefs About Distributive Justice.* Cambridge, MA: Harvard University Press.

Hogarth, Robin N., and Melvin W. Reder, eds. 1986. *Rational Choice: The Contrast Between Economics and Psychology.* Chicago: University of Chicago Press.

Holling, Crawford S. 1979. "Myths of Ecological Stability." In *Studies on Crisis Management,* ed. C. F. Smart and W. T. Stanbury. Montreal: Butterworth.

Holmes, Bill. 1991. "Weirdos, Wimps, and Watermelons." *Earth Island Journal* 6:48.

Holt, Robert T., and John E. Turner. 1975. "Crises and Sequences in Collective Theory Development." *American Political Science Review* 69:979–94.

Holton, Gerald. J. 1968. *Thematic Origins of Scientific Thought: Kepler to Einstein.* Cambridge, MA: Harvard University Press.

Homans, George. 1961. *Social Behavior: Its Elementary Forms.* New York: Harcourt Brace and World.

Houtman, Gustaaf. 1988. "Interview with Maurice Bloch." *Anthropology Today* 4:18–21.

Hult, Karen M., and Charles Walcott. 1989. "Organizational Design as Public Policy." *Policy Studies Journal* 17:469–94.

Huntington, Samuel P. 1981. *American Politics: The Promise of Disharmony*. Cambridge, MA: The Belknap Press of Harvard University Press.

Hyman, Herbert. 1959. *Political Socialization*. New York: Free Press.

Iannello, Kathleen P. 1992. *Decisions Without Hierarchy: Feminist Interventions in Organization Theory and Practice*. New York: Routledge.

Inglehart, Ronald. 1971. "The Silent Revolution in Europe: Intergenerational Change in Post-industrial Societies." *American Political Science Review* 65:991–1017.

_____. 1977. *The Silent Revolution: Changing Values and Political Styles Among Western Publics*. Princeton: Princeton University Press.

_____. 1979. "Value Priorities and Socioeconomic Change." In *Political Action*, ed. S. Barnes and M. Kaase. London: Sage Publications.

_____. 1981. "Post-materialism in an Environment of Insecurity." *American Political Science Review* 75:880–900.

_____. 1987. "Value Change in Industrial Societies." *American Political Science Review* 81:1289–1303.

_____. 1988. "The Renaissance of Political Culture." *American Political Science Review* 82:1203–30.

_____. 1990. *Culture Shift in Advanced Industrial Society*. Princeton: Princeton University Press.

_____. 1994. "'Polarized Priorities or Flexible Alternatives? Dimensionality in Inglehart's Materialism-Postmaterialism Scale': A Comment." *International Journal of Public Opinion Research* 6:289–92.

Inglehart, Ronald, and Paul R. Abramson. 1994. "Economic Security and Value Change." *American Political Science Review* 88:336–54.

Inkeles, Alex, and David H. Smith. 1974. *Becoming Modern: Individual Change in Six Developing Countries*. Cambridge, MA: Harvard University Press.

Jantsch, Erich. 1979. *The Self-organizing Universe: Scientific and Human Implications of the Emerging Paradigm of Evolution*. Oxford: Pergamon.

Jenni, Karen. Forthcoming. "Defining Attributes for Multi-attributive Risk Evaluation." Ph.D. diss., Carnegie Mellon University.

Jenssen, Anders Todal, and Ola Listhaug. 1988. "Postmaterialisme og Valg i Norge." *Norsk Statsvitenskapelig Tidsskrift* 4:153–171.

Johnson, Branden B. 1991. "Risk and Culture Research: Some Cautions." *Journal of Cross-cultural Psychology* 22:141–49.

Johnson, Chalmers. 1982. *MITI and the Japanese Miracle*. Palo Alto, CA: Stanford University Press.

Johnson, Harry G. 1965. "A Theoretical Model of Economic Nationalism in New and Developing States." *Political Science Quarterly* 80:169–85.

_____. 1967. "The Ideology of Economic Policy in the New States." In *Economic Nationalism in Old and New States*, ed. Harry G. Johnson. Chicago: University of Chicago Press.

Johnson, James. 1993. "Rational Choice, Interpretation, and the Cultural Analysis of Politics." Paper presented at the annual meeting of the American Political Science Association, Washington, DC.

Johnston, Hank, and Bert Klandermans, eds. 1995. *Social Movements and Culture.* Minneapolis: University of Minnesota Press.

Kamieniecki, Sheldon, S. Dulaine Coleman, and Robert O. Vos. 1995. "Analyzing the Characteristics and Effects of Radical Environmentalists in Varying Contexts." Paper presented at the annual meeting of the Western Political Science Association, Portland, OR.

Katzenstein, Peter J. 1987. *Policy and Politics in West Germany: The Growth of a Semisovereign State.* Philadelphia: Temple University Press.

Kaufman, Herbert. 1971. *The Limits of Organizational Change.* University, AL: University of Alabama Press.

Kenski, Henry C., and Margaret C. Kenski. 1980. "Partisanship, Ideology, and Constituency Differences in Environmental Issues in the U.S. House of Representatives: 1973–1978." *Policy Studies Journal* 9:325–35.

Key, Valdimer Orlando Jr., and Alexander Heard. 1949. *Southern Politics in State and Nation.* New York: Alfred A. Knopf.

Khaldûn, Ibn. 1967. *The Muqaddimah: An Introduction to History.* Abridged ed. Translated by Franz Rosenthal. Princeton: Princeton University Press. (Originally written in 1377.)

Kiel, Douglas L. 1994. *Managing Chaos and Complexity in Government: A New Paradigm for Managing Change, Innovation, and Organizational Renewal.* San Francisco: Jossey-Bass.

King, Gary, Robert Keohane, and Sidney Verba. 1994. *Designing Social Inquiry.* Princeton: Princeton University Press.

Kingdon, John. 1993. "Politicians, Self-interest, and Ideas." In *Reconsidering the Democratic Public,* ed. George E. Marcus and Russell L. Hanson. University Park: Pennsylvania State University Press.

Kleinfeld, Judith. 1983. "First Do No Harm: A Reply to Courtney Cazden." *Anthropology and Education Quarterly* 14:282–87.

Klitgaard, Robert. 1976. "Institutionalized Racism: An Analytic Approach." In *Racial Conflict, Discrimination, and Power,* ed. William Barclay, Krishna Kumar, and Ruth P. Sims. New York: AMS Press.

———. 1994. "Taking Culture into Account: From 'Let's' to 'How.'" In *Culture and Development in Africa,* vol. 1, ed. Ismail Serageldin and June Taboroff. Washington, DC: World Bank.

———. 1995. "Including Culture in Evaluation Research." *New Directions for Program Evaluation* (Fall 1995):135–46.

Knoke, David, and George W. Bohrnstedt. 1994. *Statistics for Social Data Analysis.* 3d ed. Itasca, IL: F. E. Peacock.

Knutsen, Oddbjørn. 1986. "Political Cleavages and Political Realignment in Norway: The New Politics Thesis Reexamined." *Scandinavian Political Studies* 9:235–63.

Kreps, David. 1990. "Corporate Culture and Economic Theory." In *Perspectives on Positive Political Economy,* ed. James Alt and Kenneth Shepsle. Cambridge: Cambridge University Press.

Krusselberg, Hans-Gunter. 1986. "Markets and Hierarchies." In *Guidance, Control, and Evaluation in the Public Sector,* ed. Franz-Xaver Kaufman, Giandomenico Majone, and Vincent Ostrom. New York: W. de Gruyter.

Ladd, Everett C., and Seymour M. Lipset. 1975. *The Divided Academy.* New York: McGraw-Hill.

Lafferty, William M., and Oddbjørn Knutsen. 1985. "Postmaterialism in a Social Democratic State: An Analysis of the Distinctness and Congruity of the Inglehart Value Syndrome Norway." *Comparative Political Studies* 17:411–30.

Laitin, David D. 1988. "Political Culture and Political Preferences." *American Political Science Review* 82:589–93.

———. 1995. "The Civic Culture at 30." *American Political Science Review* 89:168–73.

Lakatos, Imre. 1978. *The Methodology of Scientific Research Programmes,* vol. 1 of *Philosophical Papers,* ed. John Worrall and Gregory Currie. Cambridge: Cambridge University Press.

Lalman, David, Joe Oppenheimer, and Piotr Swistak. 1993. "Formal Rational Choice Theory: A Cumulative Science of Politics." In *Political Science: The State of the Discipline II,* ed. Ada W. Finifter. Washington, DC: American Political Science Association.

Lamont, Michele, and Robert Wuthnow. 1990. "Betwixt and Between: Recent Cultural Sociology in Europe and the United States." In *Frontiers of Social Theory: The New Synthesis,* ed. George Ritzer. New York: Columbia University Press.

Landa, Janet Tai. 1978. "A Theory of the Ethnically Homogeneous Middleman Group: An Institutional Alternative to Contract Law." *Journal of Legal Studies* 10:349–62.

———. 1994. *Trust, Ethnicity, and Identity.* Ann Arbor: University of Michigan Press.

Landau, Martin. 1969. "Redundancy, Rationality, and the Problem of Duplication and Overlap." *Public Administration Review* 29:346–58.

———. 1972. *Political Theory and Political Science: Studies in the Methodology of Political Inquiry.* New York: Macmillan.

———. 1973a. "Federalism, Redundancy, and System Reliability." *Publius* 3:173–96.

———. 1973b. "On the Concept of a Self-correcting Organization." *Public Administration Review* 29:533–42.

Landau, Martin, and Russell Stout Jr. 1979. "To Manage Is Not to Control: Or the Folly of Type II Errors." *Public Administration Review* 39:148–56.

Lane, Robert. 1991. *The Market Experience.* Cambridge: Cambridge University Press.

Lane, Ruth. 1992. "Political Culture: Residual Category or General Theory?" *Comparative Political Studies* 25:362–87.

LaPalombara, Joseph. 1987. *Democracy, Italian Style.* New Haven: Yale University Press.

La Porte, Todd R. 1971. "The Recovery of Relevance in the Study of Public Organization." In *Toward a New Public Administration,* ed. Frank Marini. Scranton, PA: Chandler Publishing Company.

Larkey, Patrick D., Chandler Stolp, and Mark Winer. 1981. "Theorizing About the Growth of Government: A Research Assessment." *Journal of Public Policy* 1:157–220.

Latour, Bruno. 1987. *Science in Action: How to Follow Scientists and Engineers Through Society.* Cambridge, MA: Harvard University Press.

Laufer, Romain. 1993. *L'entreprise face aux risques majeurs.* Paris: Harmattan.

Lauman, Edward O., John Gagnon, Robert T. Michael, and Stuart Michaels. 1994. *The Social Organization of Sexuality.* Chicago: University of Chicago Press.

Lave, Lester. 1981. *The Strategy of Social Regulation.* Washington, DC: Brookings Institution.

Lazarsfeld, Paul F., Bernard Berelson, and Hazel Gaudet. 1944. *The People's Choice.* New York: Duell, Sloan, and Pierce.

Lazarsfeld, Paul F., and Wagner Thielens. 1958. *The Academic Mind: Social Scientists in a Time of Crisis.* Glencoe, IL: Free Press.

Lenski, Gerhard. 1961. *The Religious Factor: A Sociological Study of Religion's Impact on Politics, Economics, and Family Life.* Garden City, NY: Doubleday.

Lerner, Daniel. 1958. *The Passing of Traditional Society: Modernizing the Middle East.* Glencoe, IL: Free Press.

Lévi-Strauss, Claude. [1955] 1965. *Tristes Tropiques.* Translated by John Russell. New York: Atheneum.

Lichtenstein, Sarah, Paul Slovic, Baruch Fischhoff, Mark Layman, and Barbara Combs. 1978. "Judged Frequency of Lethal Events." *Journal of Experimental Psychology* 4:551–78.

Lijphart, Arend. 1984. *Democracies: Patterns of Majoritarian and Consensus Government in Twenty-one Countries.* New Haven: Yale University Press.

Lincoln, Yvonna S. 1985. *Organizational Theory and Inquiry: The Paradigm Revolution.* Beverly Hills, CA: Sage Publications.

Lindblom, Charles. 1959. "The Science of Muddling Through." *Public Administration Review* 19:79–88.

———. 1977. *Politics and Markets: The World's Political-Economic Systems.* New York: Basic Books.

Linnerooth-Bayer, Joanne, and Kevin B. Fitzgerald. 1996. "Conflicting Views on Fair Siting Processes." *Risk, Health, Safety, and Environment* 7:119–34.

Lipset, Seymour Martin. 1995. *Continental Divide.* New York: W. W. Norton.

———. 1996. *American Exceptionalism.* New York: Basic Books.

Lockhart, Charles, and Gregg Franzwa. 1994. "Cultural Theory and the Problem of Moral Relativism." In *Politics, Policy, and Culture,* ed. Dennis J. Coyle and Richard J. Ellis. Boulder: Westview Press.

Lowi, Theodore J. 1984. "Why Is There No Socialism in the United States? A Federal Analysis." In *The Costs of Federalism,* ed. Robert T. Golembiewski and Aaron Wildavsky. New Brunswick, NJ: Transaction Books.

Luce, R. Duncan, and Detlof von Winterfeldt. 1994. "What Common Ground Exists for Descriptive, Prescriptive, and Normative Utility Theories?" *Management Science* 40:263–79.

Lyotard, Jean-François. 1984. *The Postmodern Condition: A Report on Knowledge.* Minneapolis: University of Minnesota Press.

Mackie, Gerry. 1996. "Ending Footbinding and Infibulation: A Convention Account." *American Sociological Review* 61:999–1017.

Mahdi, Muhsin. 1964. *Ibn Khaldûn's Philosophy of History: A Study in the Philosophic Foundation of the Science of Culture.* Chicago: University of Chicago Press.

Maine, Henry Sumner. [1861] 1864. *Ancient Law: Its Connection with the Early History of Society, and Its Relation to Modern Ideas.* New York: Henry Holt & Company.

Majone, Giandomenico. 1986. "Mutual Adjustment by Debate and Persuasion." In *Guidance, Control, and Evaluation in the Public Sector,* ed. Franz-Xaver Kaufman, Giandomenico Majone, and Vincent Ostrom. New York: W. de Gruyter.

Manes, Christopher. 1990. *Green Rage: Radical Environmentalism and the Unmaking of Civilization.* Boston: Little, Brown and Company.

Mannheim, Karl. [1928] 1952. "The Problem of Generations." In *Essays on the Sociology of Knowledge,* edited and translated by Paul Keksmeti. London: Routledge & Kegan Paul.

Mansbridge, Jane J., ed. 1990. *Beyond Self-interest.* Chicago: University of Chicago Press.

March, James G. 1978. "Bounded Rationality, Ambiguity, and the Engineering of Choice." *Bell Journal of Economics* 9:587–608.

March, James G., and Johan P. Olsen. 1979. *Ambiguity and Choice in Organizations.* Bergen: Universitetsforlaget.

———. 1984. "The New Institutionalism: Organizational Factors in Political Life." *American Political Science Review* 78:734–49.

_____. 1988. "The Uncertainty of the Past: Organizational Learning Under Ambiguity." In James G. March, *Decisions and Organizations*. Oxford: Basil Blackwell.

_____. 1989. *Rediscovering Institutions: The Organizational Basis of Politics*. New York: Free Press.

March, James G., and Herbert A. Simon. 1958. *Organizations*. New York: John Wiley and Sons.

Margolis, Howard. 1982. *Selfishness, Altruism, and Rationality: A Theory of Social Choice*. Cambridge: Cambridge University Press.

_____. 1993. *Paradigms and Barriers*. Chicago: University of Chicago Press.

_____. 1996. *Dealing with Risk: Why the Public and the Experts Disagree on Environmental Issues*. Chicago: University of Chicago Press.

Maslow, Abraham K. 1954. *Motivation and Personality*. New York: Harper & Row.

McKelvey, Richard D., and Peter C. Ordeshook. 1984. "Rational Expectations in Elections: Some Experimental Results Based on a Multidimensional Model." *Public Choice* 44:61–102.

Mead, Margaret. 1953. "National Character." In *Anthropology Today: An Encyclopedic Inventory*, ed. Alfred L. Kroeber. Chicago: University of Chicago Press.

Mead, Margaret, ed. 1954. *Cultural Patterns and Technical Change: A Manual*. Paris: United Nations Educational, Scientific, and Cultural Organization (UNESCO).

Mead, Margaret, and Rhoda Metraux. 1954. *Themes from French Culture*. Palo Alto, CA: Stanford University Press.

Mercier, Jean. 1994. "What Level of Government for Ecologists?" *Public Administration Review* 54:349–56.

Merton, Robert K. 1952. "Bureaucratic Structure and Personality." In *Reader in Bureaucracy*, ed. Robert K. Merton, Ailsa P. Gray, Barbara Hockey, and Hanan C. Selvin. Glencoe, IL: Free Press.

Merton, Robert K., David L. Sills, and Stephen Stigler. 1984. "The Kelvin Dictum and Social Science: An Excursion into the History of an Idea." *Journal of the History of the Behavioral Sciences* 20:319–31.

Metz, Dan. 1995–1996. "Environmental Political Activism: Dissecting the Voluntary Human Extinction Movement." *The Gypsy Scholar: Journal of Undergraduate Scholarship* (Willamette University), 123–48.

Milbrath, Lester W. 1984. *Environmentalists: Vanguard for a New Society*. Albany: State University of New York Press.

Miller, Warren E., and M. Kent Jennings. 1986. *Parties in Transition: A Longitudinal Study of Party Elites and Party Supporters*. New York: Russell Sage Foundation.

Mills, C. Wright. 1956. *The Power Elite*. Oxford: Oxford University Press.

Mitchell, William C. 1969. "The Shape of Political Theory to Come: From Political Sociology to Political Economy." In *Politics and the Social Sciences*, ed. Seymour Martin Lipset. New York: Oxford University Press.

Mitchell, William C., and Randy T. Simmons. 1994. *Beyond Politics: Markets, Welfare, and the Failure of Bureaucracy*. Boulder: Westview Press.

Moe, Terry M. 1980. *The Organization of Interests: Incentives and the Internal Dynamics of Political Interest Groups*. Chicago: University of Chicago Press.

Monroe, Kristen Renwick, ed. 1991. *The Economic Approach to Politics: A Critical Reassessment of the Theory of Rational Action*. New York: HarperCollins.

Montesquieu, Charles de Secondat, baron de. [1748] 1977. "An Essay on Causes Affecting Minds and Characters." In *The Spirit of Laws*, ed. David Wallace Carrithers. Berkeley: University of California Press.

Morgan, Edmund M. 1956. *Some Problems of Proof Under the Anglo-American System of Litigation.* New York: Columbia University Press.

Morgan, Glenn. 1990. *Organizations in Society.* New York: St. Martin's Press.

Muller, Edward N., and Karl-Dieter Opp. 1986. "Rational Choice and Rebellious Collective Action." *American Political Science Review* 82:471–87.

Nash, Roderick Frazier. 1989. *The Rights of Nature: A History of Environmental Ethics.* Madison: University of Wisconsin Press.

Newman, Katherine. 1980. "Incipient Bureaucracy: The Development of Hierarchies in Egalitarian Organizations." In *Hierarchy and Society: Anthropological Perspectives on Bureaucracy,* ed. Gerald M. Britain and Ronald Cohen. Philadelphia: Institute for the Study of Human Lives.

Nie, Norman, Sidney Verba, and John R. Petrocik. 1979. *The Changing American Voter.* Cambridge, MA: Harvard University Press.

Niskanen, William A. 1980. "Competition Among Government Bureaus." In *Making Bureaucracies Work,* ed. Carol H. Weiss and Allen H. Barton. Beverly Hills, CA: Sage Publications.

North, Douglass. 1981. *Structure and Change in Economic History.* New York: W. W. Norton.

——. 1990. *Institutional Change and Economic Performance.* Cambridge: Cambridge University Press.

Nozick, Robert. 1974. *Anarchy, State, and Utopia.* New York: Basic Books.

Odhiambo, Thomas R. 1967. "East Africa: Science for Development." *Science* 158:876–81.

Odum, Eugene P. 1969. "The Strategy of Ecosystem Development." *Science* 164:262–70.

——. 1971. *Fundamentals of Ecology.* Philadelphia: W. B. Saunders.

Olson, Mancur. 1965. *The Logic of Collective Action.* Cambridge, MA: Harvard University Press.

Opp, Karl-Dieter. 1986. "Soft Incentives and Collective Action: Participation in the Antinuclear Movement." *British Journal of Political Science* 16:87–112.

——. 1989. *The Rationality of Political Protest.* Boulder: Westview Press.

Orloff, Ann Shola, and Theda Skocpol. 1984. "Why Not Equal Protection? Explaining the Politics of Social Spending in Britain, 1900–1911, and the United States, 1880s–1920." *American Sociological Review* 49:726–50.

Osgood, Charles E. 1958. "Behavior Theory and the Social Sciences." In *Approaches to the Study of Politics,* ed. Roland Young. Evanston, IL: Northwestern University Press.

Osgood, Charles E., G. J. Suci, and P. H. Tannenbaum. 1957. *The Measurement of Meaning.* Urbana: University of Illinois Press.

Ostrander, David. 1982. "One- and Two-Dimensional Models and the Distribution of Beliefs." In *Essays in the Sociology of Perception,* ed. Mary Douglas. London: Routledge & Kegan Paul.

Ostrom, Elinor. 1986. "A Method of Institutional Analysis." In *Guidance, Control, and Evaluation in the Public Sector,* ed. Franz-Xaver Kaufman, Giandomenico Majone, and Vincent Ostrom. New York: W. de Gruyter.

Ostrom, Elinor, Roy Gardner, and James Walker. 1994. *Rules, Games, and Common-Pool Resources.* Ann Arbor: University of Michigan Press.

Ostrom, Vincent. 1973. *The Intellectual Crisis in American Public Administration.* Birmingham: University of Alabama Press.

Ostrom, Vincent, Charles M. Tiebout, and Robert Warren. 1961. "The Organization of Government in Metropolitan Areas: A Theoretical Inquiry." *American Political Science Review* 55:831–42.

Otway, Harry J., and Philip D. Pahner. 1976. "Risk Assessment." *Futures* 8:122–34.

Ouchi, William. 1980. "Markets, Bureaucracies, and Clans." *Administrative Science Quarterly* 25:129–41.

Packenham, Robert. 1992. *The Dependency Movement: Scholarship and Politics in Latin American Studies.* Cambridge, MA: Harvard University Press.

Padgett, Stephen. 1989. "The Party System." In *Developments in West German Politics,* ed. Gordon Smith, William E. Paterson, and Peter H. Merkl. Durham, NC: Duke University Press.

Paehlke, Robert C. 1989. *Environmentalism and the Future of Progressive Politics.* New Haven: Yale University Press.

Parsons, Talcott. 1959. "Voting and the Equilibrium of the American Political System." In *American Voting Behavior,* ed. Eugene Burdick and Arthur J. Brodbeck. New York: Free Press.

Parsons, Talcott, and Edward Shils, eds. 1951. *Toward a General Theory of Action.* Cambridge, MA: Harvard University Press.

Peltzman, Sam. 1980. "The Growth of Government." *Journal of Law and Economics* 23:209–88.

Perrow, Charles. 1986. *Complex Organizations: A Critical Essay.* 3d ed. New York: Random House.

Peterson, Richard A., ed. 1990. "Symposium: The Many Facets of Culture." *Contemporary Sociology* 19:498–523.

Pfeffer, Jeffrey, and Gerald R. Salancik. 1978. *The External Control of Organizations.* New York: Harper & Row.

Phelps, Edmund S., ed. 1975. *Altruism, Morality, and Economic Theory.* New York: Russell Sage Foundation.

Picciotto, Robert, and Ray C. Rist, eds. 1995. *Evaluation and Development: Proceedings of the 1994 World Bank Conference.* Washington, DC: World Bank.

Pickett, S.T.A., and P. S. White, eds. 1985. *The Ecology of Natural Disturbance and Patch Dynamics.* Orlando, FL: Academic Press.

Pizzorno, Alessandro. 1966. "Amoral Familism and Historical Marginality." *International Review of Community Development* 15:55–66.

Platt, John R. 1967. *The Step to Man.* New York: John Wiley and Sons.

Popper, Karl R. 1972. *Objective Knowledge.* Oxford: Clarendon Press.

Powell, Walter, and Paul DiMaggio, eds. 1991. *The New Institutionalism in Organizational Analysis.* Chicago: University of Chicago Press.

Pressman, Jeffrey L., and Aaron Wildavsky. [1973] 1984. *Implementation: How Great Expectations in Washington Are Dashed in Oakland.* 3d ed. Berkeley: University of California Press.

Pulzer, Peter. 1989. "Political Ideology." In *Developments in West German Politics,* ed. Gordon Smith, William E. Paterson, and Peter H. Merkl. Durham, NC: Duke University Press.

Putnam, Robert D. 1993. *Making Democracy Work: Civic Traditions in Modern Italy.* Princeton: Princeton University Press.

Pye, Lucian W. 1965. "Introduction." In *Political Culture and Political Development,* ed. Lucian W. Pye and Sidney Verba. Princeton: Princeton University Press.

———. 1988. *The Mandarin and the Cadre: China's Political Cultures.* Ann Arbor: Center for Chinese Studies, University of Michigan.

Pye, Lucian W., and Mary W. Pye. 1985. *Asian Power and Politics: The Cultural Dimensions of Authority.* Cambridge, MA: Harvard University Press.

Pye, Lucian W., and Sidney Verba, eds. 1965. *Political Culture and Political Development.* Princeton: Princeton University Press.

Quattrone, George, and Amos Tversky. 1988. "Contrasting Rational and Psychological Analysis of Political Choice." *American Political Science Review* 82:719–36.

Radnitzky, Gerard, and Peter Bernholz, eds. 1987. *Economic Imperialism: The Economic Approach Applied Outside the Field of Economics.* New York: Paragon House.

Rawls, John. 1971. *A Theory of Justice.* Cambridge, MA: Harvard University Press.

Rayner, Steve. 1992. "Cultural Theory and Risk Analysis." In *Social Theories of Risk,* ed. Sheldon Krimsky and Dominic Golding. New York: Praeger Publishers.

Renn, Ortwin. 1991. "Risk Communication and the Social Amplification of Risk." In *Communicating Risk to the Public,* ed. Roger E. Kasperson and Pietr Stallen. Dordecht: Kluwer.

Richardson, Stephen A. 1956. "Organizational Contrasts on British and American Ships." *Administrative Science Quarterly* 1:189–207.

Rigg, Jonathan. 1991. "Grass-Roots Development in Rural Thailand: A Lost Cause?" *World Development* 19:199–211.

Riker, William. 1962. *The Theory of Political Coalitions.* New Haven: Yale University Press.

Riker, William, and Peter C. Ordeshook. 1968. "A Theory of the Calculus of Voting." *American Political Science Review* 62:25–42.

Rogowski, Ronald. 1974. *Rational Legitimacy: A Theory of Political Support.* Princeton: Princeton University Press.

———. 1978. "Rationalist Theories of Politics: A Midterm Report." *World Politics* 30:296–323.

Rohrschneider, Robert. 1994. "Report from the Laboratory: The Influence of Institutions on Political Elites' Democratic Values in Germany." *American Political Science Review* 88:927–41.

Rose, Carol M. 1983. "Planning and Dealing: Piecemeal Land Controls as a Problem of Local Legitimacy." *California Law Review* 71:837–912.

Rosenau, Pauline Marie. 1992. *Post-modernism and the Social Sciences: Insights, Inroads, and Intrusions.* Princeton: Princeton University Press.

Rosenberg, Shawn W. 1995. "Against Neoclassical Political Economy: A Political Psychological Critique." *Political Psychology* 16:99–136.

Rothschild, Joyce, and J. Allen Whitt. 1986. *The Cooperative Workplace.* Cambridge: Cambridge University Press.

Rothschild-Whitt, Joyce. 1979. "The Collectivist Organization: An Alternative to Rational-Bureaucratic Models." *American Sociological Review* 44:509–27.

Rothstein, Paul F. 1981. *Evidence in a Nutshell: State and Federal Rules.* 2d ed. St. Paul, MN: West.

Rudolph, Frederick. 1956. *Mark Hopkins and the Log: Williams College, 1836–1872.* New Haven: Yale University Press.

Sale, Kirkpatrick. 1986. "The Forest for the Trees: Can Today's Environmentalists Tell the Difference." *Mother Jones* 11:25–33, 58.

Schelling, Thomas C. 1960. *The Strategy of Conflict.* Cambridge, MA: Harvard University Press.

———. 1978. *Micromotives and Macrobehavior.* New York: W. W. Norton.

Schmutzer, Manfred E.A. 1994. *Ingenium und Individuum: Eine Sozialwissenschaftliche Theorie von Wissenschaft und Technik.* New York: Springer-Verlag.

Schmutzer, M.E.A., and W. Bandler. 1980. "Hi and Low—In and Out: Approaches to Social Status." *Journal of Cybernetics* 10:283–99.

Schoemaker, P.J.H. 1982. "The Expected Utility Model." *Economic Literature* 20:529–63.

Schwartz, Barry. 1991. "A Pluralistic Model of Culture." *Contemporary Sociology* 20:764–66.

Schwarz, Michiel, and Michael Thompson. 1990. *Divided We Stand: Redefining Politics, Technology, and Social Choice.* London: Harvester Wheatsheaf.

Scitovsky, Tibor. 1976. *The Joyless Economy: An Inquiry into Human Satisfaction and Consumer Dissatisfaction.* Oxford: Oxford University Press.

Scott, W. Richard. 1981. *Organizations: Rational, Natural, and Open Systems.* Englewood Cliffs, NJ: Prentice-Hall.

Sears, David, and Carolyn L. Funk. 1990a. "The Limited Effect of Economic Self-interest in the Political Attitudes of the Mass Public." *Journal of Behavioral Economics* 19:247–71.

_____. 1990b. "Self-interest in Americans' Political Opinions." In *Beyond Self-interest,* ed. Jane J. Mansbridge. Chicago: University of Chicago Press.

Sears, Paul. 1959. *Deserts on the March.* 3d ed. Norman: University of Oklahoma Press.

Seers, Dudley. 1983. *The Political Economy of Nationalism.* New York: Oxford University Press.

Selle, Per. 1991a. "Culture and the Study of Politics." *Scandinavian Political Studies* 14:97–124.

_____. 1991b. "It Must Have Something to Do with 'Logic': A Rejoinder to Aaron Wildavsky." *Scandinavian Political Studies* 14:361–64.

Serageldin, Ismail, and June Taboroff, eds. 1994. *Culture and Development in Africa.* Washington, DC: World Bank.

Shin, Doh Chul, Myung Chey, and Kwang-Woong Kim. 1989. "Cultural Origins of Public Support for Democracy in Korea." *Comparative Political Studies* 22:217–38.

Shrader-Frechette, Kristin. 1991. *Risk and Rationality: Philosophical Foundations of Populist Reforms.* Berkeley: University of California Press.

Shweder, Richard A. 1991. *Thinking Through Cultures: Expeditions in Cultural Psychology.* Cambridge, MA: Harvard University Press.

Silver, Morris. 1973. "A Demand Analysis of Voting Costs and Voting Participation." *Social Science Research* 2:11–24.

_____. 1974. "Political Revolution and Repression: An Economic Approach." *Public Choice* 17:63–71.

Simon, Herbert A. 1955. "A Behavioral Model of Rational Choice." *Quarterly Journal of Economics* 69:99–118.

_____. 1956. "Rational Choice and the Structure of the Environment." *Psychological Review* 63:129–38.

_____. 1976. *Administrative Behavior.* 3d ed. New York: Free Press.

_____. 1985. "Human Nature in Politics: The Dialogue of Psychology with Political Science." *American Political Science Review* 79:293–304.

_____. 1986. "Rationality in Psychology and Economics." In *Rational Choice: The Contrast Between Economics and Psychology,* ed. Robin N. Hogarth and Melvin W. Reder. Chicago: University of Chicago Press.

_____. 1991. "Organizations and Markets." *Journal of Economic Perspectives* 5:25–44.

Simon, Julian. 1995. "Why Do We Hear Prophecies of Doom?" *The Futurist* 23:19–23.

Slovic, Paul. 1992. "Perceptions of Risk: Reflections on the Psychometric Paradigm." In *Social Theories of Risk*, ed. Sheldon Krimsky and Dominic Golding. New York: Praeger Publishers.

Slovic, Paul, and Sarah Lichtenstein. 1971. "Comparison of Bayesian and Regression Approaches to the Study of Human Information Processing in Judgment." *Organizational Behavior and Human Performance* 6:649–744.

Sowell, Thomas. 1975. *Race and Economics.* New York: David McKay.

Spicer, Michael W. 1995. *The Founders, the Constitution, and Public Administration.* Washington, DC: Georgetown University Press.

Sproull, Lee, Stephen Weiner, and David Wolf. 1978. *Organizing an Anarchy: Belief, Bureaucracy, and Politics in the National Institute of Education.* Chicago: University of Chicago Press.

Starr, Chauncy. 1969. "Social Benefit Versus Technological Risk." *Science* 165:1232–38.

Steinmo, Sven H. 1994. "American Exceptionalism Reconsidered: Culture or Institutions?" In *The Dynamics of American Politics: Approaches and Interpretations,* ed. Lawrence C. Dodd and Calvin C. Jillson. Boulder: Westview Press.

Stevens, Mitchell. 1996. "The Kingdom of Children: Institutionalization of Childhood." Ph.D. diss., Northwestern University.

Stewart, Richard. 1975. "The Reformation of American Administrative Law." *Harvard Law Review* 88:1667–813.

Stigler, George J., and Gary S. Becker. 1977. "De Gustibus Non Est Disputandum." *American Economic Review* 67:76–90.

Stinchcombe, Arthur L. 1982. "On Softheadedness on the Future." *Ethics* 93:114–28.

Stinchcombe, Arthur L., Rebecca Adams, Carol A. Heimer, Kim Scheppele, Tom Smith, and D. Garth Taylor. 1974. *Crime and Punishment: Changing Attitudes in America.* San Francisco: Jossey-Bass.

Summers, Lawrence. 1992. "Why the Rich Should Pollute the Poor." *The Guardian,* February 2, p. 8.

Swedberg, Richard. 1990. "Socioeconomics and the New 'Battle of the Methods': Towards a Paradigm Shift?" *Journal of Behavioral Economics* 19:33–38.

Tarrow, Sidney. 1992. "Mentalities, Political Cultures, and Collective Action Frames: Constructing Meanings Through Action." In *Frontiers in Social Movement Theory,* ed. Aldon D. Morris and Carol McClurg Mueller. New Haven: Yale University Press.

Taylor, Frederick W. 1911. *The Principles of Scientific Management.* New York: Harper & Row.

Taylor, Michael. 1987. *The Possibility of Cooperation.* Cambridge: Cambridge University Press.

Thayer, James B. [1896] 1969. *A Preliminary Treatise on Evidence at Common Law.* Hackensack, NJ: Rothman Reprints.

Thom, René. 1972. *Stabilité structurelle et morphogénèse.* Paris: Benjamin.

Thompson, James D. 1967. *Organizations in Action.* New York: McGraw-Hill.

Thompson, James D., and Arthur Tuden. 1959. "Strategies, Structures, and Processes of Organizational Decision." In *Comparative Studies in Administration,* ed. James D. Thompson, Peter B. Hammond, Robert W. Hawkes, Buford H. Junker, and Arthur Tuden. Pittsburgh: University of Pittsburgh Press.

Thompson, Michael. 1979. *Rubbish Theory: The Creation and Destruction of Value.* Oxford: Oxford University Press.

———. 1984. "Among the Energy Tribes: A Cultural Framework for the Analysis and Design of Energy Policy." *Policy Sciences* 17:321–39.

_____. 1992. "The Dynamics of Cultural Theory and Their Implications for the Enterprise Culture." In *Understanding the Enterprise Culture: Themes in the Work of Mary Douglas*, ed. Shaun Hargreaves Heap and Angus Ross. Edinburgh: Edinburgh University Press.

_____. 1993. "Good Science for Public Policy." *International Development* 5:669–79.

_____. 1996a. "Inherent Relationality: An Anti-Dualist Approach to Institutions." LOS-Centre (The Norwegian Research Centre in Organisation and Management, Bergen), Report No. 9608.

_____. 1996b. "Unsiteability: What Should It Tell Us?" *Risk, Health, Safety, and Environment* 7:169–79.

_____. Forthcoming. "Cultural Theory and Integrated Assessment." *Environmental Modelling and Assessment*.

Thompson, Michael, Richard Ellis, and Aaron Wildavsky. 1990. *Cultural Theory*. Boulder: Westview Press.

Thompson, Michael, and Alex Trisoglio. 1997. "Managing the Unmanageable." In *Saving the Seas: Values, Scientists, and Governance*, ed. L. Anathea Brooks and Stacy D. Van Deveer. College Park, MD: Maryland Sea Grant College.

Thompson, Michael, and Aaron Wildavsky. 1986. "A Cultural Theory of Information Bias in Organizations." *Journal of Management Studies* 23:273–86.

Tocqueville, Alexis de. [1835 and 1840] 1945. *Democracy in America*. 2 vols. Edited by Phillips Bradley. New York: Alfred A. Knopf.

_____. 1969. *Democracy in America*. Garden City, NY: Anchor.

_____. 1990. *Democracy in America*. 2 vols. New York: Vintage Books.

Tsebelis, George. 1990. *Nested Games: Rational Choice in Comparative Politics*. Berkeley: University of California Press.

Tucker, Robert C. 1973. "Culture, Political Culture, and Communist Society." *Political Science Quarterly* 88:173–90.

Tullock, Gordon. 1971. "The Paradox of Revolution." *Public Choice* 11:89–99.

Tversky, Amos, and Daniel Kahneman. 1981. "The Framing of Decisions and the Psychology of Choice." *Science* 211:453–58.

_____. 1986. "Rational Choice and the Framing of Decisions." In *Rational Choice: The Contrast Between Economics and Psychology*, ed. Robin N. Hogarth and Melvin M. Reder. Chicago: University of Chicago Press.

Twining, William. 1990. *Rethinking Evidence: Exploratory Essays*. Evanston, IL: Northwestern University Press.

Uhlaner, Carol Jean. 1989a. "Rational Turnout: The Neglected Role of Groups." *American Journal of Political Science* 33:390–422.

_____. 1989b. "'Relational Goods' and Participation: Incorporating Sociability into a Theory of Rational Action." *Public Choice* 62:253–85.

United Nations Educational, Scientific, and Cultural Organization (UNESCO). 1991. "Working Document." Meeting of Experts on the Cultural Dimensions of Development. CC-91/CONF.602/3.

Van Liere, Kent D., and Riley E. Dunlap. 1980. "The Social Bases of Environmental Concern: A Review of Hypotheses, Explanations, and Empirical Evidence." *Public Opinion Quarterly* 44:181–97.

Verba, Sidney, and Norman Nie. 1972. *Participation in America: Political Democracy and Social Inequality*. New York: Harper & Row.

Verba, Sidney, Norman H. Nie, and Jae-on Kim. 1978. *Participation and Political Equality: A Seven-Nation Comparison.* New York: Cambridge University Press.

Verba, Sidney, Kay Lehman Schlozman, and Henry E. Brady. 1995. *Voice and Equality: Civic Voluntarism in American Politics.* Cambridge, MA: Harvard University Press.

Viscusi, W. Kip, ed. 1994. "The Mortality Costs of Regulatory Expenditures." Special issue, *Journal of Risk and Uncertainty* 8:1–122.

Waldrop, Mitchell M. 1992. *Complexity: The Emerging Science at the Edge of Order and Chaos.* New York: Simon & Schuster.

Walker, Jack L. 1969. "The Diffusion of Innovations Among the American States." *American Political Science Review* 63:880–99.

Walzer, Michael. 1983. *Spheres of Justice: A Defense of Pluralism and Equality.* New York: Basic Books.

Ward, Lester. 1973. "Waste and Inefficiency in the Economy of Nature." In *American Environmentalism: The Formative Period, 1860–1915,* ed. Donald Worster. New York: John Wiley and Sons.

Warner, Sir Frederick. 1992. "Calculated Risks." *Science and Public Affairs* 7:44–49.

Warren, Edward, and Gary Marchant. 1993. "More Good Than Harm: A First Principle for Environmental Agencies and Reviewing Courts." *Ecology Law Journal* 20:379–440.

Watkins, John. 1984. *Science and Scepticism.* London: Hutchinson.

Weber, Max. 1930. *The Protestant Ethic and the Spirit of Capitalism.* Translated by Talcott Parsons. New York: Charles Scribner's Sons.

———. 1946. "Bureaucracy." In *From Max Weber: Essays in Sociology,* ed. H. H. Gerth and C. Wright Mills. New York: Oxford University Press.

———. 1947. *The Theory of Social and Economic Organization.* New York: Oxford University Press.

———. 1978. *Economy and Society.* 2 vols. Edited by Guenther Roth and Klaus Wittich. Berkeley: University of California Press.

Weber, M. 1993. "Recent Developments in Modelling Preferences: Uncertainty and Ambiguity." *Journal of Risk and Uncertainty* 5:325–70.

Weick, Karl E. 1976. "Educational Organizations as Loosely Coupled Systems." *Administrative Science Quarterly* 21:1–19.

———. 1979. *The Social Psychology of Organizing.* Reading, MA: Addison-Wesley.

Werlin, Herbert, and Harry Eckstein. 1990. "Political Culture and Political Change" [An exchange]. *American Political Science Review* 84:249–59.

Wheatley, Margaret. 1992. *Leadership and the New Science: Learning About Organizations from an Orderly Universe.* San Francisco: Berrett-Koehler.

Wibecke, Brun. 1994. "Risk Perception: Main Issues, Approach, and Findings." In *Subjective Probability,* ed. George Wright and Peter Ayton. New York: John Wiley.

Wigmore, John Henry. 1940. *A Treatise on the Anglo-American System of Evidence in Trials at Common Law.* 10 vols. Boston: Little, Brown and Company.

Wildavsky, Aaron. 1964. *The Politics of the Budgetary Process.* Boston: Little, Brown and Company.

———. 1972. "The Self-evaluating Organization." *Public Administration Review* 32:509–20.

———. 1976. "Economy and Environment/Rationality and Ritual: A Review Essay." *Accounting, Organizations, and Society* 1:117–29.

_____. 1979. *Speaking Truth to Power: The Art and Craft of Policy Analysis.* Boston: Little, Brown and Company.

_____. 1981. "Rationality in Writing: Linear and Curvilinear." *Journal of Public Policy* 1:125–40.

_____. 1984. "From Political Economy to Political Culture, or Rational People Defend Their Way of Life." Typescript. University of California, Berkeley.

_____. 1985a. "Change in Political Culture." *Politics: Journal of the Australian Political Science Association* 20:95–102.

_____. 1985b. "The Logic of Public Sector Growth." In *State and Market,* ed. Jan-Erik Lane. London: Sage Publications.

_____. 1987a. "Choosing Preferences by Constructing Institutions: A Cultural Theory of Preference Formation." *American Political Science Review* 81:3–21.

_____. 1987b. "A Cultural Theory of Responsibility." In *Bureaucracy and Public Choice,* ed. Jan-Erik Lane. London: Sage Publications.

_____. 1987c. "From Political Economy to Political Culture, or Why I Like Cultural Analysis." Typescript. University of California, Berkeley.

_____. 1988a. *The New Politics of the Budgetary Process.* Glencoe, IL: Scott, Foresman.

_____. 1988b. "Political Culture and Political Preferences." *American Political Science Review* 82:593–96.

_____. 1988c. "Teaching and Talking: A Seminar on Cultural Theory." *Political Science Teacher* 1:3–5.

_____. 1988d. *Searching for Safety.* New Brunswick, NJ: Transaction Books.

_____. 1989. "A Cultural Theory of Leadership." In *Leadership and Politics: New Perspectives in Political Science,* ed. Bryan D. Jones. Lawrence: University of Kansas Press.

_____. 1990. "Administration Without Hierarchy? Bureaucracy Without Authority?" In *Public Administration: The State of the Discipline,* ed. Naomi B. Lynn and Aaron Wildavsky. Chatham, NJ: Chatham House.

_____. 1991a. "Resolved, That Individualism and Egalitarianism Be Made Compatible in America: Political-Cultural Roots of Exceptionalism." In *Is America Different? A New Look at American Exceptionalism,* ed. Byron Shafer. New York: Oxford University Press.

_____. 1991b. "What Other Theory Would Be Expected to Answer Such Profound Questions? A Reply to Per Selle's Critique of Cultural Theory." *Scandinavian Political Studies* 14:355–60.

_____. 1991c. "Can Norms Rescue Self-interest or Macro Explanation Be Joined to Micro Explanation?" *Critical Review* 5:301–23.

_____. 1991d. *The Rise of Radical Egalitarianism.* Washington, DC: American University Press.

_____. 1992. "Are American Political Parties Pretty Much the Same as They Used to Be in the 1950s, Only a Little Different, or Are They Radically Different? A Review Essay." *Journal of Policy History* 4:228–47.

_____. 1993–1994. "Politically Correct Hiring Will Destroy Higher Education." *Academic Questions* 7:77–79.

_____. 1994a. "Why Self-interest Means Less Outside of a Social Context: Cultural Contributions to a Theory of Rational Choices." *Journal of Theoretical Politics* 6:131–59.

_____. 1994b. "How Cultural Theory Can Contribute to Understanding and Promoting Democracy, Science, and Development." In *Culture and Development in Africa,* ed. Ismail Serageldin and June Taboroff. Washington, DC: World Bank.

Williamson, Oliver E. 1975. *Markets and Hierarchies: Analysis and Antitrust Implications: A Study in the Economics of Internal Organization.* New York: Free Press.

_____. 1979. "Transaction-Cost Economics: The Governance of Contractual Relations." *Journal of Law and Economics* 22:233–61.

_____. 1981. "The Economics of Organizations: The Transaction Cost Approach." *American Journal of Sociology* 87:548–77.

Wilson, Richard W. 1992. *Compliance Ideologies: Rethinking Political Culture.* New York: Cambridge University Press.

Wilson, Woodrow. 1887. "The Study of Administration." *Political Science Quarterly* 2:197–222.

Wood, Gordon S. 1993. *The Radicalism of the American Revolution.* New York: Random House.

Worster, Donald. 1990. "The Ecology of Order and Chaos." *Environmental History Review* 14:1–16.

Wuerthner, George. 1985. "Tree Spiking and Moral Maturity." *Earth First! Journal* 5:20.

Wuthnow, Robert, James Davison Hunter, Albert Bergesen, and Edith Kurzweil. 1984. *Cultural Analysis.* London: Routledge & Kegan Paul.

Wuthnow, Robert, and Marsha Witten. 1988. "New Directions in the Study of Culture." *Annual Review of Sociology* 14:49–67.

Wynne, Brian. 1982. *Rationality and Ritual: The Windscale Enquiry and Nuclear Decisions in Britain.* Chalfont St. Giles: British Society for the History of Science.

_____. 1989. "Sheepfarming After Chernobyl." *Environment* 31:11–15, 33–39.

_____. 1992. "Risk and Social Learning." In *Social Theories of Risk,* ed. Sheldon Krimsky and Dominic Golding. New York: Praeger Publishers.

Zaleznik, Abraham. 1970. "Power and Politics in Organizational Life." *Harvard Business Review* 48:47–60.

Zeeman, E. Christopher. 1977. *Catastrophe Theory: Selected Papers, 1982–1977.* Reading, PA: Benjamin.

Zeuli, J. S., and R. E. Floden. 1987. "Cultural Incongruities and Inequities for Schooling: Implications for Practice from Ethnographic Research?" Occasional Paper No. 117, Institute for Research on Teaching, College of Education, Michigan State University, Lansing.

Zey, Mary. 1992. "Criticisms of Rational Choice Models." In *Decision Making: Alternatives to Rational Choice Models,* ed. Mary Zey. Newbury Park, CA: Sage Publications.

About the Book

Culture Matters explores the role of political culture studies as one of the major investigative fields in contemporary political science. Cultural theory was the focal point of the late Aaron Wildavsky's teaching and research for the last decade of his life, a life that profoundly affected many fields of political science, from the study of the presidency to public budgeting. In this volume, original essays prepared in Wildavsky's honor examine the areas of rational choice, institutions, theories of change, political risk, the environment, and practical politics.

About the Editors
and Contributors

Gabriel A. Almond is Professor Emeritus of political science at Stanford University. His many books include (with Sidney Verba) the landmark *The Civic Culture* (1963).

Sun-Ki Chai is an assistant professor of sociology at the University of Arizona. He is the author of *Choosing an Identity: A General Model of Preference and Belief Formation and Its Application to Comparative Development* (forthcoming).

Dennis J. Coyle is an associate professor of political science at the Catholic University of America, Washington, D.C. He is the author of *Property Rights and the Constitution: Shaping Society Through Land Use Regulation* (1993) and coeditor (with Richard J. Ellis) of *Politics, Policy, and Culture* (1994).

Mary Douglas is Professor Emeritus and former Avalon Professor in the Humanities at Northwestern University. Her many books include *Purity and Danger* (1966), *Natural Symbols* (1970), *Risk and Culture* (1982), and *How Institutions Think* (1986).

Harry Eckstein is a professor of social science at the University of California, Irvine. His most recent book is *Regarding Politics: Essays on Political Theory, Stability, and Change* (1992).

Richard J. Ellis is an associate professor of politics at Willamette University, Salem, Oregon. His most recent books are *American Political Cultures* (1993) and *Presidential Lightning Rods: The Politics of Blame-Avoidance* (1994).

Gunnar Grendstad teaches in the department of comparative politics at the University of Bergen, Norway. He is coeditor (with Per Selle) of *Kultur som levemate* [Culture as a Way of Life] (1996).

Robert Klitgaard is a professor of economics at the University of Natal, South Africa. His books include *Choosing Elites* (1985), *Controlling Corruption* (1987), and *Tropical Gangsters* (1990).

Charles Lockhart is a professor of political science at Texas Christian University and the author of *Gaining Ground: Tailoring Social Programs to American Values* (1989).

Howard Margolis is a professor in the Harris Graduate School of Public Policy at the University of Chicago. His books include *Dealing with Risk* (1996) and *Selfishness, Altruism, and Rationality* (1984).

Elinor Ostrom is Arthur F. Bentley Professor of Political Science and codirector of the Workshop in Political Theory and Analysis at Indiana University. She is currently president of the American Political Science Association. Her books include *Governing the Commons: The Evolution of Institutions for Collective Action* (1990) and *Rules, Games, and Common-Pool Resources* (1994).

Vincent Ostrom is Professor Emeritus of political science at Indiana University and codirector of the Workshop in Political Theory and Analysis at Indiana University. His many books include *The Political Theory of a Compound Republic* (1987) and *The Intellectual Crisis in American Public Administration* (1989).

Per Selle is a professor of political science at Bergen University, Norway. He has published widely on voluntary organizations and is coeditor (with Gunnar Grendstad) of *Kultur som levemate* [Culture as a Way of Life] (1996).

Arthur L. Stinchcombe is John Evans Professor of Sociology at Northwestern University. His many books include *Constructing Social Theories* (1968), *Information and Organization* (1990), and most recently, *Sugar Island Slavery in the Age of Enlightenment: The Political Economy of the Caribbean World* (1995).

Fred Thompson is Grace and Elmer Goudy Professor of Public Management at the Atkinson Graduate School of Management, Willamette University, Salem, Oregon. His most recent book is *Reinventing the Pentagon* (1994).

Michael Thompson is director of the Musgrave Institute and an adjunct professor at the University of Bergen, Norway. Among his books are *Rubbish Theory* (1979) and (with Michiel Schwarz) *Divided We Stand: Redefining Politics, Technology, and Social Choice* (1990).

Index

Academia, 121, 132, 194. *See also* Universities
Accountability, 81, 129
Acquiescence bias, 157
Adams, John, 205
Africa, 192, 193, 195, 199–200
Agent Orange, 145
Aid, 204, 205
Air Force $500 hammer, 141–142
Akerlof, George, 52
Alliances, 13. *See also* Coalitions
Almond, Gabriel, ix, 30–31, 32, 100, 104(n1)
Altruism, 47, 49, 50, 51, 53, 54
Anarchy, 71, 78(n9)
Anchor-and-adjust process, 144, 145, 146
Ancient Law (Maine), 85
Anomie, 23, 24, 25
Anthropology, 115–116, 122, 123, 153,
    193–194, 198, 199, 201
Antianthropocentrism, 172
Approval, 50
Archaeology, 111
Arrow, Kenneth J., 7
Arthur, Brian, 213
Assumptions, 38, 47–48, 49, 53, 55, 56, 82,
    124, 151, 155, 193, 210
Attitudes, 23, 47, 49, 108, 153, 162, 175
Audubon Society, 171, 180, 182, 183, 188(n11)
Austria, 211, 212
Authoritarianism, 157, 162
Authority. *See* Power/authority
Axioms, 23–25, 38, 125. *See also* Assumptions

Baker, Kendall L., 100
Balandier, Georges, 193
Baltic Sea, 204
Bandler, Wyllis, 6–7
Banfield, Edward, 12

Barnes, Samuel, x
Baron, Jonathan, 147(n4)
Barth, Fredrik, 8
Bastide, Roger, 194, 198, 199
Beck, Ulrich, 132
Becker, Gary S., 50
Beckman, Peter, 170
Beliefs, 4, 6, 10, 11, 26, 45, 46, 47, 48–49, 51,
    52, 53, 54, 61, 77, 92, 97, 100, 125, 145,
    147(n3), 153, 155, 175
    formation of, 55
Benectin, 145
Bentham, Jeremy, 114
Biologism, viii
Bismark, Otto von, 95
Black boxes, 113, 115, 116, 117, 118, 118(nn 2, 3)
Blame, 129, 130, 131, 142, 144. *See also*
    Scapegoating
Bloch, Maurice, 194
Boltanski, Luc, 108, 117
Bramwell, Anna, 184
Brent Star structure, 210
Brown, Robert, xv
Bureaucracies, 63, 65, 68, 69, 70, 72

Campbell, Donald, 33
Cancer, 133–134, 137, 138, 141–143, 144, 145
Capitalism, ix, 100, 170, 174, 184, 204
Capital punishment, 106
Carman, John, 206
Causality, 5, 10, 11, 49, 62, 104(n1), 139, 140,
    142, 144, 145, 208
Celebrities, 109, 110, 117, 118
Change, 1, 13–14, 14–15, 16, 52, 76, 105–118,
    153, 155–156, 193, 195, 196–199, 206,
    215
    adaptive, 25–26, 94, 98

illusion of, 110, 111, 112
in institutions, 94–95, 96, 100, 106
intergenerational, 100
organizational, 64, 65
political, 91–103, 130
in scientific theory, 34, 133
and surprise, 92–94
in technology, 213, 214(fig.)
Changing American Voter, The (Nie, Verba, and Petrocik), 106
Chaos theory, 208, 216(n2). *See also* Complexity
Chilton, Stephen, 54
Choices, 49, 67, 92, 141, 146, 195. *See also* Decisionmaking; Policy issues
Christianity, vii
Civic culture, 30–31, 153
Class struggle, viii
Clements, Frederic, 76
Coalitions, 27–28, 63, 72, 88, 101, 103, 130
shifting, 97–99
Cognitive science, 124
Cohort analysis, 107
Collective action, 48, 50, 51, 52, 56
Colonialism, 198, 199
Common law, 71, 78(n10)
Communications, 76
Comparative advantage, 198
Comparative analysis, 80, 81, 82, 152
Competition, 5–6, 68, 70, 74, 75, 84, 128, 129, 204, 213
Complexity, 17, 208, 215
Comte, Auguste, viii, 21–22, 34, 36, 43
Conflict, xvi–xvii, 4, 50, 81, 84, 152
Congruence, 28–29
Consensus, 17, 54, 56, 67, 69, 74, 105–106, 117
Consonance/dissonance, 29–30, 31, 55, 85
Consumption, 55, 81, 205
Contracts, 71, 72, 73, 85
Contradictions, 60
Converse, Philip, 106, 107
Coolidge, Calvin, 109
Cooperation, 50, 51, 54, 84, 160
Cornell, Stephen, 18
Cost-benefit analysis, 22, 128, 132
Crime, 105, 106
Cultural bias, 4, 10, 13, 53, 55, 60, 77, 93, 94, 102, 128, 132, 156, 160, 166, 170, 174, 175–176(tables), 180, 183(table)

hybrid, 96, 99, 101, 182
See also Political bias
Cultural coordination, 51–52
Cultural dialogue, 129
Cultural functionalism, 31
Cultural science, 23–34
Cultural Theory, xiii–xvii, 4, 8–9, 11, 12–13, 16, 17, 67, 75, 80, 84–86, 88, 92, 97, 101, 103, 128, 206, 209, 215
axioms, 23–25
vs. conventional theory, 206–208, 207(fig.), 211–212
debates within, 166(n1)
and environmental attitudes, 166. *See also* Egalitarianism, and environmentalism
and grid-group theory, 10, 62, 166(n1)
measuring, 161(table), 164(table)
and postmaterialism, 151–166, 154(table), 161(table), 163(table), 164(table)
vs. utility theory, 22
Cultural Theory (Thompson, Ellis, and Wildavsky), 86, 93, 178, 206
Culture-themes, 31–32
Culture wars, 184
Curvilinearity, 215
Customs. *See* Manners/customs

Dalton, Russell J., 100
Dealing with Risk (Margolis), 133, 137, 140, 145
Decisionmaking, x, 27, 53, 54, 60, 61, 62, 72, 152, 157, 209
Deep ecology. *See under* Environmental issues
Deep structures, 43
Definitions of culture, xiii–xiv, 26
Democracy, xvii, 30, 40, 75, 88, 92, 100, 136, 199. *See also* Political participation; Voting
Democracy in America (Tocqueville), 83, 88
Demographics, 174, 176(table)
Demonstrations, 48, 50
Denhardt, Robert, 60
Dependency school, ix
Despotism, 64, 74, 77, 78(n5)
Devall, Bill, 177
Development, 195. *See also* Economic growth/development
Diamond, Larry, xi
Diminishing marginal utility (DMU), 155

Discrimination, 50, 52, 201
Distribution issues, 169, 171, 201
DMU. *See* Diminishing marginal utility
Dominant Social Paradigm (DSP), 175, 176
Do No Harm, 145–147
Douglas, Mary, xiv, xvi, 2–6, 10, 31, 53, 85,
    127, 137
Downs, Anthony, 40
Dread, 125, 133–134, 142–144
DSP. *See* Dominant Social Paradigm
Dunlap, Riley, 172, 175, 176
Durkheim, Emile, viii, 2, 153

Earth First!, 171, 180, 182, 188(n11), 206
Earth Island Institute, 171, 180, 182, 183,
    188(n11)
Eckstein, Harry, 94
ECOCON. *See* Environmental issues,
    ecological consciousness
Economic efficiency, 211, 212, 215
Economic growth/development, 102, 156,
    158, 159, 163, 165, 172, 193
Economics, 37–38, 41, 52, 55, 69, 80, 81, 195,
    208, 213
    social economics, 42–43
Economic security, 153, 155, 160
Economics of Discrimination, The (Becker), 50
Education, 105. *See also* Universities
Egalitarianism, xv, xvii, 3, 7, 16, 54, 60, 64,
    66–67, 69, 73–76, 91, 93, 96, 97, 98,
    99–100, 101, 102, 152, 211, 214, 215,
    216(n9)
    and environmentalism, 158, 159, 163, 165,
        170, 171, 172–173, 173(table), 174–175,
        184, 186(n3), 187(n7), 206, 210, 212
    and human nature, 179
    and illiberalism, 177–178, 178(table)
    and postmaterialism, 159, 162
    and technology, 179–180, 181(table)
Elazar, Daniel, 54
Elites, 51, 68, 70, 96, 100, 102, 184
Ellis, Richard, 86
Empirical evidence, 39, 40–41, 47, 111
England, 52, 97, 121, 166(n4), 210
*Environmentalism and the Future of
    Progressive Politics* (Paehlke), 169–170
Environmental issues, xv–xvi, 16, 74, 93, 127,
    128, 130–131, 152, 164(table), 191,
    204–205

deep ecology, 177, 187(nn 7, 8)
ecological consciousness (ECOCON), 172,
    173, 177, 177
environmentalism and its subdimensions,
    167–168
future of environmental politics,
    183–184
and general public, 180, 182, 183, 188(n11)
New Environmental Paradigm (NEP), 172,
    176, 187(n3)
and political ideology, 169–170
    See also Egalitarianism, and
        environmentalism; Hazardous wastes;
        NATSOC1/NATSOC2 surveys; Nature;
        Ozone depletion
Environmental Protection Agency (EPA), 138,
    143
EPA. *See* Environmental Protection Agency
Epstein, T. Scarlett, 196
Equality, 85, 86, 99–100, 160, 171, 175, 215.
    See also Egalitarianism
Essentialism, 34, 35, 37, 40
    modified, 39, 44(n11)
    See also Metaphysics
Ethical bias, 128
Etzioni, Amitai, 62, 64
Eucken, Walter, 12, 80, 81
Europe, 184, 199, 216(n9)
European Court of Justice, 52
Evans-Pritchard, E. E., 78(n9)
Exit, 62–63, 64
Expectations, 49, 52, 54, 156

Fairness, 140, 145, 146, 147, 171, 204, 209,
    211–212, 214, 215
Families, 85, 96, 106
Family planning, 196
Fatalism, 3, 7, 53–54, 64, 78(n5), 93, 94, 210,
    214, 215, 216(n9)
    and environmentalism, 159, 163, 165,
        206–208
    and postmaterialism, 162
Federalism, 72–73, 98
Federalist Papers, viii, 98
Feminism, 194
Ferejohn, John, 37, 52
Fiske, Alan, 54
Flanagan, Scott C., 157, 162
Force, 64

Foreman, Dave, 169
Formalization, 112–113, 116–117, 117–118
Foundations of Economics, The (Eucken), 80
Fragmentation. *See under* Theories
Frameworks, 82–83, 84, 85, 86
France, 132
Friedman, Milton, 38, 44(n9)
Functionalism, 153, 155
Fungibility, 140, 143, 144, 146

Galbraith, Kenneth, 81
Games, 37, 47, 84
Gardner, Roy, 84
Garrett, Geoffrey, 52
Geertz, Clifford, 26
Generalizations, 2, 23, 28, 31, 59
Germany, viii–ix, 92, 99–101, 104(n3), 132,
        166(n4), 169
Goldwater, Barry, 107
Governmental growth, 102–103
Great Depression, 13, 94, 103
Greatness, 108–110, 117
Green, Donald, 36, 39, 44(n8)
Greenpeace, 206, 210, 216(n4)
Greens, 132, 158, 169
Gretschmann, Klaus, 75
Grid-group theory, 2–6, 3(fig.), 6(fig.), 9, 12,
        13, 18, 31, 53–54, 69, 77, 85, 86, 87(fig.),
        91, 92, 127, 128
    and organizations, 59–61, 62(fig.), 63–64,
        65, 68, 70, 76
    See also under Cultural Theory
Gross, Jonathan, 18
Gulf War syndrome, 145
Gun control, 105, 106
Gurr, Ted R., 29

Hardin, Russell, 52
Hartz, Louis, 97, 102
Hazardous wastes, 211–213, 216(n6)
Heiner, Robert, 18(n2)
Hermits, 3, 5, 7, 9
Hierarchy, 3, 7, 12, 54, 60, 93–94, 97, 98,
        99, 100, 101, 102, 129–130, 179,
        182, 187(n9), 210, 211, 214, 215,
        216(n9)
    and environmentalism, 159, 163, 165, 212
    and materialism/postmaterialism, 159, 162
    See also under Markets

Hildebrandt, Kai, 100
Hill, Polly, 193
Hirschman, Albert O., 62, 63, 64, 197–198
Historicists, viii
House of Representatives banking scandal,
        141–142
Human nature, 46, 54, 86, 88, 178–179, 180,
        182(table), 205
Huntington, Samuel, xi

Ibn Khaldûn, 82–83, 84
Ideology, 51, 175–176(tables). *See also*
        Political ideologies
Impossibility theorem, 6–7, 9
Incrementalism, xvi, xvii, 130, 198, 215
India, 196
Individualism, xvii, 3, 7, 54, 75, 76, 93, 94, 96,
        97–98, 98–99, 101, 102, 130, 153, 170,
        179, 182, 214, 215, 216(n9)
    and environmentalism, 159, 163, 165,
        174–175, 184, 211, 212
    and materialism/postmaterialism, 159, 162
    and technology, 188(n10)
Individuality, 7–8, 9
Indonesia, 200
Industrialization, 95, 102, 158
Inertia theorem, 25–26
Inglehart, Ronald, ix, x, 18, 151, 158. *See also*
        Postmaterialism
Inkeles, Alex, ix
Institutions, x, 11–12, 42, 53, 60, 83, 92,
        94–95, 96, 100, 101, 104(n1), 106, 122,
        152, 155, 156, 178, 179, 206, 209
Interests, 8, 92, 129
International Social Science Programme, 160
Interpretation, 22, 26–28, 32, 44(n3), 77
Intuition, 144–145, 146, 147
Ireland, 166(n4)
Italy, xi, 12, 18, 166(n4)

Jackson, Andrew, 98
Japan, 95–96
Jefferson, Thomas, 98
Joint implementation, 205
Justice, 123, 127, 132

Kaase, Max, x
Kahneman, Daniel, 124, 141
Kalt, Joseph, 18

Kamieniecki, Sheldon, 170
Kenya, 196
Kierkegaard, Soren, 122
Knight, Frank, 116
Kuhn, Thomas, 133

Lakatos, Imre, 38
Landau, Martin, 72
Language, 86, 108, 110, 117, 123
La Porte, Todd, 60
Lauman, Edward O., 110
Law and order, 157, 160
Lazarsfeld, Paul, ix, 107
Leadership, 63, 64, 68, 69, 74, 78(n5), 109, 171
Learning, 15, 24–25, 42, 91–92, 107, 117, 201, 212
Legality, 30, 41, 42, 83, 86
    law of evidence, 113–114, 118
Lenski, Gerhard, 106
Liberalism/illiberalism, 107, 108, 177–178, 178(table), 187(nn 8, 9)
Libertarianism, 63, 66, 69, 71, 74, 77(n4), 157
Lindblom, Charles, 12
Linnerooth-Bayer, Joanne, 211
Lipset, Seymour Martin, xi

McGovern, George, 107
Machiavelli, Niccolò, vii
Mackie, Gerry, 52
Madison, James, 98–99
Maine, Henry Sumner, 85
Making Democracy Work (Putnam), xi
Malinowski, Bronislaw, 201
Manners/customs, 83, 86, 88
Mannheim, Karl, 107
Markets, 12, 41–43, 72, 75, 76, 78(n12), 80, 100, 130, 174, 175, 183, 184, 210, 211, 213, 216(n6)
    and hierarchy, 63, 65, 66, 67–68, 69, 70–71, 73, 74, 205–206
    market economies, 81, 84, 205
Marxism, viii, ix
Maslow, Abraham, 16, 152, 155
Materialism, viii, 47, 48, 50, 152, 153, 155, 157, 158, 159, 165, 166(n4)
    measuring, 161(table)
    See also Postmaterialism
Mauss, Marcel, 193
Mead, Margaret, 32, 193

Meaning, 18, 23, 24, 26, 33, 40, 44(n3), 60, 122, 125
Mechanical process, 115
Mediterranean world, 83
Merton, Robert K., 67
Metaphysics, 21, 22, 34, 35, 36–37, 38, 40
Metraux, Rhoda, 32
Metz, Dan, 171
Milbrath, Lester, 172, 176, 177
Models, 80, 82, 84, 123–126, 201–202
Monopolies, 73
Montesquieu, Charles de Secondat, baron de, vii–viii
Moral Basis of a Backward Society, The (Banfield), 12
Munro, William B., viii

Nash, Roderick, 187(n7)
National Socialism, viii, ix
NATSOC1/NATSOC2 surveys, 171, 173(table), 173, 176(table), 177, 178(table), 180, 185–186, 187(n7), 188(n10)
Natural Symbols (Douglas), 85
Nature, 110, 111, 112, 159, 165, 170, 179, 180, 184, 199, 200
    social construction of, 206
    See also Environmental issues
Nature and Society (surveys). *See* NATSOC1/NATSOC2 surveys
NEP. *See* Environmental issues, New Environmental Paradigm
Netherlands, 166(n4)
New Left, 152, 157, 159
New Right, 157
Nie, Norman, 106, 107
Niskanen, William A., 72
Norms, 30, 41, 42, 60, 71
Norway, 27, 160, 166(n4), 210
Null hypotheses, 40

Objectivity, 131
Observation of culture, 32–34
Ocean Arks, 213
Odhiambo, Thomas Risley, 199–200
Odum, Eugene, 76
Optimism, 54, 77, 94, 178
Organizations, 59–77
    degrees of, 71(fig.)

and environments, 65–68, 69, 75, 76
    See also under Grid-group theory
Orientations, 22, 23–24, 30, 31, 32, 94, 95
    inferences of, 33
    reorientation, 25, 26, 92
Osgood, Charles, 33
Ostrom, Elinor, 72, 84
Ostrom, Vincent, 69, 70, 83
Otway, Harry, 122
Ozone depletion, 206–207

Padgett, Stephen, 104(n3)
Paehlke, Robert, 169, 172, 184, 188(n12)
Pahner, Philip, 122
Paradigm shifts, 133
Parsons, Talcott, 111
Particularity, 32
Perception, 125, 132. *See also under* Risk
Perpetual vain abstraction, 113, 114–115, 116
Perrow, Charles, 65
Pessimism, 53–54
Petrocik, John R., 106, 107
Pizzorno, Alessandro, 12
Pleasure, 50
Pluralism, 96, 97
Poland, 204, 205
Policy issues, 191–202, 203–216
    conventional policy analysis, 211–212
Political bias, 126, 127, 128. *See also* Cultural
    bias
Political correctness, 67
Political culture, vii, x, xiii, 21, 27, 49, 91–103,
    132, 151, 152, 153
    as term, 1, 30
Political ideologies, 172–173
    political left/right, 169–170. *See also* New
        Left; New Right
Political opposition, 123
Political participation, 152, 159, 162
Political parties, 106–107, 109, 172, 176(table)
Politics of the Budgetary Process, The
    (Wildavsky), xvi
Popper, Karl, 34, 35, 39
Populism, 127, 128
Positive Philosophy, The (Comte), 21
Postmaterialism, 16, 18, 151–166, 166(n4)
    and environmentalism, 158, 163,
        164(table), 165, 166
    measuring, 161(table), 164(table)

Postmodernism, xvii, 77, 155
Power/authority, 3, 4, 29, 54, 60, 68, 73, 74,
    77, 81, 88, 98, 129, 159, 160, 162, 163
Precepts, 203, 209–211, 214, 216
Predictions, 11, 18, 24, 27–28, 35, 41, 42,
    44(n9), 46, 47, 48, 49, 53, 59, 84, 191,
    202, 208, 209, 214
    risky, 36
Preferences, xv, 1, 7, 8, 9, 11, 18(n2), 45, 46,
    47–48, 49–50, 52, 53, 54, 60, 67, 75, 92,
    205
    expressive, 50
    formation of, 55, 103
Prices, 157, 159, 162, 165
Privatization, 73
Problem-solving, 94–96
Production functions, 195
Progress, 165. *See also* Economic
    growth/development
Project design, 197–198
Property, 99, 160, 163, 175, 184
Protestant Ethic and the Spirit of Capitalism
    (Weber), 42
Psychocultural theory, ix
Psychologists, 122
Psychometrics, 123–126, 131–132, 202(n). *See
    also* Risk,
    psychometric dimemsions
Public administration, 68–69, 70, 72
Public choice movement, x, 75
Public opinion, 141
Public sector, 102–103
Putnam, Robert, xi, 18, 32
Pye, Lucian, xi, 32

Racial issues, viii, 105, 113
Radical critics, 130—131
Radiation, 139, 142–143
Radon, 143–144
Ranking/rating procedures, 156–157
Rational choice theory, x, 1, 11, 22, 36, 45–56,
    103, 124
    and political culture theories, 92
    thin version of, 48–49, 52
    See also Utility theory
Rationality, ix, 21, 55, 65, 76, 87, 122, 208
    bounded, 60–61, 70, 156
    of lay risk intuition, 134
Rationality and Society, 39

Rawls, John, 75
Rayner, Steve, 18, 129, 130
Reagan, Ronald, 107, 109
Reality, 121, 122
Reductionism, vii–ix, 129, 200
Reflexivity, 210, 211–213
Reforms, 130
Regularities, 4–5, 17, 37
Regulations, 71, 73, 74, 93, 97, 99, 146, 174
Relativism, 69
Religion, 106
Renaissance, vii
Richardson, Stephen, 69
Rigg, Jonathan, 197
Rights, 99
Risk, 121–132, 133–147, 158, 170, 191, 207, 208
    aversion, 53, 54, 75, 132
    and bias, 139
    definitions, 122
    expert/lay conflicts concerning, 133, 134, 138, 139, 140
    perception, 15, 123–131, 132, 137(fig.), 137, 139, 140
    psychometric dimensions, 134, 135(table), 136, 138, 139, 147(n2)
    qualitative/quantitative aspects of, 134, 136–139, 137(fig.), 138
    social amplification of, 126–127, 129, 130, 132
    social construction of, 123, 137
Risk: Analysis, Perception, and Management (Royal Society), 121, 123, 130
Risk and Culture (Douglas and Wildavsky), 127, 179
Risk and Rationality (Shrader-Frechette), 127
Rogowski, Ronald, 91, 92, 100, 101
Royal Society, 121, 123, 130

Salam Bombay (film), 94
Salem-Yamhill residents (Oregon), 171, 172, 182, 187(n7), 188(n11)
Salience, 125, 127, 129, 137, 141, 143
Salzman, Lorna, 170
Scapegoating, 142, 145. *See also* Blame
Scarcity hypothesis, 152
Schelling, Thomas, 127
Schmutzer, Manfred, 6–7
Schwartz, Barry, 215

Science, 21, 22, 32, 33, 34, 35, 39, 43, 70, 76, 111, 114–115, 116, 117, 128, 142, 179–180, 188(n11), 199, 200, 209. *See also* Technology
Science and Public Affairs, 122
Scott, Richard, 64
Sears, Paul, 76
Self-interest, 1, 47, 63, 68, 74, 75, 83, 103
Sex, 109, 110, 118(n1), 194
Shapiro, Ian, 36, 39, 44(n8)
Shrader-Frechette, Kristin, 127–128
Shweder, Richard, 104(n2)
Sierra Club, 171, 180, 182, 183, 188(n11)
Signals, 126–127, 129, 130
Simon, Herbert, 60–61, 69
Slavery, 87–88
Slovic, Paul, 123
Smith, Donald, ix
Social amplification. *See under* Risk
Socialization, 91, 152, 155
Social relations, 4, 10, 12, 49, 54, 60, 63, 67, 75, 85, 87, 101, 128
Social utility, 195
Sociology, 47, 112, 193, 194
Solidarity, 10, 64, 74–75, 152, 158, 159
Soviet Union, 210–211
Spirit of the Laws (Montesquieu), vii
Starr, Chauncy, 124
Structural-functionalism, 152, 153
Subcultures, 28, 29, 106, 107, 153
Subjectivity, xvii, 18
Subsidiarity, 73
Suicide (Durkheim), 2
Summers, Lawrence, 211, 213
Surprise, 156. *See also under* Change
Survey research, 156–157, 166, 170–171, 211, 214. *See also* NATSOC1/NATSOC2 surveys; Voluntary Human Extinction Movement
Sweden, 204

Technology, 130, 179–180, 181(table), 188(nn 10, 11), 210, 213–214
    inflexibility of, 214
Thailand, 197
Theories, 34–36, 38, 39, 48, 59, 82, 84
    comparison of rival, 151
    fragmentation of, 14, 15, 117
    general theories of culture, 52–56, 80–82

of order, 81
of risk perception, 123–131
   See also Cultural Theory; Grid-group
      theory; Rational choice theory
Thévenot, Laurent, 108, 117
Thick description, 26–27
Thielens, Wagner, 107
Third World, 16
Thompson, James D., 62, 77(n4)
Thompson, Michael, 65, 86, 93, 94, 129
Tiebout, Charles, 83
Tocqueville, Alexis de, viii, 2, 59, 78(n10), 84,
   85, 86, 87–88
Todd, John, 213
Togo, 201
Trade, 204, 205
Tradition, 153, 159, 160, 162, 163, 196, 197
Transaction costs, 66, 72
Transaction theory, 8–9, 75
Trust, 32, 66, 68, 134, 209, 211
Tuden, Arthur, 62, 77(n4)
Tversky, Amos, 124, 141
Typology, 2, 30–31, 32, 44(n4). *See also* Grid-
   group theory

Uncertainty, 67, 72, 74
UNESCO. See United Nations Educational,
   Scientific, and Cultural Organization
United Nations Educational, Scientific, and
   Cultural Organization (UNESCO), 193,
   196
United States, 103
   colonial/post-colonial, 97–99, 102
Universals, 28–30, 37, 153, 156
Universities, 75, 107, 110, 132. *See also*
   Academia
Utility theory, 11, 21, 22
   core postulate of, 37
   critque of, 34–43
   See also Rational choice theory; Social utility

Values, xvi, 4, 6, 8, 10, 42, 61, 62, 63, 66, 68,
   78(n15), 92, 97, 100, 105, 106, 108,
   147(n3), 152, 155, 156, 175

Van Liere, Kent, 172, 175, 176
Verba, Sidney, ix, x–xi, 30–31, 32, 100, 106,
   107
VHEMT. See Voluntary Human Extinction
   Movement
Voice, 62–63, 64
Voluntarism, 64, 134
Voluntary Human Extinction Movement
   (VHEMT), 171, 177, 178(table), 180,
   187(nn 3, 6, 7), 188(n10)
Voting, ix, x, 39–40, 44(n13), 48, 50, 56, 107,
   108, 153. *See also* Democracy; Political
   parties

Wagner, Adolf, 102
Walker, James, 84
Ward, Lester, 70
Warner, Sir Frederick, 121, 122
Warren, Robert, 83
Weber, Max, 26, 42, 44(n3), 65
Weimar Republic, viii, ix, 100
Weingast, Barry, 52
Welfare states, 95
Wheatley, Margaret, 76–77
Whistleblowers, 94
White, Gilbert, 123
Wildavsky, Aaron, xiii–xviii, 12, 31, 65, 69,
   72, 78(n5), 79, 80, 86, 88, 91, 102, 127,
   133, 134, 136, 137, 147, 151, 152, 170,
   174, 178, 180, 183, 191–192, 215,
   216(n9)
Williamson, Oliver, 12, 63, 66
Wilson, Richard, 54
Wilson, Woodrow, 65, 84
Women, 118(n1), 152, 171, 196
World Bank, 211
World War II, 103
Wynne, Brian, 122, 126

Young people, 101, 107–108, 109, 117,
   155

Zalenik, Abraham, 63, 68